Studies in the History of Medieval Religion

VOLUME XV

THE LAST GENERATION OF ENGLISH CATHOLIC CLERGY

Parish Priests in
the Diocese of Coventry and Lichfield in
the Early Sixteenth Century

A central paradox of the English Reformation is that the call to the Catholic priesthood was never more eagerly answered than on the very eve of religious upheaval. In this important new study, based on the records of the third largest diocese in the country, covering six counties of the midlands and north-west, Dr Cooper traces the careers of the pastoral clergy from their preparatory education to old age. In this highly 'clericalised' society, in which ten new priests were ordained each year for every arising vacancy, priests *without* livings were the main point of contact between the church and its people. This 'clerical proletariat' and, indeed, the majority of parochial incumbents emerge as conscientious servants of their native communities, only distinguishable from their neighbours by a sacramental function in greater demand than ever before. As such, an interpretation of the English Reformation as founded on popular anticlericalism is difficult to sustain.

Dr TIM COOPER has taught history at the universities of Sheffield, Manchester and Hull.

Studies in the History of Medieval Religion

ISSN 0955–2480

General Editor
Christopher Harper-Bill

Previously published volumes in the series
are listed at the back of this volume

THE
LAST GENERATION OF
ENGLISH CATHOLIC CLERGY

Parish Priests in
the Diocese of Coventry and Lichfield in
the Early Sixteenth Century

TIM COOPER

THE BOYDELL PRESS

© Tim Cooper 1999

All Rights Reserved. Except as permitted under current legislation no part of this work may be photocopied, stored in a retrieval system, published, performed in public, adapted, broadcast, transmitted, recorded or reproduced in any form or by any means, without the prior permission of the copyright owner

First published 1999
The Boydell Press, Woodbridge

ISBN 0 85115 752 1

The Boydell Press is an imprint of Boydell & Brewer Ltd
PO Box 9, Woodbridge, Suffolk IP12 3DF, UK
and of Boydell & Brewer Inc.
PO Box 41026, Rochester, NY 14604–4126, USA
website: http://www.boydell.co.uk

A catalogue record for this book is available
from the British Library

Library of Congress Cataloging-in-Publication Data
Cooper, Tim, 1961–
 The last generation of English Catholic clergy : parish priests in the diocese of Coventry and Lichfield in the early sixteenth century / Tim Cooper.
  p. cm. – (Studies in the history of medieval religion, ISSN 0955–2480 . v. 15)
 Includes bibliographical references and index.
 ISBN 0–85115–752–1 (hardback : alk. paper)
 1. Catholic Church. Diocese of Coventry and Lichfield (England) – Clergy – History – 16th century. 2. Coventry Region (England) – Church history – 16th century. 3. Lichfield Region (England) – Church history – 16th century. I. Title. II. Series.
BX1495.C68C66 2000
282'.242'09031 – dc21   99-32793

This publication is printed on acid-free paper

Printed in Great Britain by
St Edmundsbury Press Ltd, Bury St Edmunds, Suffolk

Contents

List of Maps, Graphs and Tables	vii
Acknowledgements	xi
Abbreviations	xiii
Context	1

1	Preparing for Priesthood	7
	Education	7
	Examination	13
	Titles	19
	The ordination ceremonies	28
	Numbers	30
2	Acquiring a Living: The Beneficed	37
	Availability of benefices	37
	Patronage, preferment and presentation	39
	Admission, institution and induction	52
	Tenure and mobility	56
	Pluralism and non-residence	62
	Unions of benefices and pensions	72
	Standards of living	77
	Ordination and opportunity	92
3	Making a Living: The Unbeneficed	94
	Numbers and jobs	94
	Provenance and status	103
	Employment mobility	106
	Stipends and standards of living	113
	A 'clerical proletariat'?	127
4	Priests and People	129
	I. The Clerical Community	129
	Priesthood and status	129
	Sacramental priesthood	133
	Defenders of faith	137
	The clerical community: caste, status-group or profession?	148

II. Priests as People	155
Temporal kinship: family connections	156
Spiritual kinship: godchildren	159
Charity and community	161
Pastor and neighbour: the local economy	164
Pastor and neighbour: social integration	169
Pastor and neighbour: social disintegration	178
Construct	184
Appendix: Clerical Wills and Inventories Cited in the Text	190
Bibliography	194
Index	205

Maps, Graphs and Tables

Maps

1.	Dioceses of England and Wales in the early sixteenth century	xiv
2.	Diocese of Coventry and Lichfield c.1531, showing main administrative and jurisdictional divisions, collegiate churches, schools and communications	xv
3.	Major providers of monastic titles	xvi

Graphs

1.	Ordinations of secular acolytes and priests	31
2.	Ordinations of secular subdeacons and deacons	32
3.	Total ordinations 1504–1530	33

Tables

1.	Examination of ordinands	18
2.	Most significant regular providers of titles	22
3.	Length of tenure of benefices in the archdeaconry of Stafford, 1503–31	57
4.	Clergy instituted to livings in the archdeaconry of Stafford 1503–31 holding them for over thirty years	58
5.	Comparative incidence of pluralism	62
6.	Provenance of titles of employed unbeneficed clergy in the archdeaconry of Stafford 1531, by county	104
7.	Unbeneficed stipends, 1533	114

For My Parents
Mary and Nigel Cooper

The financial assistance of the Marc Fitch Fund
towards the publication of this book
is gratefully acknowledged

Acknowledgements

The nature of modern academic employment has meant that much of the writing of this book has been done away from home and family, a situation that has heightened what is, of necessity, a solitary experience. At the same time the pleasure of acknowledging the assistance of family, friends and colleagues in bringing the undertaking to completion is similarly increased.

My greatest intellectual debt is to Robert Swanson, whose patient and thorough supervision of the thesis from which the book has developed has greatly enhanced any value it might have. It was he who, from his extensive knowledge of the available materials in the field, suggested the general area of research and additionally made the principal sources available to me through the extended loan of his own microfilms. His influence on my work, and the standard he set for his research student, will be immediately obvious from a glance at the footnotes and bibliography; I hope the end result will not reflect too badly on him! The examiners of my thesis, Professors Barrie Dobson and Chris Dyer, made numerous helpful suggestions for turning it into a book, some of which, at least, I hope I have been able to incorporate. My understanding of various aspects of the lives of the sixteenth-century clergy has also benefited from discussions with Peter Heath and Peter Marshall and the importance of their work, along with that of Margaret Bowker, is, again, reflected in the footnotes.

The publishers have demonstrated exemplary patience and understanding of the problems faced by a member of the 'academic proletariat' in making the time to bring his research to fruition; as their 'frontperson', Caroline Palmer has shown herself to be the human face of modern publishing and her sympathetic treatment of this particular delinquent author has been greatly appreciated. I am also particularly grateful to the series editor, Christopher Harper-Bill, who originally brought my manuscript to the publishers' attention and has provided most welcome encouragement where others have doubted the viability of a work straddling the apparently inviolable border between medieval and early-modern history. Others who have provided support in the face of adversity include my friends in the Sheffield Friday Afternoon Seminar; in particular Bill Aird, David Roffe, Len Scales, Vanessa Toulmin and Alex Woolf. In addition, Dr Toulmin shared her expertise in seeking sources of funding and in the history and topography of her native Lancashire, the part of the medieval diocese with which I was least familiar.

The staff of Lichfield Joint Record Office have been continually helpful, most recently in responding to requests for photocopies at short notice, and their good humour has always made my visits enjoyable; the same can be said of the staff of the old British Library Manuscript Room. My visits to London were facilitated in no small way by John Kennedy who both put me up and put up with me on many occasions for no greater reward than a pint in one of the pubs off TCR. In Hull, John Rickard and Kevin Hall have provided some vital computer assistance – particularly at the critical moment when my mouse died following a prolonged illness – and John has proved that, despite widely-held assumptions of natural law, two medievalists *can* share a flat together and to mutual intellectual advantage! As I prepare to leave Hull after three years I should also like to thank the numerous part-time degree students on my courses *English Society in the Later Middle Ages* and *Religion and Society in Sixteenth-Century England* who were subjected to my often idiosyncratic interpretations of the periods and put up with them with good humour and frequently helpful comments.

No-one has experienced the anti-social nature of book writing in the last two years more than my immediate family and I hereby promise them that it will be some time before they again have to share holiday accommodation with a lap-top and a box of index cards. My wife, Pauline Cooper, will be more relieved even than the publishers that this book is finished, but without the time she spent in the few weeks before our first son was born filing the 11,000 or so scraps of paper into shoe-boxes to provide the basis of my analysis of Blythe's ordination register, it would not have been written at all. I have not had the courage since to tell her that, if I knew then what I know now, it could all have been done on a computer and am grateful for the fact that, as a psychologist, she is less likely than some to suffer the emotional damage that could be caused by such a mind-numbing task. She has had to put up with a lot, and I will always be grateful. Finally, my parents have given me their support ever since the day when, against all reason and acting upon an impulse of a peculiarly private nature, I came home from work at the bank and told them that I had decided I wanted to become an ecclesiastical historian. Even when I have had cause to doubt my own instincts, their belief and encouragement have been unfailing. This, my first History Book, is for them.

T.N.C.
Pearson Park, Hull
December, 1998

Abbreviations

For full details see Bibliography

BL	British Library
BRUC	A.B. Emden, A *Biographical Register of the University of Cambridge to 1500*
BRUO	A.B. Emden, A *Biographical Register of the University of Oxford to 1500*
BRUO 1501–1540	A.B. Emden, A *Biographical Register of the University of Oxford, A.D. 1501 to 1540*
CPL	*Calendar of Papal Letters*
JEH	*Journal of Ecclesiastical History*
Le Neve, *Fasti*	J. Le Neve, B. Jones, *Fasti Ecclesiae Anglicanae 1300–1541, vol. X, Coventry and Lichfield Diocese*
LJRO	Lichfield Joint Record Office
M.	Master (denoting graduate)
SCH	*Studies in Church History*
SHC 1915	W.N. Landor, *Staffordshire Incumbents and Parochial Records (1530–1680)*, The William Salt Society, Collections for a History of Staffordshire, 1915
Valor	*Valor Ecclesiasticus*
VCH *Staffs*	*Victoria History of the County of Stafford*
Venn	J. & J.A. Venn, *Alumni Cantabrigienses*

Map 1. Dioceses of England and Wales in the early sixteenth century.

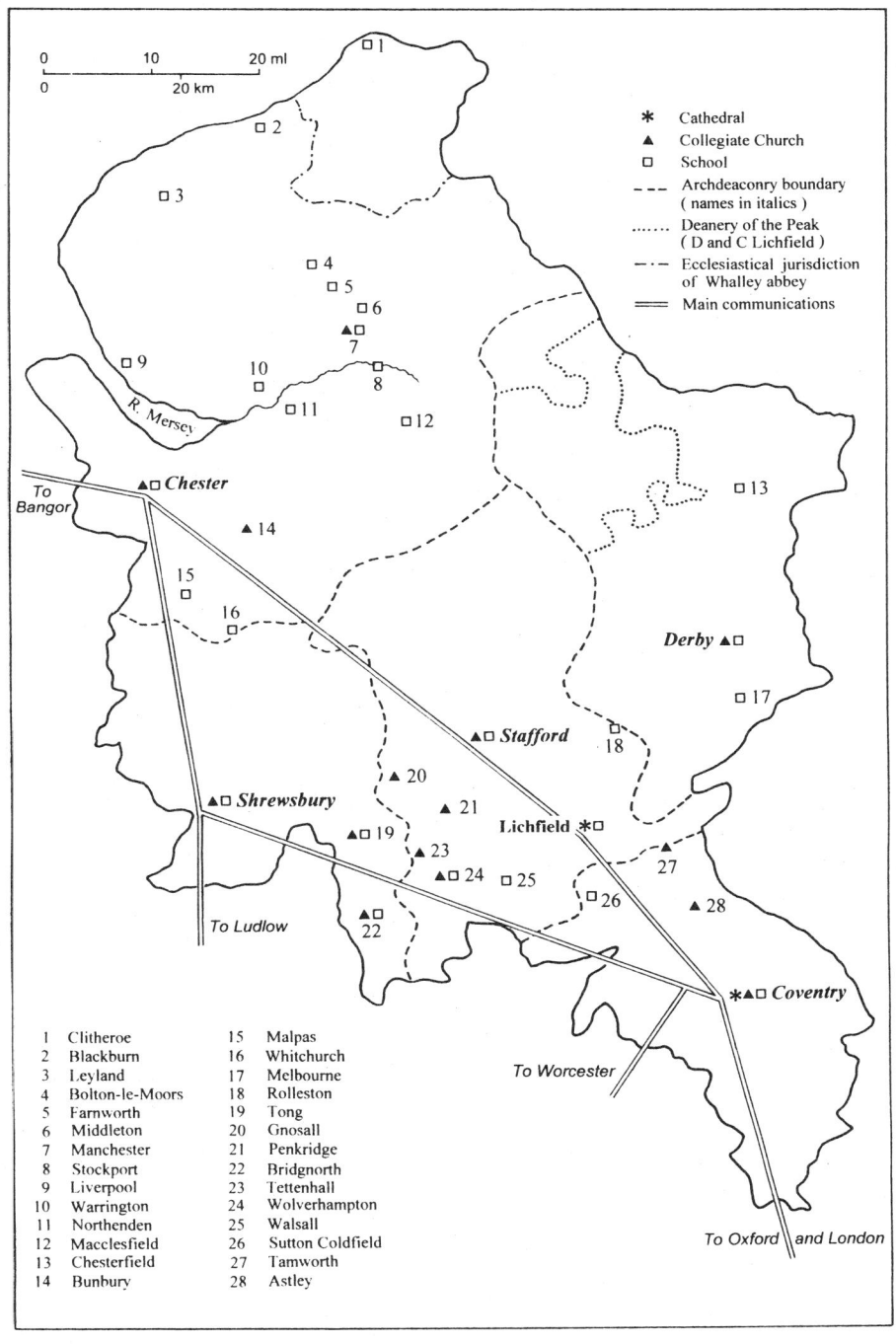

Map 2. Diocese of Coventry and Lichfield c.1531, showing main administrative and jurisdictional divisions, collegiate churches, schools and communications.

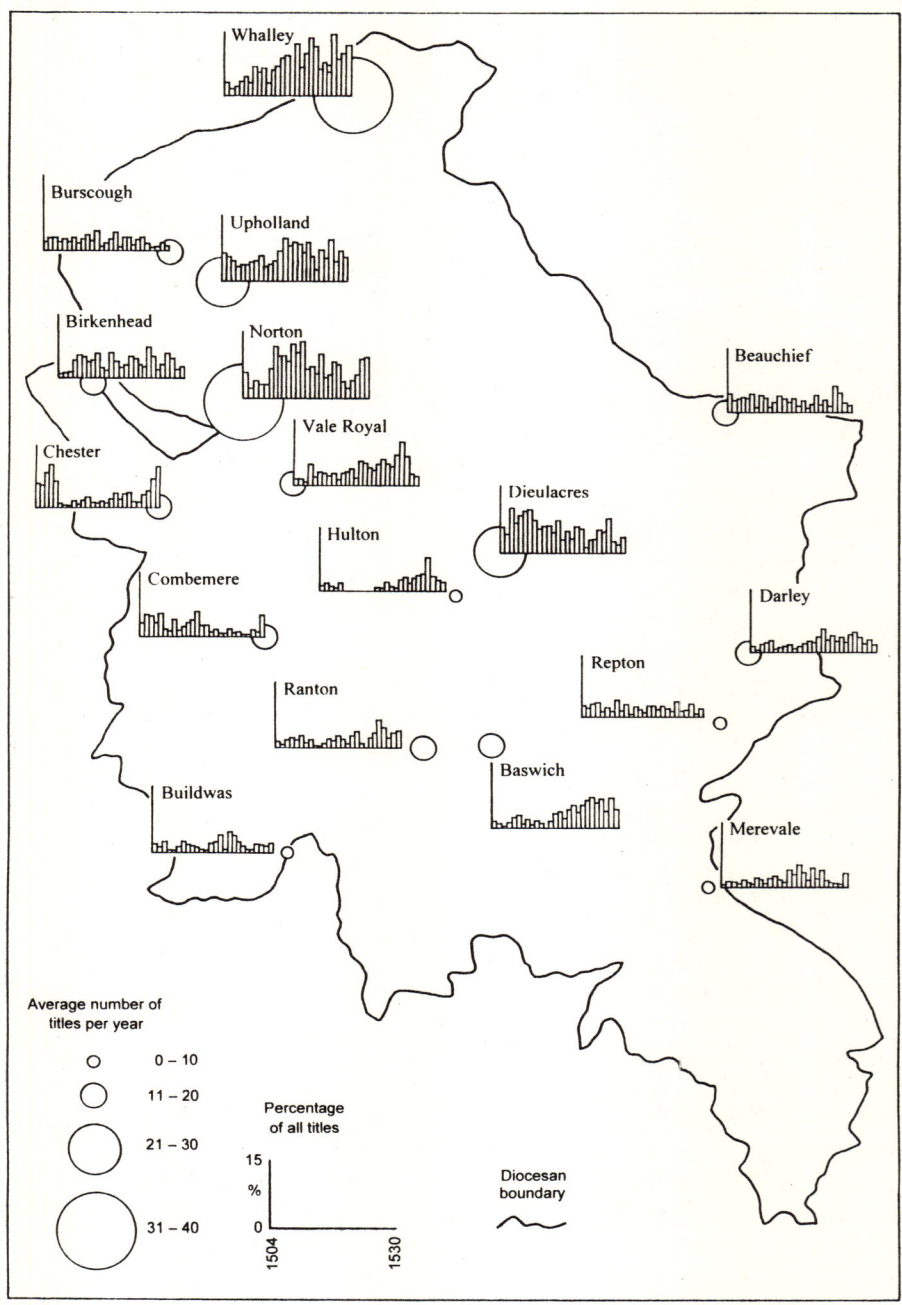

Map 3. Major providers of monastic titles (see pp. 19–27).

Context

Modern scholarly interest in the parish clergy of pre-Reformation England commenced with the work of A. Hamilton Thompson, published fourteen years after its original presentation as the Ford Lectures of 1933.[1] Drawing on the detailed examination of a broad range of archival material, from which examples were drawn by way of illustration, Thompson sketched a clear outline of the administrative structure of the late-medieval English church from the episcopate down through the cathedrals, collegiate churches and monasteries to the incumbents, curates and chaplains working in the parishes. His work, particularly the attention it drew to the rich variety of material available for study in the diocesan archives, inspired a new generation of scholars to develop on it. Prominent among these were Margaret Bowker and Peter Heath whose own researches, coincidentally published within the space of a single year, both drew on facets of Thompson's approach. Bowker's study, based on a thorough examination of the records of Lincoln diocese between 1495 and 1520, comprised an outline of its administration as well as a consideration of the recruitment patterns of its secular clergy, their general quality and economic position.[2] Heath's work was concerned more exclusively with the parochial clergy and, adopting a broadly similar archival methodology to Thompson, was based on 'strategic raids on key material' from a number of dioceses in order to produce a general overview of the quality of the pre-Reformation clergy and their economic and social position.[3] A significant strength of the work was the attention paid to the unbeneficed clergy, those who did not enjoy the security of a church living. Set against this, in terms of comparative application, was the question of the extent to which the evidence of his 'strategic raids' could be taken as typical.

This question was first tackled by a number of articles based on regional studies which appeared in the twenty years following the publication of the work of Bowker and Heath. These dealt mainly with particular aspects of the problem including ordination levels, standards of living and the significance of the unbeneficed clergy, and shared the common aim of testing general

---

[1] A.H. Thompson, *The English Clergy and their Organization in the Later Middle Ages* (Oxford, 1947).
[2] M. Bowker, *The Secular Clergy in the Diocese of Lincoln, 1495–1520* (Cambridge, 1968).
[3] P. Heath, *The English Parish Clergy on the Eve of the Reformation* (1969).

hypotheses against the evidence collected in local case studies.[4] In addition, in another book on the diocese of Lincoln continuing the story to the end of the reign of Henry VIII, Margaret Bowker looked at how the early stages of the English Reformation were implemented at local level.[5] However, scholarship of the past fifteen years has been revolutionised by Jack Scarisbrick's milestone work of 'revisionism', based mainly on the evidence of wills and other local records, in which he challenged the picture of the English Reformation that had held sway for the previous twenty years[6] by presenting the phenomenon as a state-sponsored attack on a genuinely popular and thriving religious culture.[7] Whilst one major local study subsequently appeared to challenge aspects of Scarisbrick's conclusions,[8] much recent work has been in agreement with his general thesis.[9] A common theme has been a challenge to the assumed inevitability of Reformation changes and the existence of widespread 'anticlericalism', a theme that has been stated most forcefully in the work of Christopher Haigh and Eamon Duffy.[10] Duffy's book, a detailed analysis of the religious culture of the English people between 1400 and 1580 in terms of 'traditional' religious practice and the attacks made upon it, has assumed prominence within the 'revisionist camp' and has informed all subsequent scholarship.

With specific regard to the parish clergy, important recent works have attempted to place them more fully in the context of social and religious culture.[11] However, despite Peter Marshall's assertion that 'after many years of ill-deserved neglect, the early sixteenth-century clergy have been well served by historians'[12] many of the methodological problems that faced an earlier generation of scholars (and thus the question of what and where was typical) remain. Whilst Martha Skeeters adopted the single-locality approach (in a

---

4 Of particular importance was the work by J.F. Fuggles, A.K. McHardy, J.A.H. Moran, N.P. Tanner and M.L. Zell (see bibliography).
5 M. Bowker, *The Henrician Reformation: The Diocese of Lincoln under John Longland, 1521–47* (Cambridge, 1981).
6 Exemplified by A.G. Dickens, *The English Reformation* (1964) and C. Cross, *Church and People, 1450–1660: The Triumph of the Laity in the English Church* (1976).
7 J.J. Scarisbrick, *The Reformation and the English People* (Oxford, 1984).
8 R. Whiting, *The Blind Devotion of the People: Popular Religion and the English Reformation* (Cambridge, 1989).
9 See in particular the work collected in C. Haigh, ed., *The English Reformation Revised* (Cambridge, 1987).
10 Ibid., *English Reformations: Religion, Politics, and Society under the Tudors* (Oxford, 1993); E. Duffy, *The Stripping of the Altars: Traditional Religion in England 1400–1580* (Yale, 1992).
11 M.C. Skeeters, *Community and Clergy: Bristol and the Reformation c.1530–c.1570* (Oxford, 1993); P. Marshall, *The Catholic Priesthood and the English Reformation* (Oxford, 1994); ibid., *The Face of the Pastoral Ministry in the East Riding, 1525–1595*, University of York Borthwick Paper No. 88 (York, 1995).
12 Marshall, *Catholic Priesthood*, 2.

novel departure, that of an individual city), Marshall chose a range of material covering the country as a whole, akin to Heath's 'strategic raids'. His thematic selection of 'eight paradigms of priestly function' made for an especially coherent study, though one that perhaps over-stressed the extent of the clergy's separation from lay society.

My own investigation into the careers and social position of the parish clergy is based on the records of a single diocese and is essentially prosopographical; whilst it would be naïve to pretend that collective biography will approximate more closely to the 'truth', it was my wish to avoid a survey of an overly impressionistic nature. The area chosen was the diocese of Coventry and Lichfield which, despite being the third most extensive in pre-Reformation England, has been largely neglected by historians, to a certain extent as a consequence of the poor survival of its records.[13] However, the potential rewards of the endeavour were obvious. Not only was the diocese the third largest in the country (after York and Lincoln) but it comprehended a geographically diverse area and could thus be argued as being particularly representative of the country as a whole. Extending from north Warwickshire through the midland counties of Staffordshire, northern Shropshire and Derbyshire to the north-western counties of Cheshire and Lancashire south of the Ribble, and bordering on Wales to the west, it comprised a varied topography, including areas of both lowland and upland agriculture. In terms of settlement, it ranged from small nucleated villages in the south-east to the sprawling parishes containing a multitude of small hamlets to the north-west and, whilst not being dominated by a single urban centre, contained the important cities of Coventry and Chester as well as some developing towns such as Birmingham (see Maps 1 and 2).

The principal sources chosen for study were those that emanated from the pontificate of Geoffrey Blythe, bishop of Coventry and Lichfield from 1503 to 1531, a period for which a sufficient range of material survives, in conjunction with the clerical subsidy returns of 1531 and 1533 and the *Valor Ecclesiasticus* of 1535. The subject of enquiry, and hence the title of the book, is those men either ordained as secular priests and/or who can be identified as having obtained parochial employment during this period of a little over a quarter of a century, a duration commonly seen as comprising a single generation. Thereafter, the choice of material was dictated simply by the aim of gathering as much information as possible for a collective biography of this body of men. In addition to the obvious sources such as the bishop's main register and supporting diocesan material, this included a small number of surviving wills and inventories, a sample for which the selection criteria were identical to the main subject group. Effectively therefore,

---

[13] The northern part of the diocese was included in Christopher Haigh's groundbreaking local study *Reformation and Resistance in Tudor Lancashire* (Cambridge, 1975).

the chronological scope of the book broadly encompasses the period from the first ordination ceremony in 1503 to the death of the last identifiable ordinand in 1567.

Geoffrey Blythe obtained the see of Coventry and Lichfield by papal provision on 5 May 1503, and was consecrated bishop on 20 September of the same year. Although he was born within the diocese, at Norton in Derbyshire, he was to be absent for much of his pontificate. As a nephew of Archbishop Thomas Rotherham of York, he was destined for ecclesiastical preferment and it was not long before he also came to the attention of the crown. His qualities were apparently much admired by Henry VII who sent him on a number of important foreign embassies towards the end of his reign, and under Henry VIII he acted as Lord President of Wales from 1512 to 1524. His personal activities within the diocese were largely restricted to a small number of ordination ceremonies and occasional, but very thorough, visitations of the cathedral and religious houses as well as presiding over the heresy trials conducted at Coventry in 1511 and 1512.[14] In his absence the diocese was ably administered by vicars-general and suffragan bishops and, at the local level, business such as institutions to benefices was carried out by the various archdeacons and their officials.

During most of the period of the study the diocese was divided for administrative purposes into five archdeaconries: Coventry (comprising the northern, 'Arden' portion of Warwickshire), Shrewsbury (comprising northern Shropshire), Chester (comprising Cheshire, Lancashire south of the Ribble and a few parishes across the Welsh border) and Stafford and Derby, both coterminous with their county boundaries. Of these, the archdeaconry of Chester enjoyed a large degree of administrative independence during the period[15] and constituted the major part of the new diocese of Chester at its creation in 1541. Each archdeaconry was further sub-divided into around half a dozen deaneries comprising various numbers of parishes. It was felt that identification of place names by county on all occasions in the text would be over-intrusive and readers should therefore refer to the index for questions of identification; all places have been identified according to their designations prior to the boundary changes of 1974. In accordance with contemporary practice, the designation of the diocese is frequently abbreviated to 'Lichfield'. Personal surnames, which were not subject to written uniformity in the early sixteenth century, have been standardised, either to the most common modern form or, in the case of testators, to the form used

---

14 BRUC, 67–8; J. Fines, 'Heresy Trials in the Diocese of Coventry and Lichfield, 1511–12', *JEH*, 14 (1963), 160–74. The preliminary hearings took place at the bishop's manor at Maxstoke.
15 P. Heath, 'The Medieval Archdeaconry and Tudor Bishopric of Chester', *JEH*, 20 (1969), 243–52.

in their wills. For the same reason, and for ease of communication between their world and ours, spelling and punctuation in quotations has generally been modernised and dates have been rendered in modern form.

1

Preparing for Priesthood

Why did an Englishman in the early sixteenth century decide to become a priest? Little as is known of the lives of the parish clergy of this period we know least of all concerning the fundamental considerations underlying this decision. Whilst it is a fair assumption that most took the step at an early stage in their adult lives, and one that receives some implicit support from the evidence,[1] it is little more than that. Throughout its history the Catholic Church has regarded ordination in terms of vocation, a direct calling from God, but matters of such a vital individual nature have left no impression on its administrative records. The rhetoric of contemporary apologists leaves no doubt that vocation was no less an ideal during a period that witnessed a growing, and seemingly insatiable, demand for the services of priesthood.[2] But the very reason for the frequent reassertion of the ideal was that the reality was influenced by the implications of that demand; that priesthood could be seen in functional terms and its rewards more material than spiritual. Furthermore, even if motivation were primarily economic, or inspired by a wish for social betterment, such considerations would often have been influenced by the requirements and aspirations of family, rather than being a matter of entirely individual choice. However, whether the decision to embark on a clerical career reflected real personal commitment or a desire for the associated status or remuneration, one thing is certain: the journey from the lay to the clerical state, from an entirely secular existence to the halfway house between the temporal and spiritual worlds that was encapsulated in priesthood, was one for which the traveller needed to be adequately equipped.

Education

It is now clear from research carried out over the past fifty years that educational provision, and thus the level of literacy within society, was greater in the early sixteenth century than has been traditionally assumed and that

---

[1] See below 57 and n. 102, 58, 82, 190–3.
[2] Marshall, *Catholic Priesthood*, 59.

such provision was expanding at a dramatic rate.³ In addition, the evidence from ordination registers such of those of the diocese of York, which record the ordinand's place of origin, and the very numbers that offered themselves for ordination, make it virtually certain that education at least at an elementary level was available in villages as well as towns, and that those who were able to benefit from it would have included boys from the lower end of the social spectrum.⁴ A memorial inscription of the period, from the village of Spofforth in Yorkshire, suggests that the nature of the distinction that members of the community made between those who had received elementary education and those who had not was essentially between those who were able to recite the *de Profundis* from the funeral liturgy and those who were restricted to a knowledge of the *Pater Noster, Hail Mary* and Creed.⁵ This assertion receives further support from the numerous wills of the period that made provision for children, sometimes described as 'little clerks', to recite or sing *de Profundis* around the hearse; wills such as that of the vicar of Abbots Bromley, Thomas Wylson, who in 1543 left money for 'every child that can say *de Profundis*' at his funeral.⁶ Such a distinction is of course particularly interesting in that it derives from an ability, albeit at a restricted level, to take part in the liturgy rather than simply recite the prayers that were the most basic requirement of any lay person's catechism. In other words, even at the most elementary level, education was of a type that prepared boys for the practice of priesthood and would have led even the humblest of young parishioners quite naturally towards a clerical career. The source of such education would have been one, or more, of the priests of the parish. Whilst such a role had perhaps always been expected of urban incumbents,⁷ by the early sixteenth century a wider clerical involvement in elementary education was envisaged. In 1529 a directive of the Canterbury Convocation stated that 'rectors, vicars and chantry priests after divine service shall employ themselves in study, prayer, lectures or other honest affairs or

---

3   See in particular J.A.H. Moran, *The Growth of English Schooling 1340–1548: Learning, Literacy, and Laicization in Pre-Reformation York Diocese* (Princeton, NJ, 1985).
4   C. Cross, 'Ordinations in the Diocese of York 1500–1630', in C. Cross, ed., *Patronage and Recruitment in the Tudor and Early Stuart Church*, Borthwick Studies in History, 2 (York, 1996), 5; Moran, *English Schooling*, 175, where she points out that the 1405/6 enactment of the Statute of Labourers includes the clause that serfs were to be 'free to set their son or daughter to take learning at any manner school that pleaseth them within the realm'; and 181, where she suggests a 'highly provisional and tentative' estimate that 12% of the total population of York diocese had been through at least elementary education by 1530. She offers the figure 'only as a minimal estimate'.
5   Ibid., 52.
6   Ibid.; will of Thomas Wylson (for references to all cited clerical wills from the diocese, see appendix).
7   See S. Townley, 'Unbeneficed Clergy in the Thirteenth Century: Two English Dioceses', in D.M. Smith, ed., *Studies in Clergy and Ministry in Medieval England*, Borthwick Studies in History, 1 (1991), 62, where he discusses the involvement of priests in education in the dioceses of Hereford and Worcester in the 13th and 14th centuries.

business which becomes their profession: namely, by instructing boys in the alphabet, in reading, in singing, or in grammar'.[8] Since such 'schools' were rarely formally endowed their existence is only occasionally identifiable in the historical record. The wills of a number of York priests, for example, reveal that they had been involved in education, like Robert Morres who had started by running a school associated with St John's Gild and by the end of his career had become the master of the Ouse Bridge Civic School; or John Lee, whose involvement in the teaching of children is recorded only in the money owed to him at his death in 1549.[9] A similar case in Lichfield diocese was the Chesterfield curate Richard Whitworth who made a bequest of school fees owing to him when he drew up his will in 1559.[10] Such schools were frequently associated with chantries and the Edwardian returns demonstrate that they were often set up at the initiative of parishioners rather than as part of the formal endowment of the chantry.[11] At least 10% of chantries in Lancashire and Staffordshire had schools attached to them and it has been suggested on the basis of such evidence that there were probably well over 200 such schools in the country as a whole by the 1540s.[12]

Based in often informal schools associated with a single priest as master, the syllabus of much elementary education was founded on the catechism and, as children progressed, on the liturgy.[13] A surviving printed *ABC* from c.1538 contains, in addition to the alphabet, table graces, the Seven Corporate Acts of Mercy, the Ten Commandments and the Seven Deadly Sins, all in English. Young scholars then progressed through the *Pater Noster, Hail Mary* and *Creed*, all given in Latin and English, and finally to sections of the Latin antiphoner which the children would presumably have been expected to learn by rote. The book makes explicit its dual purpose as an educational tool and one that would prepare the early steps to a clerical career by noting that the sections from the antiphoner were designed 'to help a priest to sing'. Also used in elementary education were primers both in Latin and English and, occasionally, books of hours. From these the reading scholar would progress to the committal to memory of the *de Profundis*, other parts of the funeral and daily masses, particularly the hours of the Virgin, and finally to

---

8   Quoted in Moran, *English Schooling*, 143.
9   C. Cross, 'The Incomes of Provincial Urban Clergy, 1520–1645', in R. O'Day and F. Heal, eds, *Princes and Paupers in the English Church 1500–1800* (Leicester, 1981), 75.
10 Will of Richard Whitworth.
11 Moran, *English Schooling*, 50, 167.
12 Heath, *English Parish Clergy*, 84; B.A. Kümin, *The Shaping of a Community: The Rise and Reformation of the English Parish c.1400–1560* (Aldershot, 1996), 161.
13 For the following see Moran, *English Schooling*, 41, 44, 46–8, 52; Heath, *English Parish Clergy*, 82–6. The grammar exercises produced by masters themselves were frequently based on material of a more secular nature, such as childhood reminiscences: see N. Orme, 'Schoolmasters, 1307–1509', in C.H. Clough, ed., *Profession, Vocation and Culture in Late Medieval England: Essays Dedicated to the Memory of A.R. Myers* (Liverpool, 1982), 233–7.

learning the entire psalter. Whilst not necessarily requiring a full understanding of the grammar, through work on the psalter the scholar would be expected to demonstrate skills of recognition and pronunciation. Again, statements made in wills that have been studied in the diocese of York suggest that young people of a parish described as scholars would be expected to have learned the entire psalter in Latin. The provisions drawn up by the foundation of a chantry school in Berkshire in 1526 show that a reading knowledge of Latin was to be acquired, specifically through the teaching of the alphabet, the main prayers, table graces and, significantly, in terms of education for a future clerical career, the collects, psalms, prayers for the dead and 'everything necessary to help the priest at mass'. The close link between elementary education and the parish church is again reinforced by evidence such as the restriction placed on the parish clerk of St Nicholas, Bristol, in 1481 from removing any book from the choir for use in teaching children without express permission, and the bequest of thirty books in 1524 to the church of All Saints in the same city by its clerk, who included the condition that 'no children should be taught upon the said books'.

Whilst it is clear, therefore, that much elementary education had a liturgical basis and was directed mainly towards reading, the curriculum was probably only limited by the particular interests and skills of the teacher. The master of the children's school at Rolleston, Staffordshire, was also teaching writing and the preparation of accounts in the 1520s and the chantry certificates of 1546–48 provide several examples of clergy teaching writing as well as reading and grammar.[14] William Bridges, a chaplain at Macclesfield and master of the grammar school there, was responsible for the early education of no less a figure than Raphael Holinshed who went on to become one of the foremost historians of his age.[15] Further educational opportunity for the children of the diocese was likely to have come from the monasteries either directly, through their almonry schools, or indirectly by their charitable provision for the support of children's education in other institutions, of the type suggested by the maintenance of fifty boys at York Minster Grammar School by St Mary's Abbey.[16] More direct evidence from Lichfield diocese comes from the thriving cathedral choir school established by the later fifteenth century and its associated library, completed at the beginning of the sixteenth century, showing that a culture of quality education was at least in existence in the spiritual centre of the diocese. Additionally it is quite likely that the residentiary canons of the cathedral were involved in more general education of boys, at least those from the more

---

[14] Moran, *English Schooling*, 50.
[15] Described in Bridges' will of 1536 as 'Raufe Holynzed, my scholar' the recipient of 6s 8d and the chaplain's horse. Holinshed's *History of England* was published in 1577; see footnote in the appendix for the identification.
[16] Ibid., 176.

privileged classes, in their own households.[17] The teaching of song, a vital part of the education of a prospective priest, was probably quite distinct from a general reading and grammar education, the training being directed towards the mastery of plainsong and, increasingly, polyphony. Although at its highest level such education was probably the reserve of monasteries and aristocratic households as well as the cathedral, it would also have been available in many collegiate institutions, parish churches and their associated chantries.[18] When, in about 1503, the citizens of Walsall learned that one of the chantry patrons, Sir Henry Vernon, was about to remove his chaplain John Staple to employment elsewhere, they wrote an imploring letter to him, claiming, among other things, that 'he has kept a school, and taught the poor children of the town of his charity, taking nothing for his labour'. Whatever else he might have taught, Staple would almost certainly have been involved in the teaching of song, since books of pricksong feature prominently in the inventory of church goods drawn up in 1515.[19]

It has now been established beyond doubt that there was a dramatic growth in the provision of elementary and secondary education throughout the country from about the mid fifteenth century to the mid sixteenth, to the extent that one recent writer has spoken of 'an early sixteenth-century explosion in grammar education'.[20] The number of grammar schools in the diocese of York increased almost threefold between 1500 and 1548, though by the latter date they were still outnumbered by elementary schools by about two to one.[21] A thorough survey of educational provision in the diocese of Coventry and Lichfield has not, to date, been carried out, and is beyond the scope of this book; nevertheless, as well as the parochially based, virtually *ad hoc* schooling that appears to have been available over a wide area of the diocese, around thirty formally established and endowed schools have been identified, the majority being grammar schools. The greatest number, fourteen, have been identified in the archdeaconry of Chester, of which the majority were in Lancashire, including a cluster of endowed

---

[17] VCH Staffs., iii, 164–5, 166; Moran, English Schooling, 107 (quoting R.B. Dobson); D. Lepine, A Brotherhood of Canons Serving God: English Secular Cathedrals in the Later Middle Ages (Woodbridge, 1995), 129–30. For general comments regarding the role of secular cathedrals in education and the recruitment of prospective secular clergy see N. Orme, Education and Society in Medieval and Renaissance England (London, 1989), 203–4.
[18] Moran, English Schooling, 53, 60.
[19] Ibid., 81; G.P. Mander, ed., Churchwardens' Accounts of All Saints, Walsall, 1462–1521, William Salt Society, Collections for a History of Staffordshire, 3rd series (1930), 249.
[20] Moran, English Schooling, 221. In the words of Nicholas Orme: 'It is now a well established fact that schooling was available all over England during the fourteenth and fifteenth centuries. Many institutions existed from which it could be obtained, and a wide variety of people spent their time providing it'; Orme, 'Schoolmasters, 1307–1509', 218.
[21] Moran, English Schooling, 117–22.

grammar schools in the vicinity of Manchester.²² The indenture for Manchester Grammar School itself, drawn up in 1515, was remarkably broad in its scope, specifying that the master should 'teach and instruct others, as well youths and grown-up persons, in his learning and wisdom'.²³ The endowed grammar school at Warrington started out as a free school attached to the chantry of Sir Thomas Butler in the parish church. In his will of 1521 Butler stipulated that the establishment of the school was aimed at providing education for the promotion of piety 'in order that men's sons might learn grammar, to the intent that they thereby might better learn to know Almighty God and serve him according to their duties'. Butler's nominee as first master, Richard Taylor, was still in post in 1569.²⁴ Thomas Hatton and John Latham, masters of the endowed grammar schools at Farnworth and Malpas respectively, were both local men who had been educated at Oxford. Hatton supplicated for his degree of Bachelor of Grammar in 1514 after twelve years' study and had been ordained priest eight years previously; Latham was admitted to the bachelor's degrees in grammar and arts after eighteen years' study and fifteen years spent as a school teacher and was ordained priest in 1521 to the same title as Hatton, that of Norton priory. Both men were thus well qualified to impart high quality secondary education to the boys in their charge, many of whom would doubtless have subsequently embarked on clerical careers themselves.²⁵

The examples of Hatton and Latham serve to remind us of the commitment of time, let alone money, that would have been required to follow elementary and grammar or song schooling with the acquisition of a university degree, and it should thus be no surprise that graduates remained a minority group within the parochial clergy of the early sixteenth century, albeit one that, largely in response to the directives of the ecclesiastical hierarchy and calls from lay commentators, was increasing in size. Nationally, the proportion of known graduates being admitted to benefices by the mid sixteenth

---

22 N. Orme, *English Schools in the Middle Ages* (1973), *passim*; ibid., *Education and Society*, *passim*; for location see Map 2.
23 Moran, *English Schooling*, 66.
24 F.R. Raines, ed., *A History of the Chantries within the County Palatine of Lancaster*, vol. 1, Chetham Society, Remains Historical and Literary Connected with the Palatine Counties of Lancaster and Chester, vol. lix, 58. Christopher Haigh, who offers a low assessment of the quality of Lancashire elementary and grammar education during the period ('The number of schools was small, and the quality of the education they gave *cannot have been high*' – my italics), describes Taylor as 'a violent, quarrelsome and disobedient priest whom the church courts could not control'. Presumably his opinion of Taylor, like that of Edward Molyneux (below, 68), is based on his appearance in court records, a form of evidence that must be used with caution in providing character evaluations. The reasons for his opinions of educational standards generally are less clear, particularly given his appreciation of the ability of the county to produce high numbers of ordinands; Haigh, *Reformation and Resistance*, 38, 41–3.
25 LJRO, B/A/1/14, fos. 16v, 20v, 24v, 139r, 140v, 142v, 145r; BL, Harleian Ms 594, fos. 148r, 149r; *BRUO 1501–1540*, 274, 343.

century was between 10 and 33 per cent, the variation in estimates being partly as a result of differences of opinion as to whether holders of both bachelor's and master's degrees should be included as graduates.[26] Using the wider definition, out of 410 admissions to livings within the diocese of Coventry and Lichfield between 1503 and 1531, ninety-five, or just under 25%, were of clerks holding university degrees. To this should be added the unquantifiable number of graduates who did not obtain a benefice and thus do not usually surface in the records, and a further group of men who attended university without proceeding to graduation, estimated at perhaps two-thirds of those who matriculated.[27] Given the quality and availability of elementary and secondary education that has been argued for this and other dioceses, it would be inappropriate to regard such men as uneducated. They would doubtless have included many such as William Green, the Lincolnshire labourer's son whose educational tribulations are charted in the records of the Norwich Corporation for 1521. Having been taught grammar for two years at a school in his village of Wanlet he spent five or six years working with his father before moving to Boston where he continued to work to earn the fees for part-time schooling. After a further two-and-a-half years he went to Cambridge, again taking part-time jobs such as ale-carrying and saffron-picking in order to pay for tuition. Some time later he travelled to Rome in an unsuccessful attempt to receive ordination and returned to Cambridge where he was able to obtain a licence to collect subscriptions towards a further year's education. Unfortunately he only collected funds sufficient for eight weeks' schooling and his attempted forgery of a new licence and a certificate of ordination from Rome made him the subject of a criminal enquiry in Norwich. Whilst nothing is known of his ultimate fate, it is certain that he was not the only young man from a humble background who attempted to persevere against the odds in order to gain an education and entry into a clerical career.[28]

Examination

Once the decision had been taken by an individual to seek ordination, the initial purpose of his education would be to prepare him for the process of examination prior to being admitted to orders. Canon law, backed up in England by the decree of the thirteenth-century Council of Oxford, placed requirements both on the examinees and the examiners. As a minimum the candidate would be required to demonstrate that there was no impediment to his receiving orders; he was to be of free and legitimate birth, have

---

[26] S. Brigden, *London and the Reformation* (Oxford, 1989), 58; Bowker, *Secular Clergy*, 45; Heath, *English Parish Clergy*, 81; Marshall, *Pastoral Ministry in the East Riding*, 12.
[27] Bowker, *Secular Clergy*, 45.
[28] Cited in Moran, *English Schooling*, 176.

reached the canonical minimum age (eighteen for subdeacons, nineteen for deacons and twenty-four for priests), unmarried, not a homicide, not seeking preferment through simony or fraud, and not suffering from physical disability, although a case could be made for papal dispensation from most of these if the candidate was prepared to undergo the cost and effort.[29] Of the examiners the law required thorough application of procedure; a bishop who knowingly ordained unsuitable candidates was judged to have sinned as gravely as the man attempting ordination by means of deception.[30] The examinations usually took place in a period of a few days before the ordination ceremony itself although, as is apparent from the evidence from Lichfield diocese, there was scope for departure from this practice.[31] It was customary for the examinations to be conducted by an archdeacon but again, a bishop was free to delegate responsibility to other suitably qualified and eminent persons as might be expedient.[32] Increasingly, expediency dictated that personal scrutiny might occasionally be replaced by the presentation of adequate letters of testimony, though whilst these might have been commonplace as regards statements of freedom from canonical impediment, there is little evidence to suggest that they entirely superseded *viva voce* examinations, at least in the case of candidates for secular orders. Where such documents *were* admitted they were probably themselves scrutinised for authenticity by an official.[33]

There is evidence that by the end of the fifteenth century greater emphasis was being placed on the examination of intellectual attainment in addition to a judgement of personal credentials and moral suitability.[34] In part, this probably came in response to public criticism in some quarters of the numbers of unsuitably qualified candidates allegedly being admitted to orders. Perhaps the most telling criticism of educational standards, since he was addressing an audience of ordinands himself, came from William Melton, chancellor of York, in a sermon published c.1510.[35] In this exhortation to new parish priests in his diocese, Melton spelled out the need for raising

---

[29] Heath, *English Parish Clergy*, 15; R.N. Swanson, *Church and Society in Late Medieval England* (Oxford, 1993 edn), 58. Obtaining dispensations was, of course, a less arduous matter whilst Wolsey exercised his legatine power although only one such dispensation is recorded in Bythe's list of institutions, that from defect of birth displayed by Richard Comberford at his presentation to the vicarage of Hartington in 1528: LJRO, B/A/1/14, fo. 41v. However, compare the number of dispensations issued for reception of multiple orders below, 29.

[30] W.J. Dohar, 'Medieval Ordination Lists: The Origins of a Record', *Archives*, 20, no. 87 (1992), 21.

[31] Ibid., 23–4; Heath, *English Parish Clergy*, 16.

[32] H.S. Bennett, 'Medieval Ordination Lists in the English Episcopal Registers', in J. Conway Davies, ed., *Studies Presented to Sir Hilary Jenkinson* (1957), 23; Dohar, 'Medieval Ordination Lists', 23.

[33] Dohar, 'Medieval Ordination Lists', 22–3.

[34] Bowker, *Secular Clergy*, 43–4.

[35] W. Melton, *Sermo Exhortatorius Cancelarii Ebor[acensis]*, W. de Worde, sig. Aiii.

intellectual and moral standards if the clergy were to rise above an increasing volume of educated lay criticism, though the fact that he chose to convey this important message in Latin is suggestive of the level at which he viewed the minimum educational attainment of candidates for orders. Indeed, it was fluent Latinity, of a kind that could have been mastered by a good grounding in secondary education, on which Melton placed greatest emphasis. But his arguments were equally concerned with the perceived moral failings of many of the young men who were being ordained in his time, a theme in which he received support from his friend John Colet, dean of St Paul's, and their contemporary Sir Thomas More. Writing a little after Melton, Colet seems generally satisfied with intellectual competence and stressed that there should be more rigorous examination of an individual's level of devotion and commitment to godly living; sentiments echoed by More in his assertion in 1526 that 'there should be more diligence used in the choice not of their learning only, but much more specially of their living'.[36] Thus, despite the fact that the writers of the most widely consulted pastoral manuals, William of Pagula and John de Burgh, agreed with the canonists that examination should not be over-exacting and should aim primarily at a demonstration of a reasonable level of literacy applicable to liturgical performance,[37] contemporaries appear to have been generally satisfied that examinations were being conducted with sufficient intellectual rigour.[38]

The problem faced by historians is that there is so little surviving evidence of examination procedures from this period, although the fact that they had taken place was recorded quite regularly in the diocese of Lincoln from 1532 onwards.[39] The survival of four lists of examinees in the diocese of Coventry and Lichfield therefore assumes some relative importance.[40] The fact that they were recorded not in the ordination register but among material relating to the bishop's visitations suggests that in Lichfield diocese examination was part of visitation procedure rather than the routine of the ordination ceremonies, unless of course the very survival of these lists derives from their atypical nature. The examinations were conducted in August 1521 at the collegiate church of Manchester and the Augustinian priory of Norton, Cheshire, and at the Benedictine monastery of Upholland, Lancashire, in the same month and again in August 1524, presumably arranged in both cases to precede the September ordination ceremonies. As well as containing the names of examinees, which can then be collated with references in the ordination register, the examiners are also identified, seven individuals being commissioned in all. In keeping with common episcopal practice,

---

[36] Colet and More quoted in Heath, *English Parish Clergy*, 15.
[37] Dohar, 'Medieval Ordination Lists', 22.
[38] Heath, *English Parish Clergy*, 18, is more sceptical.
[39] M. Bowker, *The Henrician Reformation*, 39.
[40] P. Heath, ed., *Bishop Blythe's Visitations c.1515–1525*, Staffordshire Record Society, Collections for a History of Staffordshire, 4th ser., 7 (1973), lxiii–lxiv, 104–6, 166.

two of these, Joachim Bretunner and Richard Strete, were archdeacons, of Shrewsbury and Derby respectively. Bretunner was a non-resident canon of Lichfield Cathedral and fellow of King's Hall, Cambridge, who held a doctorate of theology from the University of Turin.[41] In addition to being a resident canon of the cathedral, Richard Strete was dean of the collegiate church of St Chad, Shrewsbury, and a canon of the collegiate church of St John, Chester. The holder of an Oxford MA, he was appointed as guardian of the see *sede vacante* following the death of Bishop Blythe in 1531.[42] The most senior of the other examiners was Ralph Cantrell who, as well as being a residentiary canon of the cathedral and dean of St John's, Chester, was the bishop's vicar-general and holder of a doctorate of canon law from the University of Cambridge.[43] William Clyff (who is believed to have held a doctorate but the discipline is unknown) and George Colyer, the holder of an Oxford BA, were successive wardens of the collegiate church of Manchester and Colyer was also a canon of the collegiate church of Stafford.[44] Thomas Sparke was another doctor of canon law and Henry Trafford held a master's degree and was rector of Wilmslow and a chaplain in the collegiate church of Manchester.[45] The group of examiners thus comprised some of the senior academic clergy of the diocese, and the inclusion of doctors of canon law and theology suggests examinational rigour as does the fact that each examiner was responsible for only a small number of candidates at each session. It is likely that Cantrell, Clyff and Strete were among the chief examiners for the diocese; in the case of the first two because they were responsible for a large proportion of the ordinands and were examining in each location. Although Richard Strete was responsible for conducting only five of the examinations, his position as archdeacon of Shrewsbury, yet examining in the north of the diocese, suggests that he was probably employed extensively. It is probable that George Colyer and Henry Trafford were responsible for examinations held at their own institution, Manchester Collegiate Church, and that senior clergy in other places were employed on a similar *ad hoc* basis.[46]

---

41 BRUC, 92.
42 BRUO 1501–1540, 546.
43 BRUC, 121.
44 *Blythe's Visitations*, 105, 106.
45 Ibid., 106, 166. Whilst Sparke's qualification as an examiner of intellectual and doctrinal aptitude is beyond question, his suitability as a judge of clerical morality might be questioned by his fathering of an illegitimate son whose future was a major concern of his will drawn up in 1527. The boy's name, Justinian, suggests, however, that Sparke was not overly concerned by future questioning of his parentage: *Blythe's Visitations*, 104; G.J. Piccope, ed., *Lancashire and Cheshire Wills and Inventories from the Ecclesiastical Court, Chester: The First Portion*, Chetham Society, Remains Historical and Literary connected with the Palatine Counties of Lancaster and Chester, xxxiii (1857), 16–17.
46 Dohar, 'Medieval Ordination Lists', 23.

A total of ninety-three candidates were examined over the four sessions;[47] subsequent references in the ordination register reveals that their titles (see below) derived almost exclusively from monasteries in Cheshire and Lancashire, suggesting that the men were being examined within their own locality.[48] Collation of the names of the examinees with references in the ordination register tends to confirm the suggestion that these were men who had been previously admitted to the last of the minor orders, acolyte, and were being examined for admission to the subdiaconate.[49] This, the first of the major, often referred to as holy, orders, was the most significant stage in a man's clerical career. Up to this point he would still be able to marry; afterwards he was committed to celibacy and, most likely, a progression towards priesthood. As such, the lists would seem to confirm that the examination procedure was taken seriously by the diocesan authorities since candidates were being examined by senior episcopal officials at an early stage in their clerical careers.[50] Subsequent examinations were likely to have taken place for entry to the diaconate, by which time candidates would be expected to display sound scriptural, musical and liturgical knowledge, and the priesthood, at which stage competent Latinity would be tested.[51]

The seriousness of the step up from the minor to the major orders is further emphasised by the fact that admission to the subdiaconate was often delayed, sometimes for a term of years, a situation that was probably encouraged by the authorities as a time for testing the strength of vocation and commitment.[52] Only nine of the examinees cannot be subsequently traced in the ordination register up to 1531.[53] Some of these might have failed the examination and either abandoned or delayed plans for a clerical career; others might have delayed progress for a time beyond the period of seven to ten years between the dates of the examinations and the termination of Blythe's register; some might have had no intention of proceeding further. Of the remaining candidates, a few can be traced through to the diaconate only, but the majority, to priesthood. Few proceeded to the subdiaconate without some delay. Table 1 takes as a sample the fifty-eight candidates

---

[47] This compares with approximate annual ordination figures for 1521 of 140 acolytes and 180 subdeacons, and for 1524 of 130 acolytes and 145 subdeacons: see Graphs 1 and 2 below, 31, 32.

[48] The exceptions were Launde Priory (Thurstan Cokke, George Pynnyngton, George Plumton), Repton Priory (John Coke), Dieulacres Abbey (William Pickering, Thomas Ashley), Stratford-at-Bow, London and Vale Royal Abbey (William Hadfield).

[49] T.N. Cooper, 'The Secular Clergy of the Diocese of Coventry and Lichfield in the Early Sixteenth Century', unpublished Univ. of Birmingham Ph.D. thesis (1992), 20–22.

[50] *Blythe's Visitations*, lxiii; Heath, *English Parish Clergy*, 14–15.

[51] Dohar, 'Medieval Ordination Lists', 22.

[52] Swanson, *Church and Society*, 42; Heath, *English Parish Clergy*, 14.

[53] Robert Coryer, John Wyttour, William Sterky, John Weyme, Hugh Utley, Robert Longton, William Hoskayne, Matthew Chelwaw, Oliver Taliare, Robert Hobbroyle, and Geoffrey Warton.

known to have been ordained subdeacon following their examination and shows the numbers admitted at each subsequent ceremony.

Table 1. Examination of ordinands

Examination of August, 1521		Examination of August 1524	
21.9.21	5	24.9.24	—
22.12.21	9	17.12.24	1
15.3.22	5	11.3.25	—
13.6.22	5	10.6.25	4
20.9.22	2	22.9.25	—
15.12.22	—	23.12.25	—
27.2.23	4	24.2.26	—
30.5.23	—	26.5.26	—
19.9.23	7	22.9.26	1
19.12.23	1	22.12.26	—
20.3.24	5	26.3.27	—
21.5.24	1	15.6.27	—
24.9.24	1	21.9.27	—
17.12.24	—	21.12.27	—
11.3.25	1	7.3.28	—
10.6.25	—	6.6.28	—
Beyond this	4	Beyond this	2
Total	50	Total	8

These figures confirm that the examination was more than a mere formality after which the candidate proceeded immediately to higher orders. Assuming that the majority of candidates were successful in the examination, a significant proportion were not taking the next step towards priesthood until two, three or more years afterwards. Although an apparent under-recording of the admission of acolytes in some years renders exact statistics impossible (see Graph 1 on p. 31), it is clear from a collation of the names of clergy recorded in the 1533 subsidy with their ordination records that a gap before entry to the subdiaconate of one or more years was not unusual. Indeed, it could be considerably longer; an extreme case was William Yate who appears to have waited no less than twenty-one years following his admission as an acolyte to progress to the major orders at subsequent ceremonies in 1529.[54]

[54] Ordained acolyte 21 July 1508, subdeacon 22 May 1529, deacon 18 September 1529, priest 18 December 1529; LJRO, B/A/1/14ii, fos. 51v, 201v, 204r, 206r. It is, of course, possible that two individuals are involved here, but with the coincidence of one being ordained only as acolyte and the other having only the major orders recorded. Further

Titles

The significance of the progression from acolyte to subdeacon is further emphasised by the fact that it was at this stage that the candidate was required to present evidence of title. This was the canon law requirement that each ordinand should be able to present proof of his ability to support himself financially up to the time of gaining employment, so as not to become a burden on the resources of the diocese. Theoretically at least, evidence of such a title was a matter of the utmost gravity, since any bishop ordaining a candidate with inadequate title would himself be liable as guarantor of his future financial security.[55] The title in its original sense was one to a benefice, by which the candidate could demonstrate that his future living was secure. Alternatively, proof of a private income, sometimes stipulated at around five marks per annum was acceptable, which would be recorded as title deriving from the candidate's patrimony.[56] This two-tier system could only function adequately at times of a limited supply of priests relative to the number of available benefices. Even by the time of the earliest surviving episcopal ordination registers, the vast majority of titles were to the candidate's patrimony rather than to a benefice.[57] By the fourteenth century, a further change had occurred. During this period the number of titles based on patrimony or the sponsorship of an individual patron declined dramatically in favour of those provided by religious institutions. The change occurred remarkably quickly; in some areas even suddenly.[58] Two possible reasons for this procedural change present themselves. The thirteenth century had witnessed an ever-growing number of appropriations of parish churches by the religious houses and other religious corporations. One corollary of this development was that such institutions now became the major patrons of parochial livings. As the supply of priests moved towards a point of surpassing the number of available benefices, the emphasis for the provision of titles shifted to the religious houses as patrons. Theoretically, though a candidate might be unable to show that his future support derived from his actual tenure of a benefice, the religious patron would act as guarantor until such time as a living in its gift became available.[59] Under such a system it

---

suggestion of a single individual derives from the fact that the name occurs in the ordination register on these occasions only.
55 Bennett, 'Medieval Ordination Lists', 26.
56 R.N. Swanson, 'Titles to Orders in Medieval English Episcopal Registers', in H. Mayr-Harting and R.I. Moore, eds, *Studies in Medieval History Presented to R.H.C. Davies* (1985), 236.
57 Ibid.
58 Ibid., 233.
59 Bowker, *Secular Clergy*, 61. One suggestion is the possibility that ordinands served short stipendiary contracts in parishes appropriated to the house providing the title, though no corroborative evidence of such an arrangement has been found in the present study: J.C.H. Aveling, 'The English Clergy, Catholic and Protestant, in the

would be expected that those orders which commanded the greatest share of patronage would have provided the greatest number of titles. If this were not the case, then the charge could be made that the majority of monastic titles were no more than at best a legal fiction, at worst fraud, involving the house in no actual responsibility to act as an individual's financial guarantor, for which the onus would still rest with the ordaining bishop.

An alternative explanation has been offered based largely on the speed and near-completeness of the change in procedure.[60] This would be difficult to account for except in the context of official sanction or even instigation. Thus it is argued that the episcopate, faced with the increasing difficulty in enforcing titles provided by individual presenters and determining their validity, delegated a more general responsibility for the selection of ordinands to the religious houses.[61] Rather than acting themselves as guarantors of financial security, the monasteries were operating as a form of 'clearing house'. The candidate would initially be required to present himself to the house with proof of his capacity for financial independence, or to be presented by a third party who was to act as his security. In both cases, such evidence could be incorporated in a document which would also treat as to the general character and suitability of the candidate for priesthood. This document could be checked by the house which would then pass on approved candidates to the ordaining bishop, possibly after also administering a preliminary examination. Therefore the religious houses would not be providing the actual title themselves but the guarantee that the necessary deeds had been examined and validated. On completion of this administrative change, the separate recording of the initial presenter of the candidate disappears from the registers to be replaced simply by the name of the 'clearing' institution. The main deficiency in this argument is a lack of direct evidence for the operation of such an administrative procedure; indirect evidence, however, can be shown to support it. In the following discussion the relative merits of these two hypotheses will be examined.

Whilst in some dioceses it would appear that registration of titles was a somewhat random affair, those for ordinands in Coventry and Lichfield during this period were meticulously recorded, providing a sound basis for a comparative study of procedure.[62] In line with developments in other parts of the country, candidates were ordained almost exclusively to the title of religious corporations; in the great majority of cases, monasteries. Between 1504 and 1531 there is evidence of only just over forty exceptions. All but five of these were to the title of a benefice; a rectory, vicarage or prebendal

16th and 17th centuries', in W. Haase, ed., *Rome and the Anglicans: Historical and Doctrinal Aspects of Anglican-Roman Catholic Relations* (Berlin, 1982), 64.
[60] For the following, see Swanson, 'Titles to Orders', *passim*.
[61] Dohar, 'Medieval Ordination Lists', 27.
[62] Heath, *English Parish Clergy*, 17, suggests a laxity in recording of titles in some episcopal registers.

stall in a collegiate institution. The exceptions include John Sharp of Glasgow diocese, ordained deacon in 1511 to the title of ten pounds[63] and M. Peter Legh in 1514 and Nicholas Holland in 1526, for whom it was recorded simply that title was to the ordinand's patrimony.[64] John Paplowe's (*alias* Poppye), title to ordination as subdeacon in 1526 was to his patrimony but supported explicitly by the Augustinian abbey of Croxden in Staffordshire.[65] Two candidates appear to have been ordained to the title of lay sponsors: in 1512 William ap Jenyns of the diocese of York was ordained priest to the title of Sir William Gre[en], and in 1522 William Cusmere was ordained subdeacon 'per Thomas Fitz'.[66] University graduates would occasionally, though not always, be ordained to the title of their college fellowship, thus a small number of titles derive from the Oxford colleges of All Souls, Magdalen and Balliol and, at Cambridge, King's Hall, Jesus and St John's. It is likely that those graduates from the diocese who appear in the ordination register represent the minority; most would probably have been ordained by letters dimissory by the bishop of Lincoln, in the case of Oxford, and of Ely in the case of Cambridge.[67]

The vast majority of titles, however, derived from religious houses. Evidence of the location in which ordinands eventually received benefices, and from wills, suggests that the provider of the title was usually an institution in the vicinity of the candidate's place of origin.[68] This suggestion is further supported by the fact that the great majority of the ordinands examined in Lancashire were subsequently ordained to titles of monasteries within that county.[69] Over the twenty-six years for which the ordination register is complete, an average of one hundred different houses provided titles to ordinands each year. The maximum number occurred at the beginning of the period, with no fewer than 119 separate institutions providing titles in 1506, and did not fall below the total of 91 for 1521. All but a small minority of the houses providing titles were within the diocese. Most of the exceptions were monasteries close to the diocesan border; among the regular providers of titles were six houses in Nottinghamshire, four in Leicestershire, two in Northamptonshire and one each from Herefordshire and Worcestershire. To

---

[63] LJRO, B/A/1/14ii, fo. 81v.
[64] Ibid., fos. 96r, 172r.
[65] Ibid., fo. 183v. Similarly, only two men were ordained to patrimonial titles in the diocese of Lincoln between 1495 and 1520; Bowker, *Secular Clergy*, 61.
[66] Ibid., fos. 92r, 152v. The use of the abbreviation suggests that this was probably the precentor of Lichfield Cathedral, Thomas Fitzherbert.
[67] Ibid., 39.
[68] Similarly, in the diocese of Lincoln; Bowker, *Secular Clergy*, 61. This might also add indirect support to the suggestion that monasteries provided titles to *alumni* of their schools as might the testamentary bequest of a Yorkshire priest to the monastery which provided his title: Aveling, 'The English Clergy', 64; Cross, 'Ordinations in the Diocese of York', 7. See below, 104.
[69] See above, 17.

facilitate an analysis of significant regular providers of titles, the average annual total of one hundred houses providing titles can be reduced by half by excluding those institutions which did not account for a minimum of 0.5% of the total number of titles provided during the period as a whole. These regular providers of titles are listed in order of their total provision over the period in the table below, in which the totals comprise each recorded grant of a title. Titles to individuals for each of the major orders have not been collated, so a rough estimate of the number of individuals involved requires division by three.

Table 2. Most significant regular providers of titles

Key to orders
A: Augustinian; B: Benedictine;
C: Cistercian; P: Premonstratensian

Key to columns
A: Valued at over £200, 1535
B: Valued above average for order, 1535
C: No. of presentations and % of total
D: Greater proportion of total titles than presentations
E: No. of presentations of candidates to whom title provided

	House	Order	Total	A	B	C	As %	D	E
1.	Norton	A	926		+	2	1.2	+	—
2.	Whalley	C	919	+	+	1	0.6	+	—
3.	Dieulacres	C	713	+		—			—
4.	Upholland	B	708			1	0.6	+	—
5.	Vale Royal	C	451	+	+	2	1.2	+	1
6.	Birkenhead	B	436			—			—
7.	Chester	B	425	+	+	23	14		—
8.	Baswich	A	363			2	1.2	+	—
9.	Beauchief	P	348			1	0.6	+	—
10.	Darley	A	293	+	+	—			—
11.	Burscough	A	290			—			—
12.	Combermere	C	286	+		2	1.2	+	—
13.	Ranton	A	283			1	0.6	+	—
14.	Repton	A	265			1	0.6	+	1
15.	Merevale	C	264	+	+	2	1.2	+	—
16.	Buildwas	C	238			—			—
17.	Croxden	C	192			1	0.6	+	—
18.	Lilleshall	A	187	+	+	2	1.2	+	—
19.	Dale	P	179		+	—			—
20.	Newstead	A	167			3	1.8	+	—
	Hulton	C	167			—			—
22.	Halesowen	P	160	+	+	—			—
23.	Rocester	A	158			2	1.2	+	—
24.	Brewood	A	156			1	0.6	+	—

PREPARING FOR PRIESTHOOD   23

	House	Order	Total	A	B	C	As %	D	E
25.	Burton	B	146	+		4	2.4		—
26.	Church Gresley	A	132			1	0.6	+	—
27.	Launde	A	131	+	+	4	2.4		—
28.	Canwell	B	130			—			—
29.	Polesworth	B	125			2	1.2		—
30.	Tutbury	B	119			3	1.8		—
31.	Langley	B	116		+	—			—
32.	Combe	C	112	+		—			—
33.	Derby	B	106		+	3	1.8		—
34.	Haughmond	A	104	+		6	3.6		—
35.	Dudley	B	95			2	1.2		—
	Breadsall Park	A	95			—			—
	Stone	A	95			—			—
	Thurgarton	A	95	+	+	—			—
39.	Farewell	B	92			—			—
40.	Garendon	C	88			—			1
41.	Basingwerk	C	85			—			—
	Wombridge	A	85			1	0.6	+	—
43.	Shrewsbury	B	82	+	+	6	3.6		3
44.	Trentham	A	77			1	0.6	+	—
45.	Sandwell	B	75			—			—
46.	Calwich	A	74			1	0.6		—
47.	Kenilworth	A	73	+	+	18	11		—
	Alvecote	B	73			—			—
49.	Cockersand	P	59		+	—			—
50.	Much Wenlock	B	58	+		—			—

Totals from Table 2
Valued over £200:   17 = 34%   Valued above average for order: 16 = 32%

Augustinians   *Benedictines*
Average 1535 value   £169   Average 1535 value   £434
Total for order   4049   Total for order   2786
% of total   36%   % of total   25%
Average per year   150   Average per year   103
No. of houses   20   No. of houses   15
Average per house   202   Average per house   186

Cistercians   *Premonstratensians*
Average 1535 value   £233   Average 1535 value   £140
Total for order   3515   Total for order   746
% of total   32%   % of total   7%
Average per year   130   Average per year   28
No. of houses   11   No. of houses   4
Average per house   320   Average per house   187

Valuations derived from D. Knowles, R.N. Hadcock, *Medieval Religious Houses in England and Wales* (1971)

The table highlights a number of significant features concerning monastic provision of titles during the period. As in other dioceses which have been studied, only a small proportion of the titles were provided by the more wealthy houses.[70] It is of particular interest that a number of the richer institutions in the diocese feature low down the list. Among the Augustinians, the wealthiest house, Kenilworth, is almost at the bottom and Haughmond is below halfway. Although the Cistercians provided a high proportion of the titles, Combe abbey, second only in the diocese to Whalley within its order, is thirty-second. Of the Benedictine houses Burton upon Trent comes exactly halfway, while Shrewsbury Abbey, valued at twice as much in 1535, is forty-third; and Coventry Cathedral Priory, compared to which only Chester abbey was valued higher within the order in 1535, and despite being the twin seat of the bishopric, did not provide a single title to ordination during the period. The same can be said for the orders taken as a whole, since the relative importance of each of the three main orders which feature in the list is in inverse proportion to the average value, in national terms, of their houses. So whatever factors were important in deciding which monasteries were the major providers of titles, the wealth of the house can be all but discarded, with implications for any view of the title as a firm financial guarantee.[71]

A further sample of the providers of monastic titles can be taken for analysis. These are the seventeen houses at the top of the list which meet one or both of the following criteria: a total provision over the period of at least 200 titles or a minimum share of 5% of the total number of titles in at least one year. As such, these institutions can be said to be the major regular providers of titles to orders for clerks ordained in the diocese. For the purpose of discussion, the proportion of the total number of titles provided in a given year by an individual house will be described as its *market share*. Among these major providers, seven were Cistercian houses, six Augustinian, three

---

70 Heath, *English Parish Clergy*, 17, Swanson, 'Titles to Orders', 242. Virginia Davis refers to 'poverty-stricken houses offering vast numbers of titles' and ventures a tentative suggestion that the titles might have had a relationship to chantries, but, given the numbers involved, this is unlikely to account for more than a minority. The point was first made by A.H. Thompson, but apparently without the sort of (albeit limited) evidence that Davis has; V. Davis, 'Medieval Clergy Database', *History and Computing*, 2 (1990), 84; Thompson, *The English Clergy*, 143. For the objections to the argument see Swanson, 'Titles to Orders', 235–6. A possible clue as to the incentive on the part of the poorer houses might lie in an obscure source and be rather dependent on exact interpretation of meaning. The will of Thomas Atkinson, a yeoman of Clint (Yorks.), of 1538, makes arrangements that his son 'may follow the school unto such time that he may get orders and be priest, and that he shall have his *title and singing gear bought* at the cost of my said wife' (my italics and modernised spelling): were these houses selling the required documents? J.A.H. Moran, who cites the document, is of the opinion that the meaning of the testator 'is clear'; J.A.H. Moran, 'Clerical Recruitment in the Diocese of York 1340–1530: Data and Commentary', *JEH*, 34 (1983), 30–1.
71 Cross, 'Ordinations in the Diocese of York', 7.

Benedictine and one Premonstratensian. The contribution of these houses to the provision of titles is highlighted in Map 3 which shows the fluctuating market share of each house over the period in percentage terms and the relative importance of houses geographically in terms of their average annual provision. The fact that these seventeen houses were regularly providing a majority share of the titles lends weight to the suggestion that certain institutions might have been deliberately designated for this purpose. The map shows that the greatest density of these major providers was towards the north-west of the diocese and away from the south-east. If the hypothesis that ordinands received titles from a designated institution within the locality of their origin is correct, then this must reflect higher levels of recruitment from these parts of the diocese.

The graphs in Map 3 demonstrate that the market share of these houses was rarely stable and in some cases fluctuated quite noticeably; if certain houses were being designated as main providers of titles it does not appear to have been on the basis of a fixed quota. In some cases definite trends can be discerned. Whalley Abbey commanded an ever-increasing share of title provision during the period as did Baswich Priory and Hulton Abbey's share started to increase from a very low level (and in a number of years, none at all) after about 1520. Whilst Merevale Abbey displays a marked increase in volume during the middle of the period, it is these years where Chester Abbey's share declined significantly from a high level which was regained at the end of the period. In some cases the trends suggest a phenomenon of 'competition' between houses in a particular locality; for instance it could be tentatively hypothesised that, during the middle part of the period, Norton, Upholland, and, to a lesser extent, Birkenhead, were increasing their market share at the expense of Chester and Vale Royal abbeys. In the middle area of the diocese, a similar phenomenon might have been occurring between the Cistercian houses of Dieulacres and Hulton. Significantly, Beauchief Abbey, which was the only major provider of titles in north Derbyshire, maintained quite a steady market share of around three per cent. Provision of titles in the south of the diocese was dominated by the Cistercians and Augustinians, and insofar as any trend can be detected, it could be said that the Augustinians were gradually increasing their market share at the expense of the Cistercian houses.

If it was not the comparative wealth of institutions that determined their allocation of titles, was it, perhaps, their command of patronage of benefices? In her study of the clergy of the diocese of Lincoln, Margaret Bowker suggested that the move towards monastic titles was in response to their becoming the most important holders of advowsons.[72] However, when a comparison was made of the orders which provided the bulk of titles with those that made the greatest number of presentations, it was concluded that

---

[72] Bowker, *Secular Clergy*, 61.

no relationship appeared to exist between the two. Whilst the Augustinians and Cistercians dominated the provision of titles, the Benedictines made a higher proportion of presentations to benefices.[73] In Lichfield diocese the Benedictines came second to the Augustinians in terms of the proportion of monastic presentations which they made, 39% and 45% respectively. However, the Cistercians, who could be said to have been the most significant providers of titles, accounted for only 5% of the total monastic presentations to livings. Margaret Bowker discovered a similar lack of correlation between those individual houses which made the most presentations and those which offered the greatest number of titles. From Table 2 it is apparent that a number of the houses that made presentations to benefices during the period feature low down the list of provision of titles, and in a number of cases these are houses which were responsible for a greater share of presentations than they were for provision of titles. Among the houses at the top of the list, only Chester Abbey was responsible for a really significant proportion of presentations. Six houses from within the diocese which made presentations do not feature on the titles list at all. These were Maxstoke Priory, which made five, Coventry Cathedral Priory and Polesworth Abbey, which made two apiece, and Arbury Priory and Stoneleigh Abbey which made a single presentation each. Similarly, sixteen of the houses which were regular providers of titles made no presentations during the period. Equally indicative of the fact that there was little correlation between the provision of titles and presentations to benefices is the fact that, during the entire period, only four houses made presentations of clerks to whom they had provided the title. Three of these were made by the Benedictines of Shrewsbury and one each by the Augustinians of Repton and Maxstoke and the Cistercian house of Vale Royal. Amongst those presented, John Wolley and William Butler were the most fortunate in that they received their benefices within two years of ordination.[74] Roger Grene was presented to his living within five years and Thomas Hopkins, six. Ralph Francis, who like Butler, was a graduate, had to wait nine years before the provider of his title presented him to a benefice, and Richard Hill no less than thirteen.[75]

---

[73] Ibid., 63.
[74] LJRO, B/A/1/14ii, fos. 65v, 68r; B/A/1/14, fo. 56v (Wolley, presented by Vale Royal Abbey to the vicarage of Frodsham in 1511); B/A/1/14ii, fos. 75r, 77v, 81v, 86v; B/A/1/14, fo. 46v (Butler, presented by Shrewsbury Abbey to the vicarage of Wrockwardine in 1514). For references to Butler's will see *passim* and appendix; for a possible connection between him and the abbey see below, 43, n. 28.
[75] Ibid., B/A/1/14ii, fos. 167r, 169v; B/A/1/14, fo. 50v (Grene, presented to the perpetual curacy of Rodington by Shrewsbury Abbey in 1529); B/A/1/14ii, fos. 162r, 169r, 171r; B/A/1/14, fo. 18v (Hopkins, presented to the vicarage of Long Itchington by Maxstoke Priory in 1531); B/A/1/14ii, fos. 77r, 79v, 82r; B/A/1/14, fo. 43v (Francis, presented to the vicarage of Willington by Repton Priory in 1531); B/A/1/14ii, fos. 69v, 72r, 74v; B/A/1/14, fo. 48v (Hill, presented to the vicarage of Donnington by Shrewsbury Abbey in 1524).

What conclusions can be drawn concerning the provision of titles to orders by religious houses? There have been allegations by both contemporaries, notably Thomas More, and recent historians, that the system was no more than a fraudulent legal fiction.[76] Certainly the evidence, especially of the large numbers of poorer houses involved, could be used to support this view. However, there is no evidence in the surviving records of any appeals made by clerks against failed or inadequate titles that one might expect if so many poorer institutions were taking part in a wholesale fraud. By contrast, such evidence does exist from earlier periods, albeit to a small extent.[77] Generally, there is no direct evidence that monastic titles represented a real guarantee of financial support in themselves. Indeed, the evidence of the relatively small proportion of titles provided by the wealthier houses could be said to point away from this. The more persuasive argument, albeit largely from the silence of the sources, is that the titles were evidence of an investigative system already undertaken by the time the candidate presented himself for orders. Upon presentation to one of the houses in his area which issued titles, the candidate would have his personal particulars, including his financial credentials checked, probably as a preliminary to any examination of learning. It could be said that the surviving evidence of examination procedure hints at this; although very few of the examinees were recorded as being ordained as acolytes in the registers, collation of their subsequent progress through the orders suggests that they were being grouped under particular examiners according to the provenance of their subsequent title. A candidate might have been passed on the basis of satisfying the house that he had at least a subsistence income.[78] For providing such a service, significantly cutting down the work which would have to be undertaken by the bishop and his agents, it is possible that these 'clearing houses' might have received a fee, which could explain why the poorer houses were particularly favoured, or eager to take part in the system.[79] If a monastic title was in itself no financial guarantee, but just the evidence that the candidate had been deemed to be financially self-sufficient and worthy, this might explain the ordination to the priesthood of William Bosworth in 1511, despite having his title recorded as 'furgotton'.[80] By this stage, the detail was no longer important.

---

[76] For a summary of the debate, see Swanson, 'Titles to Orders', esp. 234–5.
[77] Ibid., 238.
[78] Ibid., 244.
[79] For the suggestion of fees, see Swanson, ibid. For a suggestion that titles were 'sold', see above, n. 70.
[80] LJRO, B/A/1/14ii, fo. 78v. This is, incidentally, further evidence that ordination procedure involved candidates delivering their name and titles verbally to the registrar at the ceremony (see below) and of the fact that, given the large numbers involved, the procedure was conducted swiftly without much time for checking detail. Cross, 'Ordinations in the Diocese of York', 4–5, makes the obvious but useful observation that

The Ordination Ceremonies

Suitably educated, canonically qualified and equipped with a valid title, men of the diocese would present themselves as ordinands before a bishop, usually their own, at a ceremony of ordination. Notice of intention to hold such ceremonies would be issued throughout the diocese in advance through the agency of the archdeacons and rural deans.[81] The bishops of Coventry and Lichfield generally followed the procedure, customary throughout England, of holding ordinations at four distinct points in the liturgical year being the Ember Days, that is the Saturdays in the third week of Advent, the first week of Lent, the vigil of the feast of the Trinity and following the vigil of the Nativity of the Virgin.[82] Thus ordinations were regularly held in December, February or March, May or June and September of each year. Only once during the period of Blythe's pontificate was there a departure from this general rule – ordinations of acolytes only on three successive weeks in July 1508[83] – and in all, ordination ceremonies were held on 121 separate occasions. Whilst the conferral of Holy Orders required episcopal status, very few diocesans were regularly ordaining in person during this period and Blythe was no exception in leaving the task to suffragans on all but seventeen occasions.

The first ceremony during his pontificate was conducted by John, bishop of Mayo, who was subsequently to be employed in the service of John Longland, bishop of Lincoln.[84] Most were conducted by two successive suffragan bishops of the title *Panadensis*;[85] Thomas Wele, a benefice holder within the diocese and, after 1520, another by the name of William.[86] On a single occasion, in 1521, Roger, bishop of the title *Ludensis* officiated.[87] The great majority of ceremonies were held in the cathedral church at Lichfield; the exceptions were the episcopal manors of Longdon and Eccleshall (seven and four times respectively), Repton Priory (three times), Alvecote Priory (twice), and the Franciscan friary at Lichfield, Warrington Austin Friary, Norton Priory, Shrewsbury Abbey, the collegiate churches of Manchester and Shrewsbury and the parish churches of Rugeley and St Peter's, Derby, at

---

'the ceremonies themselves must have lasted a considerable time' and 'would have proved a real test for [the ordaining bishop]'.
81 Dohar, 'Medieval Ordination Lists', 20.
82 Ibid.
83 LJRO, B/A/1/14ii, fos. 50r–v.
84 Ibid., fo. 1r; Bowker, *The Henrician Reformation*, 38.
85 Banados, in Thrace.
86 LJRO, B/A/1/14, fo. 11r; BL, Harleian Ms 594, fo. 153r.
87 LJRO, B/A/1/14ii, fo. 142r. Most probably Roger Smyth, abbot of Dorchester, suffragan bishop of Lydda in Palestine, commissioned by John Longland, bishop of Lincoln, in 1514 and 1521, and who also appears to have acted within the diocese of Salisbury; Bowker, *Secular Clergy*, 24 and n. 6.

each of which a single ordination ceremony was held.[88] On only five occasions did Blythe officiate in person in his cathedral church, the rest of his ordinations being held at his manors.[89] Thus despite the fact that suffragan bishops were being employed, they rarely moved around the diocese for the purposes of ordination any more than did the largely non-resident ordinary, and candidates from the northern part of the diocese were only convenienced on three occasions and these were all when, uniquely, acolytes alone were ordained.[90] In addition to having to obtain a title and undergo examination, ordinands from the north and west of the diocese were making an additional commitment to their clerical careers simply by having to undertake the long journey to Lichfield.

In almost all cases candidates would be admitted to a single order at one ceremony, each order symbolically representing a stage in the ministry of Christ.[91] The reception of multiple orders on a single day required papal dispensation and five clerks were dispensed by Wolsey's legatine authority, all towards the end of the period: William Whitbroke (subdeacon and deacon; December, 1525), M. George Plancknay (subdeacon, deacon and priest; September, 1527), Robert Francklyn (deacon and priest; September, 1528), Anthony Sherington (subdeacon and deacon; June, 1528) and Roger Hulton (acolyte and subdeacon; September, 1529).[92] Otherwise, apart from quite common delays between acolyte and subdeacon discussed above, most clerks advanced from the level of acolyte to priest in little more than a year.

The large numbers involved must have meant that the average ordination ceremony in this period was a fairly routine affair. A working copy of the ordination register itself might have been used as a roster,[93] though the frequent variations in spellings of a single candidate's name from one ceremony to the next (of the type that has Miles Huddleston on one occasion being entered as Miles Suddleston and one ordinand as variously Fazacurley, Phazakaley and Vasacurley) suggests that more probably the candidates gave their name in person, or had it announced, for the scribe to enter in the record.[94] Having been summoned before the officiating bishop, the latter would demand of the archdeacon whether the ordinand was worthy of admission to the order that he sought and, if answered in the affirmative, would confirm his admission by the laying on of hands and, in the case of a

---

[88] LJRO, B/A/1/14ii, fos. 4v, 19r, 21v, 25r, 30v, 32v, 44r, 46v, 37r, 50r–v, 66r, 72v, 77r, 99r, 102v, 105r, 141r, 166r, 181v, 199v, 201r, 209r, 211r, 219r.
[89] Ibid., fos. 119r, 130r, 139v, 183r, 219r.
[90] Above, n. 81.
[91] J.H. Crehan, 'Medieval Ordinations', in C. Jones, G. Wainwright, E. Yarnold, eds, *The Study of Liturgy* (1978), 324.
[92] LJRO, B/A/1/14ii, fos. 175r, 190r, 193v, 204v; B/A/1/14, fos. 47r, 61r, 114r.
[93] Dohar, 'Medieval Ordination Lists', 29.
[94] LJRO, B/A/1/14ii, fos. 91r, 93v, 114r, 116r, 118v; above, n. 80.

priest, investiture with chasuble, paten and chalice, symbolic of his newly attained status and power.[95]

Numbers

On the first of June, 1504, Blythe's first full year as bishop, fifty-four secular priests were ordained at a single ceremony at Lichfield Cathedral and by the end of the year over 160 new priests had been ordained within the diocese.[96] Nine years later, in 1513, almost half as many again were admitted to priest's orders[97] and in total, over the twenty-seven years of Blythe's pontificate, over 4,500 men entered the priesthood, an average of 167 a year.[98] While such a figure is extraordinary, high levels of recruitment were not an entirely novel phenomenon in this period; ordinations had been climbing steadily from the mid fifteenth century and then more rapidly towards its end, with 218 secular priests being ordained in 1498. However, although numbers remained high throughout Blythe's pontificate, with about ninety new priests being ordained in 1531, admissions fluctuated quite significantly. Until 1518 the trend was upwards; thereafter, numbers declined, though rallying quite significantly in 1522 and 1524 and the number of new priests in 1531 was the lowest level of recruitment since the end of the fifteenth century (see Graphs 1 to 3).[99]

The diocese of Coventry and Lichfield was not alone in witnessing this great expansion in admissions to the priesthood in the later fifteenth and early sixteenth centuries.[100] In virtually all parts of the country there was a steady increase in the number of candidates coming forward for ordination from about the middle of the fifteenth century, and in those dioceses which have been studied in detail it has been shown that the upward trend increased dramatically towards the end of the fifteenth century and into the sixteenth. In the diocese of Lincoln 2,609 men were ordained priest between 1495 and 1520, an average of just over one hundred per year, and in the period 1514 to 1521 this number rose to just over 170. The high point in ordinations was in 1522, a few years after that in Lichfield, and declined to an average of 130 per year down to 1535. The start of the upward trend in the diocese of York was in the 1460s and thereafter followed a similar pattern

---

[95] Cross, 'Patronage and Recruitment', 4; Dohar, 'Medieval Ordination Lists', 24.
[96] LJRO, B/A/1/14ii, fos. 4v–11v.
[97] Ibid., fos. 89r–94v.
[98] Ibid., *passim*.
[99] Swanson, *Church and Society*, 35–6.
[100] Nor, historically, was it an entirely novel phenomenon since numbers had been rising quite dramatically in many areas from the later thirteenth century to the arrival of the Black Death in the mid fourteenth. However, on this occasion, clerical recruitment was in advance of still quite stagnant national population figures. Ibid., 32–4; Townley, 'Unbeneficed Clergy', 47.

Graph 1. Ordinations of secular acolytes and priests

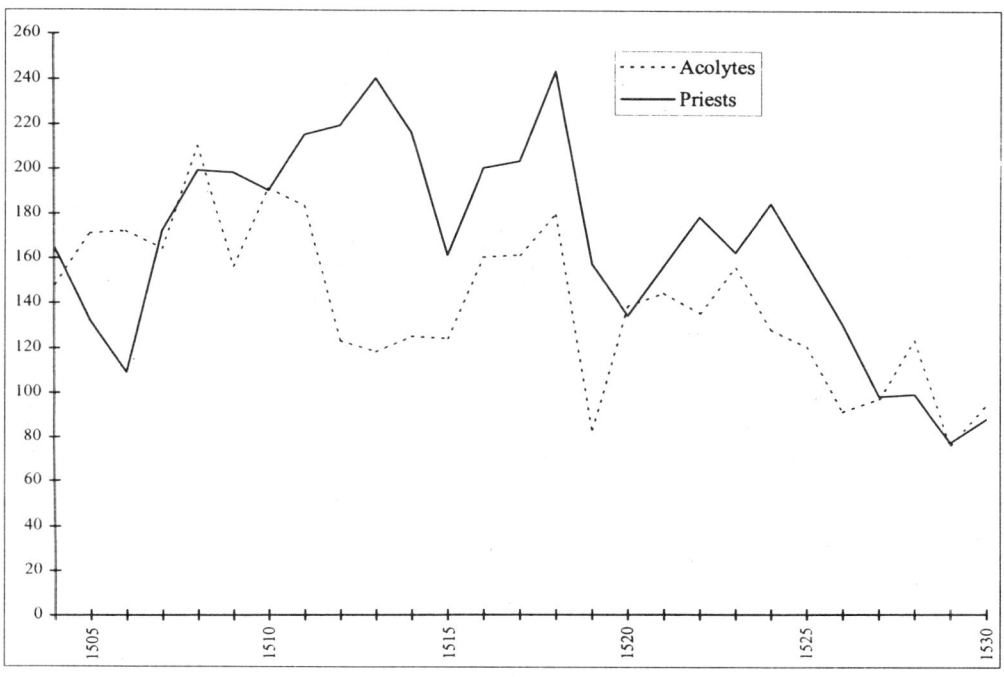

to Lincoln although the annual totals were even higher. Between 1501 and 1527 an average of 187 new secular priests were ordained each year with the high point of 363 being attained in 1508, and the increase in the clerical population of the diocese between 1377 and 1500 is estimated to have been in the region of 75%. It was in the early sixteenth century that the steadily increasing ordination figures for the diocese of London started to rise significantly, with 98 secular priests being ordained in 1502 and a total of 645 by 1510. Towards 1520 the trend was gradually downwards and accelerated markedly in the third decade of the century. A similar trend, with a high point at the beginning of the sixteenth century, has been discerned for the diocese of Winchester.[101]

Since an explanation of the huge increase in ordinations is not to be

[101] M.L. Zell, 'Economic Problems of the Parochial Clergy in the Sixteenth Century', in R. O'Day and F. Heal, eds, *Princes and Paupers in the English Church 1500–1800*, 22; V. Davis, 'Rivals for Ministry? Ordinations of Secular and Regular Clergy in Southern England c.1300–1500', *SCH* 26, 99–109; Ibid., 'Medieval Clergy Database', 77; Moran, 'Clerical Recruitment in the Diocese of York', 19–54; Bowker, *Secular Clergy*, 38–9; Ibid., *The Henrician Reformation*, 40; R.L. Storey, 'Ordinations of Secular Priests in Early Tudor London', *Nottingham Mediaeval Studies*, 23 (1989), 122, 124, 128–9; Marshall, *Catholic Priesthood*, 229–30; Cross, 'Patronage and Recruitment', 2–3.

Graph 2. Ordinations of secular subdeacons and deacons

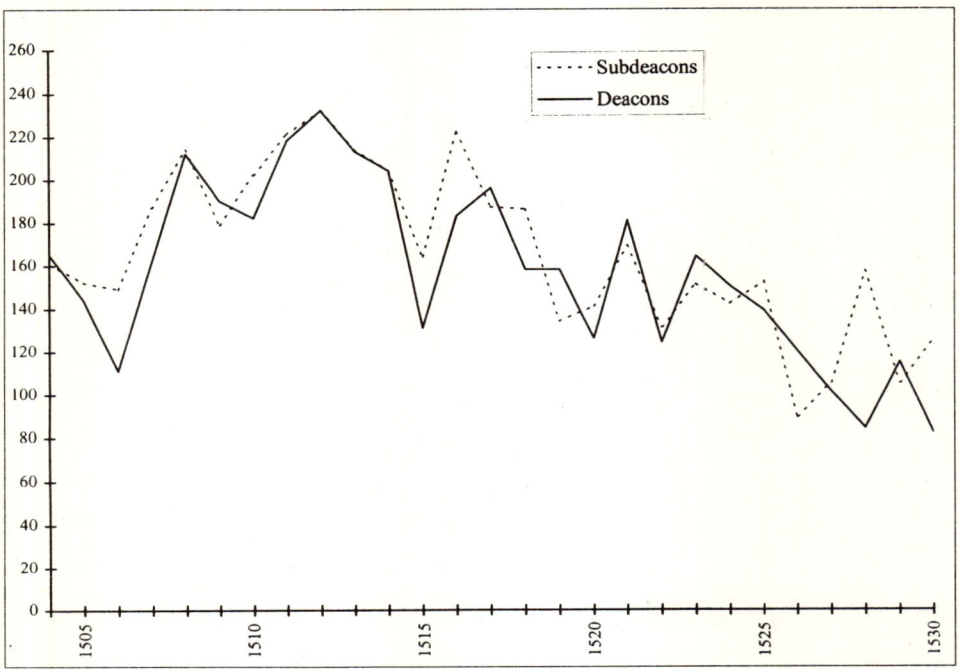

found in the demography of the period, where might the answer lie? Although the vast majority of Lichfield ordinations were of men from within the diocese, some were from outside, and a possible explanation might be that figures were inflated by the numbers of men being ordained outside their diocese of origin by the use of letters dimissory, a form of dispensation issued by bishops releasing candidates for the priesthood from this particular obligation. Over the period, the number of men ordained in the diocese under letters dimissory varied from two to fifteen per cent but despite the fact that the 1520s saw a slight growth in the number of ordinations of outsiders, the average was just 6% per year, insufficient to account for the large increase in the general volume of ordinations. In the diocese of York a fairly significant increase had occurred in the last two decades of the fifteenth century but thereafter there was little appreciable growth in the numbers coming into the diocese to be ordained. In the diocese of Lincoln no more than 10% of those ordained in the first three decades of the sixteenth century were outsiders and a large proportion of these would have been students at Oxford; in the same way, the disproportionate influence exercised by the University of Cambridge within the small diocese of Ely accounts for the high level of ordinations there, since 75% were of candidates with letters dimissory.[102]

---

[102] Bowker, *Secular Clergy*, 39.

Graph 3. Total ordinations 1504–1530

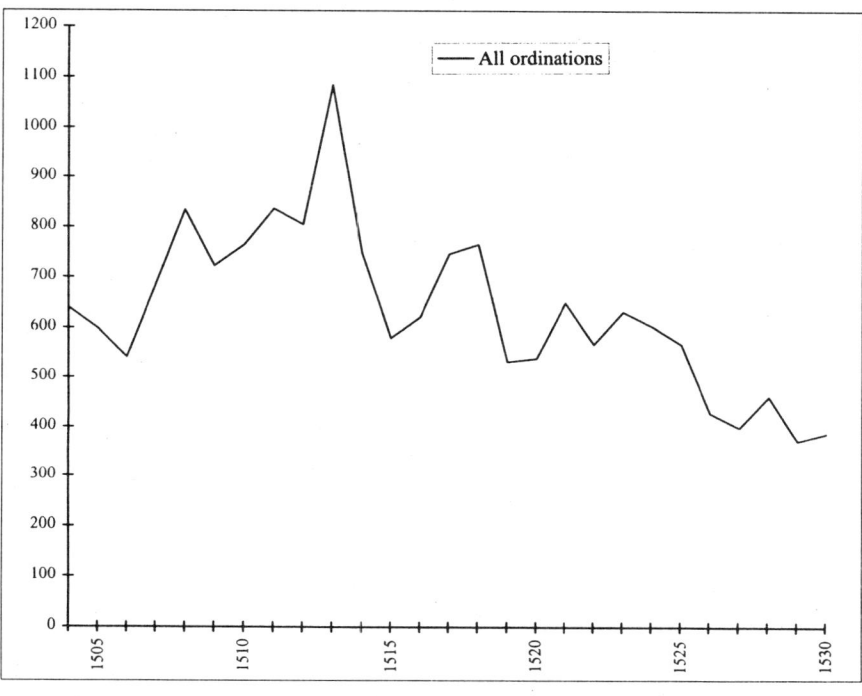

Similarly, the diocese of London, which exerted enormous economic influence out of proportion to its size, continued to act as a magnet for clerical immigration into the sixteenth century. However, despite the fact that its own clerical ranks were swelled each year by migrants particularly from the dioceses of York and Lichfield, in the case of the latter, this represented a high point of only twenty-seven men leaving the diocese in the period 1515 to 1519.[103] So whilst such clerical emigration was likely to have had a significant impact on recruitment within the capital, and implications for its religious and social culture,[104] its effect on the men's dioceses of origin would have been minimal and there is little evidence to suggest that the great majority of new clergy in the midlands and north were not staying within that region. In fact, the most significant phenomenon of migration was within the diocese itself. The high proportion of titles to orders that were being issued by monasteries in Lancashire and Cheshire would tend to suggest that these areas provided a relatively greater volume of new recruits in the diocese of Lichfield during this period, and whilst many of these were likely to have moved north and east into the large diocese of York, a good

[103] Storey, 'Ordinations of Secular Priests', 129.
[104] Ibid., 130, where Storey makes the astute observation that '[in London] it would seem, the population was accustomed to viewing the priesthood as a calling more suited to immigrants from the country's deprived regions'.

number would doubtless have moved south into the midland area of their own diocese.[105]

An obvious explanation of the dramatic rise in entry to the priesthood could of course be that there was a deliberate recruitment drive on the part of the ecclesiastical authorities. However, there is no direct evidence for such a policy; indeed, as we have seen, senior ecclesiastics such as William Melton and John Colet were seeking, if anything, to stem the tide of ordinations by equating increase in numbers with decrease in quality. Their call was taken up by a number of contemporary lay commentators and polemicists. In 1528 Sir Thomas More felt moved to complain that:

> The time was I say, when few men dared presume to take upon the high office of a priest, not even when they were chosen and called thereunto. Now runneth every rascal and boldly offereth himself for able.[106]

The argument against the swelling clerical ranks was taken up most vociferously by the polemicist Simon Fish in his *Supplicacyon for the Beggers* of 1529 in which he demanded 'who is able to number this idle, ravenous sort . . .?',[107] and even a neutral observer like the Venetian ambassador reported in 1531 that London was populated by 'an infinite number of priests'.[108] This latter statement is particularly suggestive. The evidence from all the dioceses that have been studied shows that, apart from the numbers themselves, another novel feature of ordination patterns in the later fifteenth and early sixteenth centuries is that the great majority of those who were admitted to the lower orders went on to become priests; and it was the number of *priests*, as opposed simply to *clerks*, that attracted contemporary comment. The massed ranks of clergy, which to men like More were seen as a growing weakness in the armour of clerical apologists, were not men who had taken merely the first step required to qualify for clerical status. Whatever might have been the attractions of a departure from the lay state, the majority of men sought to take it to its full conclusion. The most convincing explanation for such a phenomenon is based on the growing importance of the Mass as a focus of devotion in the fifteenth and early sixteenth centuries. More particularly, the mature development of the doctrine of purgatory led to an inevitable increase in demand for intercessory masses for the dead, evidenced most conspicuously by the proliferation of religious gilds, chantries, and testamentary obits which continued unabated into the sixteenth century. In a time of growing literacy among the population as a whole, to be a clerk was

---

[105] As expressed by Christopher Haigh, 'It appears that early Tudor Lancashire was playing modern Ireland to the pre-Reformation church, providing large numbers of clergy who moved to serve in other areas': Haigh, *Reformation and Resistance*, 38.
[106] Quoted in Moran, 'Clerical Recruitment', 54.
[107] A.G. Dickens and D. Carr, eds, *The Reformation in England to the Accession of Elizabeth I* (1967), 16.
[108] Quoted in S. Brigden, *London and the Reformation*, 47.

not necessarily to demonstrate attributes lacking among the laity. But to be a priest was to have the ability to perform the act central to contemporary devotion and to recreate the miracle which united the communities of living and dead. Whether or not it would be right to explain the ordination trend in terms of a simple economic response to the growing demand for the services of priesthood is debatable; but the demand was certainly there and it is probably not an exaggeration to describe it as virtually insatiable.[109]

It would also be valid to make a connection between the rise in ordinations and the growth in educational provision since the two trends correspond so closely, though here it is perhaps more difficult to discern cause and effect. It is possible that the increase in demand for priests promoted the establishment of both endowed and more transient schools, and it has been noted how some benefactors specifically aimed at an increase in the provision of clergy. In addition, the use of devotional and liturgical texts in elementary education and the pedagogic slant towards producing children who could assist at divine service and, more particularly, funerary masses, was bound to influence growing numbers to follow that calling themselves.[110] The sheer number of ordinations mean that perhaps more than at any time in the history of the pre-Reformation English church, the priesthood was recruiting from across the whole social spectrum. Despite the lack of direct evidence for such an assertion, in addition to the numbers involved, the overwhelming majority of rural backgrounds of ordinands that has been noted in some areas and the tiny minority that were ordained to patrimonial titles or family-held benefices, would tend to support a view of the parochial clergy as no longer drawn mainly from the gentry class, if they ever had been.[111] In early Tudor England the clerical profession represented the largest employer of male labour outside agriculture[112] and it was from an agricultural background that an increasing proportion of its members were drawn.

If the reasons behind the remarkable increase in the number of ordinations at the beginning of the period are obscure, equally so are those for the similarly dramatic decline which can be observed in most areas of the country by about 1520. Some traditional explanations no longer seem convincing. The statute of 1512 limiting Benefit of Clergy, which might have been a popular move a century earlier when large numbers of men were remaining in lower orders, was largely an irrelevance in a culture where admission to orders meant entry to priesthood.[113] Similarly, the evidence no longer appears to support the alleged widespread notoriety of Hunne's Case of 1514–15 and a heightened mood of anticlericalism, certainly outside

---

109 Marshall, *Catholic Priesthood*, 229–30; ibid., *Pastoral Ministry in the East Riding*, 3–5.
110 Moran, *English Schooling*, esp. 117–22.
111 Swanson, *Church and Society*, 36–7.
112 J. Youings, *Sixteenth-Century England* (Harmondsworth, 1984), 36.
113 Moran, Clerical Recruitment', 35.

London and the legal profession.[114] The 'progressive demoralization of the clergy'[115] which was a feature of parliamentary activity from 1529 onwards was bound to have been a factor but fails to explain the earlier onset of the downward trend. One intriguing possibility, but one that will probably remain impossible to prove, is that those like Melton, Colet and More who argued for a restriction on admissions to the priesthood through more exacting entry requirements ultimately prevailed, though the timing of the decline would have meant a remarkably swift response to the cries of Melton and Colet and came too soon to be realistically attributed to More.[116] Without denying the significance of such arguments to the long-term trend, the call for fewer and better priests was not entirely novel and in the short term, the requirements of More's paymaster, the crown, were likely to have been of greater significance in this regard than the chancellor's own scruples. The second decade of the sixteenth century witnessed clerical taxation on an unprecedented scale and not only was the frequency of exaction increasing, from already high levels in the later fifteenth century, but the net was also widening. From the 1520s not only were those who held livings subjected to regular taxation, but so too were the curates, chantry priests and stipendiary chaplains who constituted the majority of those in clerical employment.[117] As will be seen below, the holders of such posts rarely commanded incomes in excess of their lay neighbours, yet they shouldered a disproportionate burden of taxation. Whilst it would be unwise to argue for an entirely economic explanation of recruitment patterns,[118] the earlier attraction of regular employment as a 'mass priest' was likely to have been tempered by the prospect of a lifetime of heavier and more constant taxation than would be faced by the laity. Those who would be hardest hit, and might have to face poverty and debt, were precisely those whose entry to priesthood was prompted by 'consumer' demand; for whilst the popular appetite for intercessory Masses might have been insatiable, access to secure clerical employment was decidedly limited.

---

114 Dickens, *The English Reformation* (1967 edn), devotes no fewer than ten pages to the Hunne affair (131–40).

115 Marshall, *Catholic Priesthood*, 230.

116 R.N. Swanson, 'Problems of the Priesthood in Pre-Reformation England', *English Historical Review*, 417 (October, 1990), 861–3.

117 Bowker, *Henrician Reformation*, 43–4. Both northern and southern convocations had granted *ad hoc* taxes from chaplains during the fifteenth century. In four such grants between 1406 and 1435 the average payment by stipendiaries was 6s 8d: A.K. McHardy, 'Clerical Taxation in Fifteenth-Century England: The Clergy as Agents of the Crown', in R.B. Dobson, ed., *The Church, Politics and Patronage in the Fifteenth Century* (Gloucester, 1984), 168–92.

118 A point made by Marshall, *Catholic Priesthood*, 230.

2

Acquiring a Living: The Beneficed

Availability of Benefices

Between 1503 and 1531 an average of 167 men were ordained priest in the diocese each year. In terms of qualification, each of these men had acquired clerical status to the highest degree appropriate to parochial employment and could aspire to the possession of a benefice which would provide them with an income for life. For the majority, however, the security of an ecclesiastical living was not a realistic expectation. The clerical subsidy for the diocese compiled in 1533 lists a total of 414 rectories, vicarages and perpetual curacies in which the new recruit to the priesthood might hope for employment. In addition, there were just over thirty perpetual chantries counted as benefices for taxation purposes and about 165 posts such as wardenships and fellowships of colleges and hospitals, canonries and prebends, usually reserved for those with the highest academic qualifications or best connections. Thus, in the face of limited opportunity, the stark reality which faced the newly-ordained priest was that for a job to exist, a vacancy had to arise.[1] Livings became vacant either by the resignation of the incumbent, his dismissal or death. Realistically, the best opportunity for the new priest was provided by the latter; as in the dioceses of Lincoln and Canterbury during this period, the majority of livings, about 65%, fell vacant due to the death of the incumbent.[2] Only an event so final created a definite opening since the resignation of a benefice might mean that its holder was moving to another, so that in overall terms, no new opportunity was created. Such was the level of demand for livings that even in the event of death the diocesan authorities might require proof of vacancy. For example, John Walker was only admitted to the vicarage of Wombourne in 1510 following the archdeacon's scrutiny of the last will and testament of the previous incumbent.[3] As for dismissals, these were rare indeed. The only recorded deprivation from a parochial

---

[1] Simon Townley has demonstrated that similar pressure within the clerical employment market existed in the late 13th century: Townley, 'Unbeneficed Clergy in the Thirteenth Century', 47.
[2] Bowker, *Secular Clergy*, 89; Zell, 'Economic Problems', 29.
[3] LJRO, B/A/1/14, fos. 21r, 102r.

living in Blythe's register was the removal of William Whittington, vicar of Mancetter, in 1528 following repeated incidents of immorality.⁴

A small number of vacancies which did arise were not in practice available to newly-ordained secular priests since they were of livings appropriated to houses of Augustinian canons which presented members of their order. Thus successive vacancies in the vicarage of Ormskirk, in 1506 and 1530, were filled by canons of Burscough, and in 1529 the vicarage of Lullington was taken by a canon of Church Gresley Priory, while in 1514 the vacancy of the rectory of Eckington provided the opportunity for no less a figure than the prior of Newborough, Thomas Barker, to be instituted.⁵ A further limitation on the number of available benefices was caused by the actions of pluralists within the diocese, and among those instituted to benefices during the period were at least twelve clerks who held more than one living.⁶ The important consideration, therefore, is not the number of benefices which existed within the diocese, but the number of occasions on which they became available. Over the twenty-eight year period of Blythe's pontificate some 410 vacancies in parochial livings (excluding chantries) were filled, an average of fifteen vacancies a year.⁷ Expressed in different terms, quite apart from the backlog of unbeneficed clergy which would have been building up over the years, each year ten new priests were being ordained for every living which became vacant, and on average, each parochial living in the diocese was vacant only once during the period.⁸ About one-third of the benefices in the diocese do not appear to have fallen vacant over the entire period of Blythe's pontificate.

The majority of those ordained therefore, if they were ever to obtain a benefice, were faced with waiting for an opportunity to arise and would have to hope in the meantime for some untenured employment. A very small minority, usually through family connections, avoided this problem by securing a benefice prior to ordination. Sometimes the benefice was obtained in the same year as ordination, as in the case of Edmund Strethay who was presented to the vicarage of Longford by its rector in 1514, the same year that he received the orders of subdeacon, deacon and priest.⁹ However, John Dethick was ordained subdeacon and deacon three years after being presented to the rectory of Hartshorne by his family¹⁰ and Richard Mynshull

4   Ibid., B/C/2/1, fo. 71v; B/C/2/2, fo. 44r; below, 181.
5   Ibid., B/A/1/14, fos. 36v, 42r, 54v, 66v. Eckington was not an appropriation but a rectory under the patronage of Sir James Strangeways.
6   See below, 65.
7   Whilst there are some identifiable gaps in the record of institutions, they are not sufficient to greatly affect the overall picture.
8   This compares with an annual maximum of twenty vacancies arising in the diocese of Canterbury between 1534 and 1552; M.L. Zell, 'The Personnel of the Clergy in Kent, in the Reformation Period', *English Historical Review*, 89 (1974), 525.
9   LJRO, B/A/1/14, fo. 37r; B/A/1/14ii, fos. 98r, 100r, 102r.
10 Ibid., B/A/1/14, fo. 39v; B/A/1/14ii, fos. 160r, 162v. Ordained priest to the title of Burscough Priory, 1524; B/A/1/14ii, fo. 167v.

waited five years before being ordained priest following his admission to the rectory of Warrington in 1517 in which he filled the vacancy created by the death of a relative.[11] John Redfern's possession of the vicarage of Longford prior to his ordination as priest in 1529 presumably owed much to his kinship to the rector, Edward Redfern.[12] It was connections such as those enjoyed by Mynshull, Dethick and Redfern that allowed certain clerks to emerge from the mass of their fellows and obtain the security of a benefice. Given the small supply of livings relative to the great demand for them, few would have been sufficiently fortunate to have been in the right place at the right time, and only the right connections would allow them to know when and where benefices became vacant, let alone take possession of them. Otherwise they faced the choice of staying in the area of their upbringing in the hope of being available for any future vacancy or of moving to a part of the country in which there was a greater turnover of livings. No mechanism existed by which the few could be selected from the many on a basis of merit; the main modifying agent on the forces of supply and demand, and the only sure route to preferment, was the patronage system.

Patronage, Preferment and Presentation

The origins of the system by which each ecclesiastical living was subject to a patron are to be found in the origins of the parochial system itself. The earliest parishes were organised around the churches which had been built, and were therefore owned, by manorial lords. It followed that since they viewed the church itself as part of their property, then so was the benefice; the freehold tenure of the living as a unit of economic provision for its incumbent.[13] From the twelfth century, an increasing number of parish churches were appropriated by religious houses which thus became among the most significant patrons of ecclesiastical livings in the form of presentations to their vicarages. Similarly, the bishops accrued rights of patronage either stemming from original episcopal foundations or from parishes over which they successfully enforced their superior authority within the diocese. The crown, as supreme landowner and bestower of privilege, remained throughout the Middle Ages in the position of greatest single controller of patronage of benefices. In the context of these developments the church adapted its laws

---

[11] Ibid., B/A/1/14, fo. 60r; B/A/1/14ii, fo. 149v. Some of these delays might reflect dispensations to receive university education under the papal constitution *Cum ex eo*; see L.E. Boyle, 'The Constitution *Cum ex eo* of Boniface VIII', *Mediaeval Studies*, xxiv (1962), 290–6.
[12] LJRO, B/A/1/14ii, fos. 201r, 204r, 205r.
[13] For a discussion of the origins of the parochial system in England, see C.N.L. Brooke, 'Rural Ecclesiastical Institutions in England: The Search for their Origins', in *Settimane di studio del centro Italiano di studi sull'Alto Medioevo*, 28 (1982), 685–711.

concerning the benefice to the unavoidable fact that those claiming foundation rights over churches further claimed the right to select the priest who would serve its cure of souls. This compromise was in the form of allowing the patron to present a nominee to the bishop who would, if he were found suitable and canonically qualified, admit him to the benefice and issue a mandate of institution to its freehold rights. Thus although *de facto* selection of parochial and other clergy for benefices might reside with parties other than the bishop, ultimate authority within the jurisdiction of the diocese resided with him. This was a situation which was to be only temporarily modified in the course of the Middle Ages. During the thirteenth and fourteenth centuries, papal claims to have ultimate rights over the disposal of benefices in all parts of Christendom, in the capacity of 'universal ordinary', affected the extent to which the crown and local patrons could exercise their patronage. However, from about the middle of the fourteenth century, and especially following the commencement of the Great Schism, such claims became, in practice, increasingly ineffective as the operations of papal agents were frustrated by royal authority which was able to exploit the divisions within the Holy See.[14] During the fifteenth century and into the sixteenth it was, unsurprisingly, the crown which was best placed to fill the vacuum of ecclesiastical patronage left by the retreat of papal privilege.[15]

Although the system of patronage was as inescapable and pervasive a force in the ecclesiastical scene as it was within temporal affairs, its *modus operandi* within the former is perhaps even more obscure.[16] Evidence for its operation comes almost exclusively from the administrative records of the church, in particular the bishops' registers.[17] From these, the most we can usually discern is that an individual clerk was presented to a particular living by a named patron. The process by which he came to the attention of the patron, and the qualities which might have made him an attractive proposition remain, in all but a minority of cases, elusive. At the same time, even though we might be able to suggest the connections which brought an individual clerk and his patron together,[18] we can say nothing of the innumer-

---

[14] T.N. Cooper, 'The Papacy and the Diocese of Coventry and Lichfield 1360–85', *Archivum Historiae Pontificiae*, 25 (1987), 91–3.

[15] Swanson, *Church and Society*, 69.

[16] For the best general discussion of the question for England see ibid., 64–80.

[17] Less commonly from sources such as the correspondence of the priors of Durham in the first half of the 15th century; see R.B. Dobson, *Durham Priory, 1400–1450* (Cambridge, 1973), 144–72.

[18] This might be part of the context in which to view clerical membership of civic gilds. Although it is impossible to prove, there are instances where we might suspect that associations formed within the Lichfield Gild of St Mary and St John the Baptist may have had a bearing on subsequent clerical careers. An example might be Robert Jackson who was presented by the succentor and vicars choral of Lichfield to their vicarage of Penn in 1530, four years after joining the gild of which a large number of cathedral clergy were members; LJRO, D.77/1, p. 311; ibid., B/A/1/14, fo. 28r. Between 1503 and 1531, 107 clergy joined the gild; they included Blythe himself, fifteen of the

able competitors for an individual act of patronage and why they were ultimately unsuccessful. The importance of patronage mechanisms, however, demands our attention and, deficiencies of the sources notwithstanding, must be put into context, especially in a period in which competition for benefices, and thus for preferment, was particularly fierce.[19] An analysis of the extent of the distribution of advowsons between various groups of patrons for the whole diocese within this period would be too demanding a task for the present purpose; nor would it be particularly rewarding, since little more would be learned than the extent of *potential* patronage. Discussion is more usefully limited to the actual *exercise* of patronage during the period, of which record was made in the lists of institutions to benefices in the bishop's register and the act books of the dean and chapter of Lichfield.

The greatest number of presentations during the period, about half, were made by religious houses, a situation which also obtained at this time in other parts of the country.[20] Two immediate observations follow from this. First, a large number of the secular clergy of the diocese were being selected in the first instance by regulars and second, since a significant number of houses from outside the diocese made presentations to their appropriated livings in Coventry and Lichfield, part of the selection procedure originated outside the area of Blythe's jurisdiction. Apart from these general comments, little of precision can be said concerning monastic patronage, since the process behind the presentation of particular individuals is especially obscure. It might be assumed that the original point of contact between aspirant secular clerk and a religious house would occur as the ordinand sought a title, but this was very rarely the case. Only six presentations were made during the period by houses of clerks to whom they had provided the title, of which three were made by the Benedictine abbey of Shrewsbury. The contact established between John Wolley and Vale Royal Abbey prior to ordination proved to be particularly valuable since he was presented to their vicarage of Frodsham almost immediately upon ordination to the diaconate in 1510.[21] The others had to wait for anything up to ten years before this initial contact paid off in terms of presentation to one of the house's vicarages.

It has been suggested that monasteries might have made presentations of

---

senior cathedral clergy, five priests serving its chantries and six vicars choral. Of the rest, many are styled simply as *capellanus*. Ibid., D.77/1, pp. 252–330.

[19] The importance of the system to the clergy themselves is reflected in the testamentary bequest of an item of furniture by Edmund Bachelor, rector of Sheinton, to the patron of the living to whom he owed his promotion from the ranks of the unbeneficed, in 1557; below, 92 and appendix.

[20] Bowker, *Secular Clergy*, 67; Zell, 'Clergy in Kent', 526; P. Marshall, 'The Dispersal of Monastic Patronage in East Yorkshire, 1520–90', in B. Kümin, ed., *Reformations Old and New: Essays on the Socio-Economic Impact of Religious Change c.1470–1630* (Aldershot, 1996), 127.

[21] LJRO, B/A/1/14ii, fos. 65v, 68r; B/A/1/14, fo. 56v.

clerks who could have been useful in some administrative capacity such as representation in legal matters.[22] However, if this were the case, it is doubtful that it can be proved in more than a few rare cases, though it might, on occasion, be suggested. For instance, were the successive presentations by the prior of Coventry of Thomas Orton, to the vicarage of Holy Trinity, Coventry, in 1508 and the Lichfield prebendal vicarage of Ufton Cantoris in 1511, due to his being an Oxford-trained civil lawyer?[23] Faced with no other evidence than the presentations themselves, it can be suggested as no more than a possibility. Neither can it be said that the religious houses appear to have been operating anything like a discernible patronage policy in this regard.[24] Presumably, most of those seculars who would be able to prove themselves of use to monasteries would have been graduates, particularly in civil law. Yet graduates are prominent among the presentations of only two religious houses during the period; Coventry Cathedral Priory, which, apart from Thomas Orton, presented four other graduates out of a total of twelve presentations; and St Werburgh's Abbey, Chester, which put graduates forward for eleven of its twenty-three vacant livings.

An analysis of the records of Durham Cathedral Priory has suggested that monastic patronage was not always freely bestowed. The very extent of the advowsons owned by religious houses was likely to make them prey to the crown, local secular powers and even the episcopate, and representatives of all of these were to be found exerting pressure on the priors of Durham to present their nominees in the fifteenth century.[25] Like any local secular lord, the heads of the religious houses would have had to bear in mind the effects of their patronage within the county community and would be unwise to neglect the sons of the important aristocratic and gentle families. Therefore within the archdeaconry of Cheshire, where much ecclesiastical patronage was in the hands of the powerful local families, Chester Abbey presented M. John Brereton to the rectory of Christleton in 1514 and Thomas Molyneux to a moiety of Kirby in 1529, both members of the county elite.[26] Another member of the Molyneux family was presented by Evesham Abbey to the vicarage of Leyland in 1516, and in 1525 Amer Burdet, of local gentry stock, was presented to the vicarage of Middlewich by Lenton Priory.[27] Clearly, the bare details of monastic patronage to be found in the bishop's registers may well mask the influence brought to bear by outside parties.[28]

[22] Heath, *English Parish Clergy*, 34.
[23] LJRO, B/A/1/14, fos. 5r, 6r; BRUO, 1405.
[24] A similar conclusion, for the diocese of Lincoln, is to be found in Bowker, *Henrician Reformation*, 45.
[25] R. Donaldson, 'Sponsors, Patrons and Presentations to Benefices. Particularly those in the Gift of the Priors of Durham, During the Later Middle Ages', *Archaeologia Aeliana*, 4th ser., 38 (1960), *passim*; Dobson, *Durham Priory*, 163, 172.
[26] LJRO, B/A/1/14, fos. 58v, 65v.
[27] Edward Molyneux, LJRO, B/A/1/14, fo. 59v; Burdet, ibid., fo. 61v.
[28] Monasteries might also on occasion (again mirroring the activity of secular patrons)

Whatever the motive behind individual presentations of secular clergy by the religious, a large number of the parish priests of the diocese owed their admission to a benefice to members of the religious orders and Richard Ryve, vicar of South Wingfield, would surely not have been alone in remembering his patrons, in his case the abbot and convent of Darley, in his will.[29]

Of almost equal importance with regard to the exercise of ecclesiastical patronage during the period, being responsible for about 38% of presentations, were the laity themselves. More perhaps than any other patrons, the prominent county families viewed advowsons as items of property which could be used to enhance prestige. The acquisition of rights of ecclesiastical patronage was, for example, an important aspect of the territorial policy of the Stanleys of Lathom throughout the fifteenth and into the sixteenth century, by which they sought further to consolidate their local power.[30] The offspring of such families who were to embark on a clerical career were thus at an obvious advantage relative to their more lowly-born contemporaries. About 20% of presentations made by the laity were of family members; in the archdeaconry of Chester, successive vacancies to a high proportion of livings were taken up by the prominent noble and gentle families of Cheshire and Lancashire. Edward Molyneux, who was presented to the rectory of Sefton in 1509, was one of five members of this family, lords of Sefton, who held the living successively for almost a century from 1462 to 1557.[31] Similarly, the rectory of Halsall was in the hands of members of the Halsall family from 1495 to 1571.[32] In cases where the laity did not present family members, the basis of contact between patron and clerk is more difficult to discern. In a number of cases it would appear from the evidence of titles to orders that the presentees were local men, some of whom might even have been related through the female line. Otherwise, some were likely to have been family friends or members of families with whom the patrons wished to foster good relations. Considerations of 'good lordship' might have been instrumental in the presentation by James Molyneux of Richard Sutton, son

---

have presented nominees related to senior members of the convent; however, such connections are difficult to uncover. It is possible that William Butler, presented by Shrewsbury Abbey to its vicarage of Wrockwardine in 1514, was a relative of Thomas Butler, sub-prior and later (1529) elected as abbot. If so, this might have facilitated the abbey's alleged misappropriation of income from the church, of which it was accused in 1536. However, whilst it is perhaps significant that Butler obtained this preferment within two years of ordination it is also of note that no mention of the abbot or the house is made in Butler's will, of which the executors were his household servants; LJRO, B/A/1/14, fo. 46v; B/A/1/14/ii, fo. 86v; *Blythe's Visitations*, 34, 77, 132; will of William Butler (see *infra* and appendix).

29 He left 10s. to the abbot and the same amount to be shared among the brethren. For details of his will, see appendix.
30 P. Hosker, 'The Stanleys of Lathom and Ecclesiastical Patronage in the North-West of England during the Fifteenth Century', *Northern History*, 18 (1982), *passim*.
31 Haigh, *Reformation and Resistance*, 24.
32 Ibid.

of Lord Dudley, to the valuable rectory of Walton and Liverpool in 1506, to which the previous presentation had been made of James Stanley, later to become bishop of Ely, and which subsequently returned to the hands of the Molyneux family.[33] Henry, Lord Stafford appears to have been continuing a family policy of good lordship expressed in the fifteenth century mainly towards the Stanleys, when he and his wife presented John Brereton, a member of a prominent Cheshire family, to the deanship of Astley college in 1509.[34]

Where a number of presentations were made by a single patron during the period, there is a basis for attempting to discern an active patronage policy. Such a patron was Thomas Stanley, earl of Derby, who made six presentations to livings in the archdeaconry of Chester of which he held the advowson. Apart from Richard Smyth, admitted to the rectories of Holy Trinity, Chester, in 1505 and Bury in 1507, those presented were all Cambridge graduates and it is possible that the Stanleys were deliberately sponsoring Cambridge men, probably at the instigation of the earl's wife, Lady Margaret Beaufort.[35] Robert Caulyn, presented to the rectory of Holy Trinity, Chester, in 1507, had been in Cambridge for at least the previous thirty years during which time he was admitted to a doctorate of civil law. Despite being admitted to the vicarage of St Oswald's, Chester, in 1496, a living which he held at his death in 1512, between 1500 and 1503 he rented civil law schools at Cambridge and so was obviously not continuously resident as demanded by canon law. In 1505 he was granted a papal dispensation to hold one other benefice together with St Oswald's, the terms of which he exceeded by his presentation both to Holy Trinity, Chester, and another Stanley living, Acton, at some time after 1508.[36] The evidence would seem to suggest that Caulyn's career was based in Cambridge, sponsored by the Stanleys through this succession of preferments in their gift. Peter Bradshaw would have come to the attention of the Stanleys by being a member of a prominent neighbouring family in Cheshire. After spending a number of years at Cambridge, Bradshaw received his doctorate in canon law in 1511, probably from a continental university. He resigned his first post, as vicar of Pagham in Sussex, in 1509, leaving him free to accept the rectory of Eccleston from the Stanleys and was the recipient of further preferment from the family in 1535 when he was presented to the rectory of Standish, the two livings being held in plurality until his death in 1541.[37] Thomas Pommell, who followed Caulyn as rector of Holy Trinity, Chester, in 1513, was a fellow of Clare

---

[33] LJRO, B/A/1/14, fos. 54v, 63v.
[34] Ibid., fo. 5v; Hosker, 'Stanleys of Lathom', 222–3.
[35] LJRO, B/A/1/14, fos. 54r, 55r. See M.K. Jones and M.G. Underwood, *The King's Mother – Lady Margaret Beaufort, Countess of Richmond and Derby* (Cambridge, 1992), 202–31.
[36] LJRO, B/A/1/14, fos. 55v, 58r; BRUC, 127; CPL, 660.
[37] LJRO, B/A/1/14, fo. 57r; BRUC, 86–87.

Hall, to the title of which he had been ordained in 1504. He certainly based the earlier part of his career at Cambridge, becoming Master of Arts in 1501 and being licensed as University preacher in 1509. Apart from Holy Trinity, he held no other benefice, and from the time of his admission, might actually have taken up a clerical career.[38] The most valuable living in the Stanleys' gift, indeed probably the richest parochial benefice in the country, was the rectory of Winwick, valued at £102 9s 8d in 1535. From 1495 to 1515, the living had been held by the earl of Derby's brother, James Stanley, who upon his elevation to the see of Ely in 1506 had been allowed to retain it by papal dispensation; his petition to Rome had valued the living at a maximum of 180 marks, even higher than the estimation in 1535.[39] On Stanley's death in 1515 the rectory was taken by Thomas Lark, master of Trinity Hall, Cambridge, but this presentation was unlikely to have been an act of free choice by Thomas Stanley, since Lark was chaplain and secretary to Cardinal Wolsey.[40] Following Lark's resignation in 1525, further influence from the cardinal led to the admission to the living of his bastard son, Thomas Winter, illustrating the point that family connections, even if illegitimate, were one of the surest paths to the heights of ecclesiastical preferment.[41] Yet such patronage depended on the continued influence of the patron, and following the cardinal's fall from power, Winter 'resigned' the living to allow his father's erstwhile master to take advantage of the minority of Edward Stanley to provide for his mistress's uncle, William Boleyn, who was presented in December 1529.[42]

That advowsons and rights of ecclesiastical patronage were being increasingly viewed as items of property with a market value is evidenced by the numerous transfers of patronage which are recorded during the period. Details of these were either registered at institution, or separately if they were granted during an incumbency. A total of seventy-four such transfers were recorded during Blythe's pontificate, of which 47% were between parties of laymen and 30% were grants of presentation made by religious houses to laymen.[43] The majority of transfers occurred in the form of the

---

[38] LJRO, B/A/1/14, fo. 58r; BRUC, 457.
[39] CPL, 644; Valor, v, 220.
[40] LJRO, B/A/1/14, fo. 59r; J.J. Scarisbrick, Henry VIII (Harmondsworth, 1968), 188, 189.
[41] LJRO, B/A/1/14, fo. 65r; For Winter's career see P. Gwyn, The King's Cardinal: The Rise and Fall of Thomas Wolsey (1990), 294, 299, 301–2, 307, 313, 345. For his early clerical preferments see Dickens, The English Reformation, 64–5. It might be wondered whether the previous incumbent, Thomas Lark, was a relative of Wolsey's mistress of the same surname, the mother of Thomas Winter. If so, then this would make Wolsey's use of the patronage of Winwick during these years particularly interesting. On Mistress Lark, see Gwyn, King's Cardinal, xv, 137, 351, 406.
[42] LJRO, B/A/1/14, fo. 65v.
[43] For evidence of a very similar volume of grants by monasteries in E. Yorks. see Marshall, 'The Dispersal of Monastic Patronage', 129–31. See also Zell, 'Clergy in Kent', 527, and for transfers of patronage generally, Swanson, Church and Society, 69, 73–5.

grant of next presentation and a number resulted from enfeoffments to uses which could result in a single patron transferring rights of patronage to a large group of feoffees. In 1528, for example, the enfeoffment of lands belonging to Isobel Bradburne, Lady of Boylestone, gave the right of presentation to the rectory of Boylestone to Ralph Longford esq., William Basset junior, Humphrey Comberfelh, Ralph Purdfery, Richard Coton, William Dethick and Edward Redfern, rector of Longford.[44] In some cases presentation rights to a single benefice might change hands more than once, even where no vacancy to the living occurred, such as on the three occasions during the period on which Sir Thomas Clinton alienated his rights of patronage to the rectory of Arley. In 1514 the recipients were Thomas Everard, gentleman, and John Bull, yeoman, but at the next vacancy, three years later, presentation of Richard Bull was made by Edward Poynynge, Matthew Brown, William Scot, Sir John Scot, Sir John Norton, Edward Bednigfield, James Digge and Thomas Wrewke esq. Eight months later, following the death of Richard Bull, Henry Morgan was presented by William Bull.[45] The prior of Coventry granted the right of presentation to the vicarage of St Michael in the city to a layman in 1507, presented to the living himself in May, 1520, and in October of the same year made a further grant to a local knight.[46] The right of presentation to the rectory of Frankton had been granted in April, 1529, from Richard Duke, gentleman of Nuneaton, to two laymen who presented M. Edmund Strethay, a canon of Lichfield Cathedral.[47] Duke made a further grant to three different men in 1529; they would have had to have been prepared to wait for an occasion to exercise this right, however, since Strethay was still incumbent in 1535.[48] Similarly, two grants of patronage to the rectory of Grappenhall were made by Thomas Byrom esq. in 1514 and 1515, despite the fact that no institution to the living was recorded during the period.[49] The intricate nature of some patronage connections is illustrated by the second of these two grants, which went to James Stanley, bishop of Ely, Sir John Stanley, and Ranulph Pole, who as well as being lord of the manor of Poole, was rector of Hawarden. Pole, whose family had close connections with the Stanleys, had been admitted to the benefice by the king and Lady Margaret Beaufort following the translation of James Stanley to Ely.[50]

Transfers of patronage could involve more than just the two parties of

[44] LJRO, B/A/1/14, fo. 42r.
[45] Ibid., fos. 6v, 8r. Scot was probably of the Scottes of Coventry; see C. Carpenter, *Locality and Polity – A Study of Warwickshire Landed Society, 1401–1499* (Cambridge, 1992), 665.
[46] LJRO, B/A/1/14, fos. 5r, 7r, 8v.
[47] Ibid., fo. 14v.
[48] Ibid., fo. 16r; *Valor*, iii, 62.
[49] LJRO, B/A/1/14, fos. 60v, 104r.
[50] Ibid., fo. 54r. For Pole, and his connections with the Stanleys, see D. Jones, *The Church in Chester, 1300–1540*, Chetham Society, Remains Historical and Literary

grantor and recipient. For example, in cases of minority wardship, the king could either present to the living himself or grant the right of presentation to a third party allowing for an act of patronage on his part and on that of his client. Thus the right to present to the rectory of Somersal in 1517, during the wardship of the daughters of Sir John Montgomery, was not taken by the king himself but granted to Lord Mountjoy, Sir John Gifford and John Porte, the king's solicitor.[51] Similarly, in 1527 the bishop chose not to take advantage of the vacancy in Coventry Cathedral Priory to collate to the vicarage of Holy Trinity in the city himself, but granted the right to do so to two of his cathedral prebendaries, Richard Strete, archdeacon of Derby, and his kinsman, John Blythe.[52] And on the occasion when Thomas Stanley granted the next two presentations to Galeston (Lancs.) to three gentlemen at the instance of (*ad instanciam*) Dr William Butts, the king's physician, it might be wondered exactly who was patronising whom.[53]

The recipients of grants of patronage include occasional references to lawyers, merchants and yeomen, members of those groups which increasingly aspired to positions of social rank within national and county elites. Although it was not overt, there is a suspicion that such transfers of patronage were not far from outright simony.[54] How would the social climber with no claims to ecclesiastical patronage of his own persuade the holders of advowsons to part with them, even temporarily, if money or gifts did not change hands or some form of consideration at least given? What, for example, was the inducement for the Benedictines of Hertford to grant the right of next presentation to their appropriated rectory of Stockton to Robert Barefote, a merchant of London?[55] It is doubtful that Barefote had any interest in Stockton other than the provision of an opportunity for him to exercise patronage in a society which set great store by such manifestations of rank. However, the fact that multiple exchanges of presentation

---

Connected with the Palatine Counties of Lancaster and Chester, 3rd. series, VII (1957), 23; Jones and Underwood, *The King's Mother*, 151.
[51] LJRO, B/A/1/14, fo. 39r; *Letters & Papers Foreign and Domestic, Henry VIII*, vol. II, part 2, 4657.
[52] LJRO, B/A/1/14, fo. 13v.
[53] Ibid., fo. 65r. For the close relationship between Butts and the king, and the physician's reformist views and influence at court, see J.A. Guy, *Tudor England* (Oxford, 1988), 83, 183 and D. Starkey in D. Starkey ed., *Henry VIII: A European Court in England* (1991), 143. For his influence on the patronage decisions of Anne Boleyn see M. Dowling, 'Anne Boleyn as Patron', in ibid., 110. Butts' 'knighthood and his foundation of a country family mark the moment at which medicine became a lay profession': S. Gunn, 'Medicine and Welfare', in D. Starkey, ed., *Rivals in Power: Lives and Letters of the Great Tudor Dynasties* (1990), 182. Compare the career of Thomas Linacre, below 51 and n. 73.
[54] Swanson, *Church and Society*, 65, 70.
[55] LJRO, B/A/1/14, fo. 12v. Given that another Robert Barefote was vicar of Mancetter during the period a Warwickshire connection is possible; below, *passim* and appendix.

rights frequently occurred at times when a vacancy had neither occurred nor would appear to have been imminent, as illustrated above, would tend to argue against such transactions being 'overtly simoniacal'.[56]

A patron not wishing to alienate his rights of presentation entirely could offer the privilege of nominating to a particular vacancy without a formal transfer of the advowson. Although there are few explicit references to such an arrangement, the fact that the holder of the advowson would still be recorded as the nominal presenter might mean that it was more common but is obscured by the formal statement of presentation. Both of the grants made by the abbot and convent of Leicester concerning presentation to its appropriated rectory of Rugby, were of nomination only. The first, in 1507, was taken by Lady Margaret Beaufort, and twenty years later Gilbert, Lord Talboys, lord of the manor of Rugby, was allowed to nominate his candidate for the vacancy.[57] At the presentation to the vicarage of Hampton in Arden in 1510 the transfer from monastery to layman was reversed with, in this instance, Simon Mountford of Coleshill granting nomination to the abbot and convent of Kenilworth.[58] Such arrangements could easily lead to legal complications and it was in the interests of the holders of advowsons to ensure that as well as holding the transfer document themselves, a copy was entered in the bishop's register. There are thirty-six such entries in the register, only a small number of which refer to vacancies which actually arose during the period. Since the right to tenure of the benefice depended on the incumbent being presented by the recognised patron, he too might want to ensure that a transfer of patronage was duly recorded in the register. In 1518, for example, Michaelhouse, Cambridge, granted the next presentation to the rectory of Cheadle to Richard Leche, gentleman, Robert Calton, BA, and Robert Norres, yeoman, and details of the arrangement were copied by the episcopal registrar at the petition of the rector, Richard Norres.[59] Presumably, patron and clerk were related in this instance, and not infrequently transfers of patronage allowed local families of little social standing to make presentations of their members. Thus in 1524, a grant of presentation was made to the next vacancy of a moiety of Eggington by John Booth esq. to Edmund and William Smith, who were described as parishioners of the neighbouring village of Barrow upon Trent.[60] The resignation of the incumbent rector in 1530 allowed for the presentation of Richard Smith by William Smith, enabling a local family to further its aims by intervention in the patronage market, albeit following a six-year wait.[61]

Compared to the number of presentations made by the religious houses

---

[56] Marshall, 'The Dispersal of Monastic Patronage', 96, 131.
[57] LJRO, B/A/1/14, fos. 5r, 12v.
[58] Ibid., fo. 5v.
[59] Ibid., fo. 40v.
[60] Ibid., fo. 41r.
[61] Ibid., fo. 43r.

and the laity, the patronage exercised by the senior clergy of the diocese was limited. Apart from collations to the cathedral prebends,[62] the bishop presented his nominees to parochial livings on only five recorded occasions, including two on which he acted during wardship and one on which the right of nomination had been granted for a single term, allowing the opportunity to advance the career of a close relative.[63] A similar number of presentations was made by the dean and chapter of Lichfield to their appropriated livings, mainly in the peculiar jurisdiction of the Peak.[64] In April, 1525, Robert Rawson refused to accept his nomination by the dean and chapter to their appropriated vicarage of Rugeley, but retained the vicarage of Longdon to which he had been admitted earlier in the month. However, a few months later he also resigned this living to take up appointment to the vacant chantry of St Radegund in Lichfield Cathedral. The reasons for Rawson's decision to leave the ranks of the parochial clergy seem obvious enough; the chantry was worth 10s a year more than Longdon vicarage and was over twice the paltry valuation of Rugeley in 1533. Demand for benefices was, however, sufficient to ensure that the dean and chapter were able to fill the vacancy at Rugeley within three days of Rawson's refusal.[65]

Attempts by bishop and dean and chapter to encroach on each other's rights of presentation towards the end of Blythe's pontificate led to a protracted dispute between the two parties.[66] Earlier, on the occasion of Blythe's presentation of his nominee to the vicarage of Bakewell in 1511, at the concession of the dean and chapter, the latter ensured that the bishop could not in future claim a permanent alienation of patronage by copying his letter of commendation into the register; in it, the bishop acknowledged that the grant was 'for this time' only. The document is of particular interest as the only record made by the diocesan authorities of a letter of presentation to a benefice, the bishop supporting his nominee as follows:

[62] See Cooper, 'Secular Clergy', 201–2.
[63] His presentations were as follows: Humphrey Hawardyn as vicar of Tarvin, 1511 (LJRO, D.30/3, fo. 102r); John Hopton as vicar of Bishop's Tachbrook, 1512 (LJRO, D.30/3 fo. 105r); Edward Redfern as rector of Longford, during minority of Ralph Longford, 1514 (B/A/1/14, fo. 36v); M. Robert Blythe as vicar of Shirley, nomination granted by Darley Abbey, 1515 (B/A/1/14, fo. 37r); Richard Shurley as rector of Pinxton, during minority of Ralph Longford, 1517 (B/A/1/14, fo. 39r). For will of Robert Blythe see *passim* and appendix. Sharing the bishop's birthplace of Norton, Derbyshire, (BRUC, 68) Robert was either his younger brother or a nephew, but, rather curiously, makes no reference to family members in his somewhat perfunctory will.
[64] Presentations to the chantry of the BVM in Moneyash in 1503 and 1509 (LJRO, D.30/3 fos. 72v, 97v); the vicarages of Harborne in 1505, 1507 and 1521 (ibid., 85v, 90v; D.30/4, fo. 1v); Bakewell in 1511 and 1513 (LJRO, D.30/3 fos. 102v, 109v); Chebsey in 1505 (LJRO, D.30/3, fo. 85v); Hope in 1530 (LJRO, D.30/3, fo. 62r); Rugeley in 1525 and 1530 (LJRO, D.30/4, fos. 17r, 20v) and Worfield in 1528 (LJRO, D.30/4, fo. 57r).
[65] LJRO, D.30/4, fos. 11v, 17r, 56v.
[66] VCH *Staffs.*, iii, 163; xiv, 138; T.N. Cooper, 'Oligarchy and Conflict: Lichfield Cathedral Clergy in the Early Sixteenth Century', *Midland History*, 19 (1994), 42–3.

So it is yet I commend unto you and name this bringer Master Doctor Wilcocks whose promotion I verily trust shall be to the honour of God and Saint Chad and furthermore as well to your discharge and mine.

Blythe went on to request of the dean and chapter that Wilcocks

may have and occupy such farms as his predecessor had, that he may be of better ability to keep his house and residence . . . which to do he hath faithfully made in promise as your brother my chancellor hath heard.

The parishioners of Bakewell had little opportunity to test the sincerity of Wilcocks' promise, however, since he resigned the living just over a year after his admission.[67]

The most important single patron of benefices at national level was the crown, and to attract the king's patronage was to put the clerk in line for some of the most valuable livings in the diocese. Not surprisingly, those who found favour were frequently careerists and pluralists, often prominent in the service of church or state. An example of the former was George Heneage, presented to the rectory of Sutton Coldfield in 1517. After taking his bachelor's degree in canon law at Cambridge in 1511, Heneage travelled to Bologna to further his studies, and on his return to England for incorporation at the University of Oxford was granted leave 'to wear cloaks of any costly material, lined with fur and silk, as befitted a person of such distinction'. Following his admission to Sutton Coldfield his career was based mainly in his native Lincolnshire and among his benefices were a number of Lincoln cathedral prebends. He was eventually to become dean of Lincoln and subsequently archdeacon as well as chaplain to Bishop Longland.[68] Whilst Heneage would appear to have been a genuine ecclesiastical careerist, most crown presentations were of royal servants in various capacities. For example, part of the recognition of the debt Henry VIII owed to his tutor, William Hone, was acknowledged by his installation as dean of Tamworth in 1514.[69] In 1516, no sooner had the renowned organist of St Mark's Venice, Dionisio Memo, arrived at the English court at the king's beckoning than he was provided with an income from the perpetual curacy of Henbury in the Cheshire parish of Prestbury. Such a living strictly required residence and the knowledge that this fine musician was delighting his courtly audiences in London would have been little comfort to his parishioners.[70] Roger Dyngley, presented to the vicarage of Bradley in 1528, claimed service to the crown as the reason for his non-residence in one of his benefices in the diocese of

---

67 LJRO, D.30/3, fos. 102v, 103r, 109v.
68 Ibid., B/A/1/14, fo. 7v; BRUO 1501–1540, 280–1.
69 LJRO, B/A/1/14, fo. 22v; BRUO, 956; Scarisbrick, *Henry VIII*, 20, 31.
70 LJRO, B/A/1/14, fo. 60r; Thompson, *The English Clergy*, 122; Scarisbrick, *Henry VIII*, 32. The name of a curate was not returned separately for Henbury in 1533 but there was a curate and eight stipendiary chaplains employed in the parish of Prestbury; BL, Harleian Ms 594, fo. 151v.

Lincoln and he was later given a canonry in the collegiate church of Tamworth.[71] William Knight, presented to the rectory of Bangor-is-y-coed in 1527, was the king's chaplain and principal secretary who, shortly after his presentation, was engaged in often secret embassies to Rome in an attempt to secure the king's divorce, assignments that played a part in the downfall of his spiritual superior, Cardinal Wolsey.[72] Royal patronage could also be indirectly bestowed, as in the case of the presentation of the king's physician, Dr Thomas Linacre, to the valuable rectory of Wigan by Thomas Langton esq. which could hardly have been a matter a free choice, but rather part of a high-level exchange of favours.[73] The career of John Taylor, presented by Henry VII to the rectory of Sutton Coldfield in 1504, epitomises the advantages to be gained by securing powerful patronage. Reputedly born the eldest of triplets to a poor farming family in Barton-under-Needwood, Staffordshire, Taylor's origins could hardly have been less auspicious. Of his early career we know nothing, but he must have come to the attention of a prominent patron by 1500 since in that year he received a doctorate of canon law from the University of Ferrara and in 1502 was a confrater of the English hospital in Rome. Ecclesiastical preferment in England followed swiftly upon the receipt of his doctorate and ordination to the priesthood in 1503 and by the time of his admission to Sutton Coldfield he had already entered the orbit of crown patronage since he was part of a commercial embassy to Burgundy in that year. In 1509 he was admitted to the Lichfield prebend of Eccleshall and in the same year was appointed chaplain to the new king, Henry VIII, clerk of parliament and master of chancery. In 1510 he was presented to the rectory of All Hallows the Great in London and the following year to a rectory in Northamptonshire. In 1513, he accompanied the king on his French campaign as chaplain and on his return in the following year was made prolocutor of the Canterbury convocation. In 1516 he was appointed archdeacon in two dioceses; Derby in Coventry and Lichfield, and Buckingham in Lincoln, and in the following three years was appointed Deputy Master of the Rolls, was presented to a prebend of St Stephen's chapel, Westminster, and accompanied the king at the Field of the Cloth of Gold. In 1522 he was presented to a rectory in Bedfordshire and two years later to one in Devon. By 1526 he was a senior royal diplomat, with his appointment in that year as ambassador to France and his embassy in the following year to invest Francis I with the Order of the Garter. Taylor's rise to the heights of

---

71 LJRO, B/A/1/14, fo. 27v; BL, Harleian Ms 594, fo. 141v; Bowker, *Henrician Reformation*, 118.
72 LJRO, B/A/1/14, fo. 63r; Scarisbrick, *Henry VIII*, 133, 213–15, 216–17, 266, 268–71, 272, 277, 290, 292; Gwyn, *King's Cardinal*, 67, 73, 502, 514–16, 554, 574, 579.
73 LJRO, B/A/1/14, fo. 60v. For the career of Linacre, to whom the foundation of the College of Physicians is attributed, see *BRUO*, 1146–9 and G.T.O. Bridgeman, ed., *The History of the Church & Manor of Wigan in the County of Lancaster, Part 1*, Chetham Society, New Ser., 15 (1888), 73–95. Compare his career as a clerical-careerist physician with that of Dr William Butts, above, 47 and n. 53.

royal service and ecclesiastical preferment was perhaps the most spectacular of all those men of the diocese who sought clerical preferment during the period. Only the careers of John Vesey of Sutton Coldfield, who rose through royal patronage to the bishopric of Exeter and a position as a senior diplomat, and Geoffrey Blythe himself, are comparable. But whereas Vesey was the son of land-owning gentry, and Blythe enjoyed the additional advantage of descent from the family of the archbishop of York, Taylor had not been similarly blessed. Before his death in October 1534, he gave recognition to the humble origins from which he had risen in a particularly appropriate manner; by building a church for the people of Barton-under-Needwood on the site of the cottage in which he had been born.[74]

Admission, Institution and Induction

Having managed to bring himself to the attention of a patron, and having been presented to a vacant benefice, a clerk would subsequently appear, before the bishop or his deputy, for the process of institution. The details of presentation would be copied into a letter of institution beforehand, the contents of which would be read to the clerk who kneeling, held the letter's seal in his hand. The wording of the document formally placed the clerk in charge of the cure of souls and his presentation with symbolic items such as a ring or chalice marked his formal entry to the benefice. If any pension had been arranged out of the fruits of the living by a previous incumbent the details would be added to the presentation deed which would also include the time and place of institution. Before formally instituting, the bishop would need to be satisfied that the benefice was indeed vacant, that the patron had adequate title to present and that the candidate was fully qualified under canon law.[75] At the termination of the institution ceremony the clerk had the right to take possession of his glebe and the tithes of his benefice and received a mandate of induction addressed to the relevant archdeacon or an appointed deputy. He would be further enjoined not to be absent from his living, or if he was, to ensure adequate provision for the cure of

---

[74] LJRO, B/A/1/14, fo. 3v; BRUO 1501–1540, 559–60; R. Morris, *Churches in the Landscape* (1989), 375, 464 and pl. 37. He was also a member of the Lichfield Gild of St Mary and St John the Baptist from 1505: LJRO, D.77/1 fo. 252v. On Taylor's involvement in the French campaign, see Scarisbrick, *Henry VIII*, 60, n. 44. For details of Taylor's speech to the Convocation of 1514 in which, like John Colet, he called for urgent self-reform by the English church and referred to the 'foul and dissolute lives' of the secular clergy, see Gwyn, *King's Cardinal*, 46, 339. Gwyn makes the valid observation that, although relatively ignored, Taylor's speech was more remarkable than Colet's since it came from the mouth of a prolific ecclesiastical careerist rather than a committed humanist. As such, it might suggest a widespread demand for self-reform at least among the clerical élite.

[75] Orme, *Education and Society*, 17.

souls. In the subsequent ceremony of induction the freehold rights to glebe and tithe were formalised by the touching of the church door or another part of the fabric, and by words of induction by the official which included a formula for the handing over of possession of all rights of the church with 'profits and appurtenances thereto belonging'. The new incumbent would then enter the building and traditionally, the bells would be rung to signify possession of the living to his parishioners.[76]

In the great majority of cases the new incumbent was present at the ceremonies in person. Canon law did, however, allow for institution by proxy, a provision of which nineteen clerks during the period took advantage. Thirteen of these were known graduates and were prevented from attendance at the ceremonies by reason of their being at university, engagement in secular or ecclesiastical service or simply because they were pluralists. Thus John Vesey, a prominent civil lawyer, was chancellor and vicar-general of the bishop of Exeter at the time of his admission to the vicarage of St Michael, Coventry, in 1507, and was represented at institution by Richard Collet, vicar of Holy Trinity.[77] The connection between the two men originated from being near-contemporaries in the civil law faculty at Oxford and both were prebendaries of Lichfield Cathedral. Collet soon followed Vesey to the west country and at his death in 1528 was vicar-general of the see to which his friend had been provided by the pope in 1519.[78] In 1527 M. John Davenport was represented at his institution to St Mary on the Hill, Chester, by Hugh Davenport, presumably another member of this prominent Cheshire family.[79] John Bond acted as proxy at the institutions of both M. John Pyffert to Baddesley Clinton in 1511 and M. Anthony Molyneux, admitted to a perpetual chantry in Coventry in 1528. The identity of Bond himself is uncertain[80] but some of those proxies who cannot be traced were likely to have been incumbents and chaplains within the locality such as M. Henry Sherman and Ranulph Wodnut, who when representing Humphrey Hawardyn at his institution to the vicarage of Tarvin in 1511, were rector of Mobberley and chaplain of Wybunbury respectively.[81] Proxy for William Stockwith at his institution to the vicarage of Monks Kirby in 1528 was his father, Henry, who was patron of the living; since there is no record of his ordination prior to the termination of the register in 1531, it is likely that Stockwith was presented as a minor.[82] This was certainly the reason for the institution by proxy of Thomas Mary Wingfields to the rectory of Warring-

---

[76] Heath, *English Parish Clergy*, 42.
[77] LJRO, B/A/1/14, fos. 5r, 13v.
[78] BRUO, 1882–3, where he appears as *Tollet or Talott*.
[79] LJRO, B/A/1/14, fo. 63r.
[80] Ibid., fos. 5v, 15r.
[81] Ibid., D.30/3, fo. 102r; B/A/1/14, fos. 57r, 63v.
[82] Ibid., fo. 14v.

ton in 1527, the patronage rights to which his father had previously bought to provide a good start in life for his young son.[83]

The majority of ceremonies of institution and induction were performed by the archdeacon within whose jurisdiction the benefice lay or if deputies were used they were not generally named. There are only five occasions where a named representative officiated. Four of these were institutions to the vicarage of Harborne which was appropriated by the dean and chapter of Lichfield. The deputy appointed at the first institution to this benefice during the period, of Thomas Waterward, was the vicar of Aston.[84] The following year M. Roger Ball was instituted by one Thomas Twyste, MA, whose identity and status cannot be ascertained.[85] At the next vacancy, in 1521, M. Reginald Hospis, a man who enjoyed connections with the dean and chapter, was instituted by Roger Clough, chaplain.[86] The institution of the subsequent incumbent, George Wyrral, in 1529, was performed by the chaplain of Adbaston.[87] Regardless of whether a deputy was appointed to officiate on particular occasions, ultimate authority to institute and induct to benefices resided with the bishop. This authority could only be circumvented by that of the universal ordinary, the pope. At a time when actual papal interference in the disposal of benefices was restricted, there was one person within the kingdom who was able to exercise the authority of the Holy See. Acting as papal legate *a latere*, Cardinal Wolsey had the power to institute and induct to benefices on his own behalf and he took advantage of two opportunities to do so within the diocese during the period. In 1523 he usurped the right of presentation to St Mary on the Hill, Chester, from St Werburgh's Abbey in order to institute M. Maurice Birkenshaw to the rectory which in 1535 was valued at £52.[88] Birkenshaw was tutor to Wolsey's bastard, Thomas Winter, who was himself presented to Winwick two years later.[89] The vicarage of Rostherne, also in the archdeaconry of Chester, had been ordained in 1507 following the appropriation of the rectory by Launde Priory in Leicestershire.[90] Whilst the priory had been able to present the first two vicars to the new living, its rights were usurped by Wolsey's exercise of legatine authority following the death of the incumbent, Ralph Boydell, in 1529. The connection between the cardinal and his institutee, William Hardwick, described as chaplain, is uncertain.[91]

There is no record of the scale of charges which would have been incurred in these ceremonies, and for other dioceses, references are sparse

---

83 Ibid., fo. 63r; Haigh, *Reformation and Resistance*, 24.
84 LJRO, D.30/3, fo. 85v.
85 Ibid., fo. 90v.
86 LJRO, D.30/4, fos. 1v, 61v, 71v.
87 Ibid., fo. 60v.
88 LJRO, B/A/1/14, fo. 102r; *Valor*, v, 208.
89 For Birkenshaw see N. Williams, *The Cardinal and the Secretary* (1975), 65.
90 LJRO, B/A/1/14, fo. 80r.
91 Ibid., fo. 68v.

but suggestive. The Canterbury convocation of 1421 had set a maximum charge for institution at 12s but such records of fees as have been discovered suggest that this was not rigidly adhered to. In the diocese of Norwich in the early sixteenth century the charge was either 10s or 12s (the reason for the variation is not known), though in effect the total cost could be considerably higher since archdeacons were entitled to charge a further 3s 4d for induction and the certificate of induction itself cost 1s. In the archdeaconry of Wiltshire there are references to the archdeacon charging 6s 8d, and an appeal to chancery from the period deals with the case of a clerk of Exeter diocese who claimed to have been charged £20 for induction by the archdeacon of Cornwall. Whilst this was surely an exception, the inclusion in the petition to the Commons against the clergy of 1532 of complaints against archdeacons overcharging for induction as well as requiring bonds for payments from first fruits, suggests that more than a minority of new incumbents might have faced difficulties in meeting the required sum.[92] This was a further effect of the increase in ordinations and an associated high level of demand for benefices; costs of entry to the limited number of available livings rose to the level which, in a particular area, the 'market' could stand. Thus the spiralling costs of institution and induction would have represented a further limiting factor on the number of men who, once ordained, could realistically expect to be beneficed.

Even the relatively small number of priests who did acquire benefices could face a long wait between ordination and admission. For those whose institutions are recorded in the registers during the period, the average delay from ordination to first, and often only, benefice, was seven-and-a-half years so the chances were against most priests receiving a benefice before the age of thirty. The relatively insignificant number of priests instituted to livings in the diocese but ordained outside it[93] suggests that migration between dioceses, except for those with connections, was limited, and in the vast majority of cases the first recorded institution in the diocese for a particular clerk was his first benefice. Once again those with university degrees, or whose families owned advowsons, were in a favoured position relative to the mass of their contemporaries. Thomas Blythe was almost certainly a relative of the bishop and had been ordained priest only nine months before he was presented by the king to the wardenship of the hospital of St Nicholas at Nantwich.[94] Sir William Bothe was able to present his relative Robert to the rectory of Thornton of which he was patron in 1514 within six months of his ordination.[95] In contrast, William Hordley had been ordained twenty-five years before the transfer of the right of presentation to the vicarage of Holy

---

[92] Heath, *English Parish Clergy*, 43. 6s 8d appears to have been a more generally applied fee: Swanson, *Church and Society*, 221.
[93] See above, 32–4.
[94] LJRO, B/A/1/14, fo. 55r; B/A/1/14ii, fos. 12r, 15r, 18r.
[95] Ibid., B/A/1/14, fo. 58v; B/A/1/14ii, fos. 73r, 93r, 95r, 99r.

Cross in Shrewsbury Abbey from the abbot and convent to a layman provided an opportunity for his admission to a benefice.[96] The difference that education could make in attracting a patron and jumping the queue for livings is illustrated by two presentations made during the period by the abbot and convent of Kenilworth.[97] John Pulteney, ordained in 1506, does not appear to have had the benefit of a university education, and had to wait twenty years before admission to his first benefice, the vicarage of Kenilworth. Pulteney was one of a number of clergy who, at their admission to a first benefice some years after ordination, were described as 'chaplain' or 'priest' rather than 'clerk', designations that appear to have been used to indicate that they were previously unbeneficed. By contrast, John Pyffert, MA, was presented by the same patron to its vacant rectory of Baddesley Clinton two months before his ordination to the priesthood in 1511.[98]

Tenure and Mobility

Such was the intensity of competition for benefices that, once secured, tenure was often maintained for a long period.[99] Throughout the diocese there are numerous examples of priests whose incumbencies in a single parish accounted for most, or all, of their working lives. Just over a quarter of the beneficed clergy in the testamentary group held their benefices for over thirty years[100] and by way of a more concentrated sample, the conjunction of available sources for the archdeaconry of Stafford enables the subsequent careers of clergy ordained to benefices within its jurisdiction to be traced. Fifty-nine clerks were instituted to a total of sixty parochial benefices within the archdeaconry during the twenty-eight year period of Blythe's pontificate and the range of tenures was from a few months to sixty-two years, with the average incumbency being of a duration of just under fourteen-and-a-half years. The high proportion of long tenures is demonstrated by the following table which groups incumbencies according to their duration.

---

[96] Ibid., B/A/1/14, fo. 52v; B/A/1/14ii, fos. 12v, 15r, 18v.
[97] Ibid., B/A/1/14, fo. 12r; B/A/1/14ii, fos. 20r, 22v, 24v, 25r.
[98] Ibid., B/A/1/14, fo. 5v; B/A/1/14ii, fos. 67r, 71v, 74r, 76v.
[99] A phenomenon that has been observed in other areas of the country (Marshall, *Pastoral Ministry in the East Riding*, 7); and in another period (Townley, 'Unbeneficed Clergy in the Thirteenth Century', 47).
[100] See appendix.

Table 3. Length of tenure of benefices in
the archdeaconry of Stafford, 1503–31

No. of years	No. of incumbencies
0–5	8
5–10	4
10–15	11
15–20	10
20–25	10
25–30	5
30–35	3
35–40	2
Over 40	6
Not known	1
Total	60

It can be seen that just over half of the incumbencies lasted for between ten and twenty-five years and 10% were for more than forty years; significant cut-off points occurred at five years and twenty-five years.[101] Twenty-eight of the priests in this sample, almost half, died whilst incumbent. The careers of the eleven men who held benefices for periods in excess of thirty years serve to highlight the implications of the shortage of available jobs. All but one of these men held their single benefice from shortly after ordination until their death; their *minimum* ages can be calculated on the assumption that they had at least reached the canonical minimum age, twenty-four, at their ordination to the priesthood. If their ordination is not recorded in the Lichfield register then the same assumption about age can be made from the date of institution or, in some cases, there is evidence to suggest that they were ordained before 1503 and were thus at least twenty-four by that date.[102]

---

[101] For comparative figures see Swanson, *Church and Society*, 54 and appendix A2, and Zell, 'Clergy in Kent', 529.

[102] This calculation will be used elsewhere. Its utility is confirmed by correlation of sample cases with information given in chantry returns, legal cases and other documents where age is recorded. In such cases it is clear that the age given is often rounded to, say, forty or fifty, but where a more exact age is given, it frequently corresponds to the minimum age calculated from the ordination register.

Table 4. Clergy instituted to livings in the archdeaconry of Stafford 1503–31 holding them for over thirty years

D = Deacon, P = Priest, R = Rector, V = Vicar

Name	Ordination	Institution	Benefice	Value in 1535 £ s d	End of incumbency	Reason	Duration (years)	Estimated min. age
Richard Grene[103]	P 1519	1526	V Longdon	5 5 0	1560	Death	34	65
Robert Bruce[104]	pre-1503	1530	R Kingsley	16 14 10	1564	Death	34	78
Henry Slany[105]	pre-1503	1511	V Bushbury	7 11 14	1546	Death	35	67
Thomas Wylson alias Wetton[106]		1526	V Abbots Bromley	5 0 20	1561	Death	35	69
M. Richard Norres[107]	pre-1503	1516	R. Cheadle	12 9 0	1554	Death	38	75
William Bacon[108]	D 1504	1526	R Standon	6 18 2½	1570	Deprived	44	89
William Merton[109]	D 1518	1531	R Mavesyn Ridware	7 2 10	1575	Death	44	76
Roger Jennings[110]	P 1505	1506	R Weston-under-Lizard	6 7 8	1551	Death	45	69
M. Philip Weldon[111]	P 1495	1509	R Aldridge	8 0 14	1556	Death	47	85
M. John Hall[112]	pre-1503	1505	V Chebsey	5 7 4	1558	Death	53	77
Griffin Broke[113]	P 1525	1529	R Darlaston	3 11 4	1591	Death	62	89

103 LJRO, B/A/1/14, fo. 24v; B/A/1/14ii, fos. 126r, 131r, 133r, 134r; D. 77/1, fo. 294r; Valor, iii, 149; BL, Harleian Ms 594, fo. 140v; SHC 1915, 181.
104 LJRO, B/A/1/14, fo. 28r; B/A/17/1(1), fo. 2v; BL, Harleian Ms 594, fo. 137v; SHC 1915, 136.
105 LJRO, B/A/1/14, fo. 21v; BL, Harleian Ms 594, fo. 141r; Valor, iii, 101; SHC 1915, 45; will of Henry Slany.
106 LJRO, B/A/1/14, fo. 24v; BL, Harleian Ms 594, fo. 140v; Valor, iii, 149; SHC 1915, 1; will of Thomas Wylson. Several clerks with this name were ordained up to 1531.
107 LJRO, B/A/1/14, fo. 23r; B/A/17/1(1), fo. 2r; BL, Harleian Ms 594, fo. 138v; Valor, iii, 126; SHC 1915, 53.
108 LJRO, B/A/1/14, fo. 24v; B/A/1/14ii, fo. 12v; B/A/17/1(1), fo. 4v; BL, Harleian Ms 594, fo. 139r, Valor, iii, 122; SHC 1915, 248.
109 LJRO, B/A/1/14, fo. 31r; B/A/1/14ii, fos. 113v, 122r, 124r; BL, Harleian Ms 594, fo. 140r; Valor, iii, 150; SHC 1915, 189.
110 LJRO, B/A/1/14, fo. 20r; B/A/1/14ii fos. 12v, 17v, 21r; BL, Harleian Ms 594, fo. 142v; Valor, iii, 103; SHC 1915, 313.
111 LJRO, B/A/1/14, fo. 20v, BRUC, 625; BL, Harleian Ms 594, fo. 141r; Valor, iii, 150; SHC 1915, 6.
112 LJRO, D.30/3, fo. 85v; BA/17/1(1), fo. 4v; BL, Harleian Ms 594, fo. 139r; Valor, iii, 126; SHC 1915, 56; will of John Hall, in which he describes himself as 'sick in body but of good and perfect memory, thanks be to God', suggesting a man grateful of being spared from one of the principal infirmities of advanced age.
113 LJRO, B/A/1/14, fo. 28r; B/A/1/14ii, fos. 172v, 174v; BL, Harleian Ms 594, fo. 141r; Valor, iii, 150, SHC 1915, 80.

Among the benefices held for over thirty years only two can be said to have been at all valuable. Richard Norres's rectory of Cheadle was worth £12 9s 0d a year in 1535 and Robert Bruce could expect almost £17 a year as rector of Kingsley, but eight of the eleven livings were only worth between five and ten pounds. The two longest serving incumbents in the archdeaconry, John Hall and Griffin Broke, were in receipt of annual incomes of only about £5 and £3 respectively, although Hall died with estate valued at about £40.[114] The value of over half of the twenty-three benefices held during the period for more than twenty years was less than £10 a year. Whatever the circumstances that led to a clerk staying in a single parish for the whole of his life, the desire to accumulate wealth does not appear to have been among them. Rather, for those without the opportunities for mobility afforded by education, personal wealth or good connections, the lifelong possession of even a poor living was a better prospect than to take one's chances among the swelling ranks of the unbeneficed.[115]

Some of the incumbencies at the other end of the scale can be examined by way of contrast. Two of those clerks whose tenure of benefices lasted five years or less are known to have died whilst incumbent. Of the remaining six, four were graduates, and this was probably the significant factor in their relative mobility.[116] M. William Butler, admitted to the vicarage of Pattingham in November, 1517, had resigned from the living within two months; if he is to be identified with the vicar of Wrockwardine, instituted in 1514, then it is possible that his resignation was enforced due to pluralism.[117] Robert Alen had been ordained priest in the diocese in 1519 and was presented to the vicarage of Seighford nine years later. By 1533 the living had a new incumbent and it is not known whether Alen died or resigned from the benefice; if the latter, it is possible that he might have returned to his place of origin within

---

[114] Will of John Hall.
[115] Long tenures can be observed in other parts of the diocese; for example, Robert Codgrave held the vicarage of Elmton (Derbs.) for 41 years from 1511 to 1552 and John Keldermere held the vicarage of Chilvers Coton (Warks.) for 36 years from 1521 to 1557. In all cases, the possibility that more than one individual is involved has been reduced by including in the sample only those clerks whose names are unique in the ordination register or whose identification can be ascertained by other means.
[116] However, M. Francis Kynnersley held on to the rectory of Leigh for twenty-four years, having been presented three years prior to his ordination to the priesthood in 1529, until his death in 1550. A Cambridge Bachelor of Canon Law, he also held the rectory of Blithfield (Staffs.) from 1533 until his death: LJRO, B/A/1/14, fo. 24v; B/A/1/14ii, fos. 196r, 199r, 201v, 204v; BL, Harleian Ms 594, fo, 140v; *Venn*, iii, 23.
[117] LJRO, B/A/1/14, fo. 24r. Possibly the Butler, fellow of Michaelhouse, Cambridge, in 1489, graduating BCnL in the same year, rector of a moiety in Norfolk, 1487, canon of St George's, Windsor, from 1503 until his death in 1519; in which case, the vacancy might have been incorrectly registered as due to resignation: *BRUC*, 113. For the vicar of Wrockwardine see *passim* and appendix. A William Butler was also vicar of St Werburgh, Derby, in 1533, so it is possible that up to three different individuals are involved here; BL, Harleian Ms 594, fo. 129r.

the diocese of York.[118] M. John Bulcombe is another for whom the reason for a short incumbency is unclear. He had been admitted to the rectory of Church Eaton in 1527 but by 1532 there was a new incumbent; again, as a graduate, it is possible that he obtained preferment in another part of the country.[119] M. William Collier was admitted to Alrewas vicarage in 1530 and resigned the following year. Since he was also at this time in possession of the vicarage of St Peter's, Derby, and is not recorded as holding a dispensation for plurality, again, it is likely that his resignation was enforced.[120] M. Thomas Hunt held the rectory of Mucklestone for no more than four years from his admission in 1529 since the benefice was in the hands of another clerk by 1533. It is possible that he resigned the living to take possession of the Wiltshire rectory to which he had been presented in February, 1530.[121] The reason for Gervase Bagshaw's resignation from the vicarage of Sedgley in 1534, after five years' tenure, was to allow him to take up the position as vicar of the Lichfield prebend of Colwich. The incentive for the move, however, is unclear, since it implied a fall in income of £2 a year between two benefices of meagre value.[122]

The corollary of a high proportion of long tenures was a limited level of mobility between benefices. Only sixteen clerks instituted to benefices in the diocese subsequently moved to another during the period. Exactly half of these can be identified as graduates and the same proportion were moving to a more valuable living. Twelve of the moves were within the same archdeaconry which might reflect either the desire to base a career in a particular locality or simply the fact that the clerk would be more likely to hear of a vacancy within the same area as his existing benefice, or both. No explicit evidence has been found of clergy exchanging benefices within the diocese between themselves, a practice that was common in the fourteenth century and was still occurring up to the end of the fifteenth.[123] On occasions moves between benefices appear to have provided only a small notional rise in income. M. Thomas Porte resigned from the rectory of Coddington in Cheshire to take up that of Doddleston in the same county in September 1508, bringing an increase in value of about £2.[124] John Wright resigned Kenilworth vicarage in 1504, a year after being admitted to that of Great Packington, also in Warwickshire, but the move would have brought an increase of only £1 in annual income.[125] William Merton took the opportu-

---

118 LJRO, B/A/1/14, fo. 25r; B/A/1/14ii, fos. 126r, 131r, 133r, 134r.
119 LJRO, B/A/1/14, fo. 24v. The reason might have been the annual pension of twenty marks, only about £1 less than the value of the living in 1535, which he was committed to paying for the benefice to the abbess of Polesworth; LJRO, B/A/1/14, fo. 24v.
120 LJRO, D.30/4, fo. 66r; B/A/1/14, fo. 42r.
121 LJRO, B/A/1/14, fo. 28r; BRUO 1501–1540, 305–6.
122 LJRO, B/A/1/14, fo. 28r; SHC 1915, 74, 226.
123 Swanson, *Church and Society*, 55.
124 LJRO, B/A/1/14, fos. 55v, 57r; *Valor*, iii, 207, 211.
125 LJRO, B/A/1/14, fo. 3r; *Valor*, iii, 70, 81.

nity of the vacancy of the rectory of Mavesyn Ridware in 1531 to move from his rectory in the neighbouring village of Hamstall Ridware, only a few miles away. He might have found the extra £1 2s 0d that could be expected from its fruits an attractive proposition and, as mentioned above, remained incumbent until his death in 1575.[126] Other moves brought more substantial gains. M. Thomas Lililow was able to double his expected annual income from £6 to £13 by moving between the Derbyshire rectory of Thorpe and vicarage of Hope.[127] The vicarage of St Werburgh's, Derby, was worth little more than £3 a year to John Hodgkinson when he resigned it in 1517 for the rectory of Cubley in the same county, which in 1535 was valued at over £13.[128] Richard Smyth resigned the rectory of Holy Trinity, Chester and was admitted to that of Bury in Lancashire on the same day in October, 1507; the increase in value was from £8 15s 6d to £29 11s 4d as assessed in 1535.[129] The most substantial increase in income to be gained by a move between benefices during the period was attained by M. James Beresford, a residentiary canon of Lichfield Cathedral who resigned from the rectory of Matlock at the beginning of August 1504 and was admitted to Wirksworth vicarage later in the same month. The 1535 valuation of these two livings within his native Derbyshire was £9 3s 0d and £42 7s 9d respectively.[130]

Where there appears to have been a fall in expected income from a move between benefices it must be assumed that other considerations were of importance to the clerk in question. Richard Rolleston resigned from the rectory of Weston in Derbyshire in 1504, but eleven years later was admitted to that of Stoney Stanton in the same county which was worth about half as much. If Rolleston is to be identified as the same person as M. Richard Roston who resigned from the chantry at Lea, Derbyshire, in 1520, then it is possible that his career involved a move away to university and then a return to his place of origin.[131] William Diason was admitted to the Shropshire rectory of Harley in April, 1518, and resigned that of Sheinton, a few miles away, the following month. The move was likely to have brought him a drop in annual income of about £1 but it might be that he had family ties in the one village to which he was now closer than whilst rector of the other.[132] At first sight, the resignation of M. William Darley from the rectory of Ladbroke in 1529 and retention of the vicarage of Allestree to which he had been admitted three years previously would not appear to have been a wise move. In 1535 Ladbroke was valued at £13 10s 0d whilst Allestree was only £8.

---

[126] LJRO, B/A/1/14, fo. 31r; Valor, iii, 150.
[127] LJRO, B/A/1/14, fo. 43r; D.30/4, fo. 62r; Valor, iii, 171, 181.
[128] LJRO, B/A/1/14, fos. 39r, 39v; Valor, iii, 166; BL, Harleian Ms 594, fo. 129v.
[129] LJRO, B/A/1/14, fos. 55r, 55v; Valor, v, 208, 226.
[130] LJRO, B/A/1/14, fo. 32r; Valor, iii, 169, 170.
[131] LJRO, B/A/1/14, fos. 32v, 37v, 40r; Valor, iii, 159, 164.
[132] LJRO, B/A/1/14, fo. 48r; Valor, iii, 183, 184.

However, prior to his resignation, Darley had negotiated an annual pension of no less than £12 from the Warwickshire rectory, resulting in an increase of £7 a year over his previous income.[133]

Pluralism and Non-Residence

The level of competition for benefices in the early sixteenth century was such that those who accumulated more than one were likely to have attracted even greater attention than among previous generations. Certainly, by the time of the opening of the 'Reformation Parliament' of 1529, reactions to the holding of benefices in plurality among prominent laymen had reached an extravagant level of hyperbole. Yet the arguments against pluralists were almost as old as the system of ecclesiastical livings itself and aroused the righteous anger not only of contemporaries but numerous commentators ever since. Whilst the sort of polemical rhetoric that accompanied the first systematic assault on ecclesiastical privilege was long taken at face value, more recent research has suggested that the scale of the problem has perhaps been exaggerated. Summarised below, the findings indicate a number of points of significance.

Table 5. Comparative incidence of pluralism

Area	Date	Pluralists as proportion of total incumbents
Deanery of Holderness, Yorks. E. Riding	1475–1550	6%
Archdeaconry of the E. Riding	1526	4%
Diocese of Lincoln	1518–30	25%
Archdeaconry of Leicester	1518	16.5%
	1526	11.6%
Diocese of Ely	c.1500–c.1550	25%
Diocese of Canterbury	1511	15%
	1538–9	14%
Diocese of Rochester	1523–5	22%
City of London	1521–46	34%

Source: Marshall, *Pastoral Clergy in the East Riding*, 5; Bowker, *Secular Clergy*, 90–1; ibid., *Henrician Reformation*, 42–3; Fuggles, 'Parish Clergy in the Archdeaconry of Leicester', 33; Zell, 'Personnel of the Clergy in Kent', 531–2; Brigden, *London and the Reformation*, 55.

---

[133] LJRO, B/A/1/14, fos. 12v, 15v; *Valor*, iii, 62, 81; below, 76.

First, it is apparent that there was marked regional variation in the incidence of pluralism. The earliest recent analytical survey was that by Margaret Bowker, based on one of the few surviving visitation returns, directed towards an investigation of the scale of the problem in the diocese of Lincoln. There, despite the fact that it appeared to be in decline over the period between 1518 and 1530, at no point did it fall to a level much below a quarter of the parochial clergy. However, the area most affected was the archdeaconry of Buckingham which included the University of Oxford and it seems likely that the level of both pluralism and its attendant abuse, absenteeism, was artificially inflated by the relatively high value of many of the livings of the diocese and the presence within it of a high number of non-resident scholars. Significantly, when the figures for the archdeaconry of Leicester within the same diocese were examined in isolation it was found that the incidence was considerably lower. The neighbouring diocese of Ely, in which it has been estimated that a similar proportion of clergy were pluralists as in Lincoln, would have been similarly affected by the disproportionate influence exercised within it by the presence of the University of Cambridge. This is reinforced by the fact that in the dioceses of Canterbury and Rochester, in which there were benefices available of a similar value to those in Lincoln and Ely, the overall incidence of pluralism was lower; however, the figures could still be said to have been unacceptably high and a probable reason for this, in the absence of an institution of higher learning, was the dominant presence in the ecclesiastical affairs of the south-east of England of the city of London. Here, where the richest pickings were available to those prepared to exploit the system, it has been estimated that two-thirds of parishes had a pluralist incumbent at some point during the period, many of whom held their city living with one or more in one of the neighbouring dioceses; it is thus hardly surprising that, in common with many of the actions of the 1529 parliament, the move against pluralism was strongly influenced by interest groups within the capital.[134] To date, little systematic research has been done on benefice-holding outside of these regions but the figures for the East Riding of Yorkshire are in stark contrast to the other areas, influenced no doubt in part by the relative poverty of available livings. An investigation into the situation in the diocese of Coventry and Lichfield therefore assumes some significance, since from it can be gained a comparative perspective for the midlands and north-west of the country.

Much of the significance of the Lincoln study is that it was based on the records of a thorough episcopal visitation of the parishes of the diocese undertaken between 1514 and 1521. No other diocese is so well served with such material and a study of Coventry and Lichfield must draw on a range of sources in order to build up an overall picture. Bishop Blythe's register and court records reveal only four explicit charges of pluralism or non-residence.

---

[134] C. Harper-Bill, 'Dean Colet's Convocation Sermon and the Pre-Reformation Church in England', *History*, 73, no. 237 (Feb. 1988), 210.

John Colmore, succentor of Lichfield Cathedral and vicar of Penn, was cited before the bishop's Official Principal in 1526 on a charge of unlicensed pluralism, but was able to satisfy the court by his production of a papal dispensation and documents of institution by the archdeacon of Stafford.[135] In the same year Richard Harrington, vicar of Sutton Maddock, pleaded guilty to a charge of non-residence brought by his parishioners and was warned not to be absent from his benefice in future.[136] In 1527, a number of charges of immorality and misconduct brought against William Whittington, vicar of Mancetter, also revealed that he had been absent from his parish for some time.[137] The dean and chapter of Lichfield brought a charge of absenteeism against Edmund Eyre, vicar of Tideswell, in 1529; in his defence, Eyre showed the chapter his papal dispensation for non-residence on condition that the parish was served by one priest and a subdeacon while he was resident and two priests and a subdeacon during periods of absence.[138] He had certainly complied with the terms of the dispensation by 1533 when the cure was served by four clergy, three of whom were definitely in priest's orders.[139] Licences of dispensation were usually granted for a fixed period, in most cases between one and seven years, and a distinction was made between those clerical appointments which involved the cure of souls and those, such as cathedral canonries, which did not.[140] There was an obligation on a clerk who was to be absent from a parochial cure to be represented by a proctor for the administration of the temporalities of the benefice and a chaplain to minister to the people, which, in the case of an absent rector, would usually be a vicar.[141] During the first ten years of Blythe's pontificate, for which papal registers have been published, ten clerks from the diocese were dispensed for holding benefices in plurality and a further eight papal and legatine dispensations are recorded in the bishop's register. The dispensation granted to Thomas Tomkins, rector of Quatt, in 1505, made an additional specific allowance for absence from the parish; he was not to be compelled to reside whilst at university or visiting the papal *curia*.[142] The grants made to John Gresley and John Blythe in 1505, and William Bonde, in 1508, also included dispensations from defect of age. Gresley, who had been previously dispensed by Alexander VI to hold a benefice when he was seventeen, was licensed at the age of twenty-three to hold another for life. Two years later

---

[135] LJRO, B/C/2/1, fos. 132r, 139v.
[136] Ibid., fos. 131r, 136r, 140v, 143v; B/C/2/2, fo. 29r.
[137] LJRO, B/C/2/1, fo. 111v; below, 181.
[138] Ibid., D.30/4, fo. 59v.
[139] BL, Harleian Ms 594, fo. 128v.
[140] Bowker, *Secular Clergy*, 93–4. Bishops were able to grant licences for non-residence but no such grants are recorded in Blythe's register; R.N. Swanson, 'Universities, Graduates and Benefices in Later Medieval England', *Past and Present*, 106 (February 1985), 31–2.
[141] Heath, *English Parish Clergy*, 63.
[142] CPL, 505.

he was admitted to the degree of bachelor of both laws at Oxford and in 1511 was presented to the rectory of Norton in Hales. By the following year he had also obtained the rectory of Ruthin in Denbighshire and had been ordained priest.[143] Blythe, a relative of the bishop, was granted a dispensation at the age of eighteen allowing him to receive a benefice and to hold one other when he had reached the age of twenty. On attaining the lawful age, twenty-four, he was permitted to add a third benefice or any three if he were to resign the previous two. Ordained deacon to the title of an unspecified benefice in the following year, by the end of the period he held two non-parochial appointments, the archdeaconries of Coventry and Stafford with their attached prebends of Lichfield Cathedral.[144] Bonde was nineteen when he petitioned the pope concerning his desire to become a cleric. He was granted permission to be beneficed once he had received the tonsure, and at the age of twenty was to be allowed to hold another, irrespective of whether it involved cure of souls.[145] There is no record of his having subsequently received any benefice within the diocese of his birth and thus of whether his attempt to gain a head start in the clamour for benefices was ultimately successful, but he might have pursued a career elsewhere.

In the absence during this period of sources such as the lists of pluralists which were drawn up by papal command in the late fourteenth century,[146] two approaches to an estimate of the number of clerks holding benefices in plurality can be made. The first is to consider those clerks who were instituted to more than a single parochial living during the period without resigning from their previous acquisitions; twelve such cases are recorded, accounting for about 3% of those instituted to parish benefices. Eight of these clerics are known to have been graduates and eight were in possession of two livings, whilst four held three each. Exactly half of these pluralist institutees were canons of Lichfield Cathedral, amongst whom were the chancellor, Ralph Whitehead, and the bishop's vicar-general, Ralph Sneyd. A more accurate impression of the extent of pluralism is, however, gained by a survey of the tenure of benefices within the diocese at a single point in time. The clerical subsidy return for 1533 reveals that a total of fifty livings (approximately 12% of the benefices in the diocese) were in the hands of twenty-two pluralist clerks, which represents about 5% of the incumbent parish clergy. The formulation of the acts limiting pluralism and non-residence of 1529 stated that thenceforth the abuses were to be dealt with by the secular courts which were empowered to deprive any clerk holding more than one living worth in excess of £8 a year and to impose fines of between

---

[143] Ibid., 421; LJRO, B/A/1/14, fo. 21v; B/A/1/14ii, fos. 81v, 88v; *BRUO 1501–1540*, 247.
[144] *CPL*, 516; LJRO, B/A/1/14ii, 27r; B/A/17/1(1), fo. 4r; BL, Harleian Ms 594, fos. 118v, 139r, 143r, 144v, 147r.
[145] *CPL*, 874.
[146] Swanson, *Church and Society*, 53.

£10 and £20 on absentees and those who had unlawfully procured papal dispensations. Those exempted from the strictures of the act included royal chaplains, councillors, prelates, the nobility, university scholars and pilgrims.[147] It is therefore possible that by 1533 the new legislation had already made an impact on the unquantifiable incidence of pluralism in the previous decades.

Eighteen of the twenty-two pluralists in 1533 were holding two benefices and four held more, with the greatest number of benefices held by a single individual being Richard Egerton's collection of five. Of the fifty benefices held in plurality, three-quarters (37) were rectories and one-quarter (13) were vicarages from which a strict application of canon law did not allow absence without possession of the necessary dispensation. Over half (14) of the pluralists are known to have been university graduates and some of these might have been able to gain exemption from the statute of 1529 by claiming continued study at university. The graduates included John Brereton and Anthony Draycott, who, as royal chaplains, had a further claim to exemption. Apart from the rectory of Christleton and a moiety of Malpas, both in the archdeaconry of Chester, Brereton was also in possession of the rectory of Hatford in Berkshire. In 1532 he obtained a royal pardon for his previous acquisition of a papal dispensation for plurality.[148] Draycott, rector of Checkley, to the title of which he had been ordained subdeacon in 1515, and of Draycott, of which he was probably a native, was also vicar of Wirksworth and rector of Cottingham in Northamptonshire. His pluralist career was eventually brought to an end in 1560 when he was deprived of all his benefices for failing to take the oath of supremacy.[149] Another graduate, William Throgmorton, was also in possession of a benefice outside the diocese; in addition to the rectories of Hanbury and Handsworth, both in the same Staffordshire deanery, he held the rectory of Great Houghton in Northamptonshire.[150] Four of the graduate pluralists were dignitaries of Lichfield Cathedral. M. Nicholas Darrington was a non-residentiary canon, holding three successive prebends from 1524 which were combined with tenure of the vicarages of Holy Trinity, Coventry, and Wybunbury.[151] M. Edmund Strethay, although in all probability a local man, was never admitted to residence by the Lichfield chapter but acquired two successive prebends in the cathedral in addition to the rectory of Frankton, Warwickshire, and Audlem

---

[147] Heath, *English Parish Clergy*, 49–50; Bowker, *Henrician Reformation*, 113.
[148] LJRO, B/A/1/14, fos. 5v, 58v; BL, Harleian Ms 594, fo. 148r; *BRUO 1501–1540*, 67–8.
[149] LJRO, B/A/1/14ii, 197r; B/A/17/1(1), fo. 2v; BL, Harleian Ms 594, fos. 127v, 138v, 139r; *BRUO 1501–1540*, 176. For an allegation of forced entry by Draycott and others into premises in Checkley see below, 179.
[150] LJRO, B/A/1/14, fo. 20r; BL, Harleian Ms 594, fo. 140r; *BRUO 1501–1540*, 566.
[151] LJRO, B/A/1/14, fos. 13v, 60v; D.30/4, fos. 15r, 40v, 61v; BL, Harleian Ms 594, fos. 118v, 142r, 144v, 150r, 153r.

in Cheshire.[152] M. Richard Egerton was one of the longest serving of Lichfield's resident canons and at his death in 1538, aged about eighty, had given a lifetime of service to the diocese and its mother church, though whether this was any consolation to the many parishioners to whom he would have been conspicuous by his absence, might be debatable. Apart from his cathedral dignities, Egerton held no fewer than five parochial benefices in the diocese; the rectories of Grindon, Stoke and Newcastle, Enfield, the vicarage of Frodsham and the perpetual curacy of Ingestre chapel. His sinecurist career in Staffordshire also extended to his tenure of the posts of warden of the hospitals of St. John in both Stafford and Lichfield.[153] Ralph Sneyd, a member of another prominent family of the diocese was a servant of both cathedral chapter and bishop, being vicar-general in the diocese as well as a resident canon of the cathedral. Additionally, he was in possession of the Cheshire rectories of Tattenhall and Woodchurch. At his admission to the latter benefice in 1529 he was required by the bishop to display the documents whereby he was dispensed from holding livings in plurality. He duly produced a papal dispensation licensing him to hold three simultaneous benefices which the bishop and his registrar were satisfied was valid.[154]

Evidence survives to prove that dispensations for pluralism were held in only five other cases, two of which, granted to Richard Egerton and Thomas Lililow, were licences from Cardinal Wolsey as *legate a latere*. Copies of these were made in the bishop's register, as was the papal dispensation issued to John Walker allowing him to hold the three vicarages of Wombourne, Worfield and Sheriffhales, all in the same rural deanery.[155] Over half (twelve) of the pluralists held their benefices in the same area, including five who held livings in the same deanery, which suggests that they were not simply random collections amassed for the purposes of financial gain but a deliberate concentration of a career in a particular locality. John Brereton, Edward Molyneux and Ralph Sneyd all held benefices exclusively in the archdeaconry of Chester within which their families were prominent landowners. The holding of a number of benefices within a small geographical area might have allowed for simultaneous supervision[156] and although that was unlikely to have been the case with these three clerks, priests without any obvious prominent county or national connections, such as John Walker and John Ward, who both held benefices within close proximity to each other in Staffordshire, may have intended such an arrangement.[157] Alternatively, it

---

152 LJRO, B/A/1/14, fos. 14v, 37r, 58v; D.30/4, fos. 7r, 65v; BL, Harleian Ms 594, fos. 119v, 120r, 144v, 153r; *Venn*, iv, 174.
153 LJRO, B/A/1/14, fo. 59r; B/A/17/1(1), fos. 3r, 10r; *Valor*, iii, 120; *BRUO*, 630; Le Neve, *Fasti*, 31.
154 LJRO, B/A/1/14, fos. 54v, 65v; D.30/4, fo. 58r; BL, Harleian Ms 594, fos. 121r, 147r, 148r; Le Neve, *Fasti*, 24; SHC 1915, 278.
155 LJRO, B/A/1/14, fos. 21r, 101v; BL, Harleian Ms 594, fos. 141v, 142v.
156 Bowker, *Secular Clergy*, 102.
157 For Ward see below, 69.

might reflect no more than that, once they had obtained their first benefice within a particular area, they were more likely to be aware of vacancies that arose within the locality.

In her study of the secular clergy of the diocese of Lincoln, Margaret Bowker isolated a group from among the pluralists whom she labelled 'pure pluralists'; these were clerks with education, wealth and good connections, often servants of the crown, whose sole motivation for holding more than one benefice was to amass a personal revenue commensurate with their status, or who received multiple preferments by way of reward from those to whom they owed some form of service.[158] In his work on the clergy of the archdeaconry of Leicester in the same diocese J.F. Fuggles drew a distinction between that group and those whose combination of livings was aimed at merely providing a sufficient income whom he called 'poor pluralists'.[159] The evidence from Coventry and Lichfield tends to support the validity of this distinction. The financial rewards of pluralism in the diocese varied between the extremes of the four benefices that provided Edward Molyneux with a combined annual income of almost £140, and the two livings which together yielded less than £12 to Edmund Strethay; unsurprisingly, those at the top of the earnings list included the majority of the graduates and members of the landed gentry. The act of 1529 excluded from its definition of pluralists those clerks whose first benefice was valued at under £8, and this would reduce the list of those holding more than one benefice in 1533 by nine. Furthermore, all of these clerks, with the exception of M. Robert Mainwaring and Richard Werburton, held benefices which yielded a combined value of less than £15; such men could hardly be accused of abusing the system for the purpose of amassing a personal fortune.[160] At the other end of the scale, nominally at least, considerable fortunes could be made. Yet matters were not always as simple as they might seem for those with the connections that brought them advantageous preferment. For example, Edward Molyneux's combined income of £137 11s 10d from the rectories of Walton and Liverpool, Ashton-under-Lyne, Leyland, and Sefton have been seen as compounding the alleged 'force and deceit in his financial dealings and . . . a thoroughly disreputable character', who 'had nothing to recommend him but his connections; he did not hold a university degree'.[161] In fact Molyneux, a Master of Arts, was having to pay an annual pension of no less than £80 from the fruits of Walton and Liverpool, valued at £69 16s 10d in 1535, to the

---

[158] Bowker, *Secular Clergy*, 101.
[159] Fuggles, 'Parish Clergy in the Archdeaconry of Leicester', 36.
[160] Mainwaring: rectory of Ightfield (£7 14s 8d in 1535); rectory of Alderley Edge (£24 10s 10d in 1535). Werburton: rectory of Pulford (£6 5s 10d in 1535); moiety of Lymm (£11 0s 6d in 1535). BL, Harleian Ms 594, fos. 133r, 147v, 152r, 153r; *Valor*, iii, 185, 207, 210, 215.
[161] Haigh, *Reformation and Resistance*, 26.

previous incumbent Richard Sutton, who as son of the Lord of Dudley, was similarly well connected.[162] Whatever the reputation Molyneux enjoyed as a litigant both in the local courts and Star Chamber, the financial implications of his collection of nominally valuable benefices were more complex than they would appear at first sight; and at least some of his absence from these Lancashire parishes was spent in acquiring university education, a situation readily condoned by both church and state. Such was the scale of his indebtedness at his death in 1534 that an estate of 1,000 marks was declared insufficient to meet his commitments and his creditors had to be paid proportionately.[163] On a smaller scale, the revenue potential of the two vicarages held by Nicholas Darrington were similarly affected. For the first year of his tenure of Holy Trinity, Coventry, he had been committed to providing an annual pension of £30 from its fruits to the previous incumbent, Richard Collet, who, fortunately for Darrington, died within a year of leaving the benefice for a lucrative post in the diocese of Exeter.[164] In 1535 Holy Trinity was valued at just over £26, and Darrington's decision not to resign from the vicarage of Wybunbury which he had acquired three years previously, and was valued at £13 11s 6d in 1535, might even have been based on motives of financial survival rather than covetousness. If we were to allow for any laxity in the recording of pension arrangements by the episcopal registrar, then it is possible that a greater number of the potential high-earning pluralists were similarly affected by the acquisitiveness of their predecessors.

The discussion so far has concentrated on the implications of pluralism and non-residence for the clerks who practised them. What can be said about the likely consequences of such behaviour for the provision of sacramental and pastoral care to the people of the affected parishes? Despite the limited survival of visitation material on which an impression of lay attitudes might be based, it has already been noted that a very small number of cases for the enforcement of residence were brought before the consistory court during the seven years for which records survive, or were entered in the registers. In the subsidy returns of 1531 and 1533 only John Ward, rector of Gratwich, was specifically labelled as non-resident, though, as stated earlier, limited periods of non-residence, at least, were the inevitable consequence of all holding of benefices in plurality.[165] Although not specifically returned as absent from their cures, we know that men such as the royal chaplains John Brereton and Anthony Draycott and the resident cathedral canons and

---

[162] LJRO, B/A/1/14, fo. 63v; BRUO, 598–9. For Molyneux's indebtedness to the rector of Wigan see below, 75. Pension arrangements are discussed more fully below, 74–7.
[163] Bridgeman, *History of the Church and Manor of Wigan*, 99, n. 2.
[164] LJRO, B/A/1/14, fo. 13v; BRUO, 1883.
[165] LJRO, B/A/17/1(1), fo. 2v. His other living was the rectory of Blore; BL, Harleian Ms 594, fos. 138r–v.

diocesan officials, Richard Egerton and Ralph Sneyd, would, of necessity, have been non-resident. The most frequently rehearsed allegation concerning the consequences of pluralism has been that, in the absence of the incumbent priest, care of the parish was left in the hands of underpaid, poorly supervised and by implication, poorer quality curates and other assistant clergy.[166] An approach to testing this assumption, faced with a lack of specific visitation records, must again be based on information from the subsidy returns, and inference from the court records of a slightly earlier date. It is immediately clear that, by the 1530s, the ecclesiastical and secular authorities need have had little cause for concern regarding the provision of clergy in the parishes of non-resident incumbents. Only three of the pluralist clergy in 1533 held a parish in which no other clerk was assessed for tax. In each of these cases, the one benefice was provided with at least one curate and since none of the clerks in question was in government or local service there is no reason to assume that they were not personally resident in the other.[167] Similarly, the only parish which was explicitly returned as having a non-resident incumbent, Gratwich, was being served by a curate.[168] In all, the fifty parishes subject to pluralism in 1533 were provided with a total of 113 assistant clergy, an average provision of two clerks, apart from the incumbent, per parish. Some of the well-endowed parishes enjoyed the services of a sizeable body of clergy. For instance, periods of absence of Nicholas Darrington from the vicarage of Holy Trinity, Coventry, were covered by the presence in the parish of eleven full-time stipendiaries including a curate, a chantrist and nine other clerks.[169] Walton and Liverpool, a typically large Lancashire parish, the rectory of which was in the possession of Edward Molyneux, was served by a vicar and eleven stipendiaries.[170] The five clergy attached to the parish of Malpas, the major revenues of which were divided between two rectors, included two curates and a schoolmaster.[171]

The evidence of the consistory court records, which survive for the years 1524 to 1531, does not support the assertion that the unsupervised stipendiary clergy serving the parishes of absentee incumbents were any more vulnerable to lapses of discipline or any less able to provide for the spiritual needs of their parishioners. None of the clergy attached to benefices known to have been subject to pluralism or absenteeism during the period were cited for

---

166 W.J. Sheils, for example, appears to make a direct relationship between the poor remuneration of stipendiary clergy and poverty of service which, to the mind of this author at least, is contentious; W.J. Sheils, *The English Reformation 1539–1570* (1989), 5.
167 M. Ralph Bowring, Plemstall: BL, Harleian Ms 594, fo. 148v; Richard Ryve, South Wingfield: BL, Harleian Ms 594, fo. 124r; below, *passim* and appendix; Andrew Roode, Wistaston: BL, Harleian Ms 594, fo. 154v.
168 LJRO, B/A/17/1(1), fo. 2v.
169 BL, Harleian Ms 594, fo. 118v; above, 66.
170 BL, Harleian Ms 594, fo. 150v.
171 Ibid., fo. 148r.

either moral defects or failure to minister to the souls left in their charge. Indeed, as was found to be the case in the diocese of Lincoln, the beneficed clergy feature just as prominently in the proceedings, and many of those unbeneficed who were subject to charges, either by the diocesan authorities or the laity, do not appear to have been involved in formal parochial work.[172] Other evidence also points away from a suggestion that curates and other supporting clergy were of a relatively poor quality. Only a minority of the clerks attached to the benefices of pluralists in 1533 cannot be traced in the ordination registers. Of these, some were likely to have been ordained before 1503 and would thus have been in their mid fifties and might have served the parish for much, if not all, of their working lives. The average minimum age was thirty-six, with a significant proportion in their late forties and fifties. In general, the clergy supporting these parishes represented a broad range of age, and thus by implication, experience. For example, of the eleven clergy attached to Holy Trinity, Coventry, the minimum ages of all but four can be calculated. The most senior, Thomas Morres, was fifty-two, John Dalbye was forty-five, William Bailey and the chantrist, William Molyneux, were both in their thirties, while Thomas Avery, Robert Robothum and William Lambard would all have been in their late twenties.[173] There is no reason to believe that such men would have been in particular need of close supervision from incumbents who were often younger and had less, if any, experience of parish work, than themselves. Since the great majority of these assistant clergy can also be shown to have been in priests' orders, they would have been able to take full responsibility for both pastoral and sacramental provision to the people of the parish.

Experience, however, was not well rewarded. Only a minority of curates serving the benefices of non-residents in the diocese of Lincoln during this period received annual stipends in excess of £5;[174] in Coventry and Lichfield only three were paid more than £4. These were the curates of Holy Trinity, Coventry, and Newcastle, who received £16 and £11 respectively, and John Latham, schoolmaster at Malpas who received a salary of £20 which would have been quite high for such a post.[175] In Walton and Liverpool the assistant clergy who shouldered almost the entire burden of parochial responsibility received a little over 5% of the value of the benefice to its absentee rector. It is therefore particularly surprising that none of the tensions which might be expected to have arisen between underpaid assistant and wealthy pluralist surfaced in the court proceedings of the period. That they did not is partly explained by the disadvantageous bargaining position of the unbeneficed in the light of an abundant supply of priests. It might also, of course,

---

[172] Bowker, *Secular Clergy*, 106–8.
[173] LJRO, B/A/1/14ii, 15v, 37v, 153r, 188v, 200r, 143v.
[174] Bowker, *Secular Clergy*, 103.
[175] BL, Harleian Ms 594, fos. 138r, 148r; Orme, *Education and Society*, 57–8.

point to high standards of dedication and pastoral care, qualities which leave all too little impression in the historical record.[176]

Unions of Benefices and Pensions

Despite the serious attempts that might be made by individual bishops to limit the scale and effects of pluralism and absenteeism,[177] until the introduction of secular legislation in 1529, they were impotent in the face of a clerk in possession of a valid dispensation. A determined pluralist might go one step further and petition the pope for an additional licence to combine livings so that for the purposes of canon law they would be counted as a single benefice. The arrangement was purely financial; geographical distance did not present an obstacle since there was no intention that the parishes should be served as a single unit.[178] Nationally, an increasing number of such licences were issued by the papacy during the fifteenth century, adding fairly significantly to the number of benefices which were held in plurality.[179]

The present unavailability of papal registers after 1513 precludes a full assessment of the impact of the phenomenon during the period of Blythe's pontificate, but between 1505 and 1512 licences were issued to seven clerks for union of benefices of which one was within the diocese; in no case did this apply to both livings. Five of the recipients are known to have been graduates and in three cases the grant included a specific dispensation from non-residence. These were the licences issued to John Talbot in 1505 to unite the rectory of South Walsham in the diocese of Norwich with the vicarage of Glossop; to Thomas Dalison for the union of the rectory of Avon Dassett with that of Stoke Dry in the diocese of Lincoln; and John Grygge for the union of the rectory of Wolstanton with a benefice in Winchester diocese.[180] The wording of the grants to Dalison and Grygge specifically released the petitioners from the oaths of residence that they had made before the bishop on their admission to the livings in question. No-one was henceforth to compel them to reside against their will. Grygge, certainly,

---

[176] Two historians have assessed the situation particularly neatly: 'Here [South Ockenden] is a glimpse of what must have been the usual result of legitimate non-residence; the parish was quite well served by a chaplain. Unfortunately it is usually the parishes where absence has led to scandal of one kind or another which are described in the disciplinary and episcopal records of the time'; 'As long as there was no shortage of clergy, and provided that the episcopal authorities were vigilant, pluralism and non-residence did not adversely affect the ministration of the church in the parishes'. Heath, *English Parish Clergy*, 67; C. Harper-Bill, *The Pre-Reformation Church in England 1400–1530* (Harlow, 1989), 48.
[177] Heath, *English Parish Clergy*, 69.
[178] For conditions attached to such unions, and some examples, see ibid., 164; J.A.F. Thomson, *The Early Tudor Church and Society* (1993), 175–6.
[179] Swanson, *Church and Society*, 54.
[180] *CPL*, 93, 495, 821.

was unlikely to have ever set foot in his Staffordshire benefice. As a member of the household of Christopher Bainbridge, cardinal archbishop of York, from whom he had obtained his original dispensation from pluralism, his career would have been based in Rome.[181] As with all other facets of clerical careers, good connections were the surest means of overcoming barriers to advancement. John Talbot's petition for a licence was not hindered by the fact that his descent from the noble family was illegitimate, a defect from which he was not dispensed until thirteen years later. Again, it is unlikely that he spent much time in his Derbyshire vicarage, since he appears to have enjoyed a career as an Oxford theologian.[182]

Unions of benefices were only licensed for fixed terms, usually the lifetime of the petitioning clerk, and at his death they were to revert to their original state. His retirement would similarly terminate the union. Yet this could still deprive at least one of the parishes concerned of a resident incumbent for some considerable time. Richard Roston, licensed to unite his wardenship of the collegiate church of St Lawrence, Putney, with the chantry of Lea in 1505, did not resign from the Derbyshire living until fifteen years later[183] and John Talbot's absence from Glossop appears to have lasted for more than twenty years.[184] The union of Bangor-is-y-coed with Chepping, in York diocese, that was granted to James Straitbarrel in 1506 appears to have been of a similar duration. Whilst there is no record of an institution to the benefice during the period, it was vacated, without the resigning incumbent being mentioned, in 1527. Straitbarrel, who would appear to have been a member of a prominent Cheshire family of that name, also held the rectory of St Mary on the Hill in Chester from 1506 to 1523.[185] The longest surviving union of benefices in the records is likely to have been that of the rectory of Avon Dassett with Stoke Dry in the diocese of Lincoln, granted to Thomas Dalison in 1507. This was the same year as Dalison's admission to the benefice which he is recorded as still holding in 1535. Although he resigned from Stoke Dry in 1513, Dalison held on to two of his other benefices, the vicarage of St Cleer in Cornwall, and the rectory of Clothall in Hertfordshire, until his death in 1541. If, as seems likely, he also maintained his tenure of Avon Dassett, this would mean that its union to a benefice outside the diocese, and lack of a resident incumbent, lasted for thirty-four years.[186] Despite his continuous absence from the parish, Dalison was able to claim almost £14 each year from the fruits of its greater tithes; in his place a single

---

[181] For Bainbridge's career, see D.S. Chambers, *Cardinal Bainbridge in the Court of Rome, 1509 to 1514* (Oxford, 1965).
[182] BRUO, 1844–5. For his career within the diocese of Lincoln, see Bowker, *Secular Clergy*, 41, 45, 162n.
[183] CPL, 464; LJRO, B/A/1/14, fo. 40r.
[184] BL, Harleian Ms 594, fo. 128r.
[185] CPL, 623; LJRO, B/A/1/14, fo. 63r.
[186] *Valor*, iii, 69; BRUC, 176.

curate, William Warner, received little more than a quarter of this amount to take full responsibility for its cure of souls.

Alongside the union of benefices, another development which became increasingly prominent during the fifteenth century was the levying of pensions on livings by their retiring incumbents. Ideally, the reason for the negotiation of a pension would be to provide vital sustenance for an aged and decrepit incumbent no longer able to continue his ministry within the parish.[187] Increasingly, however, the system was exploited as a further means of acquiring revenue without responsibility; servants of church and state and well-connected careerist clergy would treat the parish as little more than a milch cow for the continuing provision of income.[188] As with the union of benefices, it allowed for the enjoyment of the fruits of pluralism while avoiding its sanctions. Like pluralism, however, the propensity for clerks to enter into pension negotiations was affected by the value of available livings. Hence whereas the records of Lincoln diocese reveal an average of ten pension arrangements per year,[189] there is evidence of only fifteen in the twenty-eight years of Bishop Blythe's administration of the relatively poorer diocese of Coventry and Lichfield.[190] All but three date from the last four years of his pontificate.

What is immediately clear from the Lichfield evidence is that the size of pensions varied enormously, from those which would have provided little more than the basic requirements of a man in his retirement to sums that could support a lifestyle of considerable comfort. Yet in almost every case the pension represented significantly more than one-third of the total gross revenue of the living that was the usual arrangement in the diocese of Lincoln, resulting in a significant diminution in parochial revenues available to the new incumbent.[191] Indeed, three pensions were arranged which were worth more than the annual value of the benefice as assessed in 1535. When William Bradshaw retired from the rectory of Aughton in 1528 he committed his successor, Brian Morecroft, to providing an annual pension of £26 13s 4d against a valuation in 1535 of just £14 15s 4d.[192] Richard Collet's pension of £30, negotiated with Nicholas Darrington in 1527, was £4 more than the value of the vicarage of Holy Trinity, Coventry to its new incumbent[193] and

---

[187] Until the fifteenth century usual practice had been to appoint a coadjutor; N. Orme, 'Sufferings of the Clergy: Illness and Old Age in Exeter Diocese 1300–1540', in M. Pelling, R.M. Smith, eds, *Life, Death and the Elderly: Historical Perspectives* (1991), 66.
[188] Swanson, *Church and Society*, 56.
[189] Bowker, *Secular Clergy*, 145.
[190] The paucity of evidence might, of course, be as much a consequence of inconsistencies of record-keeping as of the relative poverty of livings.
[191] Bowker, *Secular Clergy*, 146. In the diocese of Exeter, up to 1535, pensions were largely a matter of free bargaining and resulted in almost one-quarter being below the putative subsistence level of £4; Orme, 'Sufferings of the Clergy', 68.
[192] LJRO, B/A/1/14, fo. 64v; *Valor*, v, 223.
[193] LJRO, B/A/1/14, fo. 13v; *Valor*, iii, 58.

the largest pension arranged during the period, a remarkable £80 payable from the rectory of Walton and Liverpool by Edward Molyneux to Richard Sutton from 1528, exceeded the valuation of the benefice in 1535 by more than £10.[194] Even allowing for uncertainty as to the basis of the calculations in *Valor Ecclesiasticus*, such pensions severely depleted the income available to the newly-admitted clerk, who would have had to make careful calculations as to whether the benefice was a viable proposition. The implications were of less consequence to the pluralists Darrington and Molyneux than to Morecroft who was in possession of no other benefice from which he could compensate for the burden imposed by his predecessor; little wonder that he was involved in tithe litigation against a parishioner in the following year.[195] The ability of retiring clerks to levy such sums is further testimony to the high level of demand for benefices generated by the abundance of men in orders; the attraction of freehold tenure was sufficient for new incumbents to take a gamble on the longevity of the pensioner. In Darrington's case, it paid off: Richard Collet died within a year of securing his annual allowance.[196] Edward Molyneux, on the other hand, would have had to part with over £600 before Richard Sutton's death in 1536,[197] a situation further aggravated by his grant of a substantial annuity to the rector of Wigan; it is hardly surprising therefore that Molyneux was such a frequent litigant in the royal courts.[198] Again, Morecroft's was, relatively speaking, likely to have been the greatest burden. William Bradshaw would appear to have been no older than forty at the time of his resignation of the rectory of Aughton, the advowson of which was in the possession of his family. He was certainly still alive five years later, by which time Morecroft had already had to find almost £135 for his predecessor's maintenance.[199]

Once the negotiation of a pension had become an accepted feature of the vacancy of benefices, the way was open for them to be used as part of a continuing career as well as for support during retirement. Five of those in receipt of pensions during the period went on to be admitted to further livings. Thomas Lililow resigned the rectory of Thorpe in 1530 after being in possession for three years and was immediately presented by the dean and chapter of Lichfield to their vicarage of Hope. His turnover of Derbyshire livings was quite prodigious, and by 1533 he had resigned from this and the vicarage of Chesterfield, and was in possession of the rectories of Bonsall and

---

194 LJRO, B/A/1/14, fo. 63v; *Valor*, v, 221.
195 LJRO, B/C/2/3, fo. 86r.
196 Above, 69.
197 *BRUO*, 588–9.
198 Bridgeman, *History of the Church and Manor of Wigan*, 99; above, 68–9.
199 Three ordinands of that name appear in the register, the most likely of which to be the rector of Aughton was ordained deacon in 1513: LJRO, B/A/1/14ii, fos. 93r, 95r, 181v, 184r, 202v, 212r, 214r, 217v. He was taxed as pensioner of Aughton in 1533: BL, Harleian Ms 594, fo. 149r.

Matlock as well as a prebend in the collegiate church of All Saints, Derby.[200] Richard Collet resigned from Holy Trinity, Coventry, in 1527 to further his career as an official of the bishop of Exeter but died within a year of the move[201] and following his resignation from the rectory of Ladbroke in 1529, with an annual pension of £12, William Darley retained the vicarage of Allestree, to which he had been admitted three years previously, together with a canonry in Lichfield Cathedral.[202] Thomas Wylett had been admitted to the vicarage of Mancetter following the deprivation of William Whittington in 1528 but stayed there for only two years before securing an annual pension of 40s and taking possession of the rectory of Hamstall Ridware.[203] After negotiating the annual pension of £80 from the rectory of Walton and Liverpool, M. Richard Sutton remained as rector of Birmingham, worth a further £20 a year, until his death in 1536.[204]

Those priests who actually appear to have retired from active ministry included some with the smallest pensions.[205] John Littonne resigned from the rectory of Ilam in 1505, taking an annual pension of 100s, and is not recorded as receiving another benefice in the diocese.[206] Thomas Vyes resigned from Tibshelf after being vicar for over ten years. His annual pension, which was recorded as being for life, was only two marks, and he does not appear to have entered another benefice during the period.[207] Robert Hewat had been rector of Clowne for twenty-four years and resigned in 1530 on a pension of £4 a year when he was in his early fifties; since he was not in possession of a benefice in 1533 it can be assumed that he had retired from parochial service.[208] The same applies to William Molder, who resigned from the rectory of Rolleston in 1529, but on a more comfortable pension of £10 a year.[209] Nicholas Chauntrell, who retired from Bebington after twenty-one years as rector, would have been able to maintain the lifestyle he had enjoyed as incumbent of this well-endowed benefice on his pension of £23 6s 8d.[210] Others retired from their livings but continued to supplement their income with non-beneficed posts. Robert Cartleage retired from the vicarage of Bolsover, which he had held for at least twelve years, in

---

[200] LJRO, B/A/1/14, fos. 40r, 43v; BL, Harleian Ms 594, fos. 127r, 129v.
[201] Above, 53.
[202] LJRO, B/A/1/14, fos. 4v, 12v; BL, Harleian Ms 594, fo. 121v.
[203] LJRO, B/A/1/14, fos. 17v, 31r. For the deprivation of Whittington, above, 38, below, 181.
[204] BL, Harleian Ms 594, fo. 122v; BRUO, 599.
[205] Priests who actually retired probably accounted for a substantial portion of the 23.2% of pensioners in Exeter diocese who received less than £4; Orme, 'Sufferings of the Clergy', 68.
[206] LJRO, B/A/1/14, fo. 32v.
[207] Ibid., fo. 36v.
[208] Ibid., fo. 43r.
[209] Ibid., fo. 28r.
[210] Ibid., fos. 63r, 67r.

1515, on an unspecified pension and in 1533 was employed as a chantry priest in neighbouring Dronfield.[211] Robert Newton was about fifty when he retired from Monks Kirby in 1528 after only three-and-a-half months as vicar; five years later his pension of five marks was supplemented by a prebend of All Saints, Derby.[212] William Bradshaw had secured a much more lucrative pension of forty marks prior to his retirement from the rectory of Aughton in 1528. In 1533 he was taxed as pensioner at the same rate as the incumbent rector and was possibly still active in a limited capacity within the parish. If he is to be identified with the curate of Penwortham at the same date, then his active ministry was far from over; his date of ordination, which would suggest that he was no more than forty years of age at his retirement, would also support this.[213] A pensioner who remained within the parish of his incumbency, however, risked becoming a focus of resentment among the local clergy. A graphic example is that of Richard Harrington who retired from the vicarage of Sutton Maddock in 1529 on a pension of just over £3. His twelve-year incumbency had been marked by a number of disputes with his parishioners including allegations that he had been physically assaulted and culminating in a court order to reside in his benefice. His retirement was equally fraught. Within three months of his resignation he was again present in the consistory court accusing a local chaplain, Richard Brett, with whom he appears to have been involved in a financial dispute, of attempting to strangle him.[214]

Standards of Living

Not least among the attractions of a beneficed post to the large numbers of priests recruited in the diocese each year was the steady income which would be guaranteed by freehold tenure of the living. But quite apart from the difficulties faced in obtaining a benefice there was considerable variation in the value of such livings as were available, both within the country as a whole and the diocese itself. Until the compilation of the *Valor Ecclesiasticus* in 1535, and associated fiscal experiments in the preceding decade, clerical incomes had been taxed on the basis of a national assessment produced in 1291 which had clearly come to be viewed as inadequate for the purposes of the Henrician state.[215] Taken at face value, the *Valor* reveals that for the majority of the country, away from the London area, the average annual income available from benefices was less than £15, a figure that has been estimated as the minimum that would allow an incumbent to discharge his

[211] Ibid., fo. 37r; BL, Harleian Ms 594, fo. 125v.
[212] LJRO, B/A/1/14, fo. 14v; BL, Harleian Ms 594, fo. 129v.
[213] BL, Harleian Ms 594, fo. 150v.
[214] For details of the pension arrangement, LJRO, B/A/1/14, fo. 49v; for Harrington, Brett, and problems within the parish of Sutton Maddock, see below, 180–1.
[215] Swanson, 'Standards of Livings', 154, 156–7.

various expenses and make a decent living.[216] In the diocese of Coventry and Lichfield 77% of vicarages and almost 50% of rectories were officially worth less than £10, a situation mirrored in most of the rest of the country.[217] Even within the diocese, there was considerable variation in available wealth. Whilst a high proportion of the livings within the archdeaconries of Stafford and Shrewsbury were particularly poor, over half of the thirty-one rectories valued at over £30 were within the archdeaconry of Chester. These included the rectories of Wigan, worth over £80 a year to those men whose patronage connections brought them within its orbit, and Winwick, at £102 one of the richest pickings in the entire country and a regular target of crown appointees.

The considerable variation in clerical incomes was not, however, a problem confined to the career decisions of contemporary clerics. Despite the central importance of the *Valor* to historians, remarkably little analysis has been undertaken into the underlying basis of its assessments.[218] It is certainly clear, by comparisons of its data with surviving clerical subsidy returns of the 1520s and early 1530s, that this was a period of fiscal experimentation and that the 'fossilisation' of the *Valor* figures in the historical record has lent them an aura of definitive statements which is perhaps not entirely warranted. First, it must be remembered that the figures were drawn up not as an aid to future historians but as a fixed basis for taxation of clerical wealth. As such we would not expect the assessments to be unduly favourable to the incumbent himself; in other words, they were likely to tend towards an overvaluation of real income. Yet one of the major problems with the use of the *Valor* is that we do not know how the actual process of assessment was carried out. In many cases the commissioners must have relied on statements from the incumbent himself. One of the allegations made in 1544 against the rector of Swynnerton, M. John Nowell, by a parishioner was that

> whereas the parsonage of Swynnerton has been, and is, of the clear yearly value of forty marks, and yet the said Nowell has rated the same parsonage for the payment of your [i.e. the king's] tenths at £10 only.

In his defence Nowell declared that

> upon his oath he truly presented the parsonage of Swynnerton for the payment of tenths to the king to be of the yearly value of £10 5s 0d, as the said

---

216 P. Heath, *Medieval Clerical Accounts*, St Anthony's Hall Publications, no. 26 (York, 1964), 24.
217 Heath, *English Parish Clergy*, 173; Swanson, *Church and Society*, 57–8, Bowker, *Henrician Reformation*, 134; Zell, 'Economic Problems', 32, 34–5; Brigden, *London and the Reformation*, 48; Haigh, *Reformation and Resistance*, 23–4, 26.
218 There is some discussion in Bowker, *Henrician Reformation*, 132; F. Heal, 'Economic Problems of the Clergy', in F. Heal and R. O'Day, eds, *Church and Society in England, Henry VIII to James I* (1977), 103; R.N. Swanson, 'Standards of Livings: Parochial Revenues in Pre-Reformation England', in C. Harper-Bill, ed., *Religious Belief and Ecclesiastical Careers in Late Medieval England* (Woodbridge, 1991), 154–7.

parsonage has been presented time out of mind, which is as much as the said parsonage is worth, all charges deducted, one year with another, as this defendant is ready to prove.

The valuation actually recorded in 1535 was £10 2s 4½d net.[219]

The surviving subsidy returns for the diocese of Lincoln in 1526 demonstrate that the government's experimentation in the field of clerical taxation originally envisaged a system of periodic reassessments of real income in place of the fixed statement that had been used hitherto.[220] The Lincoln returns record actual income received and its sources;[221] surviving subsidy returns for the archdeaconry of Stafford, for 1531 and 1533, whilst containing only the final value, nevertheless show that reassessments were now taking place on a national basis.[222] Furthermore, in some instances revised figures entered in the returns for a single year suggest evidence of the experimental nature of the taxation base. This process is most evident in the returns for 1531. To take as a sample the deanery of Tutbury and Tamworth in which entries for 1531, 1533 and *Valor* are most complete, eleven of its fifteen parishes have more than one assessment in that first year. In some cases the juggling of figures was minimal, as in the case of Tutbury, where a figure of £4 was replaced by one of £3 13s 4d, or Darlaston, where a final assessment of £4 10s 4d was entered following earlier drafts based on £4 5s 4d and £6. However, variations of a much greater magnitude include the entries of £15 and £35 against Rolleston, and £20, £25 and £50 under Clifton Campville. Presumably the various figures reflect experiments with different elements of allowance against tax and, in the case of Clifton Campville, might have been an attempt to deal with the relatively new and extensive house which had been built for the rector.[223] It is also apparent from the round figures involved in many of the calculations that, unlike the Lincoln returns, an estimate of value was the aim rather than an explicit statement of income for that particular year. The variation between the assessments of 1531 and 1533 can also be highlighted by the same sample deanery. In the case of Rolleston, the assessment of £16 was nearer to the lower figure of the previous calculation and with an assessment of £30 in 1533 Clifton Campville was assessed at a median of the previous range. In most cases the

---

[219] *Star Chamber Proceedings, Henry VIII and Edward VI*, William Salt Society, Collections for a History of Staffordshire (1912), 148; *Valor*, iii, 121. This would tend to support Zell's impression that 'if the *Valor* errs at all (for 1535) it is more in the direction of under- than over-assessment': Zell, 'Economic Problems', 20. For the view that 'the "clear value" declared for many parishes in 1535 overstates the real return which a rector might expect from his benefice' see Swanson, 'Standards of Livings', 157. For reference to Nowell's will of 1555 see *passim* and appendix.

[220] Swanson, 'Standards of Livings', 156–7.

[221] Bowker, *Henrician Reformation*, 132–3.

[222] The following is based on LJRO, B/A/17/1(1); D.30/18; *Valor*, iii, 100–158: see bibliography for details.

[223] Heath, *English Parish Clergy*, 139, 140.

assessments of 1535 involved further calculations. Of the thirty-seven rectories and vicarages in the archdeaconry of Stafford for which figures for all three years can be compared, just over half (twenty) were reassessed. Exceptionally, in four cases the revaluation was lower, quite significantly so in the case of the rectory of Rolleston where earlier calculations based on figures of £35, £16 and £15 were replaced by one of £13 19s 6d. However, as might be expected, the majority of the reassessments (sixteen) were upwards, and, again, on occasion the revised figures could have drastic consequences for the incumbent. Thus the rectors of Grindon and Stoke and Newcastle found the valuation of their benefices doubled from £8 to over £15 and £20 to £41 respectively. And what might have been the reaction of the rector of Checkley who, after paying tax on successive valuations of £7 10s 0d in 1531 and 1533 faced a bill three times greater in 1535 following a clear valuation of no less than £20 2s 4d?

The reasons for such variations in valuation are not readily discernible from the sources. They might be affected by the leasing of part or all of a rectory in the intervening years or by differences in the valuation of the glebe;[224] both, however, are very difficult to prove. In the case of the *Valor* they are compounded by the fact that its record of the sources of the valuation, and the allowances set against it, is not uniform. In order to gain some indication of the different sources of income open to individual incumbents, and how these and the allowances set against them are treated in the *Valor*, a sample can be taken comprising the twenty-seven clerks who can be definitely assigned to a particular benefice during the period and whose testamentary inventories survive.[225] Nineteen livings in the sample have allowances included in the calculations of their value in 1535, though they are rarely of any great significance. The largest total deduction was Edmund Bachelor's rectory of Sheinton and Thomas Alen's rectory of Kingswinford, from which deductions of just over £1, comprising synodals and annual payments to the crown and the archdeacon of Stafford, produced clear values of £6 9s 1d and £17 3s 2d respectively. At the other end of the scale, Richard Smyth's rectory of Kirk Ireton was valued at £7 10s 10d following deduction of a mere 22d for synodals and 'Chad farthings'.[226] Synodals and procurations account for the majority of deductions;[227] others, apart from the payments to the crown and local levies already mentioned, included pensions payable to appropriators and other corporations. Typically, however, they can be seen to have been negligible.

---

[224] Bowker, *Henrician Reformation*, 133; Heal, 'Economic Problems', 104.
[225] For the composition of the wills sample see above, 3, and appendix.
[226] The latter being a Pentecostal payment levied at the rate of one farthing per household in the diocese towards the upkeep of the fabric of the cathedral: *VCH Staffs.*, iii, 150.
[227] For these see Heath, *English Parish Clergy*, 143; Swanson, 'Standards of Livings', 155.

As for the sources of income itself,[228] these varied from the type of nominal assessment (probably a rental value) entered as the result of the 'demand and scrutiny (*per scrutinium et exacionem*) of the commissioners' to the type of detailed list, including nine items, which comprised the valuation of Henry Slany's appropriated vicarage of Bushbury. Significantly, the nominal values, which accounted for over a quarter of the sample, were among the lowest; William Butler's vicarage of Wrockwardine was, at £7 8s 6d, the most valuable living in the sample to be assessed in this way. On the other hand, some of the more valuable livings included a house and glebe which comprised a major component of their income.[229] Just under one-fifth of the valuation of William Campion's rectory of Breadsall, of £28 14s 8d, was made up by his house and glebe and despite the fact that John Fitzherbert's vicarage of Doveridge was appropriated to Tutbury Priory, he had a house and glebe worth one-third of the £12 clear value of the benefice. The quality of accommodation provided and the amount and quality of the glebe land attached to it varied, however, from one living to the next as did any other component of beneficial income. To Richard Rylay, rector of Swarkestone, they were worth just over £1, half the value of his small tithes and about the same as those on lambs and wool and what he could expect from his Easter dues and other offerings in a year.[230] Together, they had a clear value of exactly £5. It is, of course, this disparity between the main sources of income from one living to another which makes them so hard to compare, as it surely did for contemporaries to whom they were part of a career decision, or at the least, a regular income.[231] William Swynerton, whose rectory parsonage at Blymhill was worth no more than Rylay's house, had tithes and offerings worth a further £13, providing in total a considerably more respectable income.

Those incumbents whose income came principally from glebe and tithes, so long as they were able to avoid serious dispute with their parishioners, were likely to have weathered the inflationary pressures of the first half of the sixteenth century better than their colleagues who leased their benefices or who were dependent on other types of fixed income.[232] These would

---

[228] For a discussion of the range of sources see Zell, 'Economic problems', 33–5; Swanson, 'Standards of Livings', 162; ibid., 'Chaucer's Parson and Other Priests', *Studies in the Age of Chaucer*, 13 (1991), 64–6.
[229] For the provision of a house and glebe for some vicarages see Zell, 'Economic Problems', 33.
[230] For these see Heath, *English Parish Clergy*, 156; Brigden, *London and the Reformation*, 50. From his will and inventory it is evident that, apart from working hemp and flax, Rylay's agricultural concerns were entirely pastoral and at his death in 1539 he had manure worth one-tenth of the valuation of his house and glebe.
[231] Swanson, 'Standards of Livings', 182–3.
[232] For discussion of glebe and tithes see Heath, *English Parish Clergy*, 148, 158; Zell, 'Economic Problems', 36–8; Brigden, *London and the Reformation*, 49; Swanson, 'Chaucer's Parson', 65. For the impact of inflation on beneficial incomes see Bowker, *Secular Clergy*, 147; Heal, 'Economic Problems', 111; Zell, 'Economic Problems', 36.

probably include some of those livings returned with a nominal value in 1535. It was certainly the case with Richard Smyth's rectory of Kirk Ireton, valued at £7 10s 10d in 1535, and leased to his brother for £4 a year, £3 of which was owing at the rector's death in 1536. Those probably in an even weaker position would have included men like John Smyth, vicar of Shilton, whose income of £5 was in the form of an annual stipend payable by the appropriator, Coventry Priory, from the small tithes and offerings. However, the terms of a new lease of Prescot vicarage in 1516 allowed the vicar to have half of the corn tithe of one section of the glebe in return for an annual payment of 40s to the lessees; an arrangement that, even at this price, the vicar might have come to see as good business.[233] In 1546 Henry Slany, vicar of Bushbury, bequeathed half his corn to his cousin, a fellow-priest, on condition that he paid the rent outstanding on the land on which it had been grown.[234]

Whatever might be the main sources of income recorded in the *Valor* they were, of course, statements of potential rather than actual income. At a time of rising prices there would be those in positions of greater security than others, but, given the generally low level of assessments of livings within the diocese, there would have been few incumbents who could face each coming year with any great degree of security. In order to gain a better impression of the composition of beneficial incomes, their adequacy, and the standards of living they provided, the inventories of the sample clerks can be compared with the evidence from *Valor*. The twenty-seven priests in the sample comprised nine each with livings in Shropshire and Derbyshire, five in Staffordshire and four in Warwickshire. Obviously a testamentary inventory is not a statement of financial affairs over time but a snapshot of the level of prosperity at a particular moment; in the majority of the sample, a time close to death.[235] As discussed above, *minimum* ages of clergy at a given date can be ascertained by calculating that a priest was at least twenty-four years of age at the time of his ordination. The age range of the sample at the time of writing their wills is from a minimum of thirty-two to a minimum of eighty-eight, but with an average age of at least sixty-one and only two of the priests being under the age of fifty. For the greater part, therefore, the sample priests were mature men who had long clerical careers behind them and, given the nature of such careers, were likely to have reached something like the

---

[233] F.A. Bailey, ed., *A Selection from the Prescot Court Leet and Other Records 1447–1600*, Record Society for the Publication of Original Documents Relating to Lancashire and Cheshire, vol. 89 (1937), 6; Zell, 'Economic Problems', 38.

[234] Will of Henry Slany; see appendix.

[235] For the composition of the sample, and the value of the surviving inventories, see appendix. Caution is of course advised when using such source material due to the possibility of under-recording, undervaluation, or even misrepresentation on the part of assessors. However, inventories are invaluable supplementary material if used primarily in an impressionistic rather than statistical fashion; Cross, 'Incomes of Provincial Urban Clergy', 70.

maximum of their earning potential. Furthermore, all of these priests, including the six over the age of seventy, died whilst incumbent, so one is not dealing with retired pensioners who had spent time living off past income. Of itself, the fact that these men were prepared to carry on working as rectors and vicars, rather than take the option of a salaried assistant's post, suggests that the opportunities for amassing great wealth were generally limited.[236]

The first thing that can be said from looking at the inventories is that they bear little correlation with the *Valor* totals, perhaps reinforcing the suggestion that the latter are an imperfect reflection of clerical wealth. The highest valued inventory was that of Edmund Bachelor, rector of Sheinton, whose goods were valued at over £77 despite the fact that the living was assessed at less than £7 in 1535. Similarly, Henry Slany, whose vicarage of Bushbury was valued at under £8, had goods worth almost £43 at his death, and the poverty of John Hall's vicarage of Chebsey, worth £5 7s 4d in 1535, was not reflected in his personal estate of £40 10s 0d. Conversely, despite a combined stipendiary income of over £16 as vicar of Mancetter and gild priest of St Mary there, Robert Barefote left only £12 12s 6d at his death. Indeed, this case perhaps highlights the problems facing the incumbent on a fixed income; whilst almost a quarter of his estate was in the form of cash, he was one of the few men in the sample to have nothing in the form of livestock or agricultural produce. The poorest testator had his vicarage of Melbourne, which included house and glebe, small tithes and Easter dues, valued at £9 13s 4d, very much the middle level of wealth among the parish clergy of the diocese. Yet John Reed died with goods worth only £5 15s 10d, mostly in the form of furniture and household utensils.[237]

Almost half (thirteen) of the sample testators had their goods valued at between £10 and £20. There were four with values of between £20 and £30, two between £30 and £40 and six testators with estate in excess of £40. At the bottom of the scale were two beneficed priests who had their goods valued below £10. Of these, with possessions worth only £5 15s 10d at his death in 1534 and despite his graduate status, John Reed would have been officially classed as poor. Generally, the range of the sample would suggest

---

[236] For length of tenure of benefices see above, 57.
[237] For comparison, none of the seven surviving clerical wills from York, 1520–40, were valued at over £20 and the average value of the inventories of clergy in rural Leicestershire in the 1530s was just under £30: Cross, 'Incomes of Provincial Urban Clergy', 72, 76. There are few published surviving lay inventories from Lichfield diocese during this period which can be used for comparative purposes but three from the city of Lichfield might be cited. The goods of Charles Nedham of Wall (occupation not given) were worth £9 8s 1d in 1568; those of Thomas Whitmore, baker, were valued at £82 17s 2d in 1570 and those of Richard Harpar (occupation not given) £4 8s 8d in 1574: D.G. Vaisey, ed., *Probate Inventories of Lichfield and District 1568–1680*, Staffordshire Rec. Soc., Collections for a History of Staffordshire, 4th ser., 5 (1969), 41–4.

that there were two main bands of income as regards the beneficed clergy which broadly reflect those discerned in the *Valor*: a majority whose income would have been on a level comparable with their yeoman-farmer parishioners and another significant group whose affluence approached that of the parish gentry. The variation in the sources of income between livings, as recorded in 1535, is mirrored in differences in the main components of incumbents' inventories. Those of the five incumbents (three rectors and two vicars) whose livings were valued at over £10 all had agricultural produce, equipment, or livestock as their main single components and, as such, were among those parish clergy best equipped to face the growing problem of price inflation.[238] For John Fitzherbert, whose vicarage of Doveridge was unusual in its entitlement to a large glebe, just over half of his estate of about £60 came from the fruits of arable agriculture and the equipment used to produce it. The detailed itemisation of corn in his barn included 59 *thraves*[239] of wheat, 34 *thraves* of mixed corn and rye, 80 *thraves* of barley, 38 *thraves* of oats, 2 loads of *dredge*,[240] 25 loads of peas and 16 loads of hay. From such a list, Fitzherbert's need of his iron-bound wain is quite obvious, as also are the two ploughs with accessories and two harrows that he owned. The heavy bias in his agricultural activities towards arable production again makes him quite unusual in the sample; apart from a dozen pigs, his only livestock were the six oxen of his plough-team. The 6½ stone of wool that was also listed must either have come from his parishioners (his tithes of lambs and wool were worth one-sixth of the £12 valuation of the vicarage) or have been purchased out of his agricultural profits, though by the time of his death in 1551, involvement by clergy in marketing had been forbidden by statute for over twenty years.[241]

Other incumbents in this group were operating a more mixed economy, like Robert Blythe, vicar of Dunchurch, who, apart from his corn and hay, had a flock of fifty-eight sheep and two dairy cows with their calves; or William Swynerton, rector of Blymhill, whose glebe was stocked with twenty head of (mainly beef) cattle, and a flock of twenty sheep, in addition to the linen, hemp and flax that he was cultivating. Further evidence of such involvement in textile production is to be found in the spinning wheels and looms occasionally mentioned in inventories. But involvement in such agricultural enterprise was not limited to those in possession of the higher-value livings. For example, Edmund Bachelor, rector of Sheinton, had, at over £77,

---

[238] Even some urban clergy during this period were involved in farming: Cross, 'Incomes of Provincial Urban Clergy', 74–5. Among the clergy of the East Riding of Yorkshire it was common: J.S. Purvis, 'A Note on Sixteenth Century Farming in Yorkshire', *Yorkshire Archaeological Journal*, 36 (1947), 435–54; Marshall, *Pastoral Ministry in the East Riding*, 20. See also Heath, *English Parish Clergy*, 160–2; Swanson, 'Chaucer's Parson', 66.

[239] A measure of up to twelve sheaves.

[240] Mixed grains, often oats and barley.

[241] Heath, *English Parish Clergy*, 162.

the highest-valued inventory, despite the nominal value of his living at under £7 in 1535. Over half of his estate was in the form of livestock and agricultural produce, all recorded with close attention to detail in his inventory. His stock included 6 cows, 3 heifers, a bull, a weaning calf, a great boar, 6 young pigs, 29 sheep, 5 lambs, 4 ducks, 7 hens, a cock, 2 capons and 5 chickens. From his arable land he had amassed no less than £18-worth of mixed corn as well as hay worth 40s and a quantity of flax from which 22 *ells*[242] of cloth had been made. In addition he had produced 16 *ells* of hemp cloth, 3 lbs of lambs' wool and quantities of onions and garlic; for the latter his well-equipped kitchen included 'three garlic crushes with cords'.

Bachelor is certainly to be counted among those whose 'rural rectory represented a functioning agricultural enterprise';[243] even his 'great wood pile' was valued at 20s. Others in this category would have included Richard Rowlowe who rented out his yoke of oxen to his parishioners at Ryton, one of whom owed 48s 4d at the time of the rector's death in 1550; his two other lay debtors may have been involved in similar arrangements. On a smaller scale, John Holwaye, whose rectory of Hinstock was valued at under £6, had only one heifer, a nag and a colt listed in his inventory. But he had evidently also put a mare of his out to be sired by the stallion owned by a local gentleman and counted one and a half of the colts that were produced as his property, and both mare and the share of colts were bequeathed in his will. The affinity which many incumbents would have felt for their agricultural concerns is given eloquent testimony by the fact that four of the fifteen head of cattle owned by John Hall, vicar of Chebsey, had been given names: bullocks called 'Lyon' and 'Lombe' and cows called 'Fudge' and 'Praty'. The latter were presumably dairy cows, such as those that provided the raw material for the cheese press owned by Henry Slany, vicar of Bushbury. Even a relatively impecunious incumbent such as William Franks, vicar of Barrow upon Trent, might enjoy a remarkably mixed source of income. At his death in 1541 he was in possession of two looms and a spinning wheel with which he worked flax, hemp and wool in addition to a beehive, a cow and calf, a heifer and calf, a barren cow, three pigs and a boar.

In contrast to the close involvement of some clergy in the management of their economic affairs, others, like Richard Smyth, rector of Kirk Ireton, mentioned above, took the option of putting their rectories out to farm. However, those doing so not only took the risk associated with a fixed income but were also dependent on the ability, or willingness, of the lessee to meet his commitment. Thus Richard Webb, whose rectory of Stapleton was worth just over £6 in 1535, and who had goods valued at under £8 at his death two years later, was, like Smyth, owed outstanding rent by the farmer of his benefice. His involvement in leasing also extended to a small piece of

---

[242] The *ell*, usually given in the wills in its archaic form of *eln*, was a measure of cloth equal to the length of the arm, in England taken to be 45 inches.
[243] Swanson, 'Standards of Livings', 170–1.

land for which another layman owed him a few pence at his death. Greater problems were caused by the decision of M. George Darwin, vicar of Dilhorne, to lease out half of his vicarage, including the glebe, to laymen during the 1530s. In 1534, following his resignation, the new incumbent, Thomas Tomkinson, had allegedly agreed to continue the arrangement as a condition of his admission. Whether or not this was the case, Tomkinson was accused by the farmers of entering the glebe land with a gang and impounding their cattle, following which fourteen of them died. One of the farmers, Thomas Spever, had claimed that the cattle were the only means of support for himself, his wife and twelve children. The situation appears to have been resolved by Tomkinson's own subsequent resignation since a new vicar was in place by 1535.[244] Similar problems could also arise when incumbents themselves rented land from laity in order to augment their income. In 1538 a parishioner of Biddulph claimed that he had been attacked by the vicar, Nicholas Willock, and his accomplices, within the bounds of a certain pasture in the parish. Refuting the allegations, Willock claimed that his accuser had granted him a lease of the land for a period of ten years in 1533 and produced his part of the relevant indenture. The reason for the lease, according to the vicar, was the poverty of the living, valued at £4 9s 7d in 1535, and 'not sufficient for the maintenance of [his] household', for the remedy of which the grant had been willingly made by the lay party. Whatever the specifics of the dispute, tension had evidently arisen when an attempt was made to stop the vicar's men from putting up hedges and bringing cattle into the pasture to graze.[245] Such arrangements had probably been quite common before their official curtailment by statute in 1529, although this case demonstrates that they were still being entered into after the passing of the act.[246] But a sense of a world in transition arises clearly from the testamentary bequest of Richard Blockley, vicar of Wolvey, of his lease of 'Copston's field' to 'my lord Olyver, abbot of Combe', for the use of a third party, in 1537: two years later the monastery was surrendered to the crown and its former abbot, Oliver Adams, paid for his previous resistance to suppression by forfeiting his pension.[247]

A problem involved in the use of inventories is that the law required a statement of personal (i.e. moveable) property but not real estate and thus, apart from not always obtaining a full impression of the testator's wealth, references to property ownership are often incidental.[248] However, from the

---

244 *Star Chamber Proceedings, Henry VIII and Edward VI*, 57–8. Darwin was vicar in 1531 when the assessors for the subsidy noted that he had paid his contribution. The vicarage was valued at £8 13s 0d in 1535: LJRO, B/A/17/1(1), fo. 3r; *Valor*, iii, 127.
245 *Star Chamber Proceedings, Henry VIII and Edward VI* 121–3; *Valor*, iii, 121.
246 Swanson, *Church and Society*, 371.
247 Knowles and Hadcock, *Medieval Religious Houses*, 107. The field might have belonged to the Copston chantry in Coventry Cathedral; above, 53.
248 Cross, 'Incomes of Provincial Urban Clergy', 70. Her sample of urban clergy includes a few who had inherited or purchased property: ibid., 74. There is more evidence for property ownership among the unbeneficed clergy; below, 118.

inquest taken following the death of Sir Alexander Standish knt, in 1508, it is evident that the rector of Wigan, M. Richard Wyott, was the owner of at least two burgage-plots valued at four marks and a messuage worth 100s a year in the town, which he had rented to Standish and his wife for 27s and 6s 3d respectively.[249] Ownership of property, leasing of land, and involvement in agricultural production could all result in accumulations of cash, but also, as in some of the cases above, in a list of debtors. It was presumably largely as a rector who had farmed out his benefice that Richard Smyth had been able to amass the tidy sum of forty marks (£26 13s 4d) in cash which, at the time of his death, amounted to over half the total value of his estate. In contrast, it might have been Richard Webb's problems with his debtors that restricted his cash accumulation to 22s 6d; even so, this represented a significant proportion of his estate. As vicar of Mancetter and gild priest of St Mary there, Robert Barefote was in possession of two small houses, the rent collected from which probably contributed to the £4 0s 16d in cash counted by the appraisers of his goods. The £3 9s 0d accredited to William Campion at his death probably owed much to his close involvement with his rectory of Breadsall as an agricultural enterprise, mentioned above. There is evidence to suggest that the £5 6s 0d in gold and silver belonging to William Brewster, vicar of Etwall, at his death, might have come partly from involvement in the local wool market. He had certainly sold some of his tithe hay to one of his parishioners and would appear to have been an important source of cash credit in his village; his will included the solemn statement that he forgave 'every man being in my debt that is my parishioner of . . . Etwall the third part of that he oweth me, except Sir John Porte, knight, for he may pay well enough'.

A significant distinction between the standards of living enjoyed by incumbents would have been the quality of their accommodation, if indeed any was provided.[250] Whilst the *Valor* returns of twelve of the incumbents in the sample included houses, it is clear that they varied considerably in their quality,[251] although this is partly due to the usual inclusion of the glebe valuation in with that of rectory houses. Both glebe and house together were worth £5 4s 8d in 1535 to William Campion as rector of Breadsall but only 22s in the case of Richard Rylay's rectory of Swarkestone. Whilst we would not be able to discern the quality of Campion's house itself from the *Valor* entry alone, it might be significant that its layout is not mentioned in his inventory, which might be expected in the case of a superior parsonage. Certainly, with a combined value of 22s the Swarkestone rectory house and glebe could not be put in this category. At the same time, the layout of Edmund Bachelor's house is described in his inventory despite the fact that a

---

[249] Bridgeman, *History of the Church and Manor of Wigan*, 72. Wyott had been presented to the rectory by the king in 1506; LJRO, B/A/1/14, fo. 54v.
[250] Heath, *English Parish Clergy*, 138.
[251] Ibid., 139.

rectory house is not even mentioned in the low nominal value of his living of Sheinton in 1535. From the *Valor* alone we would not know that he was living in a six-roomed house comprising hall, parlour, buttery, kitchen and two upstairs chambers nor, significantly, that almost half the total value of his inventory was in the form of household items which included 'half a garnish of new London pewter'. Similarly, the nominal valuation of Richard Rowlowe's rectory of Ryton, at £5 11s 11d in 1535, did not include what must have been the quite substantial accommodation evidenced by his testamentary bequest of a sheep to 'every child and servant in my house'.

Apart from instances such as the provision of glebe land as well as a house for John Fitzherbert's vicarage of Doveridge by the appropriating monastery, vicarage houses were generally of lower value in the 1535 assessments. In the absence of glebe, differences in valuation of vicarage houses are mainly attributable to the existence or otherwise of attached land, however negligible this might be. As vicar of Barrow upon Trent, William Franks enjoyed the possession of a house and garden worth 10s 7d and the existence of a garden at John Reed's Melbourne vicarage led to its valuation of 6s. In contrast, William Richardson was assessed for a house alone at his vicarage of Crich which was worth a mere 2s in 1535. As in the case of rectories, the *Valor* may omit specific reference to accommodation in its valuation of vicarages. Thus the vicarage and 'guild house' between which the property of Robert Barefote was divided at his death, were presumably included in the respective stipends of £10 13s 4d and £6 payable to him as vicar of Mancetter and gild priest. Whilst the gild house appears to have comprised relatively simple accommodation, probably consisting of a single room, the vicarage comprised two chambers, a carpeted hall, buttery and kitchen. At his death in 1537 he was owed rent by two men who would appear to have been graduate clerics and who were presumably lodging in the premises.[252]

Further evidence of the nature of clerical households comes through the mention of servants,[253] who feature in the wills of just over one-third of the sample incumbents. The degree to which they were valued is evidenced by occasional bequests of as much as ten marks and frequent references to the quality of service that they had provided during their master's tenure of the benefice. This was obvious in the case of Richard Rylay's servant Joan. Whereas his other servants received 2d each in his will, she was his single greatest beneficiary, receiving two acres of rye and substantial quantities of other produce, as well as feed for her cow, clothes and household items,

---

[252] M. George Bradocke and M. John Glover. Bradocke cannot be traced in the records of the English universities but a John Glover, of Worcester diocese, was warden of All Souls, Oxford, in 1497–8 and admitted to MA in 1502; there were priests of the same name ordained to the titles of Merevale, Alvecote and Hulton in 1512, 1513 and 1523 respectively and a chaplain at Nantwich in 1533: LJRO, B/A/1/14ii, fos. 87r, 92v, 159r; BL, Harleian Ms 594, fo. 153r; *BRUO*, 774–5.

[253] For general comments see Heath, *English Parish Clergy*, 142.

which included 'the bed that she doth lie in'. William Richardson and Thomas Wylson similarly bequeathed female servants their beds, a favour that seems to have been rarely bestowed on men. An exception was 'Old Randall', a servant of the rector of Swynnerton, John Nowell, who was left his bed and a black frieze coat; another aged manservant, 'Old Mackelond', was given a similar coat and a pair of canvas sheets and a towelling sheet. Thomas Wylson's generosity to his two female servants was comparable to Rylay's; whilst one received stock and substantial quantities of household stuff, both were the beneficiaries of the residue of his estate. Whilst Richardson's servant Margaret got her bed, and she and other female servants received some stock and household items, his single male servant was rewarded with a scythe, an axe, a hatchet, an iron wedge, the vicar's 'riding knife' and 5s. John Holwaye's manservant, William Johnson, was similarly rewarded with the rector's sword and bill which he had been 'wonte to wear' as well as substantial quantities of corn and some clothes. The 'little William' who also received some clothes might have been a child of Johnson and his wife Margaret, and possibly a boy-servant of the type that are occasionally mentioned in clerical wills. William Corveser, vicar of Stanton-upon-Hine-Heath, was another incumbent who made a distinction between his female and male servants, leaving household goods to the former but an ox each to the latter. One of these manservants acted as a witness to his will, whilst the trust that William Swynerton, rector of Blymhill, and William Butler, vicar of Wrockwardine, felt towards their servants, was expressed not only in terms of generous bequests but through their appointment as executors to the will itself.

Whilst the large numbers of servants attached to the households of incumbents such as John Fitzherbert, Richard Rowlowe and William Corveser attest to some degree of comfort, as well as the need for help with their more temporal affairs, they were also an added expense. Accordingly, decisions would presumably have had to have been made balancing the need for assistance or the desire to maintain a certain lifestyle (Fitzherbert was, after all, a member of a prominent gentry family) against the costs involved in their employment. These would have been reduced to some extent by the common practice of servants living in, a situation demonstrated by some of the evidence cited above, and also suggested by the amount of bedding mentioned in some wills. This might also reflect the expectation that incumbents would offer hospitality where required,[254] though this is an area of potentially significant expense about which there is little direct evidence. The fact that John Fitzherbert had his brother living with him might not be seen in this category but it *was* an extra mouth to feed. Some of the less wealthy incumbents might have needed servants but experienced difficulty in meeting the cost, which seems to have been the case with William Butler,

---

[254] 'About a third of a beneficed clerk's income was expected, ideally, to be disbursed on hospitality and alms': ibid., 141.

from whose estate of a little over £10, £2 had to be found to meet the outstanding wages of two of his three servants.

The other expense associated with an incumbent's house would be repairs and maintenance. Very often such an inconvenience was likely to have been left as an added problem to be faced by a new incumbent. However, while such costs might have been quite burdensome, they leave very little mark in the records except where an episcopal monition was involved.[255] William Brewster, vicar of Etwall, bequeathed 20s and some bedding that he had left at his former vicarage in Yorkshire to his successor there on the condition that 'he give an acquittance to my executors for all manner of dilapidations there, or else to have but that the law giveth him'. The 400 roof tiles for which Richard Webb, rector of Stapleton, still owed 18d at his death in 1537, were probably associated with the building of a new house since a parsonage was not included in the valuation of his living two years previously and he owned no household goods whatsoever. If no rectory house was provided, then Webb would have had to have found accommodation elsewhere, an added cost to be met from a benefice valued at only a little over £6. William Butler, vicar of Wrockwardine, was probably in the same situation; there was no house attached to his vicarage and at his death in 1550 the only household items in his possession were some bedding and various pots and pans. The outlay involved in providing for accommodation would have significantly eroded the income available from a benefice. As it was, the stipend payable to John Smyth as rector of Shilton was only £5, but he was clearly living in rented accommodation since, apart from his bedding, the only household items which he owned were a pewter basin and a kettle. Indeed, whilst at first sight, Smyth might appear to have been comfortably off, leaving estate valued at £13 15s 8d at his death in 1543, this included a cope worth £8 and other vestments valued at £3; in practical terms he had died a poor man.

Just as an incumbent would have to judge his ability to hire servants to help with the day-to-day running of his household, clerical assistance would similarly require costing. Despite the probability that an income of around £15 would be required for an incumbent employing an assistant to meet all his commitments, clergy with incomes well below that level were apparently taking on the added burden.[256] Just over half of the incumbents in the testamentary sample had curates or stipendiary chaplains working in their churches in 1533, the majority of whom were being paid a salary of £4.[257] In most cases only a single assistant was hired and an incumbent such as William Campion, rector of Breadsall, whose living was valued at over £28 in 1535, and who left estate valued at over £37, would have been able to meet this extra expense without too much difficulty. Similarly, despite the

---

[255] Ibid., 140.
[256] Ibid., 173; Swanson, 'Standards of Livings', 180.
[257] See below, 114–15, Table 7.

fact that Robert Blythe's vicarage of Dunchurch was worth only half the value of Breadsall, the £20 estate which he left at his death in 1547 would suggest that he was able to afford the generous salary of over £8 that he paid to his curate.[258] However, it is two of the less wealthy incumbents who were involved in the greatest expense in this regard. Unless payment was coming from other sources, the employment of two stipendiaries at Crich was costing the vicar, William Richardson, £8 a year, to be met from a living officially valued at just £6 10s 10d.[259] There is some ground for doubt, however, that such costs were usually met by incumbents themselves. Of the 313 stipendiary chaplains listed in the archdeaconry of Chester in 1542, only one-third received their salary from the incumbent, compared to just under half who were supported by individual laypeople.[260] And whilst the terms of the ordination of the vicarage of Prescot had required that the vicar was to provide all the chaplains for the parish, at the time the list was drawn up he was personally supporting only one; of the remaining eight, the stipends of two were paid by a layman, three were supported by the offerings of the laity, one received the profits of certain lands, and two, the chaplains of Rainford and Farnworth, appear to have been paid out of chapel receipts.[261] But the potentially crippling costs involved are highlighted by the case of John Reed, vicar of Melbourne. A university graduate, Reed also held the rectory of Broughton Astley, Leicestershire, and at a visitation held not long before his death in 1534, he offered no reason for his absence from this living other than that he was resident in Derby, some five miles to the north of Melbourne. Reed was thus having to find replacement clergy at both of his livings, which at Melbourne involved the employment of no fewer than three stipendiary priests at a total annual cost of £12, against the valuation of the vicarage at £9 13s 4d. The costs involved could not be met without running into debt, a situation which had forced Reed to sell goods worth £3 8s 5d, including a dresser and other large items of furniture, as well as his set of silver spoons, an heirloom which, like most men of his age, he would have preferred to pass on to a favoured beneficiary of his will. In the event, Reed's estate amounted to just £5 15s 10d and his only possessions of any real value were his two cows, worth £1 in total.[262]

The examples of incumbents such as John Reed and William Butler, vicar of Wrockwardine, who died in 1550 with goods worth just over £10 but also

---

[258] BL, Harleian Ms 594, fo. 120r.
[259] Ibid., fo. 129r.
[260] W.F. Irvine, ed., *A List of the Clergy in Eleven Deaneries of the Diocese of Chester, 1541–2*, The Record Society for the Publication of Original Documents Relating to Lancashire and Cheshire, xxxiii (1896), ix–xi, 1–45.
[261] *Prescot Records*, 3; *Clergy in the Diocese of Chester*, 15. See also below, 117.
[262] BL, Harleian Ms 594, fo. 126v; Bowker, *Henrician Reformation*, 115; will of John Reed, see appendix. Reed had been ordained priest in 1508 to the title of Daventry Priory (Northants) and would have been at least fifty at the time of his death: LJRO, B/A/1/14ii, fo. 55v.

over £4 in debts, serve to highlight the problems facing even those fortunate few among the hundreds of priests ordained each year throughout the country who were able to secure a beneficed post.[263] Against the security of a job for life and at least some sort of steady income they would have to face the same changes in fortunes as their parishioners with the added costs associated with their status and the unrelenting incidence of taxation that it attracted. But the range of fortunes, and the ability of some to prosper in spite of the uncertainties, is also in evidence in the career of Edmund Bachelor who, as a stipendiary priest in Cound, had been paid a salary of just £4 in 1533. Having subsequently been appointed to the rectory of Sheinton, he died in 1557 in his mid fifties, with an estate that put him among the wealthiest parish clergy in the diocese. He would have been well aware of the part played by personal connections in his change of circumstances and prominent among the beneficiaries of his will was the patron of the living. However, most of his wealth had come from the personal and effective exploitation of an agricultural concern which, in the view of the commissioners twenty-two years previously, had been of little value. His consciousness of the close association between the community which he had been chosen to serve and his spectacular rise in fortune was reflected not only in his request for burial in the chancel of its church but in the money he left towards the rebuilding of the church and steeple, the penny doles to be given to all who attended his funeral, and the bequest of part of the residue of his estate to the poor of his parish.

Ordination and Opportunity

The early sixteenth century witnessed a huge increase in the number of men who put themselves forward, and were accepted, for the priesthood. Once ordained, the majority faced almost insurmountable odds against obtaining the security for life of the freehold tenure of a benefice. The number of available livings was strictly limited and developments such as appropriation, pluralism, unions of benefices and pension arrangements, served to restrict opportunities for their acquisition even further. Nor did the hierarchy of ecclesiastical advancement allow for each new ordinand to find the place merited by his ability within the formal structure of a career; indeed, to talk of clerical careers would be to limit the discussion to a relatively small elite within the clerical body. What mattered, if progress was to be made and security obtained, was essentially to be in the right place at the right time: the right place to come to the attention of a patron; the right time to be

---

[263] For the question of clerical poverty, and economic problems generally, see Heath, *English Parish Clergy*, 163, 173; Bowker, *Secular Clergy*, 136–7, 143–4; ibid., *Henrician Reformation*, 137; Thomson, *Early Tudor Church and Society*, 173–7; Heal, 'Economic Problems', 101.

available when that rare event, a vacancy, arose. Certain men started with an advantage: those with wealthy families; those whose relatives owned the advowsons of churches and could present them to a vacancy even before they were ordained; those who, through family connections, had a prior claim on the patronage that was available. Such men were better placed to take advantage of university education by which they might be more noticeable among the clerical crowd to those who had livings in their gift. The rest would have to make what living they could, perhaps for the rest of their lives, by performance of the functions which set them apart from lay society, wherever there was a demand.

The predicament which faced the newly ordained in this period is most vividly illustrated by taking as a sample those clerks admitted to the priesthood at a particular ceremony. On the first of June 1504, fifty-four seculars were ordained priest.[264] Only eight of these can be subsequently traced with any degree of certainty in the administrative records of the diocese. Richard Harrington was admitted to the vicarage of Sutton Maddock in 1517, Ralph Grene was presented to the rectory of Chetwynd in 1527, Henry Flemyng became vicar of Brewood at some time before 1533 and at the same date James Brook was a fellow of the collegiate church of Bunbury.[265] The others, Robert Taylor, John Wilson, John Byrde, and Hugh Smyth, are all to be found in non-tenured stipendiary posts.[266] If this sample is at all typical, and in fact it was a below-average year with regard to ordinations to the priesthood, then no more than about 7% of the secular clergy of the diocese could expect to obtain a benefice, certainly not for many years following ordination. The rest were destined to serve out most, and probably all, of their professional lives among those workhorses of the late medieval English church: the unbeneficed.

[264] LJRO, B/A/1/14ii, fo. 5v.
[265] Ibid., B/A/1/14, fos. 48r, 50r; BL, Harleian Ms 594, fos. 140v, 153r.
[266] Ibid., B/A/17/1(1), fo. 3r; BL, Harleian Ms 594, fos. 124r, 130v, 139v, 144r.

3

Making a Living: The Unbeneficed

However many of the newly-ordained men of the diocese may have aspired to the acquisition of a church living, the high level of recruitment to the priesthood in the early sixteenth century meant that such ambitions would be realised by very few. The rest, a group which historians usually refer to as 'the unbeneficed', had to make a living for most, or all, of their working lives without the security of a rectory, vicarage, collegiate post or even a perpetual chantry. Many would have to seek employment outside the formal parochial structure and an equally unquantifiable group might have spent time without employment at all. Since the principal sources for our knowledge of the clergy of this period, the episcopal registers, are concerned in the main with admissions to benefices, the significance of those outside this structure has, until recently, been overlooked. Yet 'to ignore the existence of the unbeneficed is to produce a gravely distorted picture of the late medieval church'[1] and reference to other sources is gradually revealing something of the true significance of those clergy who worked on the margins of the parochial structure.

Numbers and Jobs

It is the sheer numbers of clergy operating without the security of a living in the early sixteenth century that demands that they be given attention. The clerical subsidy return for the diocese in 1533 records the names of over 930 stipendiary clergy compared to a little under 420 with parochial livings; in other words, the unbeneficed clergy in formal employment alone outnumbered their beneficed colleagues by more than two to one. A similar situation obtained in the East Riding of Yorkshire in which 364 assistant clergy were employed in 1525 compared to about 200 incumbents and in the diocese of Lincoln where it has been estimated that the unbeneficed consti-

---

[1] McHardy, 'Careers and Disappointments', 115. For other surveys see Zell, 'Clergy in Kent' and for a comparison with the situation before the Black Death see Townley, 'Unbeneficed Clergy in the Thirteenth Century' which helps to put many of the problems into historical perspective.

tuted about 60% of the active clerical population.² Indeed, every part of the country that has been studied has been shown to have been supporting large numbers of assistant clergy in the early sixteenth century.³ In fact the situation was not an entirely novel one. Analysis of the poll tax returns of the later fourteenth century has revealed that the unbeneficed constituted anything in the range of 56% of the clerical population in the diocese of Carlisle, between 55% and 66% in the diocese of Hereford, 72% in the diocese of Lincoln, to 80% in the archdeaconry of Chester, and recent research has suggested that the numbers of unbeneficed were far higher than had been previously appreciated as far back as the mid thirteenth century.⁴ Thus by the early sixteenth century, if not at many times before, the typical priest was not a parochial incumbent but one of the unbeneficed. Whilst it is tempting to view the situation in terms of oversupply of priests and thus overmanning, such an assertion assumes the existence of optimum levels of provision.⁵ Certainly the earlier episcopal vision of a priest in every parish had been surpassed,⁶ but such was the level of demand for the services of priests that levels of supply continued to rise unabated in the first two decades of the sixteenth century. Those able to find employment within the parochial structure included the curates, chaplains and those referred to simply as 'parish priests' whose names were entered in the clerical subsidy return for 1533. Although, strictly speaking, the term *curatus* referred to a priest with cure of souls, in other words a parish incumbent, in England it had long been customary shorthand for *capellanus curatus*, a hired assistant who was given charge of the cure of either the parish of a non-resident incumbent or a chapel which had not been formally ordained as a vicarage.⁷ Quite a large number of these existed in the diocese, particularly in Shropshire and Staffordshire, and in most cases the priest in charge of them was referred to as a curate rather than a chaplain, the churches themselves often being described as 'perpetual curacies'.⁸ Most parishes in the diocese enjoyed the services of at least one assistant,⁹ though the number of stipendiaries attached to benefices was not uniform throughout the diocese. The highest incidence of assis-

---

2   Zell, 'Economic Problems', 21; Fuggles, 'Parish Clergy in the Archdeaconry of Leicester', 26.
3   See, for example, Zell, 'Clergy in Kent', 516, giving minimum figures for the diocese of Canterbury of 293 employed stipendiaries compared to 225 incumbents between 1538 and 1541, and 118 in the diocese of Rochester compared to 85 incumbents between 1533 and 1535. Even in the 1540s there were about 360 secular priests working within the approximately forty parishes of the county; Zell, 'Economic Problems', 21.
4   McHardy, 'Careers and Disappointments', 112–15. For the earlier period, see Townley, 'Unbeneficed Clergy in the Thirteenth Century', esp. 49, 52, 57, 64.
5   A point made by Marshall, *Pastoral Ministry in the East Riding*, 4.
6   Moran, *English Schooling*, 131; Townley, 'Unbeneficed Clergy in the Thirteenth Century', 49.
7   Thompson, *The English Clergy*, 122–3.
8   Ibid., 123, n. 2.
9   The same was true for the East Riding of Yorkshire where there was an average of 3.6

tant clergy was in the archdeaconry of Chester, with an average of three per parish, a figure that is significantly affected by the great size of many of the parishes of Lancashire and northern Cheshire. For example in 1533, in addition to its resident vicar, the great parish of Prestbury in the Cheshire deanery of Macclesfield was served by fifteen assistant clergy, including a curate and eight stipendiaries at the parish church itself, a curate and four assistants at the perpetual curacy of Macclesfield and two assistants and a curate at the chapel of Pot Shrigley.[10] Similarly, in Frodsham deanery, the eleven stipendiaries at the parish church of Great Budworth (three of whom had the same surname) were in addition to a curate and two assistants at the chapel of Lower Peover and a curate at Witton; and on the other side of the Mersey, in the Lancashire deanery of Warrington, the parishes of Ormskirk, and Walton and Liverpool, both employed eleven assistants.[11] In the Lancashire parish of Whalley, the largest and most northerly in the diocese, the vicar was assisted by a curate and two other clergy in addition to the priests employed at eight outlying chapels. Of these, Altham and Church were served by curates alone in 1533, but the others all employed assistants, including two each at Clitheroe and Colne and three at Burnley.[12] In total, there were 414 stipendiary chaplains employed in the archdeaconry in 1533, amounting to about 45% of the provision for the diocese as a whole.[13] But

secular priests per parish, Marshall, *Pastoral Ministry in the East Riding*, 3, and Bristol, where the average was 4; Skeeters, *Community and Clergy*, 111, Table 6.

10 BL, Harleian Ms 594, fos. 151v–152r.
11 Ibid., fos. 149v–150r, 153r.
12 Ibid., fo. 151v. They included the chaplains of the royal forests of Pendle, Trawden, Rossendale, Bowland and Blackburnshire who served chapels at Pendle, Whitewell, Clitheroe Castle, Goldshaw Booth and the 'new chapel' in Rossendale and who constituted the clerical component of the juries that met in exercise of the abbot of Whalley's exempt jurisdiction over the area; A.M. Cooke, ed., *Act Book of the Ecclesiastical Court of Whalley 1510–1538*, Chetham Society, Remains Historical and Literary Connected with the Palatine Counties of Lancaster and Chester, new ser., 44 (1901), xix–xxii.
13 The change in provision over time, however, is highlighted by the fact that only 313 were listed eight years later, by which time almost 60% of the parishes within the archdeaconry had undergone a change in provision of assistant clergy, over 65% being less well provided than formerly. Examples of significant reductions in staffing between 1533 and 1541 include Nantwich (from 9 to 5), Bolton (from 9 to 3), Walton and Liverpool (from 11 to 4), Ormskirk (from 12 to 6) and Sefton (from 7 to 2). But conversely, a minority of parishes saw an increase, such as Astbury (from 0 to 3) and Lawton (from 0 to 1). An interesting case is Rostherne (Chesh.) for which a vicarage had been ordained following its appropriation by Launde Priory in 1507; the vicar was assisted by two chaplains in 1533 but by eight in 1541. BL, Harleian Ms 594, fos. 147v–154r; *Clergy in the Diocese of Chester*, xxxiii (1896), ix–xi, 1–45; LJRO, B/A/1/14, fo. 80r. A comparison of the 1533 list, the *Valor*, the list of 1541/2 and the chantry returns of 1546–8 suggests that comparatively few of the clergy listed in 1533 and 1541 were chantrists, and where they were, this was usually indicated in the margin. The reductions in staffing are thus not accounted for in the main by a decline in the foundation, and ultimate demise of, chantries.

such high level of clerical provision was not an entirely northern phenomenon. The figures for the archdeaconries of Stafford and Shrewsbury are slightly higher than those for Coventry and Derby because of the greater number of dependent chapels, but large numbers of clergy can be found even in some of the relatively smaller parishes of Warwickshire, such as the three chaplains who, along with the vicar, served Bishop's Itchington in place of the non-resident Lichfield prebendary, Thomas Fitzherbert.[14] Elsewhere in the county, the concentration of clergy was in most cases a reflection of either the size of a parish, as at Polesworth which was served by a vicar and five chaplains,[15] and Aston, where the parish church and six outlying chapelries were served by a curate and four assistants in addition to the vicar,[16] or its urban nature. In Coventry the vicar of St Michael's enjoyed the assistance of no fewer than fifteen clergy including a curate, quite apart from the curates who served the parish's numerous outlying chapels, and the church of Holy Trinity was staffed by nine stipendiary priests in addition to a curate and priest of a perpetual chantry.[17] At Birmingham there were seven assistant clergy including a curate at the parish church.[18] To a certain extent the provision of assistant clergy would also reflect variations in lay wealth since some would have been hired directly by parishioners either to assist the incumbent at times of particular need such as Easter, or for longer periods.[19]

There is evidence to suggest that an increasing number of the parishioners who made provision in their wills for temporary or semi-permanent chantries during the period were aiming to meet the needs not only of their own souls after death, but of clerical provision within the parish. The terms of such testamentary provision would normally include the payment of the priest's stipend for a period of between one and ten years, during which time he would be expected to play a full role in the liturgical and ceremonial life of the parish.[20] On occasions, failure to fulfil such duties would lead to action

---

[14] BL, Harleian Ms 594, fo. 121r.
[15] Ibid., fo. 123r.
[16] Ibid., fo. 122r.
[17] Ibid., fos. 118r–v.
[18] Ibid., fo. 122r.
[19] Swanson, *Church and Society*, 46–7, 50; Zell, 'Clergy in Kent', 524. For evidence of financial support of assistant clergy by parishioners see B. Kümin, 'Parish Finance and the Early Tudor Clergy', in A. Pettegree, ed., *The Reformation of the Parishes – The Ministry and the Reformation in Town and Country* (Manchester, 1993), 49, and the same author's *Shaping of a Community*, 43, 130, 132.
[20] C. Burgess, 'Strategies for Eternity: Perpetual Chantry Foundation in Late Medieval Bristol', in C. Harper-Bill, ed., *Religious Belief and Ecclesiastical Careers in Late Medieval England* (Woodbridge, 1991), 3–4. An explicit example is the endowment by Sir Thomas Butler knt, of a stipendiary at the parish church of Warrington, effectively the family mausoleum, 'to celebrate there forever'. Of course, a primary function of such a priest was to promote remembrance of the benefactor and, particularly in this case, to assist the schoolmaster of Warrington in saying obituary masses for Butler and his wife; Raines, ed., *History of the Chantries*, vol. II, 251. In addition, such endow-

being taken by the community, and certainly the chantry returns of 1546–48 frequently mention the contribution made by chantry priests to the parochial cure.[21] Sometimes such duties might be made explicit as in the requirement of a Hull chantry priest to 'minister sacraments when the vicar is absent' and that of other Yorkshire chantrists to help in administering communion and other sacraments in populous parishes.[22] Where the funds set aside for the support of the priest by the original benefactor were insufficient, additional financial support for such extra duties might be provided by the parish community.[23] One role that might be easily filled by a chantry priest would be the musical augmentation of the liturgy and the teaching of song to children of the parish, and a significant contribution to the dramatic growth in local educational provision during the period would have been a result of the efforts of such priests. They would have included men like the Walsall chaplain, John Staple, whose impending loss to the parish was the subject of an impassioned plea from the parishioners in 1503.[24] Staple had

> always been ready to maintain the service of God. He has caused charity amongst the people, where else there would have been much discord and debate. He has kept a school and taught the poor children of the town of his charity, taking nothing for his labour. He has done many more good deeds, specially to the poor people. That he should thus depart were the greatest loss to the poor town of Walsall that it has ever had by the departure of any priest.[25]

The problem, of course, for the parishioners of Walsall was that the priest who made such a valuable contribution to the life of their community was in the pay of an individual patron and was ultimately beholden to his wishes, the type of arrangement that might occasionally have been made manifest by the priest's wearing of his master's livery.[26] Even so, the presence in a parish of men such as Staple and the Wigan chaplain Hugh Cockson, described as

ments might provide an occasion for the employment of family members, such as Robert Adderton, employed by John Adderton esq., at Leigh, and Christopher Ireland, employed by Thomas Ireland at Childwall, in 1541; *Clergy in the Diocese of Chester*, 14, 16. Even if not employed directly by their own family, stipendiary employment could favour those with family connections, such as Nicholas Taylor, presented to the restored Butler chantry at Warrington in 1554, whose brother, Richard, was the parish curate. The prominence of the Taylors is reflected by Nicholas' presentation to the rectory itself later in the same year, being in the right place at the right time to benefit from the deprivation of M. Edward Keble; Raines, *History of the Chantries*, 60.

21 Kümin, *Shaping of a Community*, 160–1, though it is unlikely that many parish communities would be prepared to take action as extreme as that of Sandwich, Kent, where available sanctions included imprisonment of the recalcitrant priest; ibid., 166. For the evidence of chantry returns see Marshall, *Pastoral Ministry in the East Riding*, 5.
22 Ibid.
23 Burgess, 'Strategies for Eternity', 4; Kümin, *Shaping of a Community*, 160.
24 See above, 11.
25 Quoted in Moran, *English Schooling*, 81.
26 C. Burgess, 'The Benefactions of Mortality: The Lay Response in the Late Medieval

being in the hire of Thomas Gerrard esq., must usually have made itself felt among the wider community;[27] this was certainly the case with Richard Asche, chantry priest of Beighton, who, in addition to his bequests in 1539 to two altars in his own church left 4d 'to either of my other churches'.[28]

Another major source of employment of priests within the parochial framework were the parish confraternities or religious gilds, civic gilds and other lay corporations such as the Lichfield Gild of St Mary and St John the Baptist which employed a group of priests, probably on an annual basis, to serve its altar in St Mary's chapel.[29] As with chantry chaplains, the priests hired by gilds either on a temporary or semi-permanent basis might prove useful to the wider parish community and attract additional financial support from its members.[30] Evidence of the activities of such priests within the diocese is unfortunately sparse, but references to clergy attached to religious gilds elsewhere during the period is suggestive both of their importance to the confraternities themselves and the greater community within which they worked.[31] By the late fifteenth century, for example, the gild of St Mary in Boston (Lincs.) had ten chaplains in its hire and there were four working for the Trinity Gild, Wisbech, in the 1520s, one of whom was a schoolmaster.[32] Whilst his contribution to parish life would have been quite conspicuous, the annual hire of two additional priests by the gild to take part in the celebration of the anniversary of one of its founders would, as well as providing employment to the chaplains concerned, have added to the liturgical provision of the parish. John Hobard, the priest employed by the Trinity Gild in Bassingbourne made himself additionally useful to the community by writing up the churchwardens' accounts, copying out primers for use in the church and making corrections to its mass book. His considerable involvement in the life of the parish in the early sixteenth century also included the direction of the annual St George play, and the more mundane tasks of fetching wood and wax for the church and raising money towards its funds from the sale of crab-apples.[33] The importance in the parish of Robert Parson, a gild priest of Gamlingay, was rewarded by a generous testamentary bequest by its vicar in 1542 in recognition of 'the great pains that he has taken with me in times past'.[34]

Outside of the formal parochial structure a significant number of clergy

---

Urban Parish', in D.M. Smith, ed., *Studies in Clergy and Ministry in Medieval England*, Borthwick Studies in History, 1 (1991), 72.
[27] Bridgeman, *History of the Church and Manor of Wigan*, 112, n. 4.
[28] Will of Richard Asche.
[29] Swanson, *Church and Society*, 50.
[30] Kümin, 'Parish Finance', 49; *Shaping of a Community*, 130.
[31] V. Bainbridge, *Gilds in the Medieval Countryside: Social and Religious Change in Cambridgeshire c.1350–1558* (Woodbridge, 1996).
[32] Ibid., 70.
[33] Ibid., 73–4.
[34] Ibid., 74.

would have found employment in the households of nobility, gentry and higher clergy and, increasingly, those of the more prosperous members of the mercantile class. A considerable proliferation of licences for private oratories and domestic chapels from the middle of the fifteenth century has been observed in the diocese of York,[35] and that this was part of a nationwide phenomenon is suggested by the vociferous complaint of Sir Thomas More that one of the chief evils of his day was the debasement of the office of priesthood resulting from the fact that 'every mean man must have a priest in his house to wait upon his wife, which no man almost lacketh now'.[36] The employment of domestic chaplains does appear to have been moving gradually down the social scale, with two priests coming to be seen as the normal requirement of a medium-sized household.[37] In Lancashire about a dozen gentry families can be seen to have employed priests during the period, but much research needs to be undertaken before the true scale of the phenomenon is recognised.[38] A vivid impression of the varied duties required of domestic chaplains is to be found among the regulations of the household of Henry Percy, fifth earl of Northumberland, written in the early years of the century for use at his Yorkshire castles of Wressle and Leckonfield.[39] There were to be eleven chaplains in all, each required to be in priest's orders, and remunerated at the rate of five marks for graduates and 40s for non-graduates. The senior chaplain, who was required to be either a doctor of laws or bachelor of divinity, was to hold the position of dean of chapel, under whom was a subdean with the specific duty of 'keeping the choir in my lord's chapel daily' and two priests whose jobs were 'singing of Our Lady's mass in the chapel daily' and 'reading the gospel in the chapel daily'. The duties required of the remaining seven chaplains were of an altogether more secular nature. They comprised a surveyor of the earl's lands; a riding chaplain accompanying him on his travels; a chaplain for his eldest son, to 'wait upon him daily'; a clerk of the closet; a master of grammar; a secretary and an almoner.[40] The relative importance attached to the domestic duties of household chaplains over priestly functions is given further stark emphasis in a letter of introduction written by Thomas Warley to Lady Lisle in 1534, recommending a chaplain for her service:

> ... pleaseth it your ladyship to understand that here is a priest, a very honest man, which would gladly do service to my lord and your ladyship. And these properties he hath: he writes a very fair secretary hand and text hand

---

[35] Moran, *English Schooling*, 136.
[36] Ibid.
[37] K. Mertes, *The English Noble Household 1250–1600* (Oxford, 1988), 143.
[38] Haigh, *Reformation and Resistance*, 65.
[39] T. Percy, ed., *The Regulations and Establishment of the Household of Henry Algernon Percy, The Fifth Earl of Northumberland, at his Castles of Wressle and Leckonfield in Yorkshire, begun Anno Domini MDXII* (1905).
[40] Ibid., 47, 244, 311–13, 316–17.

and Roman, and singeth surely, and playeth very cunningly on the organs; and he is very cunning in drawing of knots and well seen in grafting and keeping of cucumbers and other herbs. I judge him very meet for to do my lord and your ladyship service.[41]

As part of a growing trend, domestic service would undoubtedly have provided employment for many of the swelling ranks of secular clergy, but it is not difficult to discern the basis of More's fears of a consequent threat to clerical status, and unlike gild and chantry chaplains, few would have had the freedom to provide service outside the confines of their establishments. Employment more in keeping with the dignity of priesthood would have been available in the service of monastic oratories and as chaplains attached to religious houses and, more specifically, to their abbots and priors. A definite requirement for the services of secular priests existed among the communities of female religious in the diocese.[42] The Benedictine nuns of Nuneaton employed three chaplains and those of Chester, two, while the White Ladies of Brewood had a single chaplain to say mass for them and one or more of the five chaplains employed within the parish of Polesworth might have combined parochial duties with service at the altar of the Benedictine nunnery there.[43]

The extent to which priests who were unable to find formal employment either within or outside the parochial structure of the diocese remained unemployed depended on continuing high levels of demand for their intercessory services. Yet limiting factors existed even in the market for such casual employment since some testators specified that the work was to be undertaken by named individuals, sometimes priests already in formal employment.[44] Writing his will in 1534, Ralph Tatton, rector of Barlborough, specified that the priests who were to say a trental of masses and dirige for his soul should be his brother Richard, cousin Thomas, and John Stolys, a gild priest of neighbouring Repton. In any case Tatton was not offering particularly attractive remuneration, directing that the men should 'be content of such rayment and bedding not before bequeathed'. In the same year Richard Bexwyke, curate of Middleton, Lancashire, made provision for four named priests to say mass and dirige and pray for his soul following his death, two of whom were chaplains who had already been employed at the church. Short-term employment such as this attracted remuneration of only 16d compared to the 10s that Bexwyke offered to Roger Ireland, curate of neighbouring Radcliffe, in return for saying a trental of masses at Middleton under the terms of the same will. If Ireland were not to be granted leave from his curate's post then the work was to be given to 'another poor priest that is out

---

41 M. St. Clare Byrne, ed., *The Lisle Letters* (Harmondsworth, 1985 edn), 39; I have modernised the spelling.
42 Townley, 'Unbeneficed Clergy in the Thirteenth Century', 57.
43 BL, Harleian Ms 594, fos. 122v, 123r, 140v, 147r.
44 For details of wills, see appendix.

of service'. When Richard Ryve, vicar of South Wingfield, established his obit in 1537 he attempted to direct the work to a particular individual but made provision should this fail, instructing his executors:

> I will that Sir William Hood, priest, shall have the preferment there before any other if he so will, he doing his duty like an honest man, and I will that the said Sir William or any other priest that shall so celebrate ... shall always be at the appointment of the overseer of my will.

In the same year the priest employed under the terms of the will of Richard Webb, rector of Stapleton, was to be Thomas Turner, who in 1533 had been employed as a chaplain at neighbouring Coundon. The fact that he was expected to say a trental of masses in return for a book of psalms and a worsted hood, rather than cash, suggests not only that he was probably a friend of the vicar but also that he was still in formal employment. In 1538 William Swynerton, rector of Blymhill, stipulated that the man who should 'sing a year at Blymhill church, to pray for my soul and my father and mother's soul' should be John Collins, described as 'my priest'. He is probably the same as the curate of neighbouring Sheriffhales in 1533 and, from the description, might have enjoyed connections with Swynerton of long standing, probably, since later in the will he is described as 'my ghostly father', as his confessor. For the year's service Collins was to have £5 on the condition that 'my goods will perform it'. Similarly in 1548 George Gregory, chaplain of Rossendale, nominated Henry Ramsbothom, who had been working as a chaplain at Bolton in 1533, 'to pray devoutly for the salvation of my soul' in return for 3s 4d.

Other testators were prepared to leave the appointment of their intercessors to the discretion of their executors and thus more open to competition, perhaps even tender. In addition to his appointment of William Hood, Richard Ryve also left 20s towards the hire of a priest to say mass for an unspecified period at the church of Brailsford some twelve miles away, while Alexander Legh, curate of Ryton-on-Dunsmore, set aside £3 for the hire of a priest for six months and Richard Podmore, curate of Dawley, left a sum of money (unfortunately indecipherable in his will of 1541) for 'a priest to sing for a year'. Smaller sums could be earned simply by attendance at funerals. Richard Blockley, vicar of Wolvey, made provision in 1538 for four priests to attend his funeral at 8d each and the residue of his estate to support a priest for three months, and in 1539 the Coventry chaplain, John Wells, promised 4d to any priest that 'do bear me to the church' on the day of his funeral. In 1543 Richard Dodycotte, chaplain of Wroxeter, directed that on the day of his burial 'priests and clerks that come to pray for my soul' should be paid 'according to the custom of the church'. Richard Bryddocke and Thomas Wylson each left 8d, in 1556 and 1561 respectively, for every priest that attended their funerals, whilst in 1549 William Brewster requested that his executors give out a total of 40s in funeral doles, to be shared between attending clergy and the local poor. The Macclesfield chaplain and schoolmaster William Bridges was eager to secure a good send-off in his will, directing that

> Upon the day of my burial there be thirty priests to sing and say St Gregory Trental the same day, if so many can be conveniently gotten . . . to the extent above said shall sing and say placebo and dirige overnight and the commendation in the morning, and every priest so doing to have 8d and every parson, vicar and parish priest . . . 12d.

In addition, on his 'month's mind' his executors were to

> cause a trental of masses to be said and sung for my soul . . . if so many can conveniently be gotten, and if not then it may be in the next day following fulfilled and accomplished, and that every priest being [present] and singing of the said trental to have every of them 6d and every parson and vicar being of the same number to have 8d.

By the time Bridges wrote his will in 1536 recruitment to the priesthood was in rapid decline and he was perhaps justified in sounding a note of caution concerning the numbers that would be attracted by the relatively small sums that he was offering. However, in 1524 when Lord Mounteagle had made provision for the same number of clergy to be present at his funeral in return for a modest dole, no fewer than eighty priests turned up in the hope of receiving payment.[45] At that time, certainly in the north of the diocese, there was evidently a regular supply of eager takers of casual employment. But whilst it would be true to say that there is little evidence of the kind of social unrest that might be expected had a large body of men remained unemployed for a long period,[46] ten years after Edward Stanley had been buried, another Lancastrian, Henry Turton, fellow of the collegiate church of Manchester, could still feel moved to leave his two breviaries 'to some poor priest new made to pray for me'.[47]

Provenance and Status

Despite the evident ubiquity of unbeneficed clergy within early Tudor society, the fact that without the legal status that accrued from the tenure of a benefice they were of comparatively little interest to the ecclesiastical authorities means that their presence within the historical record is generally obscure. Much of what we can say about them derives, paradoxically, from the fact that from the 1520s onwards, secular government expressed a relatively greater level of interest as it widened its tax net to include all the unbeneficed clergy within formal ecclesiastical employment. The best

---

[45] Heath, *English Parish Clergy*, 25.
[46] A comment made regarding the 13th century in Townley, 'Unbeneficed Clergy in the Thirteenth Century', 60.
[47] *Lancashire and Cheshire Wills*, 13.

starting point for a general investigation is thus the clerical subsidy returns, and since these survive for the archdeaconry of Stafford for both 1531 and 1533, the clergy of this area provide a useful sample for study. The 1531 list returns the names of 201 unbeneficed clergy of whom 128 (64%) can be traced in Bishop Blythe's ordination register. Apart from a single individual who was ordained to the title of his choral vicar's stall in Lichfield Cathedral,[48] all of these men obtained their titles from religious houses, representing forty-two different institutions. Nine houses provided five or more of the titles each; these were Norton (Cheshire), Buildwas (Shropshire), Halesowen (Worcestershire), and the Staffordshire houses of Dieulacres, Croxden, Hulton, Ranton, Brewood White Ladies and Baswich. It has been argued above that priests usually obtained their titles from a monastery in the near vicinity of their place of origin, and in the case of the Staffordshire sample the breakdown of the source of titles is set out below.

Table 6. Provenance of titles of employed unbeneficed clergy in the archdeaconry of Stafford 1531, by county

Staffordshire	89	(70%)
Cheshire	12	(9%)
Derbyshire	8	(6%)
Shropshire	8	(6%)
Warwickshire	7	(5.5%)
Lancashire	1	(0.8%)
Worcestershire	1	(0.8%)
Oxfordshire	1	(0.8%)
Lichfield vicar choral stall	1	(0.8%)

Most of the unbeneficed clergy employed in the archdeaconry of Stafford at this time would thus appear to have been natives of the county. This impression is further enforced by the numerous examples of stipendiaries being employed in a parish within the immediate vicinity of the house which provided their title or, at the very least, within the same part of the county. A few examples serve to illustrate the point. Stephen Atkinson was ordained priest in 1512 to the title of Croxden Abbey and in 1531 was employed as a chaplain in the neighbouring parish of Bramshall;[49] John Bellet, ordained deacon to the title of Hulton Abbey in 1527, was employed four years later

---

[48] Richard Borows, ordained to the title of his stall in 1517; LJRO. B/A/1/14ii, fo. 120r.
[49] Ibid., fos. 71r, 79r, 81v, 84v; B/A/17/1(1), fo. 2v. There was a Thomas Atkinson and family living in the village c.1532; A.J. Kettle, *A List of Families in the Archdeaconry of Stafford 1532–3*, Staffordshire Record Society, Collections for a History of Staffordshire, 4th ser., 8 (1976), 69.

at Cheadle;[50] Thomas Flemyng, ordained priest to the title of Sandwell Priory in 1515, was a chaplain at Walsall by 1520 and was still working within the parish eighteen years later;[51] Robert Gryme was ordained priest in 1512 to the title of Baswich Priory and twenty-six years later was curate of Acton Trussell, at a distance of just a mile or so from the house, a position that he had held for at least the previous seven years;[52] Thurstan Bradshaw and Richard Forde both obtained titles from Dieulacres Abbey and found employment at Cheddleton, just a few miles away,[53] and Thomas Whitehead and William Hill, who received titles from the nunnery of Farewell, near Lichfield, both found employment within the city.[54] It is possible that Ralph Machyn might never have had to leave the parish of Stone of which he was probably a native, since twenty-four years after obtaining his title to the priesthood from the priory there he was one of two curates employed in the parish church.[55] The sample of wills provides further evidence that a significant proportion of the stipendiary clergy were working within the locality of their origin. Of the twenty-four chaplains and chantry priests in the sample it is possible to trace the titles of twelve; all of them were from institutions within the immediate vicinity of their place of employment.[56] The same conclusion has been reached in studies based on Kent, Lancashire and County Durham and in many cases it has been shown that stipendiary clergy were working in the parishes within which they had been born.[57]

In terms of status, the great majority of the 128 clergy in the Staffordshire sample can be shown to have been ordained to the priesthood; there are only seventeen individuals for whom ordination cannot be proved to this level and only six of these were employed in positions with cure of souls in 1531.[58] Therefore only a minority of the employed assistant clergy of the region

[50] LJRO, B/A/1/14ii, fo. 192r; B/A/17/1(1), fo. 2r.
[51] Ibid., B/A/1/14ii, fos. 99v, 102r, 103v; B/A/17/1(1), fo. 8v; *Churchwardens' Accounts of All Saints, Walsall*, 253.
[52] LJRO, B/A/1/14ii, fos. 77r, 79v, 82r; SHC 1915, 3; *Families in the Archdeaconry of Stafford*, 92.
[53] LJRO, B/A/1/14ii, fos. 39r, 54v, 194r, 197r, 200r; B/A/17/1(1), fo. 2v; BL, Harleian Ms 594, fo. 138v; a James Bradshaw and family were resident c.1532: *Families in the Archdeaconry of Stafford*, 36.
[54] LJRO, B/A/1/14ii, fos. 13v, 20v, 23r, 52r, 55r, 56v; B/A/17/1(1), fo. 14v.
[55] Ibid., B/A/1/14ii, fos. 82r, 85r, 88r, 94r; BL, Harleian Ms 594, fo. 139r.
[56] See appendix.
[57] Zell, 'Clergy in Kent', 521; Haigh, *Reformation and Resistance*, 140; L.M. Stevens Benham, 'The Durham Clergy 1494–1540: A Study of Continuity and Mediocrity Among the Unbeneficed', in D. Marcombe, ed., *The Last Principality: Politics, Religion and Society in the Bishopric of Durham 1494–1660*, 8–9. It is further supported by occasional incidental references such as the 3s 4d that the Walsall chaplain William Starismore owed in 1495 for the burial of his parents in the parish churchyard; *Churchwardens' Accounts of All Saints, Walsall*, 234.
[58] Thomas Bakewell (deacon 1521, curate of Checkley 1531); Roger Fletcher (deacon 1521, curate of Patshull 1531); Thomas Hode (deacon 1513, curate of Calton 1531); William Schelfeld (deacon 1525, curate of [Great]Barr 1531); John Underhill (deacon

would be unable to undertake the full range of clerical duties which would frequently have been expected of them. If the unbeneficed clergy did not differ greatly from those with livings in terms of their orders, the same was not true, however, with regard to education. None of the stipendiaries in the wills sample appears to have held a degree and among the 930 employed in the diocese in 1533 only four appear to have been graduates; Richard Palin, a stipendiary at Trentham in 1531 and 1533, Maurice Wyllington, curate of Bangor-is-y-coed, and John Latham and Thomas Hatton, schoolmasters of Malpas and Farnworth respectively.[59] The phenomenon of Oxford graduates taking short-term curate's posts in the vicinity of the university appears to have been an entirely local one and a study of almost 100 wills made by Yorkshire chaplains between 1480 and 1530 has revealed that none of them held university degrees.[60] Similarly, there was only a single graduate among the 360 stipendiary clergy employed in Lancashire in 1548.[61] However, before concluding (as has been done for the unbeneficed clergy of County Durham) that their educational level was probably more similar to that of their parishioners than their beneficed colleagues,[62] it would be well to remember first, that this was a period of dramatic growth in educational provision at primary and secondary level and second, that the basis of the university curriculum was such that many clergy may have followed a significant part of it without formally proceeding to graduation.[63] And whilst it has been observed that the unbeneficed clergy of the East Riding of Yorkshire were 'virtually uniformly non-graduate', the chantry certificates for the region demonstrate that the general educational level of its auxiliary clergy was of an entirely acceptable standard.[64]

Employment Mobility

It has been seen that the level of competition for benefices meant that a large proportion of the clergy of the diocese who were able to obtain parochial livings held on to them for a long period, often for their entire careers.

1528, curate of Ingestre 1531); Hugh Walker (deacon 1521, curate of Thorpe Constantine 1531): Cooper, 'Secular Clergy', appendix. This excludes two clerics whose careers suggest that they had been ordained prior to the commencement of the register in 1503. Some of the six might simply have not had their ordination to the priesthood recorded or it might have taken place outside the diocese.

[59] LJRO, B/A/17/1(1), fo. 5r; BL, Harleian Ms 594, fos. 139r, 148r, 149r.
[60] Fuggles, 'Parish Clergy in the Archdeaconry of Leicester', 32; P. Mackie, 'Chaplains in the Diocese of York 1480-1530: The Testamentary Evidence', *Yorkshire Archaeological Journal*, 58 (1986), 127.
[61] Haigh, *Reformation and Resistance*, 41.
[62] Stevens Benham, 'The Durham Clergy', 14.
[63] See above, 13.
[64] Marshall, *Pastoral Ministry in the East Riding*, 12-13.

The nature of stipendiary employment means that the careers of the unbeneficed are more difficult to trace. Certainly the relative weakness of their legal position was likely to have made their hold on regular employment more tenuous. Curates and parochial chaplains, whilst receiving some legal protection from the canon law dictate that they could not be dismissed 'without just cause', could not depend on continuing employment through a change of incumbency since an incoming rector or vicar was under no obligation to retain his predecessor's assistant. The stipendiary employed by a longstanding incumbent was thus likely to have been in an advantageous position, but any change in the tenure of the living would have been an event at least as stressful for curates as for the new holder of the benefice in his need to ensure adequate title.[65] The employment of priests in the service of the many chapels dependent for their existence on the renewal of episcopal licences was even less secure. These were often issued for periods of only one year at a time and there are sufficient examples from various parts of the country of the revocation of licences to suggest that the living made by such chaplains could be a precarious one.[66] Again, the survival of clerical subsidy returns for the archdeaconry of Stafford for both 1531 and 1533 allows the unbeneficed clergy of the county to be taken as a sample and, together with evidence from the testamentary sample and other scattered evidence, enables tentative general conclusions to be drawn regarding the level of mobility between posts and the ability of stipendiary priests to hold on to employment. Of the 201 employed stipendiary clergy recorded in the archdeaconry in 1531, 165 (just over 80%) were listed again two years later. Of these about 10% had moved to a different post, and there is evidence of thirty (just under 15%) of the 1531 sample subsequently obtaining a benefice, although the possible conflation of a few individuals would render the latter figure as a maximum.[67]

The reasons for moves between stipendiary posts are obscure and are likely to have been varied. Stephen Wainwright's move from his position as chaplain in the parish of Abbot's Bromley to the curacy of Rugby in Warwickshire brought him an extra mark's salary and, probably, a little greater security.[68] Cases such as this were, however, exceptional, and other moves do not appear to have brought any discernible financial advantage. The

---

[65] Zell, 'Economic Problems', 24; McHardy, 'Careers and Disappointments', 125; Swanson, *Church and Society*, 63. Where the change in incumbent involved a pension arrangement there might be a financial disadvantage for the new incumbent to retain his predecessor's assistant: see Swanson, *Church and Society*, 56–7.
[66] McHardy, 'Careers and Disappointments', 125.
[67] This can be compared with data from a comparison of the stipendiary clergy employed in the archdeaconry of Chester in 1533 and 1541. Of the 313 listed at the later date, 105 (34%) were in the same post as ten years earlier and a further 47 (15%) had moved to another position: BL, Harleian Ms 594, fos. 146v–154r; *Clergy in the Diocese of Chester*, ix–xi, 1–45.
[68] LJRO, B/A/17/1(1), fo. 5v; BL, Harleian Ms 594, fo. 124v.

remuneration available to Thomas Whitehead as a Lichfield chaplain in 1531 was nominally the same as that offered by the same type of employment at North Wingfield, Derbyshire, to which he had moved by 1533. Since his ordination to the priesthood in 1509 was to the title of Farewell nunnery, near Lichfield, the earlier position was probably within his native region. He might have been a relative of Ralph Whitehead, the chancellor of Lichfield Cathedral, and if so, his move to North Wingfield might have owed something to the fact that its rector was the cathedral precentor, Thomas Fitzherbert, and some advantage might have been gained that is concealed by the bare figures of the subsidy returns.[69] Some clergy can be shown to have moved to other stipendiary posts subsequent to 1533 but again, the motives are often unclear. Robert Barlow, for example, was curate of Walsall in 1531 and 1533 but by 1545 held the curacy of Burton upon Trent; the reason for the move does not obviously appear to have been an increase in pay since at Walsall he would have been paid seven marks whilst the stipendiaries at Burton were being paid just £4 in 1533.[70]

Other Staffordshire assistant clergy were able, or more willing, to hold on to stipendiary posts for longer periods of time. Thomas Mere's tenure of the curacy of Norton in the Moors was for at least eleven years up to his death in 1542 and William Delf, who had been ordained priest in 1521, was curate of Newcastle-under-Lyme ten years later and held the post until his death in 1543.[71] Some long periods of tenure are revealed by the chantry certificates of 1547; Roger Fletcher, Thomas Howll and John Hyll were all in the same posts then that they had held in 1531, at Patshull, Whitmore and Burton upon Trent respectively.[72] For many clergy a long period in post obviously represented most, if not all, of their working lives. Hugh Smyth, a chaplain at Audley in 1531, still held the post in 1550 and if he is to be identified with the priest ordained to the title of Hulton, less than ten miles away, in 1504, then he would have been about seventy years old.[73] When John Abell made his will in 1553 he described himself as curate of Kingstone, a post he had held since at least 1531; he died, in his seventies, in 1558.[74] Both Thomas Drakford and Thomas Tunstall had been ordained priest to the title of Dieulacres Abbey; Drakford in 1510 and Tunstall four years later. By 1531 they were curates of Leigh and Wolstanton respectively, and held the posts until their deaths in 1565 when they, too, would have been in their seventies.[75] Ralph Parker held

---

[69] BL, Harleian Ms 594, fo. 124r. It might also be significant that Thomas had joined the Lichfield Civic Gild in 1520: LJRO, D.77/1, p. 291.
[70] LJRO, B/A/17/1(1), fo. 8v; BL, Harleian Ms 594, fo. 141r; SHC 1915, 41.
[71] LJRO, B/A/1/14ii, fos. 137v, 142r, 144v, 156v; B/A/17/1(1), fos. 3r, 4r; BL, Harleian Ms 594, fo. 138r; SHC 1915, 251, 253.
[72] Ibid., 42, 200, 253.
[73] LJRO, B/A/17/1(1), fo. 3v; B/A/1/14ii, fo. 8r; SHC 1915, 20.
[74] See appendix.
[75] LJRO, B/A/1/14ii, fos. 56r, 65v, 68r, 70v, 90v, 94v, 96v, 99r; B/A/17/1(1), fos. 2r, 3v; SHC 1915, 150–1, 317.

successive stipendiary posts in the same region for long periods. Probably the priest of that name ordained to the title of Ranton Priory in 1525, by 1531 he was a chaplain at Shenstone, a post that he held until at least 1548. By 1552 he had moved to take on the curacy of Yoxall which he served until at least 1568, having subscribed to the Act of Settlement in 1559.[76] John Berdemore had been ordained priest in 1521 to the title of Croxden and ten years later was employed at Grindon. By 1542 he had become chantry priest at Kingsley, which was converted to a curacy after the dissolution of the chantry six years later. He was still in this position, as well as undertaking the responsibilities of schoolmaster in the parish, in 1571 when he would have been at least in his mid seventies.[77] If the Robert Sutton who died as curate of Rushton in 1588 is the same as the priest appointed to the post shortly after his ordination in 1530, to the title of Hulton Abbey about ten miles away, then his tenure was for a remarkable fifty-eight years and he would have been at least eighty-two years old when he died.[78] But long tenures of stipendiary positions were certainly not confined to Staffordshire. Two Derbyshire curates, Thomas Somersall at Brampton chapel, and Richard Whitworth at Chesterfield, died in 1558 and 1559 respectively, having held their posts since at least 1533, and in the following year Richard Hatton, curate of Shifnal, Shropshire, died having held the position for the same duration.[79] In Lancashire the Wigan chaplains Henry Grange, Hugh Cockson, William Astley and Matthew Hey, recorded in 1533, were all still in position in 1550 and at Prescot Edward Garnett and Henry Colley were still active in the parish in the late 1550s.[80]

Sporadic as is the survival of evidence from the diocese of Coventry and Lichfield, however, the suggestion of the relative stability of many of the stipendiary clergy is somewhat at variance with that from areas to the south and east. A greater level of mobility has been observed in Leicestershire, Surrey and Kent; most probably due the relatively higher rates of remuneration available in those areas.[81] Statistics reflecting the ability of stipendiary clergy to be promoted to benefices is, however, remarkably consistent in all areas that have been studied. The incidence in Kent, Leicestershire and

[76] LJRO, B/A/17/1(1), fo. 9r; BL, Harleian Ms 594, fo. 141r; SHC 1915, 232, 357, 359.
[77] LJRO, B/A/1/14ii, 133v, 136r, 136v, 138v; BL, Harleian Ms 594, fo. 138r; SHC 1915, 136, 137, 361.
[78] LJRO, B/A/1/14ii, fos. 198v, 203v, 207v, 209v; B/A/17/1(1), fo. 2v; BL, Harleian Ms 594, fo. 138r; SHC 1915, 147. A James Sutton and family were resident in the village c.1532: *Families in the Archdeaconry of Stafford*, 33.
[79] Wills of Richard Whitworth and Richard Hatton; see appendix. Somersall: BL, Harleian Ms 594, fo. 124v; W.P.W. Phillimore, *Calendars of Wills and Administrations in the Consistory Court of the Bishop of Lichfield and Coventry 1516 to 1652*, Index Library, vol. 7 (1892), 102.
[80] Bridgeman, *History of the Church and Manor of Wigan*, 112, n. 4; *Prescot Records*, 108, 111, 131, 137, 138.
[81] Fuggles, 'Parish Clergy in the Archdeaconry of Leicester', 31; study by R.A. Christophers quoted in Zell, 'Economic Problems', 24, 25.

Lancashire was between ten and sixteen per cent of assistant clergy compared to the figure of just under fifteen per cent in Staffordshire.[82] In all these cases the priest in question must have come to the attention of a patron, either by his own efforts and contacts or by the aid of a third party. However, the details of such a process remain hidden and we must look for other clues as to the means by which this small proportion of the unbeneficed clergy managed to obtain a living. In many cases it is clear that, as was the case in Kent and Lancashire, for a priest to acquire a benefice within his general locality one or more moves away were required first. John Wildblood appears to have left his post at Mucklestone shortly before the compilation of the subsidy return in 1531. Two years later he was employed at Caverswall and in the same year became a vicar choral of the royal free chapel at Stafford. Admission to such a post must have necessitated his departure from Caverswall but by 1539 he had returned to become vicar and held the living until his death in 1563.[83] In 1531 and 1533 John Beche was curate of Ellenhall in the deanery of Newcastle but by 1541 he had moved south to become chaplain of Abbots Bromley. He was still there three years later but by 1558 had returned to Newcastle deanery to become rector of Maer.[84] John Goodwyn had been ordained priest to the title of Dieulacres Abbey in 1529 and in 1531 was a stipendiary at Wolstanton, one of the parishes in the vicinity of the house. By 1533 he had moved to Cheddleton chapel, perhaps with the motive of moving even closer to his place of origin.[85] By 1549 he had been instituted to the vicarage of Ilam, a few miles to the east, which he held until his death in 1571.[86]

Other Staffordshire clergy were required to move but seem to have benefited, like John Wildblood, from connections with collegiate churches in the area. For example, in 1531 Edmund Walker was a stipendiary at Stowe, attached to Lichfield Cathedral, and within two years had moved to become chaplain of Salt, a chapel annexed to the royal free chapel of Stafford. By 1548 he was serving the same establishment's chapel at Hopton and within a further eight years was admitted to the crown living of Aldridge which he held until his death in 1575.[87] The career of Thomas Fox was remarkably similar to that of Walker, including the chaplaincies of Hopton and Salt which he held by 1531 and 1548 respectively. Between 1554 and his death in 1572 he was vicar of Penn, a living to the west of the county annexed to

---

82 Zell, 'Clergy in Kent', 521–4; Fuggles, 'Parish Clergy in the Archdeaconry of Leicester', 31–2; Haigh, *Reformation and Resistance*, 37.
83 LJRO, B/A/17/1(1), fo. 3v; D 30/18, fo. 1r; BL, Harleian Ms 594, fo. 143r; SHC 1915, 51.
84 LJRO, B/A/17/1(1), fo. 4v; BL, Harleian Ms 594, fo. 139r; SHC 1915, 135, 186.
85 A Robert Godwyn, his wife Margery and son John were resident in the village c.1532: *Families in the Archdeaconry of Stafford*, 36.
86 LJRO, B/A/1/14ii, fos. 197v, 200r; B/A/17/1(1), fo. 3v; BL, Harleian Ms 594, fo. 139v; SHC 1915, 131.
87 LJRO, B/A/17/1(1), fo. 4v; BL, Harleian Ms 594, fo. 143r; SHC 1915, 6, 129.

the subchanters of Lichfield Cathedral.[88] Like Edmund Walker, Thomas Tatton was chaplain of Lichfield Cathedral's chapel of Stowe in 1533 but by 1544 he had been admitted to the chantry at the altar of St Thomas within the cathedral itself. However, the following year he was able to resign this post in favour of the vicarage of Rugeley, a living in the gift of the dean and chapter. He held the benefice for thirteen years before moving to the neighbouring parish of Colton where he was rector until his death in 1572.[89] Edward Fletcher, Tatton's successor as vicar of Rugeley, came to the living by a similar route. Having first obtained employment as chaplain of Gratwich within three years of his ordination to the priesthood in 1528, by 1541 he had become a chantry priest at Lichfield. Soon afterwards he took up the curacy of the chapel of Denston annexed to the royal free chapel of Penkridge before being admitted to Rugeley by 1558, a living which he held until his death in 1564.[90] In the absence of direct evidence, the careers of these men strongly suggest that their ability to secure a benefice followed from coming to the attention of influential ecclesiastics in the region and possibly even the crown. The presence in Staffordshire of a relatively large number of royal free chapels and other collegiate churches, compared to the rest of the diocese, further suggests that the figure of 15% mobility from stipendiary positions to benefices based on a sample from this area, if anything, overstates the opportunities available to the clergy of the diocese as a whole. In addition it must be remembered that, quite apart from those priests in stipendiary positions, there existed a great pool of clergy outside the formal parochial employment structure whose opportunities for advancement cannot be adequately assessed.

An even smaller number of Staffordshire assistant clergy was able to acquire benefices without moving far from the parish in which they were working, presumably taking advantage of being close at hand as vacancies arose. As well as having the benefit of proximity, Edmund Jackson was another priest who might have obtained preferment through a connection with Lichfield Cathedral. In 1531 and 1533 he was a stipendiary in Eccleshall, a prebendal parish of the cathedral, and in 1554 moved to the neighbouring parish of Offley, another prebend, to become vicar. He held the living until his death in 1563.[91] Andrew Bowyer's career was based exclusively within the deanery of Newcastle. Having been ordained priest in 1526 to the title of Hulton Abbey, by 1531 he had become curate of the chapel of Keele, a post he was still holding five years later. In 1548 he was admitted to the vicarage of Wolstanton and three years later to the rectory of neighbour-

---

[88] LJRO, B/A/17/1(1), fo. 12v; BL, Harleian Ms 594, fo. 143v; SHC 1915, 212–24.
[89] LJRO, B/A/17/1(1), fo. 14v; BL, Harleian Ms 594, fo. 144r; SHC 1915, 73, 158, 219. At Colton he succeeded his kinsman, George; below, 156.
[90] LJRO, B/A/1/14ii, fos. 183r, 187v, 191v, 193v; B/A/17/1(1), fo. 2v; SHC 1915, 153, 207, 219, 221.
[91] LJRO, B/A/17/1(1), fo. 6r; BL, Harleian Ms 594, fo. 140v; SHC 1915, 125.

ing Ashley, both of which he held in plurality until his death in 1574.[92] William Starismore's promotion probably occurred towards the end of his active career. Ordained priest in 1509, he held a stipendiary post at Walsall in 1531 and had become a chantry priest in the same parish by 1548 and vicar of Wednesbury by 1553 when he would have been at least sixty-eight years old.[93] Outside of Staffordshire, Edmund Bachelor was ordained priest in 1527 to the title of the Shropshire abbey of Buildwas and within six years had obtained employment as a chaplain at Cound, a few miles away; at his death in 1557 he was rector of Sheinton, a church virtually in the shadow of the monastery which had launched his career.[94]

No more than five priests in the Staffordshire sample appear to have been able to take the easiest possible step into dead men's shoes by obtaining the living of the parish in which they were employed as stipendiaries. John Byrde was another who managed to take advantage of connections with the mother church of the diocese. In 1531 he was employed as the priest of one of its chapels and in 1533 was instituted as vicar of St Mary's church in Lichfield market place. Ordained priest in 1504, he had been admitted to membership of the civic gild in 1519 and his links with both cathedral and civic community would have ideally suited him to a benefice, formerly the gild chapel, to which the dean and chapter had so recently won rights of presentation over the bishop.[95] Sampson Byrche was a fellow-member of the Lichfield Gild, having been admitted eight years after being ordained priest to the title of Baswich Priory in 1512. By the time of his institution as vicar of Stretton in 1555 he had been curate of this former chapelry of the royal free chapel of Penkridge for at least twenty-four years.[96] Thomas Bredwall, stipendiary at Stoke and Newcastle in 1531 died seven years later as its vicar[97] and John Underhill was similarly able to take over the vicarage of a former chapel of which he had been curate, being presented as vicar of Ingestre in 1538 by his employers, the fellows of the royal free chapel of Stafford. Having subscribed to the Act of Settlement in 1559 he held the living until his death in 1577.[98] Finally, the promotion of John Collins from curate of Weston-under-Lizard to rector in 1559 was interrupted by a period as chaplain in the neighbouring parish of Blymhill.[99] Evidence from the arch-

---

[92] LJRO, B/A/1/14ii, fos. 171v, 176r, 178v; B/A/17/1(1), fo. 3v; BL, Harleian Ms 594, fo. 139v; SHC 1915, 17, 136. There were Boyer families at Maer and Stoke-on-Trent c.1532: *Families in the Archdeaconry of Stafford*, 44, 53.
[93] LJRO, B/A/17/1(1), fo. 8v; B/A/1/14ii, fos. 45r, 53r, 59r; SHC 1915, 299, 305.
[94] Will of Edmund Bachelor; see appendix.
[95] LJRO, B/A/17/1(1), fo. 14v; B/A/1/14ii, fo. 8r; D.77/1, p. 290; SHC 1915, 171; VCH *Staffs.*, iii, 163; xiv, 138–9.
[96] LJRO, B/A/1/14ii, fos. 78v, 83r, 89v, 99r; D.77/1, p. 294; B/A/17/1(1), fo. 5v; BL, Harleian Ms 594, fo. 140v; SHC 1915, 208, 211.
[97] LJRO, B/A/17/1(1), fo. 4r; P/C/11, series III.
[98] LJRO, B/A/17/1(1), fo. 12v; BL, Harleian Ms 594, fo. 143r; SHC 1915, 132.
[99] LJRO, B/A/17/1(1), fo. 9v; SHC 1915, 31, 313.

deaconry of Leicester in the diocese of Lincoln has demonstrated that the wait for a benefice could be a long one.[100] Among the Staffordshire clergy this was certainly the case for Thomas Bradshaw. In 1531 and 1533 he was a chaplain of the royal free chapel of Wolverhampton as well as holding another stipendiary post in the neighbouring parish of Wombourne. He did not obtain a benefice, the rectory of Hamstall Ridware, until 1562 and died within a year of his institution. Since he had made his will before leaving Wombourne, and had requested burial in the precincts of his parish church, he had probably given up hope of ever obtaining a living.[101]

Stipends and Standards of Living

Even if he were able to obtain formal employment, the amount which a priest could expect to earn had been limited by statute in the fifteenth century which restricted curates to between eight and nine marks and chaplains and other stipendiary clergy to seven. These levels could be reduced further if the clerk were provided with free board and lodging which was sometimes available in the house of the incumbent.[102] There was a growing body of opinion among the ecclesiastical authorities that such levels of pay were inadequate; in 1538 Edward Lee, archbishop of York, asserted that increasing numbers of assistant clergy within his jurisdiction were experiencing financial difficulties.[103] The question of whether large numbers of the unbeneficed clergy faced real hardship turns on whether the statutory limits on remuneration were still being adhered to and, more difficult to determine, the extent to which curates and chaplains were dependent on their stipends for their living. If the majority of assistant clergy were more or less dependent on stipendiary income then the evidence that has been collected for various parts of the country does not allow for much optimism for clerical standards of living. As suggested by the pronouncement of Archbishop Lee, the highest stipends, between £5 and £6 a year, were obtainable in the south-east, although remuneration at the equivalent of 4d a day could hardly be called 'high' and would rank the unbeneficed clergy on an economic par with semi-skilled labourers.[104] Further north, the average salary available in the diocese of Lincoln was just over £5 in the 1520s but was only £4 in the East Riding of Yorkshire, and in 1524 the average stipendiary priest in North Lancashire

---

100 Fuggles, 'Parish Clergy in the Archdeaconry of Leicester', 32. The curate of Burrough-on-the-Hill was without a benefice fifty years after ordination in 1535; even after such a long duration, he would not have been alone.
101 LJRO, B/A/17/1(1), fos. 9v, 10v; BL, Harleian Ms 594, fo. 142v; SHC 1915, 113, 355.
102 Heath, *English Parish Clergy*, 22; Swanson, *Church and Society*, 47–8.
103 Zell, 'Economic Problems', 26.
104 Ibid.; C. Dyer, *Standards of Living in the Later Middle Ages: Social Change in England c.1200–1520* (Cambridge, 1989), 215.

was in receipt of just £2 9s 6d a year. Whilst for the south of the country Michael Zell concluded that many stipends were barely at subsistence level, and a significant number below, Christopher Haigh has argued that some of the unbeneficed clergy in the north-west of England 'were in dire poverty'.[105] Such views have not, however, gone completely unchallenged. Arguing on the basis of the surviving evidence of the Norfolk Muster Rolls, one recent writer has contended that few assistant clergy would have been entirely dependent on their stipends thus allowing a more optimistic assessment of clerical standards of living.[106]

For the diocese of Coventry and Lichfield, as for much of the country, the main sources of available evidence are the returns of the various clerical subsidies and sporadic survival of clerical wills and inventories. The former survive for the archdeaconry of Stafford for the 1531 subsidy and for the diocese as a whole for 1533. With minor exceptions the assessments recorded in these two returns are the same and, in most cases, the earlier document includes a statement of the income that was being taxed. This demonstrates that assessment was based on a calculation of one-fifteenth of salary and, applying this multiplier to the figures in the 1533 return, produces the following spread of stipendiary incomes for the diocese as a whole.[107]

Table 7. Unbeneficed stipends, 1533

Archdeaconry of Coventry		
Stipend	No. of clerks	% of total
Over £5	4	2.8
7 marks	95	66
£4	42	29
4 marks	1	0.7
£2	1	0.7
Archdeaconry of Stafford		
Stipend	No. of clerks	% of total
£5	4	2
7 marks	49	25
£4	117	60
5 marks	24	12

---

105 Zell, 'Economic Problems', 26; ibid., 'Clergy in Kent', 522–3; Haigh, *Reformation and Resistance*, 35.
106 J. Pound, 'Clerical Poverty in Early Sixteenth Century England: Some East Anglian Evidence', *JEH*, 37, no. 3 (1986), *passim*.
107 The following is based on BL, Harleian Ms 594, fos. 116r–154v.

Archdeaconry of Derby

Stipend	No. of clerks	% of total
Over £5	2	1
7 marks	12	8
£4	127	89
5 marks	1	0.7

Archdeaconry of Shrewsbury

Stipend	No. of clerks	% of total
Over £5	2	2
8 marks	6	6
£5	3	3
7 marks	15	15
£4	76	75
5 marks	2	2

Archdeaconry of Chester

Stipend	No. of clerks	% of total
7 marks	53	13
£4	293	72
5 marks	57	14
4 marks	2	0.5

Total for diocese

Stipend	No. of clerks	% of total
Over £5	8	0.8
8 marks	6	0.6
£5	7	0.7
7 marks	224	23
£4	651	66
5 marks	84	9
4 marks	3	0.3
£2	1	0.1

Taken at face value these figures suggest that average stipends in the diocese of Coventry and Lichfield were significantly lower than those available in the diocese of Lincoln and the south-east of the country, and were at a similar level to those paid to the clergy of the East Riding of Yorkshire. Clearly, over a hundred years after the formulation of the statute, salaries of eight and nine marks were still being viewed in terms of *maximum* levels of pay. Furthermore, the majority of the one-fifth of the clerks of the diocese who were paid stipends of seven marks were curates who, unlike assistant chaplains, could have expected the maximum rate of pay; evidence indeed that this was a 'buyer's market'.

The disparities in incomes which have been observed for the country as a whole are also discernible within the diocese. In relative terms those clerks in the south of the diocese fared best, with two-thirds of the assistant clergy in the archdeaconry of Coventry being in receipt of stipends of seven marks. Elsewhere, the majority were being paid £4 which was the amount received by almost the entire formally employed unbeneficed population of the archdeaconry of Derby. The lack of uniformity of rates of pay is also apparent within the archdeaconries themselves. In Warwickshire, the curates of Dunchurch and Knowle were being paid almost £8, an income in excess of some of the incumbents in the county, whilst the curate of St Michael's, Coventry, the vicar of which held one of the wealthiest livings in the diocese, was assessed on an income of £12. By contrast, the fourteen other assistant clergy in the parish were paid only seven marks.[108] Ralph Lister, curate of Norbury in Derbyshire, assessed on an income of £15, was not only the highest paid stipendiary clerk in the diocese, but one of the wealthiest priests in the archdeaconry of Derby. By contrast, Thomas Bowker and Thomas Sydall, chaplains in the Lancashire parish of Eccles were being paid only four marks while their three fellow assistant clergy were in receipt of £4. However, before jumping to an oversimplistic conclusion of a north-south divide, it should be noted that the poorest clerk in the diocese, officially at least, was Thomas Balam, a chaplain in the Warwickshire parish of Hillmorton, the most southerly in the diocese, who was paid just £2 a year. A further note of caution, concerning the exact nature of assessment of the fifteenths, is sounded by evidence relating to stipends found in surviving clerical wills and inventories. In 1533 Henry Marler, a stipendiary clerk in the parish of Holy Trinity, Coventry, was assessed on an income of seven marks but when his property was valued following his death in 1539 it was stated that he was owed 26s 8d for a quarter's wages which, if accurate, would produce an annual salary of £5 6s 8d.[109] Similarly, the Chesterfield chaplain Henry Tryge was assessed on an income of £4 in 1533 but when writing his will ten years later, claimed that he was owed £7 10s in wages for a year and a half, giving an annual stipend of £5. However, in this instance Tryge's bequests in his will of parts of his 'old' and 'new' salary suggest that his level of remuneration might have been renegotiated in the intervening years.[110] Given the greater intervening period, this might also have been the case with Thomas Tunstall, curate of Wolstanton in Staffordshire; whilst in 1533 he was assessed on an income of seven marks, at his death in 1565 he was being paid £8 13s 4d.[111] The inconsistencies in the evidence should not, however, lead us immediately to conclude that statements of income were being distorted

---

108 Other examples from the region of incumbents with apparently low incomes were the vicar of Alspath and the rectors of Baddesley Clinton and Wishaw, who were in receipt of £4, 5 marks and £2 13s 4d respectively.
109 Will of Henry Marler; for details of this and other wills cited, see appendix.
110 Will of Henry Tryge.
111 Will of Thomas Tunstall.

in favour of the stipendiary clerk. Alexander Legh, curate of Ryton-on-Dunsmore, was assessed on an income of seven marks in 1533 but in his will, written five years later, had wages outstanding from a salary of just four marks a year.[112] And whilst such cases certainly argue against taking the subsidy returns at face value, the will of George Gregory, chaplain of Rossendale in the Lancashire parish of Whalley, in which were listed outstanding payments of a salary amounting, again, to just four marks a year, would tend to substantiate the low levels of remuneration available to many of the assistant clergy of the diocese.[113]

One explanation of the discrepancies between stipends as assessed for tax and as appear in wills is that they might be composed from a variety of sources, not all of which found their way into a clerk's assessment or, conversely, into his will. Whilst Thomas Tunstall's stipend appears to have been paid by his rector, the wages outstanding at the death of Alexander Legh were payable by a layman, possibly the farmer of the living, which was a prebend of Lichfield Cathedral. As the priest in charge of the newly-founded chapel of Rossendale, George Gregory was dependent on its lay sponsors for his remuneration. These consisted of six men who appear to have borne several rather than collective responsibility for the composition of the salary, and who owed sums ranging from 9d to 8s 7½d at his death.[114] Part of the salary of the Chesterfield chaplain Henry Tryge was provided by a gild[115] and the list of 313 stipendiary chaplains in the archdeaconry of Chester drawn up in 1542 reveals that 134 (43%) were supported by individual laypeople, 106 (33%) by the incumbent, and 30 (10%) by parish offerings and church funds. A further thirty-seven chaplains did not have the source of their stipends recorded, four were listed as not being in receipt of payment from any source and one, John Sefton at Lymm, was described simply as 'celebrating for souls'. Correlation of this list with that for the diocese of 1533 would suggest a tentative conclusion that the relatively highest paid assistants were curates employed by the incumbent.[116]

As well as occasionally suggesting the problems involved in using subsidy returns as the main source for an assessment of unbeneficed incomes, clerical wills also provide fleeting glimpses into the range of activities by which the assistant clergy might supplement their salaries.[117] For instance, despite the small sample of surviving wills of unbeneficed clergy available for study, it is

[112] Will of Alexander Legh.
[113] Will of George Gregory.
[114] Ibid.
[115] Will of Henry Tryge.
[116] *Clergy in the Diocese of Chester*, xi, 1–18. Those with no stipend were Thomas Hoxleye at Audlem and Robert Wright, Thomas Hughson and William Moile at Warrington; against the name of the latter is the marginal note *apud Estham* which suggests that he might have been supported from receipts of Eastham chapel.
[117] For the use of inventories see above 82, n. 235. For the composition of the sample, and details of individual wills, see appendix.

perhaps significant that about one-fifth either owned or rented property.[118] John Bee, a chantry priest at Uttoxeter, owned the copyhold of two shops in the town, which he bequeathed to a local gentleman, and the copyhold of his garden. John Yate, a priest of Fletchamstead in Warwickshire, also owned a number of tenements which he bequeathed to his nephew in 1549, and which probably account for the large amounts of cash that were listed in his inventory. The Macclesfield chaplain, William Bridges, was also likely to have been involved in renting out property, making reference in his will to 'my tenant's wife'. A number of the chaplains in the Lancashire parish of Prescot owned property. In 1514 Lawrence Latham was one of the lord's tenants who had a licensed undertenant on his land and in the same year John Sherdeley drew up his will, bequeathing the profits of his house to the stock of Our Lady's altar after the death of his mother, who presumably shared it with him. In 1537 Edward Garnett was in possession of a small messuage and garden given to him by his father, and in 1553 two laymen testified before the manorial court that they had witnessed the surrender by the chaplain, Henry Colley, of all his messuages, burgages and lands to the use of a third party. When John Webster drew up his will in 1567 his sister was named as his heir to two messuages in the town which he held in customary tenure.[119] Despite statutory restrictions on the clergy's involvement in such activities,[120] Thomas Tunstall appears to have been quite closely involved with the property market in the Staffordshire parish of Wolstanton of which he was curate. At his death in 1565 he was renting two crofts in the village, one of them appurtenant to a linen shop, for terms of two years. It is likely that Tunstall was himself engaged on a small scale in the wool trade, since among the numerous bequests to his female servant were seven sheep and a substantial quantity of yarn. If so, then he was probably not alone in pursuing such interests. Richard Podmore, curate of Dawley, owned a flock of sixty sheep and their lambs and as well as owning twenty-two sheep outright, William More, a chaplain in the parish of Marchington, also had a share in a small flock owned by a local layman. Thomas Pyxley and Richard Dodycotte, chaplains in the Shropshire parishes of High Ercall and Wroxeter respectively, both owned small flocks of around a dozen sheep, whilst items mentioned in the wills and inventories of other stipendiary clergy also suggest involvement in the wool trade. These include the Chesterfield chaplain Henry Tryge, who owned two pairs of shears and had six pounds of

---

[118] For ownership of property by urban stipendiary clergy see Cross, 'Incomes of Provincial Urban Clergy', 74 and by Lancashire assistant clergy, Haigh, *Reformation and Resistance*, 36.
[119] *Prescot Records*, 79, 90, 123, 132, 168–9. Garnett (described as 'parochial chaplain' in 1549 and 'chaplain' in 1556; ibid., 111, 137) and Colley (as Cowley) were among the stipendiaries listed in 1533, as was Henry Sherdeley, curate, probably a relative of John Sherdeley, of whose will he had been an executor: BL, Harleian Ms 594, fo. 148v.
[120] See above, 84.

refuse wool listed in his inventory, and the curate of the same parish, Richard Whitworth, whose goods included two pairs of shears, four looms and a spinning wheel ('wool wheel'). Clergy might also have been involved in the textile end of the trade, as suggested by the seven yards of kersey, valued at 9s 4d, listed in the inventory of George Gregory, chaplain of Rossendale.

Whilst the testamentary evidence would appear to confirm that the assistant clergy were rarely involved in arable farming on a scale approaching that of their beneficed superiors, ownership of livestock appears to have been fairly common. This could range from the 'red cow and a calf' owned by Alexander Legh to the six cows, ten heifers, a mare, colt and seven pigs that Richard Podmore owned in addition to his flock of sheep, and the six cows, eight bullocks, a calf and five pigs in the possession of William More at his death in 1541. Particularly valuable were the six steers belonging to John Abell, curate of Kingstone, which were worth £11 in total, and the yoke of oxen which Thomas Tunstall hired out to his parishioners;[121] a role that, in secular terms, must have made him hard to distinguish from some of his beneficed colleagues. It is possible that some collections of livestock might have started out as a share of the incumbent's tithe as suggested by the single tithe lamb that was listed among Richard Whitworth's property along with his two cows, two pigs and two hens. On a yet smaller scale of husbandry, though not without the potential to make a useful economic return, were the four hives owned, rather appropriately, by John Bee, and the share in some hives that George Gregory held with a local layman. As in the case of those clergy who owned property, further evidence suggesting that some were involved actively in the market is the substantial sums of cash occasionally listed in their inventories, such as the 15s and £3 13s 0d left at their deaths by Thomas Pyxley and William More respectively.

As well as the possibility that some assistant clergy were supported, in part at least, with a share of the incumbent's tithe, other opportunities existed as a supplement, or alternative, to stipendiary income.[122] Curates might occa-

---

[121] For which he was owed 10s in total from two individuals at the time of writing his will.

[122] Tithe receipts were a potential source of friction between incumbents and their assistants, although there is little evidence of serious discord during the period. However, an incumbent's death might more commonly have brought matters to a head as on the occasion when action was taken by Nicholas Townley, nephew and administrator of the goods of the rector of Wigan of the same name who died in 1532, against the curate, William Astley, for allegedly taking the opportunity provided by his superior's death to steal corn and hay from the parsonage barn. As ever, the two parties' versions of events were wildly divergent; Townley claimed that the curate, aided by 'other riotous persons', 'forcibly and in manner of war with bows, staves, clubs, swords, daggers, and other weapons of war . . . menaced and threatened to beat and ill entreat' him if he tried to get in their way. For his part Astley claimed that he was acting under authority of Richard Smith, the bishop's official, and that 'in a peaceable manner without any weapon they desired the complainant to leave [the corn

sionally have been included among the lessees of farmed benefices and priests serving chapelries were sometimes allowed to retain part of the receipts.[123] Chaplains would frequently have been involved in the education of local boys,[124] as was the curate of Chesterfield, Richard Whitworth, who bequeathed his outstanding school fees to his brother, a fellow-priest. More common would have been the opportunities for performing religious duties such as month's minds and obits. Such bequests were often worth between £5 and £6 a year and were a common feature of both clerical and lay wills of the period.[125] In 1533 Alexander Legh hired a priest 'to sing for the space of half a year and he to have for his wages £3' and three years later Richard Ryve, vicar of South Wingfield, made provision for 'an honest priest to celebrate divine service for my soul and all Christian souls . . . the space of four years £20 at £5 the year' as well as for priests at two neighbouring chapels for a year each at the same rate. Even the more impecunious members of the lay community occasionally left enough for three months' hire or even just one or two masses. Additionally, clergy, and the more substantial laity, such as Lord Mounteagle mentioned above, often allocated sums of money to be given to priests who attended their funerals. Many, if not all, of these clergy would have been officially unemployed, dependent on occasions such as this, and the sporadic offerings of the laity, for their ability to make a living. Other occasional payments may have been made in return for the witnessing of wills, a function performed in some areas almost exclusively by the unbeneficed clergy. Specific mention was sometimes made in the will itself of a local clerk being a particularly trusted acquaintance and gratitude for acts of assistance might be expressed in material terms by a bequest in his favour.[126] At least two of the Prescot chaplains acted as attorneys in the manorial court and draughtsmen of legal documents and one of them, Edward Garnett, sued two laymen in 1552 to recover 5s owed to him 'for services rendered'.[127]

Occasional references in gild records, as well as complaints by bishops, suggest that stipends were sometimes augmented, and unemployed priests completely supported, by entirely secular activities such as labouring and

---

and hay] in the barn until Mr. Smith had been communicated with, William Hasteley at the same time giving a quart of wine to the complainant whom they allege to have departed forthwith "in good manner" '. Astley claimed not to have been aware of the capacity in which Townley was acting and in any case, declared that the bill of complaint was 'insufficient in the law' in that it did not specify a day on which the supposed riot had taken place: a conclusion is not recorded. Bridgeman, *History of the Church and Manor of Wigan*, 96–7. Astley was named as curate in 1533 and assessed on an income of 7 marks; the parsonage was recorded as being in the hands of the executor of M. Nicholas Townley, late rector, and was assessed at £100: BL, Harleian Ms 594, fo. 149r. In 1535 it was valued at £80 13s 4d; *Valor*, iii, 220.

[123] Swanson, *Church and Society*, 47.
[124] Cross, 'Incomes of Provincial Urban Clergy', 75; above, 8.
[125] Zell, 'Clergy in Kent', 523; 'Economic Problems', 27.
[126] Stevens Benham, 'The Durham Clergy', 27–8. For Mounteagle above, 103.
[127] *Prescot Records*, 89, 108, 121, 138.

involvement in crafts and trades.[128] Indeed, perhaps for large numbers of the unbeneficed outside the formal employment structure, their clerical status meant merely that there was something else to which they could turn by way of casual employment An indication of the range of activities in which the assistant parochial clergy might be involved is provided by the churchwardens' accounts of Prescot in Lancashire.[129] Here, Richard Potter, one of seven stipendiary clergy ministering in the parish in the absence of the non-resident vicar, Simon Matthew, features on a number of occasions in the accounts between 1523 and 1537.[130] As well as carrying out the clerical duties required of him as a priest, Potter was one of three churchwardens and thus very active in parish affairs.[131] The period for which the records survive included a dispute between Prescot and its dependent chapel of Farnworth, about three miles distant from the parish church, where the inhabitants were attempting to free themselves from certain financial obligations to the mother church.[132] In 1524 Potter was included in a delegation of laymen who travelled to Chester to hear the proceedings concerning the case in the archdeacon's court and was paid 3s 2d by way of expenses.[133] In the same year the curate of Prescot, Henry Sherdeley, was paid expenses on various occasions for visits both to Farnworth and Chester in connection with the dispute,[134] though none of this work was obviously quite in the same league as that for which the Chesterfield chaplain Henry Tryge was owed £6 14s 2d in 1543. In 1526 Potter was involved in metal-working and carpentry in Prescot church which took him and a layman three days, for which they were paid 8d and 6d for their meals and Potter was paid a further 6d 'for amyng and makyng the *shurges* iij days'.[135] In 1528 and 1529 he received payments of 5s 1d for making wax for church use and in the latter year was paid two shillings for six bushels of lime.[136] In 1530 he received various sums for making wax and candles which in total amounted to over £1[137] and in the same year, another of the stipendiaries, James Traves, was paid 4d for making decorations for the rood screen in the church.[138] In 1533 and 1536 Potter was paid 5s 4d for making candles and, in the latter year, 4d for making 'a pound of weak yarn'. He and the layman with whom he made the candles were paid a further four shillings for food and refreshments while they were

---

[128] Swanson, *Church and Society*, 62.
[129] F.A. Bailey, ed., *The Churchwardens' Accounts of Prescot, Lancashire, 1523–1607*, Transactions of the Lancashire and Cheshire Rec. Soc., 104 (1953).
[130] Ibid., 1–18. On Matthew, see Haigh, *Reformation and Resistance*, 43.
[131] *Churchwardens' Accounts of Prescot*, 2, 10.
[132] Ibid., 3; Haigh, *Reformation and Resistance*, 32.
[133] *Churchwardens' Accounts of Prescot*, 3.
[134] Ibid.
[135] I.e. for making tapers. Ibid., 10.
[136] Ibid., 11–14.
[137] Ibid., 14–15.
[138] Ibid., 15.

undertaking the task.¹³⁹ Although the work in which Richard Potter and other assistant clergy were involved was irregular and not always well paid, these examples demonstrate that we should be wary of taking clerical stipends as a full statement of income and also that their involvement in the life of the parish might go further than the mere performance of their sacerdotal duties.

Other evidence from Lancashire suggests that the augmentation of stipends did not always come from such honest toil. Stephen Smith, curate of Rossendale, was one of a group of three men fined in 1528 for illegal wool trading¹⁴⁰ and in 1530 Robert Fazakerley, curate of Walton, was accused of misappropriating dues owing to his rector Edward Molyneux, in his capacity as rector of the neighbouring parish of Sefton.¹⁴¹ Thomas Kirkby, curate of Halsall, tried a similar ruse in his parish while the rector was away at Oxford University and allegedly further supplemented his income by extortion from dying parishioners. His behaviour so incensed some of the locals that following a sermon he preached on the theme of the souls of the parish 'burning in pain of purgatory and hell' they set fire to his bed chamber.¹⁴² One of the longest cases to be heard before the Lichfield consistory court during this period was that taken by the abbot and convent of Whalley against the chaplain Richard Hayward in 1526. The accusation that he had interfered in the abbey's mortuary rights resulted in twenty-three hearings over a six-month period, but ended inconclusively, with Hayward being pronounced contumacious for his failure to appear for the final sentence. Midway through the case, the chaplain made an appeal to Cardinal Wolsey that it should be heard in a higher court since, due to the powerful position of his accusers, he was unlikely to obtain a fair hearing. Although in this he was unsuccessful, on the grounds that the appeal had been made after sentence had been delivered, at a later stage in the case the Archbishop of Canterbury intervened to prohibit the court from taking any other actions against Hayward.¹⁴³

Set against such income as the unbeneficed clergy could earn (either through conventional means or otherwise) was a similar range of costs of living to that faced by their beneficed superiors. Whilst it is clear from the fiscal evidence that some stipendiaries would have been provided with free board and lodging in *lieu* of salary, such a situation was far from universal and the need to find rented accommodation might even have been the norm.¹⁴⁴ Edward Seaman, a chaplain in the parish of Solihull, for which he received

---

139 Ibid., 16, 18.
140 Haigh, *Reformation and Resistance*, 36. He was not employed in the diocese in 1533.
141 Ibid., 35; for Molyneux's financial affairs see above, 68, 69, 75.
142 Ibid., 35–36.
143 LJRO, B/C/2/1 fos. 91r, 94r, 97v, 102v, 107r, 113r, 117v, 118r, 122v, 126r–v, 129v, 130r, 135r, 139v, 142r, 142v.
144 Heath, *English Parish Clergy*, 141.

an annual stipend of £4, was in arrears for three years' rent of a room in 1529 which he was still renting twelve years later.[145] Prior to his death in 1533 Alexander Legh, curate of Ryton-on-Dunsmore, had been living in the vacant parsonage, the rectors, as canons of Lichfield Cathedral, being non-resident. When his executors drew up his accounts they found that he was in arrears to the amount of 50s comprising outstanding payments to both the previous and current incumbent, part of which had been forgiven by the latter to enable him to pay his contribution to the previous two clerical subsidies. At some stage he had also been living elsewhere since he also owed 6s 8d to a layman for board.[146] In 1542 Robert Heynson, one of two chaplains at Middlewich, was recorded in the subsidy list as having 'a house called a Wich house'.[147] But since unbeneficed clergy seem rarely to have been in possession of their own accommodation they were less commonly burdened than incumbents with the cost of servants. Where these are mentioned in wills they were often boys who would perform light domestic tasks in return for modest remuneration, such as 'Hugh, my boy' to whom the Chesterfield chaplain Henry Tryge left a leather bucket, a mattress, a pair of sheets and a bedspread in 1543; 'Hugh Moore, my boy' who was the recipient of a short gown, a pair of hose, a doublet, a shirt, a bonnet and 6s 8d in cash from John Bee, chantrist of Uttoxeter, in 1555; or 'the boy in the house' who received 4d from Richard Hatton, curate of Shifnal, in 1560. More costly would have been Alice Hall, the servant of the Macclesfield chaplain William Bridges, to whom the bequest of 6s 8d probably represented a part of her wages, but it might be wondered whether the 'Ellyan Fines, my servant' to whom Thomas Tunstall left the greater part of his property in 1565 was more of a companion (and possibly the mother of his children) than a housekeeper.[148]

Whatever their domestic arrangements, by the 1520s all stipendiary clergy were liable to contribute to the ever-increasing number of clerical subsidies, in most cases at the rate of one-fifteenth of salary[149] which meant that two-thirds of the assistant clergy of the diocese had to find 5s 4d[150] from their salaries at regular intervals, and just over one-fifth 6s 2½d. Given the low level of average incomes and the frequency of taxation, and coming as it did on top of other regular outgoings, such demands must have put many stipendiary clergy in a position of real hardship. This might have been the reason for the chaplain William Fisher's refusal to contribute in 1527 which led to his being called before the bishop's consistory court and ultimate

---

[145] BL, Harleian Ms 594, fo. 122v; *Solihull Parish Book 1525–1720*, transcribed by G.L. Bishop, duplicated typescript, Univ. of Birmingham Dept. of Extramural Studies (1977), 5, 40–1.
[146] Will of Alexander Legh; for details of this, and other wills cited, see appendix.
[147] *Clergy in the Diocese of Chester*, 9.
[148] For servants, young and old, see Heath, *English Parish Clergy*, 142. On Tunstall, below, 158, 173.
[149] Heath, *English Parish Clergy*, 24; Bowker, *Henrician Reformation*, 43–4.
[150] BL, Harleian Ms 594, fos. 116r–154v.

excommunication for failure to turn up at any of the hearings.[151] Alexander Legh, curate of Ryton-on-Dunsmore, certainly found himself in difficulty when writing his will in 1533, by which time he had had to borrow the 6s 2½d for the previous two subsidies; on the first occasion from his landlord, the rector of the living, and the second from a layman to whom he incurred a further debt of 6s 8d in costs of legal work undertaken on his behalf.[152]

If the frequency of taxation placed great strain on unbeneficed stipends, the effect was exacerbated by the fact that those stipends were often in arrears, a significant proportion of testators being owed wages at the time of writing their wills. Thomas Tunstall, curate of Wolstanton, was owed 26s for eight weeks' service in 1565 and Alexander Legh, curate of Ryton-on-Dunsmore, and Henry Marler, chaplain of Holy Trinity, Coventry, were both owed a quarter's wages in 1533 and 1539 respectively. George Gregory, chaplain of Rossendale, was owed just over £2 in respect of three quarters' wages in 1548 and Henry Tryge, chaplain at Chesterfield, more than £14 for stipends almost two years in arrears, some of which he allocated to the beneficiaries of his will in 1543. When Henry Malabur, a chaplain in the Derbyshire parish of Lullington, had wages outstanding from consecutive non-resident incumbents in 1531, he took the matter to the consistory court which decided that a settlement should be made of 13s 4d to be shared by the current vicar and the executors of his deceased predecessor. Having won the case, Malabur found alternative employers at the royal free chapel of Stafford.[153] As well as wages, many assistant clergy accumulated debts from members of both lay and clerical communities. In addition to his outstanding salary, George Gregory was owed a total of £2 2s 10d from four laymen and a fellow-cleric and his bequest of 3s 4d to a certain laywoman was stated to be dependent on the recovery of his debts.[154] The £1 14s 4d owed to Richard Dodycotte, chaplain of Wroxeter, represented almost one-third of the total value of his inventory. Under such circumstances, accumulated debts were often written off, such as the £11 6s 8d which the Macclesfield chaplain, William Bridges, forgave to the two individuals concerned; and the Coventry chaplain Thomas Fisher listed only his 'good debts', amounting to £9. Unsurprisingly, many of the unbeneficed ended their lives with debts themselves. The three quarters' wages owed to George Gregory by the chapel reeves of Rossendale were partly offset by the 13s 4d which he owed them; William More, chaplain of Marchington died owing £7 in total to eight laymen of the parish; and the debts of £8 15s 2½d outstanding at the death of Alexander Legh, curate of Ryton-on-Dunsmore in 1533, included

---

[151] LJRO, B/C/2/2, fos. 3r, 4r, 6v. He is not named in the clerical subsidies of the 1530s.
[152] Will of Alexander Legh.
[153] LJRO, B/C/2/3, fo. 142v; B/A/1/14, fo. 42r; BL, Harleian Ms 594, fo. 143r. Malabur had been ordained priest in 1522 to the title of Grace Dieu, Leicestershire, just over the diocesan border from Lullington.
[154] Will of George Gregory.

substantial sums which he had borrowed from laypeople and an advance of 6s 8d on his salary to allow him to make a contribution to new choir stalls in the church. In 1539 a layman of Prescot parish sued the chaplain Henry Colley in the manor legal court for a 14s debt which had been outstanding for eight years.[155] Faced with such problems, it is surprising that Henry Malabur's was the only action for non-payment of salary taken before the Lichfield consistory court during the seven-year period for which its records survive.

Whilst the unbeneficed clergy were likely to have experienced similar fluctuations in their economic fortunes to many incumbents, they were rarely able to attain a comparable standard of living. The nineteen stipendiary priests with surviving inventories in the testamentary sample were all on a similar nominal income, from the £3 6s 8d paid to William More as an assistant in the parish of Marchington to the £4 13s 4d annual stipend earned by six of the group. The average minimum age at the time of writing the will was sixty-three, an age at which some would have passed their period of greatest potential earnings whilst others might have built up their extra-stipendiary income to its maximum. Thus whilst there is little variation in the level of stipends, the value of goods left by these priests ranged from the £18 3s 8d which put the curate of Dawley, Richard Podmore, on a similar standard of living to the average incumbent in the diocese, to the £1 16s 3d that undoubtedly meant that the Chesterfield chaplain Henry Tryge died a poor man.[156] The priests that fared best were those who had managed to secure a curacy and some stock or property. A large proportion of Podmore's inventory was in the form of livestock, corn and hay. The same was true of John Abell, curate of Kingstone, but even so, the fact that £11 of his total inventory of £17 8s 4d was accounted for by his livestock and that otherwise his goods were negligible, suggests that even among the curates, the situation could be quite precarious. Some might have been able to gain a degree of security for the future by the acquisition of a modest pension from the living such as that towards which Richard Bexwyke, curate of Middleton in Lancashire, was owed four marks at his death in 1534. But such cases were likely to have been rare and recognition of their relatively impecunious state at the time of writing their wills is to be found in the generally modest funeral arrangements requested by unbeneficed clergy. Where relatively elaborate obsequies *were* envisaged, such as the 'whole hearse of tapers' that was to burn over the body of Richard Dodycotte, chaplain of Wroxeter, executors might have had difficulty in fulfilling the request; in his case the inventory amounted to only £4 13s 4d, of which about one-third was debts. It is

---

[155] *Prescot Records*, 92.
[156] Most of the urban clerics whose inventories were examined by Claire Cross 'died with very modest assets'; 42% died with goods worth less than £10, and 16% worth less than £5: Cross, 'Incomes of Provincial Urban Clergy', 71, 75.

certainly questionable whether Dodycotte's generous intention of providing a dole of 8d to every cottage in the parish would have been implemented. Henry Tryge's request to be buried under the guttering of the outside wall of the chapel in Chesterfield church where he had sung daily mass was poignantly realistic given the level of his poverty. And whilst a relatively more prosperous priest like William More could probably just about afford the outlay required to carry out his intention to hire a colleague to pray for his soul for a year after his death, others, such as Alexander Legh, burdened with debt in his later years, could afford only six months and most, nothing at all. George Gregory's payment of 3s 4d to a fellow-priest 'to pray devoutly for my soul and all Christian souls' would only have secured a very limited period of service and, together with his bequest towards the repair of the chapel which he had served, might not have been sanctioned at all, given an inventory worth less than £2. There is perhaps no more eloquent testimony to the relative poverty of the majority of unbeneficed priests than the fact that so few of them could make provision for the kind of intercessory services that had been the *raison d'être* of their working lives.

Whilst over half the clergy in the sample had inventories worth less than £10, which would have meant that they were among the less affluent members of the community, five, with goods valued at under £5, would, under statute of 1529, have been officially numbered among the poor and would not have been obliged to make a will at all.[157] The two poorest testators, both with moveable goods worth less than £2, had very few material possessions to their names. In the case of George Gregory, chaplain of Rossendale, apart from his more valuable items (a foal, seven yards of kersey and two hives) they amounted to a mattress, three bedspreads, a few items of clothing and a sack, all described as 'old'. Tryge's most valuable possessions were two brass pots and a skillet worth two shillings in all. Three of these clerks were serving chantries at the time of their deaths and many others in their position must, like the assistant clergy of Prescot, have had to turn to alternative employment on many occasions, if not throughout their working lives; one of the bequests of Richard Hatton, curate of Shifnal, was a 'workday jacket', a somewhat incongruous item of clerical dress. Without obtaining the patronage that could bring a clerk to the attention of a potential employer, opportunities might be few and far between. If all else failed then the unemployed priest could turn up at a funeral such as that of the Uttoxeter chantrist John Bee, in 1555, at which he had promised that doles would be distributed 'amongst priests, clerks *and other poor people*'.[158] But impoverished clergy were certainly not limited to the ranks of the officially unemployed; as well as cases such as those chaplains mentioned above they

---

[157] Vaisey, *Probate Inventories*, 1.
[158] My italics; will of John Bee.

included men like Henry Grange, one of four stipendiary chaplains at Wigan in 1542, against whose name in the margin of the subsidy list was written *pauper*.[159]

A 'Clerical Proletariat'?

What generalisations can be drawn about the place of the unbeneficed clergy in the ecclesiastical structure and their status within broader society? First, it can be said that since they made up the majority grouping within the clerical population they demand greater attention from historians than they have hitherto received. The sheer numbers of clergy working without benefices must have meant that this group formed the main line of contact between the church and its lay members in most parishes in the country. They were usually men who had been born and brought up within the communities they served, and although the evidence suggests that many must have experienced a high degree of insecurity and a need for geographical mobility, a small but significant proportion managed to retain stipendiary posts for most, or all, of their working lives. The majority were ordained to the priesthood and had thus made a full commitment to the clerical profession and could carry out in full the duties demanded of parochial clergy by both the ecclesiastical hierarchy and their lay parishioners. What separated them from their beneficed fellows was not their qualification to act as priests but simply that most would be unable to aspire to the freehold tenure of a benefice and would be dependent on employment as assistants on a fixed stipend, perhaps with occasional supplementary income from the offerings of parishioners and casual secular employment.[160] Possession of a benefice could only be gained by attracting the attention of a patron, a process which in turn was facilitated by the acquisition of a university degree, and whilst orders were not a significant divide between the holders of livings and the unbeneficed, education was. For those without such intellectual attainments, employment mobility was likely to be geographical but not economic. No more than 15% of the stipendiary clergy were successful in the clamour to obtain benefices, and a significant proportion of those who were seem to have benefited from earlier employment within a collegiate institution through which they would either have been more visible in the patronage market, or, more directly, presented to a benefice by the institution itself. The presence of a higher concentration of collegiate foundations in the archdeaconry of Stafford than in other parts of the diocese perhaps exaggerates the stipendiary's chances of obtaining a benefice, which were likely to have been lower elsewhere.

159 *Clergy in the Diocese of Chester*, 14.
160 It has been suggested that 'an artificial bottleneck in clerical preferment, with a consequent artificial surplus of junior or less socially privileged clergy, has been a pretty constant feature of Church history': Aveling, 'The English Clergy, Catholic and Protestant', 81.

In recent historiography, the unbeneficed clergy have been generally viewed as a sub-class within the ecclesiastical hierarchy and have often been referred to as a 'clerical proletariat'. If the term is to be used generally to denote the sheer numbers working as hired assistants relative to the minority with the legal status of a benefice, then it is obviously applicable. In terms of standards of living too, the definition would usefully describe the major difference between the two groups of clergy, those with a degree of economic security and the mass of those without; an economically disadvantaged group, who, in the words of one recent commentator, would have been 'living if not from hand to mouth, then from death to death, literally singing for their suppers'.[161] However, the term has also acquired a somewhat pejorative connotation to suggest a basic inability of the unbeneficed clergy to perform the tasks required of them. Such a sense was eloquently conveyed by Christopher Haigh when describing the large-scale emigration from Lancashire of the most academically qualified clergy, leaving the pastoral care of its sprawling parishes to 'the dregs of the clerical proletariat'.[162] There is no reason to believe, however, that without having spent seven years in the study of civil or canon law the unbeneficed clergy would have been less able to provide both a sacramental and pastoral service to their parishioners. If they lacked any specific training it might have been in expository skills, though it has been shown that a great number of self-training manuals were produced in the fifteenth and early sixteenth centuries specifically to meet the requirements of the unsupervised curate or chaplain. Such an output of material is itself an indication of the importance of the unbeneficed clergy, not only in terms of numbers but also in that they shouldered the major burden of pastoral care within the parishes of later-medieval and early-Tudor England.[163] The definition of a 'clerical proletariat' does not therefore need to be framed in a wholly negative or derogatory sense. The unbeneficed clergy of County Durham in the late fifteenth and early sixteenth centuries, for example, have been shown to have been integral members of the communities they served. The fact that they were often entrusted with the care of the children of dead parishioners and featured in a significantly higher proportion of their parishioners' wills than did incumbents, is testimony to the greater closeness of their presence within the community.[164] Though many of the men who served in the parishes on low salaries and dependent on the goodwill of the laity would have been neither of high social status nor among an academic élite, they would nonetheless have been close to the needs and concerns of the communities within which they had been raised.

---

161 Swanson, *Church and Society*, 62.
162 Haigh, *Reformation and Resistance*, 41.
163 McHardy, 'Careers and Disappointments', 120.
164 Stevens Benham, 'The Durham Clergy', 11, 14, 27–8.

4

Priests and People

I. The Clerical Community

Priesthood and Status

At a time when such a high proportion of the adult male population was in holy orders, what did it mean to be a priest? This question needs to be put in two ways: how was priesthood understood by the individual ordained cleric, and how was it perceived by both wider clerical and lay society? The nature of surviving source material tends to create an imbalance in favour of the second component of the question. There was certainly no shortage at this time of eager apologists of priesthood.[1] John Fisher's defence of the priesthood was based on a traditional 'three estates' concept of the priest as defender of his flock, simultaneously mirroring the ministry of Christ himself and the assumed role of the secular élite as defenders of the common people from their enemies. Thus the priest was the first line in the defence of the people's faith who was to provide the weapons to protect them from falling into sin and, potentially worse, doctrinal error. This notion of the priesthood at the top of the hierarchical pyramid, the basis of which was as much traditionally feudal as 'Hildebrandine',[2] was taken up eagerly by other apologists and numerous lesser contemporary writers. The writers of some of the most popular preaching aids for the clergy encouraged the notion that since through his sacramental power the priest could be seen as 'the maker of his Maker' he was thus 'more blessed than angels' and 'higher than kings'.[3] John Colet's strident attacks on the failings of many of the new generation of

---

[1] Marshall, *Catholic Priesthood*, 117.
[2] Swanson, 'Problems of the Priesthood', 864.
[3] Marshall, *Catholic Priesthood*, 117–18. The concept of the priest as 'maker' of Christ is not, as is sometimes supposed, a development of the later Middle Ages. Jerome wrote of the men who 'with hallowed lips make (*conficiunt*) the Body of Christ' which he elaborated as meaning that 'on the occasion of the prayers [of the priests] the Body and Blood of Christ are brought into being': J.H. Crehan, 'Medieval Ordinations', in Jones, Wainwright, Yarnold, eds, *The Study of Liturgy*, 330.

clergy should be seen within this context; his own view of priests as 'higher than emperors' carried with it a virtually unattainable level of expectation.[4]

So how were such elevated concepts to be translated into the practical experience of the individual priest? Certainly a formal separation from the temporal world was implicit in the process of ordination. The conferring of the tonsure, by which the 'crown' of the head was shaved, and was to remain so, had been seen by Aquinas as symbolic of a simultaneous transfer of 'royal' dignity.[5] The new priest was also expected to dress henceforth in a distinctive manner by which his status would be readily distinguishable, and in English tradition he was to be addressed by the courtesy title of 'Sir', reinforcing the deliberate association of priesthood with knighthood. Just as the secular knight was expected formally to pledge his service to the chivalric ideal, the ordinand took his vow of celibacy, which perhaps most conspicuously marked his separation from the concerns of the temporal world. However, there were bound to have been problems in a highly status-conscious society associated with the attribution of quasi-chivalric characteristics to a group of men which, by its very numbers, could no longer be viewed as a *de facto* élite in the same way as the secular aristocracy. The priesthood of the early sixteenth century comprised men from probably the full range of social backgrounds. In terms of income, as we have seen, the typical parish priest was often a man of no greater means than the majority of his parishioners[6] and was often involved in the same elementary methods of gaining that income from the land. Problems of status were further compounded by the strict hierarchy which existed within the clerical body itself, most particularly between those with tenure of a living, and the unbeneficed. The nature of the surviving evidence allows us little opportunity to discern whether the elevated status of priests expounded by the apologists was reflected in high levels of deference, applied either collectively or individually. The reverse side of the coin is a commonplace of Reformation history; the defamatory words and occasional physical assaults that emerge from the records of both the ecclesiastical and secular courts, and the denunciations of priesthood itself by those who were determined on undermining it. However, given that on average only two cases of defamation between lay and clerical parties were brought each year to the Lichfield consistory court between 1524 and 1531,[7] and that even the celebrated band of Coventry heretics in 1511 had little to say against priests *per se*, even such apparently negative evidence needs to be kept in perspective.[8]

The convenience of defining clerical status in terms of sacramental and sacerdotal function was that it served to remove some of the ambiguities that

---

4   Swanson, 'Problems of the Priesthood', 864.
5   Marshall, *Catholic Priesthood*, 109.
6   Ibid., *Pastoral Ministry in the East Riding*, 19.
7   All of the fourteen cases between these dates appear to have been swiftly settled out of court: Cooper, 'Secular Clergy', 167.
8   Fines, 'Heresy Trials', *passim*.

existed among a body of men drawn from disparate social backgrounds. Just as the church authorities taught that (whatever the laity might occasionally believe) a bad priest was still a priest, so a priest who was once the son of an agricultural labourer was still a priest. But this was not to say that more refined notions of status could not simultaneously operate. Occasionally, for example, it would appear that the pseudo-chivalric form of address was deliberately parodied so as to make social distinctions which transcended the uniform concept of priesthood.[9] The evidence here, however, is almost exclusively one-sided; whilst we occasionally hear of laypeople denigrating clergy as their social inferiors, evidence of priests enforcing their status in secular terms is rare if, indeed, it survives at all. What little we can say in this regard comes from testamentary statements made towards the end of their lives, and in particular when discussing their funeral and burial arrangements.[10] The majority of the priests in the testamentary sample requested burial in the east end of their churches, in death as in life, defining their status in terms relative to the sacrament of the altar. If their graves were to be covered with a physical memorial, evidence rarely survives of its form, or whether the degree of ostentation was related to size of income. Nominally at least, Richard Ryve, vicar of South Wingfield, was one of the poorer incumbents in the diocese when his living was assessed at just £6 13s 4d in 1535. Yet when he drew up his will in the following year he requested that his grave in the chancel of the church 'be covered with a stone of alabaster with letters graven upon it' though if the 3s 4d that Ryve left towards his funeral expenses included payment for the memorial then it would have been a relatively simple affair. When William Bridges had drawn up his will in the previous year he had something more elaborate in mind for his memorial, requesting that his 'executors do cause a free stone of mason work to be laid upon my grave, with the image of a priest graduate master of grammar made of laten to be set in the same stone and a chalice of the same, with the text ascending from him *Pro passione et cruore tua libere me D[omi]ne Jesu Criste*'. From his will it appears that Bridges was a master at Macclesfield school and relatively high status undoubtedly accrued from this position as well as from his degree; as a stipendiary priest of Macclesfield on an annual salary of £4 he would otherwise have been remembered to posterity as a humble member of the 'clerical proletariat'. John Wells, a Coventry priest probably employed by one of the city gilds, would also be placed in this category, yet his funeral arrangements were the most elaborate among the sample. Explicit recognition of the intimate connection between his status and function was expressed through his request, in 1539, to be buried in the choir of his church (probably Holy Trinity) 'before the desk that the clerks sing at daily' and his sense of belonging to a wider community of clergy is

---

9 Marshall, *Catholic Priesthood*, 109, 196–7.
10 For details of wills see appendix.

reflected in the further stipulation that all the secular priests of Coventry 'fetch me to the church and sing and say dirge and commendations for my soul and all Christian souls in the choir'. A good turnout was to be encouraged by a bequest of 4d to those present at the funeral and a further 4d to those who accompanied the cortege to church. His elaborate obsequies were also to involve twelve children carrying wax tapers in a funeral procession further augmented by members of three of the main craft gilds. It may have been that the elaborate ritual of Wells' funeral was partly a reflection of his association with the gilds; however, a fellow Coventry priest, Thomas Fisher, for whom a similar association is suggested by his request for burial in the Cappers' chapel in St Michael's church, asked in the following year simply to be 'buried as convenient'.

Like Wells and Fisher, the majority of parish clergy asked to be buried in, or adjacent to, the church in which they had worked. An exception was Ralph Tatton, rector of Barlborough, who requested in 1534 that his 'simple body . . . be buried in the monastery of the Blessed Trinity in Repton near the chapel of [St] Mary [of] Pity' and left 10s for the prior and convent to say mass and dirige on the day.[11] Otherwise, the parish church and its cemetery were the usual choice of burial site, with exact location being largely a reflection of the status of the priest within the clerical hierarchy. Where a beneficed priest was not buried within his chancel or elsewhere in the church he might, like Richard Rylay, rector of Swarkestone, ask to be interred in the churchyard 'at the chancel end', and the request of John Smyth, vicar of Shilton, in 1543, to be buried in the churchyard 'where it shall happen me to take my end', was relatively unusual. For the unbeneficed, who often experienced greater proximity to the laity in life, the same was often to be true in death. Sometimes the association with the non-clerical part of the church might have been quite deliberate, as in the case of Alexander Legh, curate of Ryton-on-Dunsmore, whose body was to be buried in the churchyard 'directly before the west door'; or Henry Marler, the chaplain of Holy Trinity, Coventry, who wanted his grave to be 'under the great stone afore the holy water stoop at the west church door'. One of the more unusual burial requests among the unbeneficed clergy seems in its precision to be deliberately self-conscious of low status. Henry Tryge, a stipendiary of Chesterfield, directed his executors that his body 'be buried at the guttering in of the little porch of the south aisle [of his church] so it be not within it'. John Yate, a priest at Fletchamstead, writing his will in the second year of Edward's reign, asked simply for 'Christian burial where it shall please my executors to bury me'. Yet, in the final analysis, the terms in which priests perceived their own status remain problematic.[12] For example, when, in 1539, Thomas Pyxley, a stipendiary chaplain of High Ercall, requested

[11] See below, 153 and n. 89.
[12] John Sherdeley, a chaplain at Prescot, Lancs., requested burial in the chancel in 1514: *Prescot Records*, 132.

burial in his church after first being 'brought home according to my degree' there is a clear implication that his executors would know what was intended. But at our distance in time we can be less certain that he was thinking in terms of his generic status as a priest, his relative place in the clerical hierarchy, or his standing in society as a whole.

Sacramental Priesthood

Since a status definition of priesthood in essentially secular terms was open to such potential ambiguity it was by his sacramental function that the priest was most clearly distinguished from the lay community within which he lived. The first part of John Mirk's widely-used manual for parish priests was devoted to an exposition of the contrast between the good and bad priest – the former celebrated mass every day and conducted himself in a pious manner, whilst the latter neglected the cure of souls for a worldly interest in his benefice.[13] Significantly this passage, together with material more specifically concerned with the sacramental role, was copied into the surviving commonplace book of a York priest, Robert Burton, dateable to c.1478, the type of working notebook that would doubtless have been in the possession of many parish clergy in the early sixteenth century.[14] Yet even in this most elementary distinction the boundaries were not firmly drawn. Ownership of vestments and liturgical equipment, the basic necessities for the performance of the sacraments, is indicated in only about one-third of the sample wills and inventories, supporting the contention that such items were commonly the property of the parish church and the laypeople responsible for its upkeep, and perhaps indicative of a deliberate subordination of the sacerdotal to the communal in a society witnessing increasing self-confidence at parochial level.[15] The most common item in the possession of priests was the surplice, which is mentioned in seven wills. John Fitzherbert, vicar of Doveridge, left his to a fellow priest and the bequest by John Wells, stipendiary priest of St Michael's, Coventry, of his 'best surplice' to a colleague at Bablake College, is further evidence that this was the most basic item of clerical dress. Otherwise, references to vestments are few and far between and their frequent association with the church rather than the priest himself gains further support from the will of John Smyth, vicar of Shilton, who left his cope and other vestments to a church (not his own) 'for to serve God

---

[13] D.B. Foss, 'John Mirk's "Instructions for Parish Priests" ', SCH, 26, 132.
[14] R.M. Haines, 'A York Priest's Notebook', in R.M. Haines, *Ecclesia Anglicana: Studies in the English Church of the Later Middle Ages* (Toronto, 1989), 161, 172.
[15] Marshall, *Catholic Priesthood*, 201; perhaps there is also a slight suggestion that the secular origins of ecclesiastical vestments had not entirely been lost sight of. See W.J. Grisbrooke, 'Vestments', in Jones, Wainwright, Yarnold, eds, *The Study of Liturgy*, 489.

with as long as they will last'. Other items that feature on single occasions include an amice, rochet, and the stole which Ralph Tatton, rector of Barlborough, left to a fellow priest; and the 'priest's cap', which was listed in the inventory of the Manchester priest Robert Bryddocke, was likely to have been a 'corinal' or skull cap, a common enough item of priestly attire and probably what was meant by the 'cardinal hat' in the possession of the Derbyshire chantrist Richard Asche. Liturgical equipment and books appear to have been similarly rare possessions.[16] A chalice, together with paten, cruets and corporal case, was among the items left by Ralph Wendon to the church of Sutton Coldfield of which he had been rector, and chalices, both worth a little over £2, were owned by Thomas Alen, rector of Kingswinford and Richard Smyth, rector of Kirk Ireton. Richard Rylay, rector of Swarkestone, left his paten to a fellow priest. A more unusual item was the portable altar bequeathed by Richard Webb, rector of Stapleton, to a colleague.[17] Ralph Wendon's bequest to his church of Sutton Coldfield included one of the rare indications of ownership of service books, in the antiphoner and hymnal that he left to the choir. Richard Smyth was the only priest with a mass book, worth 3s, listed in his inventory. The more commonly-owned book was the breviary, or *porteus*, which featured in three wills; John Wells left two to a colleague and Thomas Pyxley left his 'great portices' to the church of High Ercall where he had been a stipendiary chaplain.

All priests were subject to certain canonical obligations, and restraints, regarding their prime sacerdotal duties. They were to keep the canonical hours in the church or chapel to which they were attached, to say or sing the antiphons to the Virgin Mary, and to conduct ritual processions as required. Whilst a daily mass was not required by canon law, parish communities increasingly expected it of their curates.[18] However, despite the seemingly insatiable demand for intercessory masses that followed from this, celebration of the Eucharist more than once a day was expressly forbidden by canon law, as the chaplain John Fald was reminded at a consistory court hearing in 1526.[19] As an unbeneficed priest it might have been the need for extra income which had led him to saying two masses in a single day. In any case, in his defence he showed the court a document purporting to be a dispensation from Cardinal Wolsey allowing him to act in breach of the canon, so long as it was with the consent of the rector of his parish. However, after making comparisons with other specimens the judge declared the document, which was dated Westminster and carried a copy of the cardinal's seal, to be a forgery, and ordered Fald to attend at a subsequent hearing to give reason

---

[16] No doubt in part this simply reflects the small size of the sample; contrast the evidence for late-medieval Norwich where liturgical books were common features of clerical wills. Tanner, *The Church in Late Medieval Norwich*, 37.

[17] Described as a 'super altar', suggesting use on top of a permanent, but unconsecrated, altar.

[18] Heath, *English Parish Clergy*, 4.

[19] LJRO, B/C/2/1, fos. 70v, 74r.

why he should not be punished accordingly. It is difficult to think of any potential advantage other than the pecuniary that might have led to such an elaborate attempt to deceive the church authorities; in the same year two chaplains, perhaps similarly motivated, were cited by the abbot of Whalley for celebrating mass in an unlicensed chapel within its jurisdiction.[20]

Yet whatever else the laity expected of their priests, all the evidence suggests that conscientious performance of the sacraments was of the greatest importance[21] and it is likely that such men were doing no more than responding to public demand. The explicit reason why the parishioners of Tideswell complained about the absenteeism of their vicar, Edmund Eyre, in 1529, was that they were not able to receive Communion.[22] In his defence, Eyre showed the dean and chapter of Lichfield, the appropriators of the living, his papal dispensation for non-residence on condition that the parish was served by one priest and a subdeacon while he was resident, and an additional priest during periods of absence. He had certainly complied with these terms by 1533 when the parish was served by four supernumerary clergy, including an assistant curate, and of whom three were definitely in priest's orders.[23] Unless the stipendiary clergy in the parish were as derelict in their duty as the vicar, there is thus no reason why the parishioners should not have been able to receive the Eucharist; perhaps the case emphasises the importance of parish Communion in that the parishioners expected to receive it from the man formally charged with the cure of their souls rather than one of his assistants. Certainly the Coventry heretics, whose main error in 1511 was their denial of the real presence, would appear to have held a minority view, and their secret words which included the exhortation 'may we all drink from this cup', rather than being a parody of the Mass,[24] are perhaps suggestive of the very popularity of the collective and inclusive nature of Communion which might, even among the orthodox, have occasionally bordered on utraquism.[25] Perhaps more typical were the sentiments which lay behind a dispute between Henry Kimberley, a parishioner of Newton Regis, and his rector, William Leson. Escalating friction between the two had led to a court order in 1529 for the layman to show due reverence to his priest and certainly not to disturb him in the chancel, which he

---

[20] Ibid., fos. 84r, 102r.
[21] A large section of Robert Burton's notebook deals with the priest's preparations in advance of celebration, conduct and frame of mind during the course of it, and sacramental matters more generally: Haines, 'A York Priest's Notebook', 160.
[22] LJRO, D. 30/4, fo. 59v.
[23] BL, Harleian Ms 594, fo. 128v.
[24] Fines, 'Heresy Trials', 166; J.A.F. Thomson, *The Later Lollards 1414–1520* (Oxford, 1965), 115.
[25] The inclusion of an exposition, in verse, of the doctrine of transubstantiation in Robert Burton's notebook suggests that parish clergy were expected to be able to expound its underlying basis to the laity, albeit in a necessarily simplified form: Haines, 'A York Priest's Notebook', 173.

was only to enter to receive Communion. Three years later Kimberley was back in court again, accusing his rector of denying him not only access to the chancel but to the sacrament itself.[26]

Apart from the Eucharist, the sacramental role of the priest which brought him into closest contact with his parishioners was that of confessor.[27] Whilst celebration of the Eucharist brought priest and people into greatest collective contact, the sacrament of confession brought the parties together as individuals.[28] It was thus an area which required the utmost discretion and sensitivity, an issue which was reflected in the numerous manuals that existed to assist the priest in this regard.[29] However, it also had the unique quality of being the only sacrament that was in essence a private matter and, in consequence, it is one sphere of priestly activity concerning which we have very little information. All laypeople were obliged to confess, in preference to their parish priest, at least once a year, traditionally in advance of taking Communion at Easter.[30] That it was an obligation willingly undertaken is suggested by the fact that the absenteeism of William Seller, curate of Pendle, was reported to the authorities precisely on account of his failure to hear confessions; his subsequent failure to attend a disciplinary hearing resulted in his suspension from celebration of Mass and, presumably, further cause for grievance among the lay people in his charge.[31] It is certainly remarkable that very few complaints were made by lay people concerning confessional practice. The parishioners of Bickenhill and Walsall complained in 1525 that unwarranted penance was being imposed by their priests following confession[32] and a more serious charge, that of revealing the contents of confession, was made against William Whittington, vicar of Mancetter, in the same year. Whilst he attempted to deny

---

[26] LJRO, B/C/2/1, fo. 61v; B/C/2/2, fos. 43v, 45v. Whilst such an incident is perhaps indicative of nothing more than the spilling over of a dispute of an essentially secular nature into the ecclesiastical domain, it might reflect the heightened level of tension that surrounded the moment of elevation by this period. Having been introduced in the 13th century to provide emphasis for the moment of consecration, by the later Middle Ages it had 'attracted all the ceremonial resources of the [church]'. The elevation 'became for the west what the Great Entrance had been for centuries in the east: the focal point of popular devotion, and the ceremonial high-spot of the rite': H. Wybrew, 'The Setting of the Liturgy: Ceremonial', in Jones, Wainwright, Yarnold, eds, *The Study of Liturgy*, 436.

[27] It has been argued that an important theological development of the later Middle Ages was a decline in importance of the role of the priest as confessor relative to that of celebrant: J. Hughes, *Pastors and Visionaries: Religion and Secular Life in Late Medieval Yorkshire* (Woodbridge, 1988), 160–2.

[28] As such it was likely to have 'made great emotional, spiritual and intellectual demands on ordained clergy': Hughes, *Pastors and Visionaries*, 88.

[29] Foss, 'John Mirk's "Instructions for Parish Priests"', 137–8; Haines, 'A York Priest's Notebook', 156; Marshall, *Catholic Priesthood*, 5–8.

[30] Marshall, *Catholic Priesthood*, 11–13.

[31] *Ecclesiastical Court of Whalley*, 175–6, 191.

[32] LJRO, B/C/2/1, fo. 14v.; B/C/2/2, fos. 4v, 6v.

specific charges of revelation, he was forced to admit that some of his parishioners were under the impression that they were being charged for their confessions, and acknowledged that their general reluctance to confess to him resulted from his poor reputation amongst them.[33]

In contrast to the secrecy of the confessional, the very nature of the sacrament of matrimony required a public and highly visual act in which even the priest himself was essentially a witness to a sacrament performed by the parties themselves. The importance of openness is emphasised by the citation of the chaplain James Roberts in 1517 for conducting a clandestine marriage ceremony in the new and undedicated chapel of Rossendale. He was given one week to clear himself of the charge through the compurgation of three priests and three honest men of the vicinity.[34] Two priests were charged on the same day in 1528 with failure to follow the correct banns procedure. John Wilkins, rector of Little Packington, was alleged to have solemnised marriage between a couple from outside the parish without the proper reading of banns and further, in the knowledge of evidence that the woman involved was already married. He was ordered to attend a further hearing, bringing with him both the woman and her certificate of licence to marry; a record of the following session does not, however, survive.[35] The other case, involving Henry Chorlton, a chaplain of Wellington, demonstrates the seriousness with which the authorities viewed such offences. Found guilty of conducting a marriage without following the correct banns procedure he was sentenced, on the subsequent feast of the Assumption, to carry a cross in procession around the cemetery of the church and had a further act of penance commuted to the payment of 6s 8d in two instalments to go towards the rebuilding of the cathedral choristers' house and other charitable purposes.[36] If the motivation behind Chorlton's transgression was the augmentation of his income then it cost him dear.

Defenders of Faith

In addition to the sacramental obligations imposed on the parish priest he was required to instruct his parishioners in the faith at least four times a year. That this role was seen as subordinate to the sacramental, however, is supported by abundant evidence that the laity were more likely to complain of lack of sacramental provision than failure to fulfil preaching obligations.[37]

---

[33] Ibid., B/C/2/1, fos. 66v–67r, 111v, 121r; B/C/2/2, fos. 43r, 44v.
[34] *Ecclesiastical Court of Whalley*, 52.
[35] LJRO, B/C/2/3, fos. 18v, 24r.
[36] Ibid., B/C/2/1, fos. 70v, 74r; B/C/2/3, fos. 20r–v.
[37] Swanson, 'Problems of the Priesthood', 847–8; Ibid., 'Chaucer's Parson', 71, 75–77; Marshall, *Catholic Priesthood*, 90–1. However, despite the predominance of liturgical material in Robert Burton's notebook, summaries of belief, evidently designed for catechetical purposes, also feature: Haines, 'A York Priest's Notebook', 161, 169–70.

More commonly, allegations concerning the paucity of preaching were made by the ecclesiastical establishment itself, typified by the claim of Archbishop Lee of York, in 1535, that no more than a dozen parochial clergy within his jurisdiction possessed the capacity to preach.[38] Of course we have little way of knowing the standards by which preaching ability was judged, but it is probable that such criticism went hand in hand with the call by many senior administrators for a greater number of graduate clergy. Whilst it would appear that, on average, only about 25% of the parish clergy were graduates during this period, it is likely that rather more than this had at least spent some time at university, and the growing proliferation of elementary education at the local level would tend to suggest that claims of widespread clerical ignorance were perhaps exaggerated by members of the intellectual élite. Certainly a decree of the convocation of 1530 expected that parish priests should spend two or three hours, three times a week, in studying scripture or the church fathers following the completion of the divine office.[39] In the absence of direct evidence of either intellectual attainment or preaching activity, historians have traditionally relied on the indirect evidence of ownership of books that emerges from clerical wills and inventories. However, the danger of making a simple equation between the citation of books in wills, ownership of books and level of education is highlighted by observations such as that the headmaster of Eton had no books in his will, that books might have been bequeathed before the drawing up of wills and that the lack of an itemised list might be a reflection of the large scale of a personal collection rather than the opposite.[40]

Bearing in mind the need for caution, what general conclusions can be drawn concerning the intellectual interests and expository potential of the parish clergy of the diocese from the evidence of surviving wills? First, just under half the sample have books mentioned in either, or both, of their wills and inventories, which compares with evidence from other parts of the country. However, the bequest by the curate of Chesterfield, Richard Whitworth, to his brother (a fellow-priest) of 'other my books' without any others being mentioned in either his will or inventory, does tend to support the possibility that they were often disposed of in advance of will-making. Indeed, where books are not specified by name it might be that they are the remnants of a collection rather than a full statement of ownership during a

---

38 Marshall, *Catholic Priesthood*, 96.
39 Orme, *English Schools in the Middle Ages*, 12.
40 Nicholas Bradbridge, doctor of theology, chancellor of Lincoln, 1512: 'It is inconceivable that he owned no books, yet his will does not mention them'; Bowker, *Secular Clergy*, 53–4. Similarly, the inventory of a Norwich testator during this period included a large collection of books, none of which were mentioned in his will, reinforcing the point that neither wills nor inventories, and certainly neither on their own, are fully reliable guides to either ownership of books or, by extension, intellectual interests or capacity: Tanner, *Church in Late Medieval Norwich*, 37. See also Marshall, *Catholic Priesthood*, 89, n. 20.

priest's working life. Outright statements in wills and inventories such as 'all his books' are rare but we might conclude in the case of M. John Reed, vicar of Melbourne, where they were valued at 6s 8d that his collection was, at least by the end of his life, not a large one, as compared to, say, those of John Smyth, vicar of Shilton, who owned books worth 40s at the time of his death. Low value of collections is frequently implied by such formulae as 'certain old books' or the even more prosaic 'two horse locks, books, a pair of mittens [and] two pots' which were collectively valued at 11s in the will of John Holwaye, rector of Hinstock. However, in the case of the inventory of Robert Barefote, vicar of Mancetter, the 'other old books written, nothing worth' were in contrast to his eleven specified volumes, though no value is given for either part of the collection.[41]

As for the type of books that were owned, the need for caution regarding statements made on the basis of testamentary evidence alone is emphasised by the case of Ralph Wendon, rector of Sutton Coldfield. Despite being one of only four known graduates in the sample group, and the undoubted size of the collection of books which he bequeathed to a single individual, no volumes are specified by name, mention being made only of 'all the books that were sent me from Exeter and also my other books here and at Oxford . . . and my books here at Sutton'. Edmund Bachelor, rector of Sheinton, would also appear to have had a sizeable collection though they are listed simply as 'sundry books as well of holy scripture as others'. Only two priests have collections of more than one volume itemised. That of Robert Barefote reflects a variety of interests and uses and represents what might have been the typical working library of a parish priest. He should clearly have been well versed in scripture as the owner of a four-volume bible with interlinear gloss and a separate commentary, probably on the Epistles. When faced with questions of canon law he could turn to his volume of Lyndwood's *Provinciale* and a work called *Sextus Decretalum*.[42] His role as confessor would have been aided by his ownership of a copy of the *Summa Angelica*[43] and questions of Latin by the *Ortus Vocabulorum*, a Latin/English dictionary attributed to the fifteenth-century English Dominican Geoffrey the Grammarian.[44] Problems

---

41 Sometimes books were assessed in inventories simply in terms of size, and a Leicestershire priest appears to have valued his collection as the equivalent of 12 sheep: Cross, 'Incomes of Provincial Urban Clergy', 70; Fuggles, 'Parish Clergy in the Archdeaconry of Leicester', 30.
42 For a summary of the work of William Lyndwood (c. 1375–1446) see J. Hughes, 'The Administration of Confession in the Diocese of York in the Fourteenth Century', in D.M. Smith, ed., *Studies in Clergy and Ministry in Medieval England*, Borthwick Studies in History, 1 (1991), 104. For collections of decrees see Tanner, *Church in Late Medieval Norwich*, 37.
43 In full, the *Summa de Casibus Conscientie* by the fifteenth-century Italian Franciscan, Angelo de Chivasso: Tanner, *Church in Late Medieval Norwich*, 40.
44 Ibid., 37. The notebook of the York priest, Robert Burton, included exercises in grammar and etymology: Haines, 'A York Priest's Notebook', 160.

of a more secular nature were probably the subject of a book called *Formulare Instrumentorum* and further evidence that Barefote was a man of some learning, and had wider interests than those of his immediate calling, comes from his ownership of a volume of the works of Sallust, together with commentary. An interesting omission from this collection, which of itself might paradoxically suggest a man of no little erudition, was one of the collections of prepared sermons often castigated by the humanists as a very hindrance to inspired preaching. These included the *Sermones Discipuli* 'a book bequeathed more frequently than the bible'[45] though it is mentioned by name by only one of the sample testators, William Brewster, vicar of Etwall, the other priest to have a collection individually itemised. As well as the *Sermones* his collection included two bibles (one large and one small), a concordance and a commentary on the Epistles. However, further evidence that caution should be exercised in any analysis of the ownership of books by parish clergy comes from the note in his will that over half of his collection was actually on loan from a priest at his former parish to whom the volumes were to be returned after his death. Two other priests, the Chesterfield stipendiary Henry Tryge, and Thomas Wylson, vicar of Abbots Bromley, owned collections of sermons, which in Wylson's case was that on saints' lives by the thirteenth-century archbishop of Genoa, James of Voragine, which formed the basis of the *Golden Legend*, one of the most popular works of its type among clergy and laity alike.[46] Another popular work of which Wylson had a copy was Ludolph of Saxony's *Vita Christi*, which also featured in the will of John Fitzherbert, vicar of Doveridge. One reason why many parish priests did not have large collections of books listed in their wills is that, in many cases, they probably used copies in the possession of the church, such as the nine works listed in an inventory taken by the churchwardens of Walsall in 1516.[47] Some of these parish collections might have originated in bequests made by individual clergy, such as that of a copy of St Augustine's exposition of the psalms made by the Chesterfield chaplain Henry Tryge to his church in 1543. Taken as a whole, the Lichfield evidence is perhaps too little to allow generalisations to be made regarding the connection between education, book ownership and ability to preach. However, there is sufficient variety to warn against too facile assumptions of clerical ignorance and at the same time the predominance of manuals and sermon collections suggests a priesthood placing significant emphasis on pastoral care.

Irrespective of the size and composition of his library, or the breadth of his

---

[45] Marshall, *Catholic Priesthood*, 89.
[46] Tanner, *Church in Late Medieval Norwich*, 39; Duffy, *Stripping of the Altars*, 254, 593.
[47] They comprised both devotional and instructional works and included de Burgh's *Pupilla Oculi*, the *Oculus Sacerdotis* of William of Pagula and its detachable first part, the *Pars Oculi*, used as a confessional aid, and Nicholas of Lyra's *Postillae super Bibliam* in 6 volumes, all works specifically intended as manuals or reference works for the use

learning, the parish priest was the prime agent of the promulgation of Christian principles to the lay community. He was the local 'vicar of Christ' and to many, as we have seen, a 'maker of his Maker', to whose example and erudition the people looked for guidance on their own individual and communal spiritual journeys. The last generation of English Catholic clergy had committed themselves at ordination to upholding the doctrines of the universal church, but within the lifetime of many of them the nature of those beliefs was to undergo profound change and their universality to be questioned. Whereas previous generations of clergy had played their part at parochial level in the battle against heresy, the greatest uncertainty of the early sixteenth century concerned the nature of orthodoxy itself. To many of this generation the swiftness of change must have been bewildering, yet the people in their charge would have looked to them for spiritual guidance and steadfastness as never before. But if ever there was a time to keep one's head down and weather the storm it was this; a time of intermittent state-sponsored doctrinal change led by minority interest groups in opposition to a flourishing and popular religious culture.[48] In short, there was nothing to suggest to the average parish priest that he was witnessing irreversible change against which he would have to put up a fight; in any case it was the sacramental and pastoral care of his parishioners for which he had been trained, not disputation over dogma. Another reason for keeping one's own counsel was that this was a generation of clergy ordained in the diocese of a bishop personally committed to the fight against heresy. Still, as in the East Riding of Yorkshire, only one priest came to the attention of the authorities during the Henrician period on suspicion of unorthodoxy.[49] In 1528 Richard Cotton, curate of Atcham, was accused of letting his parishioners know that he did not believe in the efficacy of child baptism, pilgrimage, or the veneration of images, and saw no scriptural basis for the observance of saints' days. Whilst there was nothing specifically among these beliefs to suggest that Cotton was any different from the Coventry Lollards who had been brought to trial in 1511,[50] by the time of his appearance in court seventeen years later the definition of unorthodoxy had taken an abrupt turn and attention was now directed against the work of a new preacher of error, Martin Luther. What had caught the particular attention of Blythe's officials was that Cotton, and a small number of other stipendiary clergy, had

of pastoral clergy. In addition, four books of pricksong were listed, which apart from being used by the parish's chantry priests, might have been used for teaching purposes: *Churchwardens' Accounts of All Saints, Walsall*, 249. For the esteem in which one clerical schoolteacher was held at Walsall, above, 11, 98.

[48] For brief summaries of the voluminous evidence for the vitality of Catholic religious practice in England in this period see C. Harper-Bill, *The Pre-Reformation Church*, passim and 'Who Wanted the English Reformation?', *Medieval History*, 2, no. 1 (1992), 66–77.

[49] Marshall, *Pastoral Ministry in the East Riding*, 7.

[50] Fines, 'Heresy Trials in the Diocese of Coventry and Lichfield', passim; Thomson, *The Later Lollards*, 107–116.

met with suspected Lutherans, including William Tyndale's associate George Constantine, had debated reformist ideas and, worse, had allegedly expounded them from the pulpit. In atonement for his error he was ordered to lead a procession around the cathedral, and subsequently at his parish church, at which the bundle of sticks he was to carry on his shoulders was to mark him out as an abjured heretic to the people who, he firmly believed, had previously held him in high esteem. Without express licence from his bishop he was forbidden from preaching to them again.[51]

The curate of Atcham and his small group of associates were, however, entirely exceptional, at least in the public airing of their beliefs. Whilst not in itself evidence of orthodoxy, to either interpretation of the faith, the great majority of the parochial clergy of the diocese practised their ministry without attracting the attention of the authorities and, in consequence, without leaving explicit record of their personal convictions. Furthermore, to take Staffordshire as an example, remarkably little evidence of doctrinal conflict between priests and people during the period surfaced in the records of the royal courts, and that which did is clouded by ambiguity. In 1544 M. John Nowell, rector of Swynnerton, was cited before Star Chamber by one of his parishioners, William Martyn, for allegedly removing the bible required by the injunctions of 1536 from the parish church.[52] The charge was that it had been removed for a period of six months 'and conveyed ... where no man can tell' on the grounds that 'it is not meet that the bible should remain in the church'. For his part Nowell denied that he had removed the bible and stated that the charge was vexatious and arose from Martyn's refusal to meet the share of the cost for its provision which the rector believed was the legal requirement. Whilst Nowell's understanding of the law was in fact incorrect,[53] there is nothing in his surviving will of 1555 to suggest that he

---

51 LJRO, B/A/1/14, fos. 51r–52r; J. Fines, 'An Incident of the Reformation in Shropshire', *Transactions of the Shropshire Archaeological Society*, 57 (1961–4), 166–8, which comments exclusively on the activities of Constantine; Haigh. *Reformation and Resistance*, 79, 81, where the incident is used to illustrate the rarity of heresy cases within the diocese to the north and west of Coventry and Birmingham; A.G. Dickens, 'The Early Expansion of Protestantism in England 1520–1558', *Archiv für Reformationsgeschichte*, 78 (1987), 187–222, where the case is cited as an isolated incident in the religious history of an otherwise conservative county. I shall argue in a forthcoming paper that the most likely explanation of the meeting between Cotton and Constantine was the proximity of Atcham to the main highway from Coventry to Chester via Shrewsbury, along which Constantine was travelling at the time to distribute copies of Tyndale's English bible; see Map 2.

52 *Star Chamber Proceedings, Henry VIII and Edward VI*, 148–9. For the further allegation that Nowell had misrepresented the value of his benefice to the royal commisioners see above, 78–9.

53 '... every parson or proprietary of any parish church ... shall ... provide a book of the whole Bible ... for every man that will to look and read thereon': Sheils, *The English Reformation*, 89. Nowell's interpretation was that 'it is set forth by the authority of his majesty that the charge of the said bible be borne between the parson and parishioners'.

was particularly conservative in his religious opinions; he made no commendation of his soul, no specific request as to his burial arrangements, no pious bequests and owned no vestments or other trappings of traditional practice. However, among his numerous generous bequests, including a disproportionate number to a single woman, was just one book: a bible which he left to the parson of neighbouring Standon.[54] If this were the copy allegedly removed from the church it might tend to confirm that Nowell's prime motivation was not doctrinal, but in the words of his accuser, by reason 'of his perverse mind'. In a similar vein, in 1551 the vicar of Ilam, John Goodwyn,[55] accused John Porte esq., lord of the manor and owner of the rectory, of breaking into the church and removing choir stalls and other furniture.[56] Despite the coincidence of this act with the promulgation of official policy reforming the furnishings and fittings of chancels,[57] the defendant claimed that he had acted merely because one side of the stalls

> was erected not like the other side and so high to the glass window as that dogs continually climbed up thereby to the same glass windows and broke the same, by reason the same John as parson was, and yet is, charged to make the same window again; therefore, to the intent that he would make the same side uniform with the other for the minister to serve in without being cumbered with any other of the parish there kneeling he himself the said John Porte removed the said [stalls].

The latter part of this statement suggests that some attempt had indeed been made to comply with the injunctions of 1551 as does his continuation

> that in the same chancel behind the high altar was a certain range with a little 'aumburye' a foot and a half broad pinned to the said range, behind which the priests have been accustomed to set alestands and other such vessels, and for that the said John Porte would not suffer such unseemly things to remain in the said chancel, he quietly took away the same.

However, tempting as it might be to conclude that Porte was acting on the basis of 'Protestant' principles, his admission that certain prominent members of the parish community, in league with the vicar, continued 'unjustly to vex' him suggests that matters were greatly complicated by long-standing disputes arising from the nature of his social position.

For what little we *can* discern of either the nature of the personal beliefs held by parish clergy, or the form in which they were expounded to the faithful, we are dependent on the preambles to their wills, although such

---

[54] For details of the will see appendix.
[55] Ordained priest to the title of Dieulacres Abbey in 1529 and formerly vicar of Wolstanton: LJRO, B/A/1/14ii, fos. 197v, 200r; BL, Harleian Ms 594, fo. 139v.
[56] *Star Chamber Proceedings, Henry VIII and Edward VI*, 187–8.
[57] See Duffy, *Stripping of the Altars*, 472–7, 492.

evidence has been used with increasing caution by historians.[58] Whilst we are well advised against reading too much of personal sentiment into documents of an essentially conventional nature, we are, nevertheless, largely dependent on testamentary evidence for any indication of religious opinion. Of the fifty surviving wills in the testamentary sample, twenty-nine (58%) are from the reign of Henry VIII, seven (14%) from that of Edward VI, eight (16%) from Mary's reign and six (12%) from that of Elizabeth I.[59] As regards questions of personal piety, the preambles of wills have conventionally been analysed in terms of reference to the saints and particularly the Virgin Mary, and through perceptible attitudes to the main agency of salvation. Thus it might be said that the majority of commendations in the Henrician wills suggest a 'traditional' or 'catholic' piety, typified by William Swynerton, rector of Blymhill, who, in 1538, entrusted his soul to 'Almighty God and to Our Lady St Mary, and to all the holy company of heaven'. In the majority of cases the invocation of the saints was a general one, though in 1537 Richard Blockley, vicar of Wolvey, included St John the Baptist in his request for intercession. His direction to be buried 'before St John Baptist in the choir' would seem conventional enough given that his church was dedicated in his honour, but the later insertion of 'the image of' before the request suggests that he was conscious of a growing theological challenge to the veneration of the saints. Otherwise, evidence of particular piety is rare, but perhaps suggested by Roger Lee's heading of his will and inventory with the sacred monogram, and that of Henry Slany, vicar of Bushbury, with the invocation 'Jesus Mercy', both of which reflect contemporary devotion towards the Holy Name and the person of the Saviour.[60] In all, 63% of the wills included a commendation to the Virgin and 78% to the saints. Only two wills from the Henrician period omitted the traditional invocation altogether. Henry Byshoppe, vicar of Moreton Corbet, and the Coventry chaplain Henry Marler, both made their wills in 1539 and commended their souls exclusively to 'Almighty God'. That these two priests might have been influenced towards reformist beliefs is perhaps further supported by the fact that their 'pious' bequests extended only to giving money towards church fabric and neither requested an elaborate funeral. Other clergy who made wills in this period reflect what has been called a 'transitional' piety, a halfway house between a belief in the intercession of the saints and one in justification by faith alone. Perhaps a classic of this 'type' is represented by the will of Richard Podmore, curate of Dawley, who in 1541 commended his soul 'to Almighty God, my maker and redeemer, and to Jesus Christ His only son, by the merits of whose passion I trust to be saved, beseeching Our Lady St Mary and [all the] company of heaven to pray for me'. Again, other evidence from

---

58 For the debate on the use of preambles to wills see Marshall, *Catholic Priesthood*, 3, n. 11.
59 I.e. the sample listed in the appendix minus those where an inventory only survives.
60 Duffy, *Stripping of the Altars*, 45.

his will might be taken to support the suggestion of a priest who was hedging his theological bets. Whilst requesting simply that he be buried in his church, without elaborate ritual, his bequests included two torches and four tapers to remain in the church and money to a priest to sing for his soul for a year. Another priest who might be put in this category was Henry Slany, who wrote in 1546 of 'being repentant of my sins, beseeching God of mercy for the same which I do faithfully believe to receive of my lord God through shedding of his precious blood, I obediently bequeath my soul to my lord God, his blessed mother, and all saints in heaven'. In this case his bequest to local priests in return for masses for his soul clearly indicates that his main leaning was towards traditional Catholicism.

Apart from the commendations themselves, other evidence from the sample of wills suggests a gradual shift away from the more conspicuous aspects of Catholic doctrine and conventions of traditional piety. A marked feature of a number of the Henrician wills is the variety of bequests for pious purposes, from the inevitable provision for intercessory masses and prayers, to gifts to religious gilds and altars within the church. More specifically the curate of Ryton-on-Dunsmore, Alexander Legh, left money in 1533 for the completion of the rood loft there. In 1535 the Macclesfield chaplain, William Bridges, left his longest towel to the church to be used at the High Altar at the time of the Easter Communion and William More, a chaplain at Marchington, left fabric to his sister in 1541 to make a cloth for St Katherine's altar and a sheet to make an alb for the priest who served there. The bequests of Richard Ryve, vicar of South Wingfield, in 1537, included money to the parish's Holy Trinity Gild and 6s 8d towards an altar for the Lady chapel. But such features are conspicuous by their absence in most of the wills made from the early 1540s onwards; similarly, the fleeting glimpses of the trappings of traditional devotion become increasingly rare over time. In the 1530s Richard Kent, chaplain of Newcastle-under-Lyme, John Reed, vicar of Melbourne, and Richard Rylay, rector of Swarkestone, had all owned sets of rosary beads, Kent having two, one of which he bequeathed to a female parishioner.[61] At the same time Robert Barefote, vicar of Mancetter, was the owner of 'a St John's head of alabaster in a tabernacle', and at his death in 1540, the goods of the Coventry priest, Thomas Fisher, included 'two little crowns of bells for saints' heads'. The last overt evidence of ownership of such devotional items comes in 1557, towards the end of Mary's reign, when Edmund Bachelor, rector of Sheinton, would presumably have been happy for the assessors of his goods to record the 'little table of imagery' worth 6d that he kept in his room. But the time was coming when such conspicuous evidence of traditional piety would no longer be acceptable and

---

[61] In 1565 the bishop of Coventry and Lichfield responded to government pressure by calling upon 'the people daily that they cast away their beads with all their superstitions that they do use' and ordered churchwardens and sidesmen to fine every person found using rosary beads a shilling: ibid., 572.

there appears to be an implicit note of caution in the bequest made by Roger Lee, the Wroxeter chaplain, of money to his church in 1540 'to make a tabernacle over Our Lady, or else at the discretion of my executors'. But it is entirely explicit in the will of William Brewster, vicar of Etwall, who in 1549 left money to both his present and previous churches for their repair and for 'such ornaments as the parish are and shall be bound to maintain there by the king's laws'.

Evidence of a shift in doctrinal emphasis over time is also apparent in the arrangements that parochial clergy made for their funeral itself. Making his will in 1533, Roger Lee was quite typical of the time in his stipulation that five tapers burn around his corpse, probably in honour of the Five Wounds, and that Mass and dirige be said 'according to the custom of the parish'.[62] In the following year, Richard Bexwyke, curate of Middleton, left 16d to each of four colleagues to say dirige and mass and offer prayers for his soul, and a further sum to the parish clerk, not only to ring the bell on the day of the funeral, but, like the priests, to offer prayers for his repose. The funerary arrangements of the Macclesfield chaplain and schoolmaster William Bridges, in 1536, were, however, particularly elaborate, and demonstrate a fully inclusive Catholic eschatology. On the day of his burial no fewer than thirty priests were to 'sing and say' a trental of masses of St Gregory, although some concession to the scale of the request is apparent in the condition 'if so many can be conveniently gotten'. The masses were to be celebrated 'for my soul, my father and mother's souls, for my Master Sir John Persyvale knight's soul and all Christian souls, and especially for all those souls that I am, and have been, bounden to pray for'. Over the following night the same priests were to 'sing and say' placebo and dirige, followed by commendation in the morning. As with Lee, contemporary devotional practice is in evidence in the five torches that were to be purchased 'in the worship of the five principal wounds of our Saviour Jesus Christ, redeemer of mankind', to be held during the service by five paupers. A further trental of masses was to be celebrated thirty days after the burial by a similar number of clergy 'praying them all of their charity devoutly to pray for my soul and the souls above rehearsed, with all Christian souls'. In death as in life, Bridges clearly wished to be seen as an intercessory focus for the community of living and dead within the parish. This particular aspect of the clerical role was not to be so evident in any of the later wills; the 'custom of the church' that dictated that a 'whole hearse of tapers' burn over the body of the Wroxeter chaplain, Richard Dodycotte, in 1543, and that 'priests and clerks . . . come to pray for my soul' was clearly one that would not long survive the doctrinal upheavals of the following reign. In 1549 William Brewster, vicar of Etwall, whilst commending his soul in a traditionally 'Catholic' manner, asked simply that his body be buried where 'it shall please God to call me to his

---

62 Prominent among the liturgical entries in Robert Burton's notebook is the form of the Mass of the Five Wounds of Christ: Haines, 'A York Priest's Notebook', 156.

mercy'. In the same year Richard Rowlowe, rector of Ryton, opened his will with a similar formula then asked to be buried in the chancel of his church simply 'at the will of my friends'. The remaining four priests who drew up their wills during Edward's reign used overtly 'reformed' commendations, either simply to 'Almighty God', or with a more explicit reference to salvation through Christ's sacrifice as in the case of Roger Leigh, rector of Lymm, who in 1551 dedicated his soul 'unto God the Father Almighty . . . in sure and certain hope of resurrection to eternal life through our Lord Jesus Christ'. Burial arrangements among this group of priests were similarly elementary. Leigh asked simply to be 'buried in the ground within the chancel' and John Yate, priest of Fletchamstead, directed in 1549 that he be buried 'in Christian burial where it shall please my executors to bury me'.

The mixed reactions which must have met the young king's death in 1553 are exemplified by those half dozen priests who made their wills during the reign of his Catholic successor. Whilst none of them made the elaborate funerary arrangements of some of their predecessors in Henry's reign, in 1556 the Manchester chaplain Richard Bryddocke left 8d to every priest that said mass for his soul, and in the following year Edmund Bachelor, rector of Sheinton, asked that the four torches and five tapers that were to be burned 'to the honour of God' at his burial should be left to his church for the same purpose 'in the time of divine service'. Making his will at the beginning of Mary's reign, in 1553, John Abell, curate of Kingstone, commended his soul to 'Almighty God, my maker and redeemer', whether as a deliberate statement of Protestant belief or simply in accordance with a convention that had been gaining acceptance. There is perhaps more than a hint of Protestant sentiment in the commendation of the former Uttoxeter chantry priest John Bee, in 1555, of his 'soul to Almighty God, my maker and redeemer, and my body to the ground'. However, the commendation made in the same year by Henry Corveser, vicar of Stanton upon Hine Heath, was conventionally Catholic, as were those of Richard Bryddocke in 1556 and Edmund Bachelor, rector of Sheinton and John Hall, vicar of Chebsey, in 1557. Again, it might be wondered whether the commendation made by Thomas Alen, rector of Kinswinford, in 1556, showed more evidence of either Catholic or Protestant sympathy, or was simply swimming with the tide, with its bequest of his soul 'to Almighty God, of whom I ask mercy for all my sins, trusting [in] faith fully to be saved through the death and passion of our saviour Jesus Christ, praying the glorious virgin our Lady St Mary and all the Saints of God, pray for me'.

The personal and professional lives of those six priests who made their wills in the Elizabethan period had witnessed profound religious change. Whilst at ordination they had been committed to defending the faith of the souls in their charge, they might, as they neared the end of their lives, have been forgiven for some confusion as to the precise nature of that faith. Certainly only one of these priests, Richard Hatton, curate of Shifnal, left any evidence of a possible commitment to the new orthodoxy in his commendation in 1560 of his soul simply 'to Almighty God' and by his funeral arrangements which included burial in the church next to his brother, a bequest to four women 'to wind me', another for the ringing of the great bell, and a stipulation that 'no more bells . . . be rung'. On the other hand Ralph Wendon, rector of Sutton Coldfield and John Holwaye, rector of Hinstock, bequeathed their souls in traditional Catholic manner in 1558 and 1559 respectively, Holwaye after mistakenly (though perhaps suggestively) dating his will to the second year of Mary's reign and then correcting it to that of Elizabeth. The remaining three commendations, whilst able to be classified as 'transitional', demonstrate that the uniform conventions of an earlier age had now gone. The will of the curate of Chesterfield, Richard Whitworth, written in 1559 and leaving his soul 'to Almighty God, my maker and redeemer, to our blessed lady St Mary the virgin, and to all the holy and blessed company of heaven' suggests that he went to his grave retaining much of the Catholic doctrine in which he had been brought up. The same can probably be said of Thomas Wylson, vicar of Abbots Bromley, who in 1561 bequeathed his soul 'to Almighty God, my maker, my redeemer, and as my very . . . and especial trust is Christ . . . at this great and most terrible day of judgement, beseeching the blessed virgin Mary and all the holy company of Heaven to pray for me'; and Thomas Tunstall, curate of Wolstanton who, despite being the father of two children, commended his soul in 1565 'to Almighty God, there to be kept with the holy company of Heaven'. But it is in their final act, their request for burial, that these two Staffordshire priests most clearly betray their response to both present and future uncertainties and their relationship to things past. Wylson's funeral was to be accompanied by the ringing of bells and attended by his godchildren who were to sing *de profundis*, after which he was to be buried in the chapel of St Nicholas 'before the place where the image of the blessed Trinity stood'. Tunstall's was to be a more simple affair, though undoubtedly attended by his son Roger and daughter Elizabeth, who were to ensure that his body was buried 'within Our Lady's chancel, before there as the altar was before time'.[63]

The Clerical Community: Caste, Status-Group or Profession?

There were a number of ways by which the parish priest could be marked out from the rest of society; by his attire, by conventional forms of address and, primarily, through his unique sacramental function. However, the question

---

[63] Thomas Johnson, curate of Farnworth in 1533 was still in post in 1565 when he was presented before the bishop for 'shriving and suffering candles to be burned in the chapel upon Candlemas day, according to the old superstitious custom': Raines, ed., *History of the Chantries*, 77, n. 4.

of status was more ambiguous, being clouded by conflicting perceptions of the sanctity of priesthood and the hierarchical structures of both ecclesiastical and secular society. Furthermore, the nature of the source material precludes definitive statements concerning how the parish clergy themselves regarded their own priesthood. Did they see themselves as separate from the rest of society, or even as individual priests distinct from their fellows, each a 'maker of God' in his own right, with no need for the kind of internal group definition that distinguished a 'caste' from a 'profession'? It has been argued in some quarters that discussion of a 'clerical profession' in the pre-Reformation period is anachronistic since the clergy did not possess the necessary 'separatist' group mentality.[64] The fact that the status of each individual priest was more readily defined in terms of his own sacramental power hindered the development of true group identity, and perhaps even led to something of an 'identity crisis'.[65] Yet such a view might be as much a product of the character of our inquiry, influenced of necessity by the nature of the evidence, as a statement of a social reality. There has been a tendency to examine the practice of priesthood in something of a social vacuum: the beliefs of individual priests, the failings of individual priests, conflict with individual priests, and so on. The focus on isolated cases has, unsurprisingly, tended to preclude the identification of group identity, let alone of a self-conscious profession. One recent writer has, however, attempted to redress the balance by examining the parish clergy in terms of a social dynamic rather than a collection of individuals, based mainly on the evidence of wills.[66] In the case of Coventry and Lichfield, fellow-clergy are mentioned in the wills of no less than 90% of the testamentary sample, in over two-thirds of which they appear as beneficiaries, and in one-third as executors and witnesses. Relationships could be formed between colleagues within a single church, between those of neighbouring parishes, or even farther afield and could consist of connections between clergy of the same or different employment status. They might have formed before the priests in question even entered employment: as village neighbours, schoolmates, fellow-ordinands, fellow-graduates. But in all cases, especially given the sheer size of the clerical population, they are a reminder of the inadequacy of viewing the exercise of priesthood in isolation.

One-third of wills in the sample mention clergy in the testator's parish, including four priests who displayed considerable trust in their close colleagues by asking them to act as executors. Robert Blythe and William Richardson, vicars of Dunchurch and Crich respectively, named parish

---

[64] R. O'Day, *The English Clergy: The Emergence and Consolidation of a Profession, 1558–1642* (Leicester, 1979), 234; Marshall, *Catholic Priesthood*, 126.
[65] Aveling, 'The English Clergy, Catholic and Protestant', 64.
[66] Skeeters, *Community and Clergy*, 14–16.

chaplains,[67] as did Richard Hatton, curate of Shifnal,[68] whilst Alexander Legh, curate of Ryton-on-Dunsmore, nominated the parson of the living.[69] Other parish clergy employed the services of their colleagues as witnesses and overseers, such as the vicars William Richardson and John Smyth, whose wills were witnessed by a chantrist and parish curate respectively;[70] and Richard Whitworth, curate of Chesterfield, whose overseer and witness was a junior colleague.[71] Close relationships between the clergy of a single parish are also indicated by some of the bequests made in wills. The incumbents William Brewster, John Fitzherbert, Roger Leigh and John Nowell all left items to stipendiary chaplains. Fitzherbert evidently enjoyed good relations with his assistants, leaving bequests in his will to both his former and present curate which, in the case of the latter, included a surplice and 'the great chair in the church, to take it away when he is not curate there'.[72] The fact that such a conspicuous item of furniture was to be left to an individual priest rather than to the church that they had both served suggests a close relationship between the two. Nowell's bequest of twenty sheep to Thomas Morrey, a chaplain who had assisted him at Swynnerton for many years and whom he referred to as 'my priest', indicates an even deeper level of relationship, on both a personal and spiritual level.[73] One of similar duration had endured between Roger Leigh, rector of a moiety of Lymm, and his curate John Fernhead to whom he left a gown, and who was later to take over a moiety of the living himself.[74] It might, of course, be argued that bequests by beneficed clergy to their stipendiaries were little more than a reflection of the ubiquity of the patronage system. But the fact that they can also be seen to have operated in the reverse direction suggests that, occasionally at least, they might have been a manifestation of genuine affection. Thus as well as nominating his vicar as an executor, Alexander Legh, curate of Ryton-on-Dunsmore, left him one of his best jackets, and the chantrist of Beighton,

---

67 'Sir John Swanne my parish priest', will of Robert Blythe. John Marett, will of William Richardson; BL, Harleian Ms 594, fo. 129r, as John Maryat, stipendiary of Crich.
68 Michael Howell: will of Richard Hatton; BL, Harleian Ms 594, fo. 135r.
69 Unnamed: will of Alexander Legh.
70 Sir Robert Swynte (will of William Richardson), probably Robert Swynestoh or Swynstoo, instituted to the perpetual chantry of the BVM, Crich, in 1515 (LJRO, B/A/1/14, fo. 37r) and stipendiary at Crich in 1533 (BL, Harleian Ms 594, fo. 129r); 'Sir Simon Bellyster, curate' (will of John Smyth).
71 Sir William Bagge (will of Richard Whitworth), stipendiary of Chesterfield in 1533 (BL, Harleian Ms 594, fo. 124r, as William Bage).
72 Sir Richard Wayne, curate of Doveridge in 1533 (BL, Harleian Ms 594, fo. 126r); Sir Richard Holme (will of John Fitzherbert).
73 Sir Thomas Morrey (will of John Nowell); stipendiary at Swynnerton in 1531 (LJRO, B/A/17/1(1), fo. 4r (as Thomas Morray).
74 Sir John Fernehed, curate of Lymm in 1533 (BL, Harleian Ms 594, fo. 153r), subsequently rector of a moiety of the living; G.J. Piccope, ed., *Lancashire and Cheshire Wills and Inventories from the Ecclesiastical Court, Chester: The Third Portion*, Chetham Soc., 54 (1861), p. 50, n. 1.

Richard Asche, set aside 4s 4d for his vicar, a significant sum in the context of a stipend of £4 a year and the valuation of his entire property at £2 14s 11d; indeed, it was his single largest bequest. Bonds are also likely to have formed between the assistant clergy of a parish; Henry Tryge at Chesterfield, and John Wells of Holy Trinity, Coventry, both left books to fellow chaplains.[75]

Just as relationships between clergy were not restricted to those of the same status, nor were they limited to those within the same parish. Whilst connections that transcended parish boundaries might be a reflection of a degree of mobility between the clergy of a particular region, certainly among the unbeneficed, they might also reflect friendships formed at an earlier stage, perhaps even prior to ordination. In general, they might be suggestive of the cordiality of relations between the parochial clergy within an area that may have gone so far as recognition of a group identity. As incumbents of neighbouring parishes, William Corveser and William Ashley, vicars of Stanton upon Hine Heath and Moreton Corbet respectively, had worked in close proximity, and evidence of a trusting relationship is suggested by Corveser's nomination of Ashley as one of his executors, and perhaps an even closer relationship by his bequest of a share in the residue of his estate.[76] Richard Rylay, rector of Swarkestone, asked the curates of two neighbouring parishes to act as witnesses to his will, to one of whom he left a book, and the other a book, a black gown and a tippet, perhaps evidence of a closer relationship.[77] In 1537 John Redfern, vicar of Longford, left his 'best short gown and a new bonnet' to Edmund Latham who, four years previously, had been working as a chaplain in the neighbouring parish of Boylestone.[78] Whilst it is possible that he later acted as an assistant to Redfern, the connection may simply have come about as priests employed in the same vicinity. Similarly, the Macclesfield chaplain and schoolmaster, William Bridges, left his 'gown lined with St Thomas worsted' to Henry Knight, who had recently been employed at Wilmslow,[79] and George Gregory, chaplain of Rossendale, included a local priest, who was one of his executors, in his bequest of 'all my part of those hives which stand at the Wolfenden Bothe' and a share in the residue of the estate.[80]

A more sizeable network of clergy within an area is suggested by those

---

[75] 'Sir Rob.(?) Whytteworth' (will of Henry Tryge), probably Richard Whitworth, curate of Chesterfield in 1533 (BL, Harleian Ms 594, fo. 124r) and see above and appendix; 'Sir John Battman' (will of John Wells), stipendiary of St Michael, Coventry, in 1533 (BL, Harleian Ms 594, fo. 118v, as John Bateman).

[76] Possibly the same as the stipendiary at Atcham in 1533 (BL, Harleian Ms 594, fo. 132v) and the chaplain accused of incest in 1528; see below, 172.

[77] 'Sir William Babyngton, curate of Stanton', 'Sir Roger Peyrson, curate of Chelaston', a post he had held in 1533; BL, Harleian Ms 594, fo. 129r (as Roger Pereson).

[78] BL, Harleian Ms 594, fo. 126r.

[79] Ibid., fo. 152v.

[80] 'Sir Thomas Holden, priest', later in the document described as 'curate' (will of

priests who mentioned more than one local colleague in their wills. Richard Webb, rector of Stapleton, left money to a local chaplain, Thomas Turner, to say a trental of masses for his and all Christian souls immediately after his burial, and he was further rewarded with the gift of a psalter. As already mentioned, Webb also left a portable altar to Thomas Tong, rector of neighbouring Myddle, who was one of the witnesses to the will. Webb had been rector of Stapleton for over thirty years when he made his will in 1537 and might have known Tong since his induction as rector of Middle in 1511,[81] an indication of the long-standing nature of some of the relationships which developed between local clergy. The will of William Brewster, vicar of Etwall, demonstrates similar connections with a number of local priests. Within the immediate vicinity he named Robert Ottaway, rector of Dawbury, as one of his executors, who was rewarded with the bequest of 'my furred winter gown and my little bible'; William Grene, curate of Barton-under-Needwood,[82] who received 20d and 'one of my tippets'; and Randall Webster, a chaplain of Mickleover who received other items of clothing. Farther afield, across the Nottinghamshire border, John Chaverham, vicar of Cuckney, was left 'a tache that I have with finalle pearlls';[83] Cuckney was situated just a few miles from Welbeck Abbey, the patrons of Brewster's living and another possible link between the two men.[84] Edmund Bachelor, rector of Sheinton, remembered friendships he had made whilst previously working as a chaplain at nearby Cound; included among the beneficiaries of his will in 1557 were its incumbent, Ralph Shaw, and an assistant,[85] as well as the parsons of neighbouring Harley[86] and Leighton.[87] The will was witnessed by Richard Wycherley who, in 1533, had been a stipendiary at Baschurch on the other side of Shrewsbury.[88] Clearly, Bachelor was a priest very firmly placed within the local clerical community.

It is certain that if a greater quantity of testamentary evidence survived from this period it would suggest more complex clerical networks than have been suggested by most of these individual wills. A rare glimpse of the multiple connections which were likely to have existed between local priests is afforded by the wills of Richard Hatton and John Holwaye, curate of

---

George Gregory), possibly the same as, or a relative of, John Holden, curate of neighbouring Haslingden in 1533; BL, Harleian Ms 594, fo. 15r.

[81] LJRO, B/A/1/14, fo. 46r.
[82] The post he held in 1533; BL, Harleian Ms 594, fo. 140r.
[83] A brooch, buckle or clasp; *finalle* in this sense probably meaning 'real'.
[84] LJRO, B/A/1/14, fo. 43v.
[85] Sir William Alcock, stipendiary at Cound in 1533; BL, Harleian Ms 594, fo. 133v.
[86] 'Sir William Dyson, priest of Harley' (will of Edmund Bachelor), rector of Harley in 1533; BL, Harleian Ms 594, fo. 133r; above, 61.
[87] 'Sir John Barnes, vicar of Leighton' (will of Edmund Bachelor), possibly the same as John Barnys who was a chaplain at Holy Cross, Shrewsbury, in 1533; BL, Harleian Ms 594, fo. 132v.
[88] BL, Harleian Ms 594, fo. 134r.

Shifnal and rector of Hinstock respectively, two adjacent Shropshire parishes close to the Staffordshire border. Both men died in 1560 having named John Moreton, rector of neighbouring Stockton, in their wills, Hatton as a witness and Holwaye as an executor and beneficiary who received numerous valuable items including his best black colt and 'any other thing as he shall think necessary for him'. To many incumbents, of course, the benefice itself would have been the main connection between them and both their predecessors and successors, and again, such relationships might have endured over a considerable period. Thus William Brewster bequeathed the bedding and other items which he had left at his former living of Austen, near Doncaster, to his (unnamed) successor as well as 'my long gown lined with black satin of Cypress, my biggest bible and 10s' to William Rogers, the parish priest there. Brewster's affinity with his previous parish and his generosity to its clergy extended to a bequest of 8d 'if there be any more priests there to each of them'. To the parish priest of his current living of Etwall he left 12d and to the man that would succeed him he left the timber and ladders remaining at the vicarage and 20s, although the condition attached to this payment, 'that he give an acquittance to my executors for dilapidations of Etwall, or else to have but that the law giveth him' suggests that the bequest was not entirely motivated by generosity of spirit. Richard Rylay indirectly acknowledged his predecessor by leaving to a layman 'the gown that I had of the parson that dead is'. As well as time and place there were other boundaries that might be transcended in relationships between clergy as suggested by their wills. These included status, as revealed by the bequest of the Coventry priest Thomas Fisher of a spruce coffer worth 4d to the bishop of Bangor, and that between seculars and regulars. In 1534 Ralph Tatton, rector of Barlborough nominated the prior of Repton, John Young, as one of his witnesses and overseers[89] and in 1543 the Coventry priest Charles Bucke left 12d to a former Carthusian of the same city to whom he still referred as 'Brother John from the Charterhouse'.

---

[89] See above, 132, for Tatton's request for burial at Repton. The relationship between Tatton and Young, whatever its basis, had become too close in the eyes of the bishop by the time of his visitation of the priory in 1518. Inquiries made then revealed that Tatton had been granted the lease of a pasture belonging to the priory, probably one of the reasons for his frequent sojourns; another might have been that he was stopping over on his way from visits to Lichfield (where he was a member of the gild and had family connections) to his Derbyshire parish. It was alleged by a number of the monks that during his stays he shared in the communal allowances of bread and ale, much to their annoyance, and, more seriously, had taken on the role of advisor to the prior, provoking discord between him and the convent. In addition, the occasions of visits had also tempted some members of the community to join him at a local inn. Another frequent visitor to the priory was the (unnamed) vicar of Ashbourne, probably at this time William Tykhill, who had been allowed his own room and stable by the prior. Blythe ordered the immediate removal of Tatton from the farm and the cessation of the arrangements for the vicar of Ashbourne; *Blythe's Visitations*, 8–10; LJRO B/A/1/14, fo. 40v; D.77/1, p. 259. For Tatton's family connections see below, 156.

Of course, it would be unrealistic to expect that relations between such a large and disparate body as the early Tudor parish clergy would have been universally harmonious and, indeed, bequests from one priest to another might even on occasion imply a desire to make up for previously strained relations rather than acts of generosity based on a mutually cordial relationship. Sometimes there were bound to have been outright disputes, which, if unresolved at a personal level, might end up as presentments before the ecclesiastical courts. Fertile ground for hostility would have been provided by the financial and other rights upon which the parochial system was founded and which lay behind the allegation made in 1529 by Thomas Shirebroke, vicar of Tibshelf, that the vicar of Mackworth was impeding his parishioners from paying their Easter dues.[90] There was always the danger that disputes of this nature could lead to accusations of defamation – as between the chaplains John Mylner and John Bralyford in 1527[91] – or worse, violence. Such an outcome was the result of one of a number of disputes in which the vicar of Sutton Maddock, Richard Harrington, was involved during the period. In 1529, by which time he had retired from the living on a pension, his complaint to a local chaplain, Richard Brett, that he had been interfering in the rights of the benefice, led to a violent assault.[92] The attack was evidently a serious one: witnesses described how Brett had confronted Harrington with the words 'art though here? I shall have my pennyworth on ye now!' before grabbing him by the gown. According to their deposition, two witnesses, Harrington's successor John Morehall and another cleric, Thomas Southall, managed to separate the two temporarily but Brett ran after Harrington 'and then leaped over the hedge into a ditch' where he found the former vicar hiding and imploring bystanders 'help, help, he kills me!' Morehall and Southall ran to the scene and saw that Brett 'had the one hand on [Harrington's] head hair, pulling his head downward awry, and the other hand at his throat'. When the two onlookers managed to drag Harrington from the clutches of his assailant the latter shouted 'nay, whoreson, I will have my pennyworth on ye now as Master Chancellor bade me!' suggesting a protest of official sanction for his actions. The conclusion of the case does not survive, but we know that Brett was suspended from celebrating mass until he had been absolved of the charge of clerical violence and it appears that little long-term harm was done to his prospects, since within four years he had achieved that feat beyond the ability of most of the unbeneficed clergy of the time and been admitted to a rectory himself.[93] But the impression that such a squalid affair, with money at the root of subsequent evil, was exceptional between clerics, is reinforced by the fact that the case contains more detailed deposition of witnesses than in almost any that came before

---

[90] LJRO, B/C/2/3, fo. 76v.
[91] Ibid., B/C/2/2, fo. 26v.
[92] Ibid., B/C/2/3, fos. 78v, 79r–v.
[93] Rushall, Staffs.; BL, Harleian Ms 594, fo. 141r.

the bishop's consistory court during the seven years for which the records survive. And although, by the nature of the source material, evidence of genuine warmth in relations between clergy is almost equally as rare, such a situation would surely have been more common. When Richard Hatton, describing himself as 'priest of the parish of Idsall'[94] drew up his will in 1560 he chose as one of his executors a fellow priest Michael Howell. Twenty-seven years previously they had both been employed within the parish, Hatton as curate and Howell as a stipendiary chaplain, and the pair were now in at least their early seventies.[95] Their lives had spanned the reigns of all five Tudor monarchs and religious upheavals on a scale they could not have imagined when, along with record numbers of eager young compatriots, they had joined the ranks of the Catholic priesthood. It is hard not to believe that like Richard Ryve, vicar of South Wingfield, referring to the two chaplains whom he nominated as the overseers of his will, they would have counted each other among their 'right trusty friends'.

II. Priests as People

Whilst it is important to consider the significance of priesthood in relation to individual ordained men and the wider clerical community, both are inadequate on their own since they impose an exaggerated isolation of the clergy from society as a whole. No seminaries as such existed in pre-Reformation England and those boys who attended a local school, or even one of the universities, were not at this stage being marked exclusively for priesthood. This was a step they took as adults, their entire formative years having been spent within the secular world and its social basis of kinship and friendship. Whatever the high ideals of clerical apologists and reformers, an awareness of this fact could not have been entirely lost, or eradicated, at ordination. Young men taking on priesthood had experienced the same range of upbringing as their peers and the traditional distinction made between clerical and lay society, especially in an age of such high levels of ordination, is to a large extent a false one: in short, priests *were* people. Even when their clerical status had defined their specific role in relation to the sacramental structure of the church they often served in the locality within which they had been raised, among the people with whom they had grown up, and for much of their working lives were engaged in the same activities

---

[94] I.e. Shifnal, commonly referred to as *Idsall alias Shifnal*.
[95] Hatton: ordained priest in 1511 to the title of Lilleshall Abbey (LJRO, B/A/1/14ii, fo. 76v), curate of Shifnal in 1533 (BL, Harleian Ms 594, fo. 135r). Howell, chaplain at Shifnal in 1533 (BL, Harleian Ms 594, fo. 135r). His name does not appear in Blythe's ordination register; if he was ordained before 1503 then he would have been at least eighty-one.

as their neighbours. Relations between priests and their flocks were bound to have been informed by this basic fact, and a polarisation of roles was most probably restricted to the performance of the sacraments. At other times both groups existed within a web of interconnected and overlapping relationships within which distinctions must often have been blurred.

Temporal Kinship: Family Connections

The most obvious set of social relationships within which the parish clergy existed was the kin group; yet even at this most basic level, interests and definitions overlapped. A priest's kin would often include his parishioners as well as the wider collective of laity in opposition to which much of the definition of priesthood was derived; it also included other clergy. Among the clerical networks which have already been observed are relationships which can be shown to have also existed through kinship, emphasising the way in which distinctions could be blurred. For example, when the vicar of Bushbury, Henry Slany, left all his books, his gowns, half of his swine and all his wood to his cousin, and half his corn to his brother,[96] both priests, was the prime motivation the family relationship or that which existed between fellow-clergy? When the inventory of Robert Dore, chantry priest of Walsall, was drawn up by the vicar John Turner and the testator's brother Edward, himself the incumbent of a benefice outside the diocese, was this important task being undertaken primarily in his capacity as a member of the senior parish clergy or as a close relative of the deceased? Similarly, the executor of John Sherdeley, priest of Prescot, was another local priest, Henry Sherdeley, presumably a relative.[97] Whole networks of clergy can occasionally be shown to have been based both on 'professional' and kin groupings as in the case of the Tattons, an interesting example of a 'clerical family' working mainly within the areas of south Staffordshire and south Derbyshire. In his will of 1534 Ralph Tatton, rector of Barlborough, Derbyshire, and also a member of the Lichfield Gild of St Mary and St John the Baptist, mentioned his brother Richard Tatton, chantrist of Lichfield Cathedral and gild member (both brothers had been admitted in 1509);[98] his cousin Thomas Tatton, curate of the chapel of Stowe annexed to Lichfield Cathedral;[99] and George Tatton, rector of Colton, Staffordshire.[100] In addition, Bartholomew Tatton had been instituted to the Derbyshire rectory of Morley in 1508.[101] Here was a group of men whose connections included kin-relationship, profession and

[96] On the condition that he paid the rent due on the land on which it was grown.
[97] *Prescot Records*, 132. The will was dated 1514. By 1524 Henry was curate of Prescot; above, 121.
[98] BL, Harleian Ms 594, fo. 144r; LJRO, D.77/1, pp. 259, 261.
[99] BL, Harleian Ms 594, fo. 144r.
[100] Ibid., fo. 140r.
[101] LJRO, B/A/1/14, fo. 33v.

gild membership, a useful reminder of the overlapping nexus of relationships within which the clergy operated and the danger of drawing artificially fine distinctions between them.

This maxim is at its most obvious as regards family relationships. It has been correctly observed that the sheer scale of clerical recruitment would have meant that few people in early Tudor England would not have had at least one priest in their family.[102] The universality of the kin relationship is demonstrated by the fact that 96% of the sample wills mention family members; most of these occur as beneficiaries, but just under one-third of testators nominated their kin as executors and 4% as witnesses and overseers. Whilst such relationships might be expressed in the most general terms, as in Edmund Bachelor's bequest of part of the residue of his estate to his 'kinsfolk', and frequent references to 'kinsman' and 'kinswoman', in most cases they were more specific, mentioning brothers, sisters, nephews, nieces, cousins and brothers- and sisters-in-law, and occasionally parents, as well as more distant relatives. Fairly typical was the will of John Holwaye, rector of Hinstock, who in 1559 bequeathed the debts that were owed to him to his cousin 'John Holway [and] my nephew, Humphrey Adams, and their sisters such as be unmarried', as well as making further bequests to a brother-in-law, a sister, and two kinswomen; the residue of the estate was to be divided between John Holway, his children and his (the cousin's) three unmarried sisters. A similar range of family ties can be seen in the will of William Richardson, vicar of Crich. He left his best bedding, best clothes, two horses, silver spoons and 20s to his brother, whose wife was to have his best pots and her daughter various items, including a cow. A bequest to another brother and his children included his second best bedding, clothes, and 20s and to every one of a third brother's children he left 3s 4d. His sister was to share all his hemp and flax with his two female servants. Not only does this will demonstrate some of the range of relationships which might be remembered as the priest neared the end of his life, it also expresses a notion of family hierarchy in relation to the disposal of the estate. However, a warning against drawing too close parallels between the concept of family and kin as understood in the early sixteenth century with our own, as well as drawing conclusions from evidence of surname alone, comes from the direction in the final line of Richardson's will, that the residue of the estate should go to 'John Heyton, my brother, to dispose for my soul like as he would I should do for him if the case or chance were like'. In this case 'brother' might refer to a fellow priest. Hierarchy might also be expressed through a distinction between relationships through consanguinity and affinity. Thus William Brewster left £5 to his sister

> as I suppose dwelleth in Maydston or thereabouts, and if she be not alive then the premisses bequeathed unto her I will be divided and given evenly

[102] Marshall, *Catholic Priesthood*, 109.

among her children, if any be alive, and if none be alive, then her husband John Turner, if he be alive shall have only 20s.

In order that his sister might be able to claim her legacy, Brewster arranged for a copy of the will to be sent to her. On occasion it might be wondered whether a testator was deliberately restricting his bequests to relatives of a single sex or if this was simply a matter of family composition and survival. Henry Slany, for example, made bequests exclusively to male relatives which, as well as his cousin, the priest Richard Slany already mentioned, included his brothers, Henry senior, Henry junior, Edmund and Nicholas who were to receive 20s each; his cousin Nicholas, who was left a cow and all his sheep; and his brother Ralph who was to have the residue. Similarly, the beneficiaries of Ralph Wendon's will were his sisters and a niece, a decision that is perhaps explained by an exclusion clause that his executors and overseers were

> to pay no penny nor pennyworth of this my legacy to them until [they] or their husbands in their behalf do seal acquittance for all demands or title that they can make to my goods or any parcell thereof by any manner or title or demand and that if they will not seal such acquittance then I will that they be excluded from all legacies, willing them to have no portion of my goods.

For obvious reasons, parents were rarely mentioned other than in the context of prayers for the departed, and Wendon's will is an exception in its request that he be buried in the chancel at Sutton Coldfield 'near where my father lyeth'. Even more unusual was the will of Thomas Tunstall, curate of Wolstanton, a parent himself. In his will of 1565 he left £10 each to his son Roger and daughter Elizabeth, as well as 6s 8d and items of clothing to each of his brothers, Ralph and Peter. Interestingly, whilst no reference is made to Tunstall's wife (she might, of course, have died) the single greatest beneficiary of his will was his servant, Ellen Fines, who received three cows, 'one day's work of rye and one hogge', two crofts (one of which incorporated a linen shop), his best bedding and 'all my *ole* [ale?; coal?] within my house and half the yarn which is in my house'.[103] Within the house of John Fitzherbert, vicar of Doveridge, was his brother, Robert Fitzherbert the younger, who had been living with him and who received 20s in his will. Relatives further afield were not, however, neglected since Fitzherbert also left 'to the house of Somersall where I was born my best *countretable*,[104] my two iron racks and my two great brooches to be and remain there as heirlooms for ever', evidence of both the importance and persistence of family ties in the life of a parish priest.

---

103 For the relationship between Tunstall and Fines see also 123, 173.
104 Most likely a sideboard.

Spiritual Kinship: Godchildren

Whilst the thoughts of an aged celibate priest might turn to the place where he had been born, they might also be directed towards his godchildren, who represented a tangible link between the relationships a priest enjoyed with his family and those which he formed within the wider community of the parish. The fact that almost half of the clergy in the sample made bequests to godchildren would tend to support the assertion that the choice of a parish priest as godfather was a widespread practice in early Tudor England, perhaps due simply to his presence on the occasion,[105] or as a deliberate step taken by lay-people to avoid potential future problems arising from spiritual affinity. The frequency of choice of priests is also suggested by the common formulaic bequest, often of 4d or 8d 'to every godchild that I have' as in the will of John Abell, curate of Kingstone. That this might have been a large number is implied in other wills such as the lump sum bequeathed by William Brewster to his godchildren in his previous and present parishes and those 'within Derbyshire'; of Richard Kent, chaplain of Newcastle-under-Lyme, of 4d to every godchild that he had 'within the town'; or of Thomas Tunstall, curate of Wolstanton, of 4d to 'every godchild that is alive'. It is certainly the implication underlying the bequest by Richard Ryve of 3s 4d to 'every one of my godchildren which be within the number of twenty'.

However, the frequency with which the parish clergy were chosen as godparents need not imply that it was an obligation undertaken without due gravity or that it was a relationship without potential for genuine affection. Edmund Bachelor, rector of Sheinton, clearly enjoyed a close relationship with at least some of his godchildren, but also appears to have viewed them within a hierarchy similar to that which has been observed as regards kin. To two of his godchildren, probably the offspring of his servant, he left 20s each and the same amount to another two goddaughters. Two named godsons were to receive '20s towards his exhibition' and 'the one half of my books' respectively. Finally, he left 12d to 'every one of my godchildren to whom I have made no bequest'. Similarly, Richard Rylay, rector of Swarkestone, left 4d to each of his godchildren but singled out his godson Roger for the bequest of a heifer. In the case of the will of Thomas Tunstall, the distinction being made might have been that between those godchildren who were related through blood and those who were not. The most favoured was his godson of the same name who was to receive 'one cow, and his three children every one of them one sheep, the which cow and sheep are in his keeping'. Another godson also shared the curate's name and was distinguished as 'Thomas Tunstall my godson Ralph Tunstall's son' and was left 6s 8d. Three other godsons, two of whom were left a sheep and one who received 3s 4d also, perhaps significantly, shared the name 'Thomas'. Thomas Wylson,

---

[105] Marshall, *Catholic Priesthood*, 209.

vicar of Abbots Bromley, made the distinction between all his godchildren 'in the town', to whom he left 4d, the four that would 'bear me unto the church' who would receive 6d and 'every child that can say *de profundis*', who were to be rewarded with a further 4d. The Macclesfield chaplain and schoolmaster William Bridges left twice as much to his goddaughters as his godsons (12d and 6d respectively), favouritism that might have had half an eye to the future as with his further bequest to his goddaughter Margaret Creswell of 40s 'towards her marriage'. His will also suggests that a priest chosen to stand as godfather at baptism might go on to act as sponsor at confirmation by his bequest 'to every godchild, son and daughter, that I have confirmed at the Bishop 4d to pray for my soul and all Christian souls', thus further enhancing the spiritual relationship between the two. Richard Blockley, vicar of Wolvey, made bequests only to godsons, presumably with a regard for their future economic security, leaving a ewe to each one within the parish and two sheep and a calf to a specified godson. In a similar vein, William Corveser, vicar of Stanton upon Hine Heath left a sheep 'to every godchild that I have, not married'.

Some clerical testators made bequests only to a limited number of godchildren, or individuals, again suggesting a relationship involving genuine affection. Richard Asche, chantry priest of Beighton, left quality gowns of different materials to three named godchildren, and John Fitzherbert, vicar of Doveridge, specified two godsons; one, the son of his servant was to receive a new coat and 'the wheat of one land in the field' and the other, 'young John Smalcher', was to have the choice of a yearling calf or 5s. The Chesterfield chaplain Henry Tryge mentioned only one godson who, as the recipient of 'my bow, three arrows, a bird bolt, a spear and a steel bonnett', was, like his father in whose keeping they had been, evidently seen as a suitable custodian for some of the priest's more secular items.[106] Even greater trust was placed by the Coventry priest Thomas Fisher in his godson chosen to act as his executor, and the closeness of their relationship is reflected in the bequest to him and his wife of 'all other my goods that God has lent me'. If such a relationship between priest and godchild is suggestive of pseudo-kinship, so too is the fact that, following a list of bequests to some half dozen named individuals, the rector of Lymm, Roger Leigh, went on to leave 4d 'to

---

[106] Much is often made of the ownership of weapons by clergy which is much more an indication that they were all at one time full members of secular society than that they teetered constantly on the brink of acts of violence; in many cases such items might themselves have been received as bequests when the future priest was in his youth. Certainly bows and arrows were mentioned in a number of wills in the sample and presumably, if used by the priest himself at all, would be fired in practice and competition at the butts. For the view that ownership of weapons equalled preparedness to do violence see for example, Haigh, *Reformation and Resistance*, 53 and Brigden, *London and the Reformation*, 46: 'The London clergy were not always peaceable. Some left weapons in their wills . . .'.

every *other* godchild that I have within the parish'.[107] The previous individuals had not been specified as the rector's godchildren and, to all intents and purposes, were treated as though they were members of his family.

Charity and Community

Just as the degree of involvement by the pastoral clergy in the economic life of the parish emerges from the details of their material possessions contained in their wills and inventories, the common choice of a member of the local clergy as a godparent is a reflection of the social ties that bound cleric and layman within the parish community. During his lifetime the priest would have been expected to extend hospitality to his lay neighbours[108] and show pastoral concern for their material as well as spiritual well-being, but whilst there is no reason to suppose that such duties were not generally undertaken they make little impression on the surviving records. Only when the priest made arrangements for the distribution of his worldly goods after his death does the nature of his social concern emerge with any clarity and whilst it can be argued that acts of deathbed charity were little more than a pious convention of the age,[109] such provision on the part of the parish clergy affords a rare insight into their own perceptions of the community within which they lived and worked.

Almost half of the clergy in the sample made charitable bequests in their wills, some as part of the general distribution of their goods, others specifically as an aspect of their funerary arrangements. Since it was priests without formal parochial benefices who were most likely to be serving communities within which they had been raised, it is perhaps significant that it was clergy from within this group that more commonly made the most inclusive bequests, that is, to every householder in the parish. In a variation on this formula, two chaplains of Wroxeter, Richard Dodycotte and Roger Lee, both remembered the wider community in their wills; Dodycotte leaving 8d to every cottage in the parish and Lee 4d to every cottage in the town, as well as putting aside 40s to be distributed in doles of bread at his funeral. William Bridges made similar provision, leaving 12d 'to every honest householder in the town of Macclesfield'. The will of Thomas Avereye, a priest of Astley, clearly suggests the intentionally inclusive nature of such provision, leaving money to every house in the parish as well as for bread, cheese and ale to be provided at his funeral, with the residue of his estate 'to be distributed in deeds of pity . . . as best to please God, for my soul, my friends' souls, and all

---

[107] My italics.
[108] Above, 89 and n. 254.
[109] According to Jonathan Hughes, best seen as penitential gestures: Hughes, *Pastors and Visionaries*, 114.

Christian souls'.¹¹⁰ Although these priests were among the poorest testators, their bequests perhaps suggest the closest links with the greater community. But such demonstrations of community spirit could also be found among the beneficed clergy. William Brewster, vicar of Etwall, devoted no fewer than four pages of his will to extraordinarily elaborate charitable provisions. They included a bequest of 12d

> to every man, woman and child and servant [of the parish] and the residue and overplus to be bestowed . . . in cows and such other cattle that the increase of the said cattle may help and discharge the common charges both of [Etwall] and Burnaston in taxes, fifteenths etc.

Writing in 1549, at the height of the first period of Tudor price inflation and a time of increasing taxation, Brewster's provisions would surely have been welcome, as, presumably, were the worn out shoes and old clothes that he set aside for distribution to the local poor.

Other priests directed their charitable intentions *specifically* to the local poor. This could either be in the form of a lump sum, such as the 20s that the curate of Shifnal, Richard Hatton, stated should be distributed among the poor of the town and parish, or the residue of the goods of Roger Leigh, rector of Lymm, to be 'disposed among the poor folks [of the] parish'; or individual payments, such as the 12d that John Fitzherbert, as vicar, left to 'every poor householder in the parish of Doveridge and Wilton'. Like William Brewster, John Redfern, vicar of Longford, intended to establish a parish stock

> in sheep or else other cattle, and the yearly residue of the same stock to be bestowed upon necessaries belonging to the same church and part thereof to be given to poor people at the direction of the churchwardens for the time being there, with the advice and consent of the parishioners of the same, for my soul, and all Christian souls.

By contrast, Richard Rowlowe, rector of Ryton, directed his executors simply to put 3s 4d in 'the poor men's box' in the church. While charitable provision such as this was of the most general kind, other priests singled out groups and individuals in particular need. Thomas Wylson, vicar of Abbots Bromley, was mindful of the requirements of the family unit, directing that 'forty of the most poorest householders within the town shall have every one of them 4d to be bestowed amongst their family'. William More, a chaplain at Marchington, made a bequest to 'every poor widow that hath but one cow 4d and other householders that hath no cows within the town of Marchington 4d'. Henry Slany, vicar of Bushbury, identified four individual parishioners, Ellen Lufner, Thomas Stokes, William Parker and 'John Turner, his

---

110 Will dated 1541, at LJRO; not included in the sample because at that time he was almost certainly a fellow of the collegiate church rather than a member of the parochial clergy. However, he might be the same as the chaplain of Holy Trinity, Coventry, in 1533; above, 71.

neighbour' as being in particular need, and left them all a *strike*[111] of rye; whilst John Bee, a chantry priest at Uttoxeter, as well as providing for a general funeral dole, singled out an individual parishioner 'which is impotent towards his house rent' for a payment of 3s. Many priests, especially among the unbeneficed, would have been involved in the education of children, and made provision for such work to continue after their death. They might have included Richard Bexwyke, the curate of Middleton, who left 12d to each of twelve poor scholars, and certainly William Bridges, who in his working life would doubtless have hoped that some of the boys in his charge would themselves have proceeded to ordination, and made provision that after his death 'every scholar resorting [to] the Grammar School in Macclesfield, them that can sing to have 2d and every other of them to have 1d'. Of course, to the majority of young parishioners, education would have been a luxury, and to some the main preoccupation would have been mere survival to adulthood. Such as these did John Nowell, rector of Swynnerton, have in mind when he left a sheep to each of twenty poor children.

Whilst the evidence would suggest that charity usually began at home, it need not be limited to the priest's immediate neighbours. John Abell, Roger Leigh and Henry Slany all included the poor of nearby villages and townships in their wills, while William Brewster made provision for those of a number of places to which a long and varied career had taken him, including an Irish parish. Some bequests were not directed towards the priest's neighbours themselves but the roads, causeways and bridges, the upkeep of which was a vital communal concern. William Swynerton, rector of Blymhill, left 4 strikes of wheat to the town 'to help mend the fows wey, if they will not stryve with my executors' and Richard Ryve, vicar of South Wingfield, left 40s for a similar purpose. John Fitzherbert, vicar of Doveridge, left 6s 8d to the bridge from which the village originally took its name, and the same sum to Tutbury bridge, whilst William Brewster's bequests included money for the repair of a bridge in the Northamptonshire village where his parents were buried and 10s 6d to be divided between maintenance of a bridge in his own parish of Etwall and the churchyard wall. The parish church itself, too, as a communal building uniting clergy and laity, was frequently the object of clerical bequests, with almost one-third of the sample testators leaving money or goods towards the fabric of their churches. The Chesterfield chaplain Henry Tryge, as well as leaving service books for the use of the church, bequeathed 12d towards the porch next to which he asked to be buried. Recognising his position within the wider diocese as well as the parish community, William Swynerton left 12d to each of the two cathedrals in return for prayers for his soul, but to his own church left a cow. Similarly Ralph Tatton, rector of Barlborough, left money to Repton Priory, Burton Lazars and the 'Rood Guild' of his parish.[112] Edmund Bachelor, rector of

---

[111] A dry measure of half a bushel.
[112] For the connection between Tatton and Repton Priory see above, 153, n. 89.

Sheinton, remembered not only the church of which he had been incumbent, but also that of the neighbouring village where he had been a chaplain some years previously, leaving 6s 8d for a cross to be used in Sheinton and the same amount towards the rebuilding of the church and steeple at Cound. As one of the few priests who made the transition from a stipendiary post to a benefice during the period, this was an apposite gesture.

Pastor and Neighbour: The Local Economy

Most obvious in the local community through his unique sacramental role, the priest was, however, also a fellow-player in the temporal affairs of the parish. His frequent involvement in agricultural and commercial interests, outlined above, must have rendered the average incumbent or parish priest practically indistinguishable from his lay neighbours. Just as he might have been in the position to hire out his plough team, as possibly one of the few members of the community with a regular cash income he was likely to be seen as a source of local credit, a role that would have brought him into close contact with the day-to-day business of his parishioners. Indirect evidence of such activity comes in the form of the lists of debtors, some quite lengthy, occasionally entered in clerical wills and inventories.[113] John Morehall, vicar of Sutton Maddock, was owed a total of £26 from eight laymen and the debts of William Bridges, chaplain of Macclesfield, included 'one silver flat piece old gilted' and five marks which he had lent to John Leghe, and a sum of £8 which he had lent to John Hall towards the marriage of his three daughters. The organised nature of some of this clerical lending is suggested by the bequest by John Holwaye, rector of Hinstock, of all the money 'which be written in my book of debts, equally to be divided' between members of his family.[114] It is no surprise, in this context, that among the memoranda collected together in the notebook of the York priest, Robert Burton, was a ready-reckoner.[115] In case of dispute some priests took pains to identify the

---

[113] The occurrence of a significant number of the surnames of creditors of Staffordshire clergy in the list of householders in their parish c.1532 supports the impression that the majority of lending was local: *Families in the Archdeaconry of Stafford*, passim.

[114] Claire Cross cites the case of a York chantrist, the majority of whose inventory consisted of money on loan which he had entered in a book: Cross, 'Incomes of Provincial Urban Clergy', 74.

[115] Haines, 'A York Priest's Notebook', 159. Whilst this might have been primarily an aid for the record of receipts it is clear that many parochial clergy were involved in money lending, and although none of the wills in the present sample provide direct evidence of lending at interest, this might have been concealed or translated into some other form of consideration. As far as usury was concerned, by the later Middle Ages the church's 'theory became divorced from reality' and 'whilst maintaining a blanket opposition to crude usury, the theologians did admit some element of compensation for the lender'; 'Lending at interest became acceptable, provided it was not

place where the money had been lent. Richard Webb, rector of Stapleton, named the owner of the house in the village where Thomas Jobbyns had borrowed 2s, and Thomas Tunstall, curate of Wolstanton, noted that he had lent 10s to James Beche 'in Our Lady's Aisle'. Tunstall serves as a good example of the significance of local clergy in providing credit for a variety of purposes to the laity; over the long period (at least thirty-four years) during which he had served the parish, he had acquired a list of debtors from among his parishioners and other local laypeople[116] owing more than £17 in total. Some impression of the scale of such lending may be gained from the consideration that his annual stipend was under £5 and the total value of his estate was just over £11 at his death in 1565.

Had parochial records survived in greater number from this period they would doubtless reveal something of the range of integration of the parish clergy in the local economy. Just as the multifarious ways in which assistant clergy augmented their incomes is demonstrated in the churchwardens' accounts of Prescot, something of the degree of their economic integration within the community is revealed by its court records. In 1534 the chaplains Edward Garnett and Henry Colley were in dispute between themselves concerning entitlement to the profit of a cow apparently owned by one of the parish stocks. In 1535 Colley was fined 2s in the manorial court for stopping up a common way called 'le milne lane' and in the following year he was one of five men in the parish ordered to cut down any of his trees 'that shadow the windmill from the wind' on pain of a 12d fine. In 1547 Edward Garnett was alleged to have felled a tree illegally.[117] Such cases, and the very means by which the majority of local clergy made their living, suggest that in economic and social terms, firm distinctions between clergy and laity were rarely drawn, and intimate involvement in the secular affairs of the parish was rarely seen as incompatible with the clerical role.[118]

Potentially more contentious involvement of the parish clergy in the local economy, however, resulted from the obligation on all parishioners to render to their incumbent a tenth of their annual income, the tithe, as well as other occasional dues. Of 101 cases between clergy and laity of the diocese that were heard in the bishop's consistory court between 1524 and 1531, half

---

exploitative.': Swanson, *Church and Society*, 194. For other evidence of clerical money-lending at parish level during this period see Cross, 'Incomes of Provincial Urban Clergy', 74–5.

[116] Writing his will in 1565, the names of all his debtors can be identified with the offspring of householders in his parish and neighbouring Newcastle in 1532 with supporting evidence coming from his own identifications of provenance such as 'of the castell' [i.e. from Newcastle] etc. For householders in 1532 see n. 113 above.

[117] *Prescot Records*, 83, 84, 86, 92.

[118] A perception of incongruity tended to arise only when the boundaries between sacred and profane were blatantly transgressed such as by the Yorkshire vicar of Langtoft's keeping of his sheep in a pen in the chancel of the church in 1571: Marshall, *Pastoral Ministry in the East Riding*, 20.

involved financial disputes, the majority of which were at the instigation of the clerical party.[119] But to put this in context, this represents an average of just seven cases proceeding to court from the greater part of the diocese each year, a similar level of litigation to that which has been observed in the ecclesiastical courts of other dioceses. For example, the 250 parishes in the diocese of Canterbury produced fourteen tithe cases in 1482 and only four in 1531.[120] In 1529 only three such cases proceeded from the 339 parishes of the diocese of Winchester and in 1524 the extensive diocese of Norwich, comprising approximately 1,150 parishes, produced just ten cases.[121] Where mortuary cases have been separated from the record of general financial disputes, a similarly low level has been detected. The court book of the archdeaconry of Chester records five mortuary cases in Cheshire between 1502 and 1515 and none at all in the Lancashire part of the archdeaconry.[122] Between 1519 and 1529 just six mortuary cases came before the consistory court of the diocese of Norwich.[123] Financial disputes should also be set within the context of evidence of the frequently harmonious relationship between parish clergy and their parishioners which emerges from the significant cumulative expenditure on priests revealed in churchwardens' accounts, a body of evidence which has only recently been brought properly into the equation.[124] Such an economic relationship worked both ways, as shown by the Walsall chaplain, Thomas Flemyng, who, as custodian of St Clement's altar, was not only charged with accounting for receipts but with overseeing its stock which, in 1527, included the requirement to provide a statement concerning its beehives.[125]

Even when cases did come before the courts, there were mechanisms for settlement built into the system and the suits which were abandoned or peacefully settled greatly outnumbered those in which a sentence was delivered. Twenty-nine of the fifty-one cases for the recovery of ecclesiastical dues do not have a recorded conclusion. In only three cases were the lay defendants found guilty and required to pay or face a sentence of excommunication; of the remaining cases where details of the progress of the suit are recorded, five were explicitly settled out of court and one by arbitration. In six cases the defendant was suspended from taking part in the Eucharist for persistent failure to attend hearings. In only three cases is there a recorded

---

119 LJRO, B/C/2/1-3, *passim*.
120 C. Haigh, 'Anticlericalism and the English Reformation', in C. Haigh, ed., *The English Reformation Revised* (Cambridge, 1987), 69.
121 Ibid.
122 Haigh, *Reformation and Resistance*, 58.
123 R.A. Houlbrooke, *Church Courts and the People during the English Reformation* (Oxford, 1979), 125.
124 'Any attempt to discuss contemporary attitudes towards the clergy without due reference to churchwardens' accounts presents only a very partial picture': Kümin, 'Parish Finance and the Early Tudor Clergy', 52.
125 *Churchwardens' Accounts of All Saints, Walsall*, 262.

decision against the defendant layman. Of these, the action brought by the vicar of Aston against John Couper makes the most pathetic reading.[126] Couper did not attend the first hearing in March 1528, and at the second was represented by his son, Henry, who claimed that his father was too ill to make an appearance at Lichfield, but refused to take an oath of payment on his behalf, resulting in a declaration of suspension against his father. At the third hearing, Henry Couper again represented his allegedly infirm father but this time stated that agreement had been reached with the vicar who would be paid the tithes in full, and made a payment of 8s to the court to cover costs. Thomas Lynsey confessed to withholding tithes from William Leson, rector of Newton Regis, in 1528 and was ordered to make full settlement of two years' small tithes valued at 11d per year. For a further offence of uttering defamatory words against the rector he was enjoined to carry a cross around the church, bare-legged and bare-foot, in the manner of a penitent.[127] In 1529 Richard Harrison failed to appear at the first hearing of the case brought against him by Thomas Shirebroke, vicar of Tibshelf, and on his failure to appear at the second the vicar's proctor petitioned that he be declared in contempt and under pain of excommunication. The sanction was effective, since Harrison made an appearance at the subsequent hearing and declared that he had been kept away from previous sessions as a result of being about the king's business. Warned to appear at the next hearing, he failed to do so, and incurred the full penalty of excommunication, which was confirmed one month later, for his failure to appear at a specified date for absolution.[128] In the same year the vicar of Tibshelf instigated another suit, for recovery of mortuaries and tithes on coal, but with even less success than he had experienced in his action against Harrison, this being the only recorded case where the decision went against the plaintiff clerk. The case dragged on for thirty-five hearings over more than a year, occasionally splintering into individual actions against some of the parishioners involved. At the end of all this the case was dismissed when it was successfully argued by the defendants' proctor that the testimony produced during the case by witnesses for the vicar had been falsely procured and was self-contradictory.[129]

The majority of cases appear to have been settled out of court, a process that is occasionally explicit in the records. In one of two tithe actions instigated by the vicar of Alstonefield it was stated that the case was being dropped at the petition of both parties.[130] In the case of the action brought by John Colmore, vicar of Penn and subchanter of Lichfield Cathedral,

---

[126] LJRO, B/C/2/2, fos. 41v, 47r; B/C/2/3, fo. 1r.
[127] Ibid., B/C/2/2, fo. 47r; for other symptoms of friction between the two parties see above, 135–6.
[128] Ibid., B/C/2/3, fos. 89r, 92r, 94r, 96r, 99v.
[129] Ibid., fos. 76r, 78v, 80r, 82v, 84r, 85v, 87r, 88r, 92v, 93r, 94r, 95r, 96r, 98r–v, 101r–v, 103r–v, 106v.
[130] Ibid., fo. 131r.

against Robert Coke, a certificate was produced in the seventh hearing to the effect that Coke's payment of 3s was sufficient for Colmore not to proceed with the case.[131] Satisfaction was said to have been reached as soon as the case brought by the rector of Myddle against a number of his parishioners reached the court in 1529, and in the mortuaries case brought in the same year by the vicar of Child's Ercoll against one of his parishioners it was stated simply that settlement had been reached.[132] The most unusual of the cases settled out of court was that between William Franks, vicar of Barrow upon Trent, and three of his parishioners in 1526. This was brought to settlement after three months following the intervention of the rector of the same living, Ambrose Layton, who appeared declaring an interest in the case and a desire to join in the defence of the laymen.[133] Presumably Franks had been making a claim to some of the greater tithes of the parish or other dues to which only the rector was entitled, and the development of a dispute between clerk and laymen into one between clerics worked to the advantage of the lay community. Also of interest is the fact that Franks was one of the poorer incumbents in the diocese. In 1535 the vicarage was valued at just £5 6s 4d of which just over £2 came from small tithes and those on lambs and wool.[134] When he died in 1541 his goods were worth a mere £10 12s 3d: only two beneficed clerks in the testamentary sample had a smaller estate. In a single case, that between John Keldermere, vicar of Chilvers Coton, and Henry Rampton in 1527, the judge called for arbitration between the parties.[135] Due to his failure to appear at the first two hearings, Rampton was barred from entering the parish church, a disciplinary measure which succeeded in securing his presence at the third. During this session, Rampton declared that he would be prepared to make some payment and two court proctors were appointed to supervise a payment of four instalments of 3d in settlement of the unpaid milling tithes. On the same day as that decision Rampton initiated an action against the vicar which, although it appears to have been taken no further, suggests that he was not entirely happy with the outcome of the case against him.[136] A single case during the period was sent forward for appeal to a higher court. At the thirteenth hearing, definitive sentence was passed in the case of the vicar of Shustoke against Agnes Onyon. However, the proctor acting on behalf of Onyon declared that agreement had already been reached before sentencing and gave notice of his intention to appeal to the court of audience of Cardinal Wolsey, which was accepted by the judge.[137] Isolated instances of litigation, of course, are

131 Ibid., B/C/2/1, fos. 7r, 8v, 10r, 11v, 12v, 14r, 17v.
132 Ibid., B/C/2/3, fos. 78v, 81r, 87r, 93v, 95v, 98r, 105v, 108r, 109r.
133 Ibid., B/C/2/1, fos. 75v, 82v, 86r, 89v, 93r.
134 *Valor*, iii, 161.
135 LJRO, B/C/2/2, fos. 13r, 15r, 17v.
136 Ibid., fo. 18r.
137 Ibid., B/C/2/3, fos. 19v, 23v, 32v, 36v, 40r, 44r, 47r, 49r, 51v, 53v, 55v, 57v, 59r, 61v, 64r, 65v, 67v, 120v, 122v.

only indicative of problems arising between two individuals, one clerical and the other lay.[138] More suggestive of greater underlying problems within the parish were those occasions where a number of cases proceeded from within a single community over a relatively short period of time. However, such problems again appear to have been relatively rare, with just six incumbents involved in more than one suit for recovery of tithe or other ecclesiastical dues between 1524 and 1531. Four of these, the rectors of Stoke-on-Trent and Yoxall and the vicars of Aston and Alstonefield, were priests enjoying an income above the average for the diocese.[139] M. Richard Egerton, rector of Stoke-on-Trent and a resident canon of Lichfield, was a pluralist on quite a grand scale. His return for the clerical assessment of 1533 shows that, potentially at least, he was a wealthy man.[140] His involvement in three tithe cases during the period suggests that his intention was to maximise that potential from parishes from which he was an absentee. By contrast, for the vicars of Tibshelf and Shustoke, who were in receipt of incomes considerably less than average for the diocese, the motivation might have been more one of survival.[141] However, of the fifty-one clergy involved in financial litigation against their parishioners during this period, only fourteen were required to contribute to the 1533 clerical subsidy at a level lower than the average for the diocese. This suggests that the more common motivation of litigants, rather than being economic hardship, was likely to have been the desire to maximise sources of potential income, often by absentees who, in any case, enjoyed no real relationship with their parishioners.

Pastor and Neighbour: Social Integration

The economic interests of the parish priest brought him into frequent contact, and occasional conflict, with his lay parishioners. At a social level, close contact is borne out by the evidence of wills; the commonly-observed frequency with which lay people turned to their local priests as witnesses and executors of their wills[142] was largely reciprocal. Over two-thirds of the clergy in the testamentary sample included laypeople in this capacity, in

---

138 For a comparative discussion of the consequences of financial litigation between clergy and laity, including the costs involved, see Heath, *English Parish Clergy*, 147, 150–1; Bowker, *Secular Clergy*, 147; ibid., *Henrician Reformation*, 135–6; Thomson, *Early Tudor Church and Society*, 173; S. Brigden, 'Tithe Controversy in Medieval London', *JEH*, 32 (1981), 285–301; ibid., *London and the Reformation*, 51; Haigh, *Reformation and Resistance*, 25, 58–62; Swanson, *Church and Society*, 212; ibid., 'Standards of Livings', 162.
139 In 1535 the values were as follows: Stoke, £41 0s 8d, *Valor*, iii, 120; Yoxhall, £17 6s 8d, *Valor*, iii, 150; Aston, £21 4s 8d, *Valor*, iii, 81; Alstonefield, £8 13s 4d, *Valor*, iii, 126.
140 See above, 67.
141 In 1535: Shustoke, 107s, *Valor*, iii, 81; Tibshelf, £4 5s 3d, *Valor*, iii, 179.
142 Stevens Benham, 'The Durham Clergy', 28.

most cases (since a place of residence is not mentioned) their parishioners, and a number of testators named exclusively lay executors and witnesses. It was certainly not the case that parish clergy restricted their social relations to members of their own calling and in the face of such evidence, an argument that lay and clerical society were essentially hostile, or at least antipathetic, is difficult to sustain. Other incidental references, from various sources, provide hints as to the degree of integration of the parish clergy within local society. A note inserted after the list of ordinations of May 1505, records the fact that Henry Ward, vicar of Mancetter, had been warned not to practise as a physician, specifically by administering medicines and inspecting urine samples,[143] and in a similar vein, but at a rather more prosaic level, one of the numerous items that the graduate rector of Swynnerton, John Nowell, bequeathed in his will to Margaret Iremongar was an alembic for distilling whisky.[144] In 1534 Thomas Dashwen, curate of Enville, was one of a party which responded to a hue and cry in the parish of Bobbington and helped to sort out a violent dispute;[145] and the twenty-eight clergy who joined the Lichfield Civic Gild of St Mary and St John the Baptist during the period, and who can be shown to have been working in various parts of the diocese by 1535, were likely to have brought greater variety to their contacts with lay society as a result, as well as perhaps helping to further their careers.[146] In general terms, priests and people at the local level usually shared a similar social background and concerns and were subject to the same agrarian, commercial and jurisdictional controls.[147] Among the more obviously spiritually inspired items in the notebook of the York priest, Robert Burton, were memoranda of an altogether more secular nature, including astronomical calculations and riddles popular among laymen of the age dealing satirically with men's eternal mysteries such as *When Will the World End?* and *What is Woman?*[148]

It was the relationship of priests to women, arising from the vow of celibacy, that served to make the most obvious secular distinction between clergy and laity. The fact that clerical households so frequently included a female housekeeper, and perhaps other female servants, demonstrates that priests and women were commonly in close contact, a situation simultaneously facilitating social integration but providing grounds for gossip. The

[143] LJRO, B/A/1/14ii, fo. 18v. Another incumbent had been instituted by the time of the admission of Robert Whittington (see below) in 1514; ibid., B/A/1/14, fo. 6v.
[144] 'A lymbecke to stylle aquavite'. A 'lambecke' was also among the goods of Richard Hatton, curate of Shifnal; see below, 187. The view that such an item was essentially medicinal might be supported by the fact that both men lived into their seventies; below, 191, 193.
[145] *Star Chamber Proceedings, Henry VIII and Edward VI*, William Salt Society, Collections for a History of Staffordshire, 1912, 72–3. Ordained priest in 1513, he was curate by 1531; LJRO, B/A/1/14ii, fo. 94r; ibid., B/A/17/1(1), fo. 10r.
[146] LJRO, D.77/1, pp. 251–330.
[147] Kümin, *Shaping of a Community*, 225.
[148] Haines, 'A York Priest's Notebook', 163, 167–8, 172.

potential for ambiguity is perhaps exemplified by the will of John Bee, chantry priest of Uttoxeter, who made bequests to a disproportionately high number of women including numerous items left to one Agnes Moore, the daughter of a local capper,[149] and various items of clothing, as well as cash, to Hugh Moore, described as 'my boy'. Although we need read no more into this than the generosity of an aged cleric towards his servants, it is clear that the domestic circumstances of many priests could have laid them open to suspicion.[150] The Warwickshire priest John Yate similarly left a large part of his goods, as well as the residue of his estate of a little over £8, to what appears to have been a single woman. The vicar of Longford, John Redfern, left £5, amounting to almost one-third of his entire estate, to one Joan Williamson, who also appears to have been unmarried, the vicar stipulating that the bequest was to be made 'if God do spare her life, and in case she do die, then I will that her father have four marks of the said five pounds'. Even where relations between priests and female parishioners did transgress the boundary of acceptability and led to a breach of the vow of celibacy, the evidence suggests that a distinction was made between isolated incidents of sexual incontinence, or more particularly of fornication or adultery, and relationships of sometimes quasi-marital concubinage which involved cohabitation and procreation.[151] It has been suggested that in the eyes of the laity the distinction might have been one of unacceptability in the case of the former, since such liaisons threatened the social fabric, and an apparent degree of tolerance towards the latter in that a cohabitational relationship was stable and restricted the transgression to the confines of an individual household.[152] However, the length of time devoted by the consistory court to cases of apparent concubinage, together with the scale of penalties imposed on the miscreant clergy involved, tend to suggest that the ecclesiastical authorities took the opposite view, most probably on account of the threat to parochial revenues implied by clerical progeny. Between 1524 and 1531, the period for which the records of the bishop of Lichfield's consistory court survive,

---

[149] There were three individuals with this name in the parish c.1532; *Families in the Archdeaconry of Stafford*, 3.
[150] Heath, *English Parish Clergy*, 106–7.
[151] A.D. Frankforter, 'The Reformation and the Register: Episcopal Administration of Parishes in Late Medieval England', *Catholic Historical Review*, 63 (1977), 212–13. A concubinal relationship seems to be suggested by the marginal entry in the list of chaplains for the archdeaconry of Chester of 1541–2 which, against the name of Richard Deane at Blackburn, records that he was 'living with a woman at Rufford' [*vivit cum muliere apud Rufford*]: *Clergy in the Diocese of Chester*, 17. When in 1526 Thomas Appleby, vicar of Atcham, was called before the consistory court following a report from an apparitor and asked to state why he should not be punished for having a woman in his house the investigation revealed a complicated set of circumstances, with the vicar claiming that it was another man who was having sexual relations with her and there was some doubt concerning the identity of the father of her children. The case was not concluded and charges were presumably dropped: LJRO, B/C/2/1, fos. 75v, 78r, 110v, 124v, 125r.
[152] Heath, *English Parish Clergy*, 108; Haigh, *Reformation and Resistance*, 50.

actions were taken against eighteen clerks of the diocese for alleged sexual offences. Twelve of these were priests with cure of souls while the remaining six were stipendiary chaplains. Apart from the single case of filiation brought by the mother of the child in question,[153] they were all office suits and would have come to court either as a result of the findings of parochial visitation or at the instigation of apparitors.[154] Yet rather than necessarily being viewed as evidence of friction between clergy and laity, the involvement of parish clergy in sexual relationships within the community can be seen as further testimony to their degree of social integration.

Between 1524 and 1531 three priests were found guilty of isolated incidents of sexual incontinence. The chaplain, Henry Heyton, was reported to the authorities in 1525 by a fellow-priest who alleged that he had had a child by a certain woman. Despite protesting his innocence, Heyton was found guilty and by way of public penance was sentenced to lead a procession around his church.[155] John Crosse, vicar of Offchurch, charged with incontinence in 1528, similarly denied the allegation and told the court that he had been previously examined by an episcopal commission before which he had successfully purged himself. The consistory court was, however, satisfied of his guilt and he was ordered to pay 3s 4d towards rebuilding work at the cathedral.[156] Thomas Smyth, vicar of Uttoxeter, confessed to adultery with the wife of the parish clerk in 1528 and, following his failure to appear at the first court hearing, was suspended from celebrating mass. His guilt was formally established at a subsequent hearing, following which he was sentenced to carry a cross around his parish church, pay 6s 8d towards pious uses and a further 8d to cover costs.[157] A more serious allegation, of incest, was made against the chaplain, William Ashley, in the same year. His precise relationship with Helen Ashley is not elucidated in the charge (which he denied) and records of the court's decision in the matter have not survived.[158] A further three clerks had charges brought against them but were cleared by the court. In 1528 the curate of Cheswardine, John Chalner, successfully purged himself of an allegation of fornication with Joanna Capper[159] and in the same year the vicar of Curdworth, Thomas Flemyng, was acquitted on a charge of incontinence when the only witness, a female parishioner, failed to appear.[160] In 1529 the rector of Cheadle, Richard Norres, was charged with making Margaret Lyngard pregnant but the case was dropped following

---

[153] LJRO, B/C/2/1, fos. 18v, 20r.
[154] Laymen in this diocese, they made a living from the commission received for making citations before the bishop's courts; as such they attracted almost universal opprobrium: Cooper, 'Secular Clergy', 230.
[155] LJRO, B/C/2/1, fo. 78r.
[156] Ibid., B/C/2/3, fo. 4r.
[157] Ibid., fos. 4v, 7r.
[158] Ibid., fos. 35v, 38v.
[159] Ibid., fo. 41r.
[160] Ibid., fos. 19v, 24r.

questioning which satisfied the judge that the allegations were unfounded.[161] The fact that such allegations could be made, however, testifies to the potency of rumour and the need for a priest to maintain a good reputation and standing within the community; the rector of Pleasley, Nicholas Harrison, based his defence in mitigation of a charge of incontinence in 1517 precisely on the fact that he had kept his relationship with Agnes Simkin secret.[162]

Those cases which took longer to be appraised by the judge, and which involved a more systematic recording of evidence, generally resulted from longer-standing relationships into which priests had entered and which sometimes suggest either explicit or implicit concubinage. Continental evidence, including the large sums that bishops were able to collect in fees for licensing, suggests that long-term sexual relationships, whilst not the norm, were treated with a high degree of tolerance.[163] Within Britain a similar situation seems still to have obtained in parts of Wales in the early sixteenth century and *de facto* acceptance has been argued for at least some parts of England.[164] The number of clergy who took advantage of the Edwardian relaxation on marriage would tend to support the argument that part of the phenomenon was a legitimisation of existing concubinal relationships.[165] It has already been noted how the only testator in the sample to mention children, Thomas Tunstall, did not explicitly refer to his wife, whilst there is a suggestion that the mother might have been a female member of his household with whom he had entered into a form of common-law relationship.[166] The vicar of Rochdale, Gilbert Haydock, similarly made provision in his will of 1554 to 'those poor children here now dwelling in my house unto whom I am father and grandfather', without mentioning their mother. He nominated as his executors 'Joan my bastard daughter, and Ann the daughter of Richard Haydok, my bastard son', descriptions required by the law as it then stood.[167]

---

161 Ibid., fo. 71v.
162 He remained in post until his death in 1548: *Blythe's Visitations*, 46.
163 Marshall, *Catholic Priesthood*, 150–1. More and Tyndale were among those contemporary commentators who conceded that the reputation of English parish clergy in this regard was higher than that of their continental counterparts; ibid.
164 Ibid.; Haigh, *Reformation and Resistance*, 50.
165 Aveling, 'The English Clergy, Catholic and Protestant', 64; Marshall, *Catholic Priesthood*, 166.
166 See above, 123, 158.
167 H.H. Howorth, ed., *The Vicars of Rochdale, by the Late Canon Raines*, Chetham Soc., new ser., 1 (1883), 38. Haydock's institution does not appear to have been recorded in Blythe's register, but he was in possession of the benefice by 1522 and was named as vicar in 1533: ibid., 29; BL, Harleian Ms 594, fo. 151v. The ability of the offspring to act in an executive capacity proves that they were born before the accession of Edward VI and thus that they were the progeny of concubinage or other type of illicit union. Haydock would appear to have been ordained prior to 1503 and was thus at least 74 at the time of writing his will.

Any sexual relationship between a priest and a laywoman for which there was evidence of more than an isolated casual encounter appears to have been treated by the court as concubinage, regardless of whether this was specifically admitted by the suspect himself. The possibility that an allegation of fornication might unearth what in the view of the authorities appears to have been seen as a more serious state of affairs, emerges from the trial of the chaplain, Gilbert Fowler, before the consistory court in 1527. His admission of guilt when faced with an initial charge of incontinence was inevitable given that the lay apparitor presenting the articles had caught him and Elizabeth Mason in bed together. However, the court was evidently dissatisfied with this simple admission and required to know how long the liaison had continued. At this point Fowler, whilst claiming an inability to remember exactly how long he had known her, admitted to having kept her as a concubine for about ten nights and maintaining her in his house for a further four days. His attempt at precision was clearly intended to influence the court that his involvement with the woman was not of the nature of a prolonged relationship, since he went on further to claim that his had been an unpremeditated act of fornication following the temptation under which he had fallen as he watched her mowing a meadow near his house. It would appear that he was successful in sowing seeds of doubt in the mind of the judge, since whilst being required to process in penitential fashion around his church, no pecuniary fine was imposed, and a temporary suspension from celebrating mass resulted most probably from further allegations of irregularity in celebration and the hearing of confessions that arose during the hearing. He certainly appears subsequently to have been able to rehabilitate himself in the eyes of the authorities since he was working as curate of Allestree four years later.[168] A similar suggestion that the bishop's judge sought to make a distinction between simple fornication and the keeping of a concubine lies behind the questioning to which Roger Luter, curate of Berrington, was subjected in 1528.[169] Following his initial denial that intercourse between him and a certain Katherine had been frequent and that she had borne him children, it was further alleged that he had provided for the maintenance of the woman and her children from church funds. The change in direction of the questioning appears to have caught Luter off guard since he answered the supplementary charge simply with an admission of being at a loss for words. However, it would again appear that the judge was unable to ascertain the exact nature of the relationship since his initial sentence was limited to a temporary suspension from celebration of mass. It was only following the revelation, during the same hearing, that Luter had violated a previous injunction by reportedly saying mass in nearby Atcham, that he was ordered to carry a cross in procession around that church. Since his name

---

[168] LJRO, B/C/2/2, fo. 32v; BL, Harleian Ms 594, fo. 123v. Fowler would have been at least 45 at the time of the accusation; LJRO, B/A/1/14ii, fo. 27v.
[169] Ibid., B/C/2/2, fos. 32r, 37r; B/C/2/3, fo. 31v.

does not appear in the clerical subsidy list drawn up for the diocese five years later, it is possible that the aggravated charges led to subsequent deprivation from the curacy.

Another priest seemingly caught unprepared by the judge's line of inquiry was William Frinde, a chaplain in the parish of Wybunbury, who admitted to carnal knowledge of Elizabeth Pyrryn in 1528, but was similarly unable to offer a defence when asked about her pregnancy. On recovering his composure he confessed to having had access to her over a period of some six months and acknowledged that there was a general rumour that she was expecting. His admission led to the sentence of carrying a cross around the cemetery of the church in the manner of a penitent on the Sunday following the feast of St Matthew.[170] In the same year another chaplain, John Morden, came before the court and, initially, at least, put up a robust defence against allegations of incontinence with Margery Leycester, Alice Curtall, another woman of the same name and Joanna Roberts, but was eventually cornered into admission to copulation with Joanna Tyler and Katherine Damport. These charges were obviously serious enough in themselves but were compounded by Morden's further admission that he had kept Damport in his house for four years and had had children by her, for which provision had been made from church income. In this instance it is perhaps difficult to discern which aspect of the transgression the court saw as the more serious, the repeated acts of fornication or the maintenance of the concubine and her children; either way, the customary penitential sentence was augmented to include carrying a cross around the church in which he was employed on two rogation days and on the third, to carry it around the parish church where the women lived. Finally, he was given a date for a further court hearing at which he was to attempt to purge himself of the charges which he had denied, though no further record of the case survives.[171]

---

[170] Ibid., fo. 21r. Probably the William Frende ordained priest in 1508 to the title of Trentham Priory, some ten miles from Wybunbury, and who was curate of Uttoxeter by 1531. He would have been at least 44 at the time of the hearing. LJRO, B/A/1/14ii, fo. 55v; ibid., B/A/17/1(1), fo. 2r; BL, Harleian Ms 594, fo. 138v.

[171] LJRO, B/C/2/3, fo. 4r. His name does not appear in the list of chaplains in the diocese in 1533. Purgation involved the accused swearing an oath as to his innocence supported by the oaths of a number of individuals, usually between two and twelve, specified by the judge and normally determined by the seriousness of the allegations. These *compurgators* were not actually required to swear to the innocence of the accused but to his general reputation. An analysis of a few surviving lists in Blythe's register of individuals who had claimed 'benefit of clergy' and the compurgators supporting them suggests that the system could be quite perfunctory, since the same names of compurgators recur repeatedly. But despite the hostility to the system of 'benefit', by this period it does not seem to have generally affected employed parochial clergy; a search of the names of the fifteen criminous clerks cited in the register between 1512 and 1529 reveals only four possibilities in the ordination register. None of those cited appear in the lists of clergy of the 1530s and it would thus appear that they were not active parochial clergy; the same is true of the compurgators them-

The evidence that emerged during the hearings against two further clerks during the period leaves no doubt that they were involved in long-term relationships. The more prominent of the two was M. Robert Whittington, vicar of Nuneaton, who can almost certainly be identified with the renowned grammarian and possible early headmaster of Lichfield Grammar School.[172] The identification is further supported by the fact that, following an initial charge of incontinence involving one of his parishioners in 1525, the case was delayed on the presentation by the apparitor of letters from Cardinal Wolsey prohibiting the hearing of an additional charge in the Lichfield consistory court; certainly a prominent position in court circles would facilitate an appeal to the cardinal's legatine jurisdiction. The failure of the co-respondent, Margery Wade, to appear, led to her excommunication which might have prompted Whittington's own appearance at the fourth hearing, at which he renounced his appeal to the higher authority. He then confessed that Wade lived in his vicarage at Nuneaton and had lived with him in a variety of places over a period of six years, during which time he had provided for the four children that she had borne him. In answer to a further article he confessed that he had previously been warned concerning these matters by the vicar-general, Ralph Whitehead. By way of punishment he was first prohibited from having any further contact with Margery Wade, on pain of deprivation of his benefice, and was to secure her attendance at court to be absolved from her sentence of excommunication. He was then to pay 40s by way of an exhibition for poor scholars in two Easter instalments.[173]

selves: LJRO, B/A/1/14, fos. 64v, 79v, 96v; Swanson, *Church and Society*, 152–3; Cooper, 'Secular Clergy', 232, 240–62. The names found in the ordination register are John Chadwick (4 individuals; two priests, one deacon and an acolyte); Thomas Banaster (1 priest); John Marshall (4 individuals; 3 priests and an acolyte); John Parr (3 individuals; a priest, a deacon and a subdeacon). For similarly low numbers of commissions to hear compurgations with regard to criminous clerks in other dioceses see Heath, *English Parish Clergy*, Appendix 4, 211–12.

[172] Instituted to Nuneaton in 1521 (LJRO, B/A/1/14, fo. 7v). For his career see *BRUO*, 2039, where the suggestion that he might be the same as the vicar of Mancetter is almost certainly incorrect; see below. However, confusion of the two individuals, and the slight possibility that they are the same, is further compounded by the fact that the vicar of Nuneaton appears to have been occasionally *alias* Thomas (the incumbent in 1533 is M. Thomas Whittington, probably the grammarian, indicating that despite his relapse he was not deprived of the benefice; BL, Harleian Ms 594, fo. 122r) and the vicar of Mancetter occasionally William, and at his institution in 1514 appears as Master (LJRO, B/A/1/14, fo. 6v). As is shown below, the vicar of Mancetter certainly was deprived, in 1528; the institution of a new incumbent, Thomas Wylett, is not recorded, but at his resignation in 1530 he was replaced by Robert Barefote; LJRO, B/A/1/14, fo. 7v. For Barefote see *passim* and appendix. Only one William Whittington was ordained during Blythe's pontificate, admitted to each of the four holy orders to the title of Kenilworth Abbey between 1506 and 1508: LJRO, B/A/1/14ii, fos. 28r, 42v, 46v, 50v. The grammarian was apparently in priest's orders by 1513 but no-one by that name appears in Blythe's ordination register.

[173] LJRO, B/C/2/3, fos. 49v, 54v, 58v, 59r.

The punishment was not effective, however, and it was presumably the security which emanated from his position at court which gave him the confidence to refuse to accept a further citation from the court on matters concerning the 'danger to, and the correction and health of, his soul' delivered some six months after this original action.[174] Clearly, Whittington was a man following an essentially secular career, an absentee sinecurist whose ordination was probably motivated more by the interests of this career than a genuine vocation. Margery Wade, his long-term companion and mother of his children, who had followed him around the country in pursuit of that career, was a wife in all but name. Their forced separation would have been a tremendous hardship and a severe punishment for a man whose ambition, and the conventions of the day, had led him to attempt to serve two masters. Humphrey Clay, vicar of Loppington, on the other hand, appears to have pursued an unexceptional career as the incumbent of a rural Shropshire parish, at least until he was called before the Lichfield consistory court in 1528 to answer a charge of fornication with Anna Molyner. If his statement to the court that she had been his companion for six years was true, then their relationship had commenced some five years prior to his ordination to the diaconate in 1527. Perhaps this admission had been an attempt to influence the court into greater leniency towards him; if so, then it was misplaced, since in the event the judge dealt with him rather more harshly than in some of the other cases, requiring that he process around his church on three separate occasions with his head bared, following which he was to pay 10s towards repairs to the choristers' house in Lichfield and an additional sum of 10s to the churchwardens of Loppington the following Easter. Concerning Anna Molyner's fate we know nothing, but the vicar was allowed to keep his benefice and was still serving the parish in 1535.[175]

Taken together these cases which came before the consistory court might be said to confirm negative stereotypes of the parish clergy during this period. However, those surveys which have been undertaken into the ecclesiastical courts of various parts of the country help to place the problem of clerical immorality in a more accurate perspective. From over fifty parishes within the jurisdiction of the dean and chapter of York in the later fifteenth century, an average of 1.5 cases were being brought before the court each year.[176] In the diocese of Lincoln between 1514 and 1521, fewer than 1% of incumbents were found guilty of immorality.[177] Eleven clerks from the archdeaconry of Winchester came under suspicion in 1528 following a visitation of its 230 parishes and in the diocese of Norwich in 1538 proceedings were

---

[174] Ibid., fos. 129r, 132r.
[175] Ibid., fo. 34r; LJRO, B/A/1/14ii, fo. 190v; BL, Harleian Ms 594, fo. 133r; *Valor*, iii, 183.
[176] Heath, *English Parish Clergy*, 118–19.
[177] Bowker, *Secular Clergy*, 116–21.

commenced against eight clerks.[178] In all of these areas very few of the charges were proven. In the diocese of Lichfield, fewer than three cases per year were being reported by an apparitorial system of laymen notorious for their willingness to act, for fees, on the merest whiff of gossip.[179] As elsewhere, the perspective of nineteen individuals facing charges out of an *employed* clerical population of over 1,600 suggests that the problem was comparatively small-scale.[180] Furthermore, none of the evidence that emerged during these hearings suggests that the cases proceeded in response to open scandal among parishioners; rather, they were the result of the actions of lay apparitors acting on commission and on behalf of the court rather than the laypeople in the priests' charge. Such an impression is reinforced by the fact that some of these clergy had been able to maintain relationships over a number of years without apparently being reported by their parishioners. Additionally, the chronological distribution of the cases (two were commenced in 1525, one in 1527, one in 1529 and six in 1528) suggests that the majority might have come about as the result of a specific drive within the diocese to cut down on clerical immorality and, in particular, concubinage. In other words, rather than being seen as evidence of hostility between laity and clergy, and widespread disapproval of clerical relationships, they might rather be interpreted as a reflection of a desire on the part of the authorities to maintain standards, and to keep the clerical body as a whole above suspicion.

Pastor and Neighbour: Social Disintegration

The relationship between clergy and laity was essentially based on a system of mutual obligations. The priest was required to celebrate mass and administer the sacraments upon which the salvation of his parishioners was seen to depend, and at the same time maintain the discipline and dignity expected of the clerical estate. For their part, the laity were expected regularly to contribute a proportion of their income for the support of the priest as well as make certain payments, such as mortuary, as dictated by ecclesiastical law and modified by local custom. The majority of disputes which arose between clergy and laity issued from a failure in one or more aspects of this relationship, though usually in specific grievances, rather than as a general challenge

---

[178] Houlbrooke, *Church Courts and the People*, 178–9.
[179] In London diocese, for example, 'the slightest indiscretion by a priest brought catcalls and charges of incontinence. Such malicious gossip often found its way to court as a criminal charge against an innocent parson'; R.M. Wunderli, *London Church Courts and Society on the Eve of the Reformation* (Cambridge, Mass., 1981), 90.
[180] Aveling concludes that 'The few surviving episcopal visitation records indicate that only a small percentage of pastoral priests were charged with 'moral' offences': Aveling, 'The English Clergy, Catholic and Protestant', 64.

to the basis of the relationship itself. Tithe disputes, for example, appear usually to have arisen where there was disagreement concerning the amount owing, on which element of income, by whom and to whom, rather than over the principle of payment itself. Neither do the church courts appear to have been used specifically as weapons for the forceful extraction of income from the laity by the clergy. In only a tiny minority of the cases which were brought before the court during this period was the lay party found guilty of withholding tithe and required to pay; the majority appear to have been settled out of court, a process which, by its very nature, must have included a significant element of negotiation and compromise.[181] In cases where the clergy were accused of failings in their pastoral duties or moral discipline, the consistory court appears to have taken its responsibilities to the lay community quite seriously. Investigation was generally thorough, in some cases revealing defects beyond the scope of the original accusation. Some offenders, including all beneficed clergy, were ordered to pay cash fines, and most were required to make a public demonstration of their guilt through visible acts of penance designed to reconcile them with the community they served. The majority of disputes which came before the courts, including a small number of cases involving influential members of the community which were heard in Star Chamber, represented flash points of conflict, isolated confrontations between priest and parishioner arising from a particular grievance. For example, in 1520 the owner of a large house in Checkley, Staffordshire, accused the rector of the parish, M. Anthony Draycott, and Thomas Wildgoose, the curate of his other living of Draycott, of leading a forced entry into the premises. For his part Draycott claimed that he and his associates had been simply on business and that their intentions had been misinterpreted.[182] Occasionally, however, a number of lawsuits involving a single community are suggestive of more general problems which might threaten the finely-balanced relationship between the priest and his people.

In most cases a central underlying element of friction can be discerned at the root of wider problems between priests and their parishioners which caused an isolated incident to escalate into a more serious conflict. It was essentially grievances of a financial nature which lay behind the long-running dispute between Thomas Shirebroke, vicar of Tibshelf, and his parishioners, and his consequent citations by the diocesan authorities. Trouble started with Shirebroke's instigation of concurrent tithe actions against various of his parishioners, as detailed above, and the temperature was raised by his citation of a neighbouring vicar for allegedly impeding his parishioners from paying their Easter tithes.[183] Edmund Lee's reasons for doing this are suggested by a fourth case in which Shirebroke was involved.

---

[181] Wunderli, *London Church Courts*, 41–2; Houlbrooke, *Church Courts and the People*, 138.
[182] *Star Chamber Proceedings, Henry VIII and Edward VI*, 14–15.
[183] LJRO, B/C/2/3, fo. 76v.

In 1529 he was accused by the Official Principal of excommunicating his parishioners from the pulpit (presumably in direct action against their alleged non-payment of tithes) and it emerged at the hearings that the vicar himself had been declared excommunicate three years previously. At this point the questioning changed direction abruptly. When it was put to Shirebroke that there were three pregnant women living in his house, he confessed to two. He admitted to the impregnation of Katherine Fowler himself and declared that he had submitted himself on a previous occasion to the correction of the bishop's official. Although a date was set for a hearing of Shirebroke's attempts to clear his name, there is no further record of the case.[184] Clearly, this was a priest whose relationship with his parishioners had seriously broken down. Perhaps significantly, the clerical subsidy return of 1533 shows that he was one of the poorest incumbents in the diocese; his income of just over £4 put him on the level of the average stipendiary chaplain.[185]

The parish of Sutton Maddock was subject to a number of disputes during the period, both between the vicar and his parishioners and between various members of the clergy themselves. The community first appears in the records in 1526, with an allegation of clerical violence by the vicar, Richard Harrington, against a man and two women. The argument with the women appears to have been settled out of court, but the case against Thomas Fowler continued, though inconclusively.[186] On the same day an action was commenced against Harrington at the promotion of his parishioners on a charge related to non-residence which resulted in a court order for the vicar to reside in his benefice.[187] Just over a year later, Harrington himself was the promoter of an office suit against a chaplain, Richard Brett, apparently on a charge of assault, and which led to Brett's suspension from celebrating Mass.[188] Subsequent to this, Harrington retired from the living, but not before securing a pension from the income of the benefice of over £5, compared to an annual value of only about £3.[189] Shortly afterwards, Harrington's successor, John Morehall, was the promoter of another office suit against the chaplain, Richard Brett, who as a result was banned from interfering both in the cure of the parish and its fruits.[190] Two months later the official brought a second case against Brett for violent assault on the pensioner Harrington.[191] These actions clearly suggest the serious problems that could result from absenteeism. Successive incumbents were using the parish as little more than a milch cow yet attempting to enforce their rights against

---

184 Ibid., fos. 77r, 78r, 80v.
185 BL, Harleian Ms 594, fo. 125r.
186 LJRO, B/C/2/1, fos. 133r, 136v, 140v, 143r.
187 Ibid., fos. 131v, 136v, 140r, 143r; B/C/2/2, fo. 29v.
188 Ibid., B/C/2/3, fo. 53r.
189 John Morehall was taxed at 6s 2½d in 1533; BL, Harleian Ms 594, fo. 135v.
190 LJRO, B/C/2/3, fo. 67r.
191 Ibid., fos. 78v, 79r–v.

their parishioners and a local stipendiary priest. Here tensions clearly rose well above the surface and led to events that could not be interpreted otherwise than as bringing scandal to the clergy involved.

By his own admission, the reputation of William Whittington, vicar of Mancetter, was poor among his parishioners. This is apparent from his first appearance before the court on a charge of sexual incontinence with one Elizabeth Walsall, brought by a lay apparitor in 1525.[192] At the first hearing of the case Whittington failed to appear and was suspended from celebration of mass. When he did present himself at a subsequent hearing he denied the charge and was set the task of purging himself with two hands. Finding one other person who was prepared to swear in court to his good reputation seems to have presented Whittington with some difficulty, since he appeared on his own at the hearing held two months later. In the same year he was called to answer charges in an office suit promoted by his parishioners in which a number of allegations were made that he both charged for, and revealed the contents of confessions.[193] During the course of this action, which continued over the following three years, he admitted to the earlier charge of intercourse with Elizabeth Walsall. He had kept her as a concubine for two years and had had two children by her, as well as keeping a certain Agnes in his vicarage. He then made a further admission of his scandalous reputation among his parishioners. Due to the seriousness of the combined charges, Whittington was ordered to face a tribunal with the bishop himself sitting as judge, and was ordered not to relapse before Blythe's arrival in Lichfield. During the hearing and until further notice, he was to spend the nights in the bishop's palace in the cathedral close at Lichfield. After being absolved from the sentence of excommunication incurred by slandering his parishioners he was warned to act reverently during the mass for the sake of their souls. He was further ordered to keep away from drink and the company of women and, at a time appointed by the court, to take up residence in another house prepared for him and to keep the company of honest men, on pain of deprivation of his living. Just over two years later, in 1528, he was cited again on similar charges by his parishioners and it was discovered that he had not been resident in Mancetter for a considerable time. An official citation on a charge of absenteeism by the bishop of London that reached the Lichfield court at this point suggests that he was a pluralist neglecting more than the single parish. Whittington refused to respond to these further charges and, after being given some time to seek absolution from the court, was deprived of his living in April, 1528.[194] This was not to be the end of the matter, however. Five months after the deprivation of his benefice, a case was brought by the new vicar of Mancetter, Thomas Wylett, alleging that he had been attacked by Whittington, who refused to appear at court to

[192] Ibid., B/C/2/1, fos. 55r, 58r, 61v.
[193] See above, 136–7.
[194] LJRO, B/C/2/2, fo. 43r.

respond to the charges. For this action of contempt his exclusion from Christian society was completed by a sentence of excommunication.[195]

The problems which might occasionally be encountered by the ecclesiastical authorities in bringing recalcitrant clergy to heel are highlighted by a case which was brought against the rector of Whitchurch, M. George Vernon, in 1526.[196] In January of that year, a notice of citation was pinned to the door of his church ordering him to appear at Lichfield to answer charges of canonical irregularity and sexual incontinence. This was an act which greatly angered Vernon who attacked the court's agent with a knife and was heard to say by a witness 'it were well done to set one of thy ears in thy hands' upon which he tore the notice down. When summoned by the court to answer charges relating to this act, Vernon refused to appear and was sentenced to excommunication. This was sufficient to prompt him into appearing at the next hearing in order to petition for his benefice following which he was absolved and set to answer the various charges. These included sexual incontinence over a period of four years and the celebration of mass in a church that was subject to interdict, a charge which suggests that he had received a sentence of excommunication before. Vernon was sentenced to lead a procession to the church, walking in front of the cross, thus publicly demonstrating that he had been cited before the bishop on the above charges, and was further enjoined to pay a total of 60s towards pious uses. Following the completion of these penitential acts, his parishioners were urged to accept him once again as their curate.

It was these more serious consequences of dispute that the church courts were designed to avoid. The overall impression gained by a reading of the surviving Lichfield consistory material is one of general fairness, exemplified by the case of the vicar whose multiple tithe suit was dismissed from court immediately it was established that he had procured statements from witnesses through improper means.[197] The evidence from London diocese and elsewhere during this period has demonstrated how generally familiar people were with the operation of the church courts, and how frequently they made recourse to them both for the settlement of disputes and to protect their standing in the community.[198] The main aim of the courts was to achieve settlement of conflict;[199] the large number of cases which disappear from the records of the Lichfield consistory before a conclusion had been reached suggest that they were often successful. It would appear that in many cases

---

195 Ibid., B/C/2/3, fos. 3v, 6v.
196 Ibid., B/C/2/1, fos. 70v, 75v–76r.
197 Above, 167.
198 In the case of London it has been concluded that 'A legal system without physical coercion, as in most cases in the London church courts, requires widespread popular support and acceptance in order for its moral sanctions to be effective': Wunderli, *London Church Courts*, 53.
199 Ibid., 42.

the very clarification of a dispute, required so that it could be presented as a lawsuit, helped the parties towards agreement without recourse to a lengthy legal process. Although there were occasional actions which were drawn out over a period of one, two or even three years, the great majority were settled, or dropped, within three hearings. By their very nature, the records of court proceedings draw attention to conflict; stability within the parish community very rarely leaves a mark in the documentary records. Yet the scale of problems which arose, as in other areas which have been studied, was small and generally it can be said that the consistory court played a useful role in the settlement of conflict, providing a safety valve for the airing and resolution of grievances which otherwise might have been left to fester, to the great peril of the parish community as a whole. It is clear from the close involvement that many parish clergy enjoyed with their parishioners that they would have wished to have been seen as promoting social harmony. Certainly some went to quite considerable length in their wills to make restitution for any ill feeling that might live on after their deaths. Writing in 1534, the curate of Middleton, Richard Bexwyke, was quite specific as to the object of possible discord, making the bequest:

> Unto four alewives, that is to say the wife of Oliver Unsworth, the wife of William Taylor, the wife of Robert Fytton [and] the wife of Robert Jakes, unto every one of them 12d to forgive me where ever I have offended them.

However, two years later the Macclesfield chaplain William Bridges envisaged a more general reconciliation:

> I will and charge my executors that where it can be proved truth that I have done any injury or wrong to any man or any thing [or] that I am in debt to any body that my said executors shall agree with them and to discharge me as much as in them lyeth.

Construct

This book has essentially been about people and it seems appropriate to conclude a work based on collective biography with a reconstruction of what little we know of the lives of some of the men who have been its subject. Of the 4,500 who were ordained in the diocese during the first three decades of the sixteenth century and the 1,350 who were working in its parishes by 1533, the wills or probate inventories of just fifty-eight are known to have survived. Of these, six, or just over 10%, served a single parish during the reigns of Henry VIII, Edward VI, Mary and Elizabeth I and thus witnessed all the major religious and social upheavals of the period. Whilst on its own such material is obviously insufficient to draw firm conclusions concerning the nature of these changes or their consequences, if history is to be seen essentially as an examination of the evidence left by past societies, then this is the best that can be done by way of enabling the people who lived through those times to offer their own testimony. They will be called to witness in the chronological order by which they are known to have taken up their parochial ministry.[1]

John Holwaye was ordained priest to the title of Lilleshall Abbey in Shropshire on 17 May 1516 and ten years later was presented to the rectory of Hinstock, eight miles away, by its appropriators, Evesham Abbey. He held the living until his death in 1560. Holwaye would have been a conspicuous member of the community, riding on his mare either to visit his parishioners or survey the harvest of oats, rye and barley from his glebe and the condition of his small flock of sheep. He was now too old and infirm to ride, but when he had recently written out his last will he had decided that the best black colt that had been sired of his mare would be a good reward for his old friend, John Moreton, who had got the parsonage of Stockton and who, on their last meeting at Weston, had agreed to act as his executor. It was just as well he had shown him the will otherwise the fact that he had put the date as 2 Mary instead of 2 Elizabeth would not have been noticed until after his death and what might people have thought?[2] With a living worth less than £6 he was no better off than many of his parishioners, but as someone who regularly handled cash some of them had turned to him in times of need and he took care to enter the sums that they borrowed in a little book. As he neared his end he had decided that this could be something to leave to his nephews

---

1 The reconstructions comprise a summary of biographical details already mentioned with some additional testamentary material. For details of wills and inventories see the appendix and for biographical summaries, the index.
2 The will is apparently holograph.

John Holwaye and Humphrey Adams and their sisters to help them until such time as they were married. Yet it would not be much and they should also have what was left of his goods. Despite the fact that young John had moved away when he married, he was his godson and the two had frequently met. He had also been asked to act in this capacity for a number of his parishioners, and towards their futures the least he could do was leave them all 4d when he died. In his last days he often wondered how his good servant, William Johnson, would fare without him. He would do his best to ensure that he did not fall on hard times by giving him a good share of his corn and since he so liked to be seen with his sword and bill, he could have them too. One day they might be passed in turn to his boy, little William, who, in the meantime, could have a full set of clothes to be growing into. As he turned from the chancel of his church for the last time his eyes fixed upon the spot that he had chosen for his burial and, looking at the walls towards the repair of which he had left a small sum, he wondered how long the building would remain above his grave. Lifting his eyes upwards yet further his thoughts returned to his day of judgement by Almighty God, his maker and redeemer, who he hoped would take him into association with his Blessed Lady the Virgin and all the saints in Heaven.

Thomas Wylson was presented by the abbey of Burton upon Trent to its Staffordshire vicarage of Abbots Bromley on 13 December, 1526 and held it until his death in 1561. It was a poor living, worth just £5, but as he neared the end of his life Wylson had attained a position of some material comfort, with corn and hay in his fields, a small amount of livestock, and flax from which he produced a good quantity of yarn. And despite the poverty of the living he had felt a close association with the church and would ask to be buried in the chapel of St Nicholas. He had shown particular devotion to the carved image of the Trinity that had stood next to its altar, and despite the fact that it had now been pulled out of its niche, the place where he used to kneel before it would be his last resting place. He had that image in mind now as he contemplated that dread day when he would meet Almighty God his maker and redeemer; yet through his especial trust in him, and with the prayers of the Blessed Virgin Mary and all the holy company of Heaven, he felt confident that he would enjoy salvation. He had the funds to ensure a good burial; his four godchildren could bear the coffin to church, there would be five bell-ringers and all these, and every child that could say *de profundis*, could share in the bread and ale afterwards. To the church he would leave his black coverlet that would surely be of use, his parchment Latin bible with its gilded decoration and his big book on the four evangelists together with 6s 8d towards the fabric. The community he had served was not a wealthy one and he had decided that after his death he would share his own prosperity to the extent that forty of the very poorest householders should all have 4d from his estate. His colleague, Richard Smyth, could have some of his clothes and his friend William Merton, the rector of Mavesyn Ridware, could have some money as well as three of his books, including his

Ludolph and his collection of Voragine's sermons. Some of the money would have to come out of that which he was owed, including that from five of his parishioners and the 54s that M. Bryan Fowler still owed him from the time that he had acted as executor to his colleague Thomas Kirkham. He had little family still alive but he would put something aside for his niece. His housekeepers, Margaret Turner and Sibyl Treton, had done him good service and in return Margaret could have his two best cows and a yearling calf which he had already bestowed on her, as well as her bed and most of the things about the house. What was left of his goods she could share with Sibyl.

John Morehall was presented to the vicarage of Sutton Maddock in 1529 by Wombridge Priory and remained as vicar until his death in 1567. The living had been overlooked by the commissioners in 1535 but he had been able to make a reasonable living from it, though he wouldn't forget his first year in a hurry. Not only had he been required to agree to pay his predecessor, Richard Harrington, an annual pension of £3, but he had also been required to help prevent Harrington from being strangled by one of the parish chaplains, Richard Brett, who had his own scores to settle. Yet there had been corn enough in the fields to see him through to old age and as he neared the end of his long life he still had thirty-two old sheep, a cow and a few horses left on his land and lambs and a few pigs and hens in the yard. In the early years he had been forced to put up with a certain amount of ill-feeling from his parishioners, caused by his predecessor's tithe suits, and he would probably not be able to reclaim the £26 that eight of them still owed him before the end of his life.

Thomas Tunstall was a Staffordshire man who had been ordained priest with a title from Dieulacres Abbey in 1514. By 1531 he had been appointed curate of Wolstanton, a parish not far from the abbey, and he ministered to its souls until his death in 1565. He was another man who felt a close association to the area in which he had been raised, and in particular to the parish church that he had served for so long and it was natural, as he was now beyond his biblical span, that his thoughts should turn to his desire for burial in its Lady Chapel where he had so often sung mass. The altar that he had served had long since been pulled down but it was fitting that his body should occupy the place where it had once stood. Much about that church had now changed and he was unsure as to what would be done with the 6s 8d that he had left to its repair. In his younger days many other priests had also served the altars there and two that he had known longest, John Copnall and John Cartwright, he had asked to be witnesses of his will. And as well as being a man with close ties to a particular place, he was a family man in more ways than one. His brothers Ralph and Peter would be remembered in his will but more would be set aside for his son Roger and daughter Elizabeth. However, the greatest beneficiary would be his housekeeper, Ellen Fines, whose bequests would include the linen shop which had enabled him to augment his living, not to a great degree, but sufficient to allow him to make substantial cash loans to many of his parishioners and neighbours. Some of the £17 that was owed to him at the end of his life was from those who had hired his plough-team and he still had a few animals on the land that he had rented next to his shop in the village. Not only did he end his life with a number of debtors but an even larger number of godchildren; to all those still alive he determined to leave 4d, except for the half dozen that had taken his own Christian name, who would be given animals as well. Tunstall could be forgiven if in his last days his thoughts turned to his children and their mother; and, partly because of them, to forgiveness itself. For this he would trust his soul to Almighty God, there to be kept with the holy company of Heaven.

Richard Hatton was ordained priest on 14 June 1511, like John Holwaye, to the title of Lilleshall Abbey in Shropshire, and by 1533 was working as curate of Shifnal, about five miles away, where he stayed until his death in 1560. In all probability this was the village in which he had been born and brought up since his last request was for burial in its church next to his brother. His funeral itself was to be a relatively simple affair; four of his female parishioners would be paid to wind him in his burial sheet and only the great bell of the church ('and no more bells') was to be rung. From his modest assets 20s was to be distributed among the poor of the town and parish, a task that was to be carried out by his executors, who were to be one of the chaplains serving the church, Michael Howell, and Richard Higgins and John Moreton, incumbents of neighbouring Kemberton and Stockton respectively. Various members of his family were remembered in his will, amongst whom Thomas Hatton was to take possession of his quiver and arrows, and what was left of his goods was to be shared equally among the poorest members of his family. In the event, he owned very little property indeed and half of his estate of under £13 was made up of cash. In addition, one of his female parishioners owed him 4s of which he was willing to forego half. Otherwise he died owning little more than his clothes, bedding, some small items of furniture, a whisky still, a few books and his 'workday jacket' which he left to a parishioner. His soul he bequeathed simply to Almighty God.

Having been ordained deacon to the title of Newstead Abbey, Nottinghamshire, in 1521, by 1533 Richard Whitworth was employed as curate of Chesterfield, some fifteen miles away in Derbyshire, in which post he remained until his death in 1559. When he was first taken on, he and the vicar, Oliver Flint, were among thirteen clergy attached to the church, one of whom, William Bagge, was to act as one of two clerical overseers of Whitworth's will. As well as being the parish curate he had held a school at the church and the fees that he was owed at the time of writing his will were one of the bequests (including some books) that he made to his brother Miles, a fellow priest. At his death his goods were worth less than £12, of which almost one-third was made up from the value of his two cows. Otherwise, Whitworth shared in the chief source of his town's prosperity, wool, being the owner of a spinning wheel, four looms, two pairs of shears and other associated equipment. Whitworth's close association with the town of Chesterfield and its famous church was to continue in death through his request for burial in 'St Katherine's Quere over the north side of the altar', there to rest until his soul was united with 'Almighty God, my Maker and Redeemer, Our Blessed Lady St Mary the Virgin and all the Holy and Blessed Company of Heaven'.

Had the satirical rhyme of the *Vicar of Bray* been sung in their time it is doubtful that its ironic connotations would have meant much to these men.[3] They were part of a highly clericalised society which, at least at the level of interaction between priests and their parishioners, and away from the capital, was remarkably well integrated and homogenous. How typical were these six individuals relative to the many whose lives have resurfaced in the writing of this book, is impossible to say; there were many more, existing on the margins of clerical employment, who have left nothing of their existence whatsoever. But one thing they certainly shared in common: an original answer to the call of the Catholic priesthood and its requirement of sacramental and pastoral provision that had been the principal sustenance of the Christian faith of the people of this country for almost a thousand years. The service that they provided had never been in greater demand, nor its burden more willingly assumed, than in the years when their ministry began. To the

---

[3] The implications of long service in a single parish by many of the Tudor clergy have been summarised by Eamon Duffy thus: 'Their conformity was not always ignoble. Christopher Trychay on Exmoor conformed and conformed again, but he was no vicar of Bray . . . it is hard to see what else such a man in such a time could have done. For him religion was above all local and particular, "rooted in one dear perpetual place", his piety centred on this parish, this church, these people.' In her review of his book Margaret Aston concluded that 'the positive momentum that brought all this [Protestant reform] about remains invisible: a novice reader might conclude that the Vicar of Bray was central to the making of the Church of England'. Of the pastoral clergy of the East Riding of Yorkshire Peter Marshall concluded that 'to deprecate such men *tout court* as Vicars of Bray would be cruelly unjust: conformism could undoubtedly be the product of positive as much as negative motives, the desire to continue to serve, or the happy conviction that in matters of such import as the reform of worship and theology the authorities knew best'. It would seem an apposite occasion to remind the 'novice reader' of the lines inspired by this incumbent of a Berkshire parish who held his living through the reigns of Henry VIII to Elizabeth I:
    And this is the law I will maintain
    Until my dying day, Sir
    That whatever king shall reign
    I'll still be the vicar of Bray, Sir.
Duffy, *Stripping of the Altars*, 592; review by M. Aston, *English Historical Review*, cix (1994), 111–14; Marshall, *Pastoral Ministry in the East Riding*, 7; *Wordsworth Dictionary of Phrase and Fable*, revised by I.H. Evans (Ware, 1994), 1128.

last generation of English Catholic clergy the people looked for steadfastness, guidance and, more than anything, constancy in the face of a terrifying acceleration in the pace of change and in spite of the inconstancy of political rule. As their world was brought down around them, the evidence would suggest that it was not by their pastors that they were deceived.

Appendix: Clerical Wills and Inventories Cited in the Text

Source: Lichfield Joint Record Office, unless otherwise stated
A = Acolyte, C = Curate, Ch = Chantry Priest, CC = Collegiate Church,
Inst. = Instituted, M = graduate, P = Priest, Pb = Prebendary, R = Rector,
S = Stipendiary Priest, Sb = Subdeacon, V = Vicar

Name	Date	Probate	Description	Ordination	Title	Estimated min. age at writing of will	Posts held etc.	Value of Inventory
Abell, John	1553	1558	C Kingstone, Staffs.	P 23.2.1510	Croxden, Staffs.	72	1531, 1533: C Kingstone	£17 18s 4d
Alen, Thomas	1557	ditto	R Kingswinford, Staffs.	P 21.7.1508	Brewood, Staffs.	72	1533: R Kingswinford, Staffs.	£50 13s 8d
Asche, Richard	1539	1541	Ch Beighton, Derbs.			62	1533: S Beighton	£2 14s 11d
Bachelor, Edmund	1557	ditto	R Sheinton, Salop	P 26.3.1527	Buildwas, Salop	54	1533: S Cound, Salop	£77 8s 6d
Barefote, Robert	1538	ditto	V Mancetter, Warks.			59	Inst. 14.10.1530: V Mancetter 1533, 1535: V & Gild P Mancetter	£12 12s 6d
Bee, John	1555	ditto	Ch Uttoxeter, Staffs.			67		£16 4s 8d
Bexwyke, Richard[1]	1534	not known	C Middleton, Lancs.	P 2.6.1515	Upholland, Lancs.	43		
Blockley, Richard	1538	ditto	V Wolvey, Warks.	P 18.9.1529	Dudley, Staffs.	33	1533, 1535: V Wolvey	£24 0s 18d
Blythe, Robert	1544	1547	V Dunchurch, Warks.	P 6.6.1506	King's Hall, Cambridge	65	Inst. 18.6.1515: Shirley, Derbs. 1533: V Dunchurch	£20 0s 0d
Brewster, M. William	1549	1558	V Etwall, Derbs.			79	Inst. 20.9.1531: V Etwall 1533: V Etwall	£22 16s 6d
Bridges, William[2]	1536	Not known	S Macclesfield, Chesh.	P 24.9.13	Norton, Cheshire	47	1533: S Macclesfield	
Bryddocke, Robert[3]	1556	ditto	S Manchester, Lancs.	P 15.12.22	Vale Royal, Cheshire	57		£93 5s 6½d
Bucke, Charles	1543	1545	P Coventry, Warks.	P 27.2.1507	Chester	62	1533: S Bablake College, Coventry	
Butler, William	1550	ditto	V Wrockwardine, Salop	P 18.9.1512	Shrewsbury, Salop	62	Inst. 2.7.1514: V Wrockwardine 1533, 1535: V Wrockwardine	£10 3s 4d
Byshoppe, Henry	1539	ditto	V Moreton Corbet, Salop			60	Inst. 23.9.1508: Moreton Corbet 1533, 1535: V Moreton Corbet	£17 10s 7d
Campion, William	1533	ditto	R Breadsall, Derbs.			54	1533: R Breadsall	£37 11s 0d

Name								
Corveser, William	1555	ditto	V Stanton upon Hine Heath, Salop	P 18.12.1507	Wombridge, Salop	68	1533, 1535: V Stanton upon Hine Heath	Incomplete
Dodycott, William	1535	ditto	R Kinnersley, Salop			56	1533: R Kinnersley	£11 5s 7d
Dodycotte, Richard	1543	ditto	S Wroxeter, Salop	Sb 5.6.27	Wombridge, Salop	38		£5 16. 4d[4]
Dore, Robert	1544	ditto	Ch Walsall, Staffs.			65	1533: Ch Walsall	£7 2s 1d
Fitzherbert, John	1551	ditto	V Doveridge, Derbs.			72	Inst. 9.1.1520: V. Doveridge 1533: V Doveridge	£60 15s 0d
Fisher, Thomas[5]	1540	ditto	P Coventry, Warks.	?Sb 30.6.31				£7 18s 9d
Franks, William	1541	ditto	V Barrow u Trent, Derbs.	D 20.2.24	Valle Crucis, Denbighshire	62	1533, 1535: V Barrow u Trent	£10 12s 3d
Gregory, George[6]	1548	Not known	P Rossendale, Lancs.			44	By 1532: chaplain, Rossendale[7]	£1 18s 0d
Hall, M. John	1557	1558	V Chesbsey, Staffs.			77	Inst. 1505: V Chebsey 1531: V Chebsey 1533: V Chebsey; Pb. Morehall, CC Gnossall (described as *magister*)	£40 10s. 0d.
Hatton, Richard	1560	ditto	C Shifnal, Salop	P 14.6.1511	Lilleshall, Salop	73	1533: C Shifnal	£12 16s 8d
Holwaye, John	1559	1560	R Hinstock, Salop	P 17.5.1516	Lilleshall, Salop	68	Inst. 23.7.1526: R Hinstock 1533, 1535: R Hinstock	£15 4s 2d
Kent, Richard	1538	ditto	S Newcastle-under-Lyme, Staffs.			59	1531, 1533: S Newcastle	£5 9s 3d
Lee, Roger	1540	ditto	S Wroxeter, Salop	A 19.9.1506		55	1533: S Wroxeter	
Legh, Alexander	1533	ditto	C Ryton-on-Dunsmore, Warks.			54	1533: C Ryton-on-Dunsmore	£7 16s 6d

1 G.J. Piccope, ed., *Lancashire and Cheshire Wills and Inventories from the Ecclesiastical Court, Chester: The Second Portion*, Chetham Society, Remains Historical and Literary Connected with the Palatine Counties of Lancaster and Chester, 51 (1860), 144–6.
2 *Lancashire and Cheshire Wills: Second Portion*, 164–8.
3 G.J. Piccope, ed., *Lancashire and Cheshire Wills and Inventories from the Ecclesiastical Court, Chester: The Third Portion*, Chetham Society, Remains Historical and Literary Connected with the Palatine Counties of Lancaster and Chester, 54 (1861), 142–3.
4 Includes debts owing of £1 14s 4d.
5 Included in the sample since there is only one individual with the name in the ordination register, although the dates would suggest that this man was probably ordained before 1503.
6 *Lancashire and Cheshire Wills and Inventories: Second Portion*, 199–201.
7 Ecclesiastical Court of Whalley, 142.

Name	Year 1	Year 2	Benefice	Location	Date		Details	Value
Leigh, Roger[8]	1551	ditto	R Lymm, Ches.			66	Inst. 21.4.1509: R Lymm 1533: R Lymm	£5 19s 4d
Marler, Henry	1539	ditto	R Coventry, Warks.			60	1533: S Coventry, Holy Trinity	£12 9s 2d
More, William	1541	ditto	S Marchington, Staffs.	Rocester, Staffs.	Sb 11.3.1514	50	1531, 1533: S Marchington	£18 6s 0d
Morehall, John	1567	ditto	V Sutton Maddock, Salop			88	Inst. 28.4.1529: V Sutton Maddock 1533: V Sutton Maddock	
Nowell, M. John	1555	ditto	R Swynnerton, Staffs.			76	1531, 1533: R Swynnerton	
Podmore, Richard	1541	ditto	C Dawley, Salop	Buildwas, Salop	P 21.9.1510	55	1533: C Dawley	£18 3s 8d
Pontisbury, Leonard	1538	ditto	V Shawbury, Salop		A 19.9.1506	53	Inst. 31.12.1518: V Shawbury 1533, 1535: V Shawbury	£19 10s 6d
Pyxley, Thomas	1539	ditto	S High Ercall, Salop		A 19.12.06	46	1533: S High Ercall	£5 16s 8d
Redfern, John	1537	ditto	V Longford, Derbs.	V Longford	P 18.12.1529	32	1533, 1535: V Longford	£18 9s 4d
Reed, M. John	1534	ditto	V Melbourne, Derbs.	Dieulacres, Staffs.	P 23.12.1508	50	1533: V Melbourne R Broughton Astley, Leics.[9]	£5 15s 10d
Richardson, William	1543	ditto	V Crich, Derbs.			64	1533, 1535: V Crich	£14 16s 8d
Rowlowe, Richard	1549	1550	R Ryton, Salop	Tong, Salop	P 2.6.1509	65	1533, 1535: R Ryton	£21 6s ½d
Rylay, Richard	1539	ditto	R Swarkestone, Derbs.	Croxden, Staffs.	P 15.12.1511	52	Inst. 15.2.1526: R Swarkestone 1533, 1535: R Swarkestone	£10 3s 5d
Ryve, Richard	1537	ditto	V South Wingfield, Derbs.	Repton, Derbyshire	P 20.9.05	56	1518: Inst. V S Wingfield 1533, 1535: V S Wingfield	£42 17s 2½d
Slany, Henry	1546	ditto	V Bushbury, Staffs.			67	Inst. 20.12.1511: V Bushbury 1533, 1535: V Bushbury	
Smyth, John	1543	ditto	V Shilton, Warks.			64	1533, 1535: V Shilton	£13 15s 8d
Smyth, Richard	1536	ditto	R Kirk Ireton, Derbs.			57	1533, 1535: R Kirk Ireton	£40 6s 8d
Swynerton, William	1538	ditto	R Blymhill, Staffs.			59	1533, 1535: R Blymhill	£34 6s 8d
Tatton, Ralph	1534	ditto	R Barlborough, Derbs.			55	1509: Lich. gild member 1533: R Barlborough	
Tryge, Henry	1543	ditto	S Chesterfield, Derbs.			64	1533: S Chesterfield	36s 3d
Tunstall, Thomas	1565	ditto	C Wolstanton, Staffs.	Dieulacres, Staffs.	P 10.6.1514	75	1531, 1533: C Wolstanton	£11 4s 0d
Webb, Richard	1537	ditto	R Stapleton, Salop	Stone, Staffs.	P 27.2.1523	52	1533, 1535: R Stapleton	£7 18s 4d
Wells, John	1539	ditto	S Coventry, Warks.	Canwell, Staffs.	D 17.5.1505	57	1533: S Coventry, St Michael	
Wendon, M. Ralph	1558	1562	R Sutton Coldfield, Warks.			79	Inst. 24.3.1527: R Sutton Coldfield 1533, 1535: R Sutton Coldfield	

Whitworth, Richard	1559	ditto	C Chesterfield, Derbs.	D 22.12.1521	Newstead, Notts.	61	1533: C Chesterfield	£11 15s 2d
Wylson, John	1543	ditto	Ch North Wingfield, Derbs.	P 23.12.1508	Wollaton, Notts.	63	1512: Lich. gild member 1533: Ch North Wingfield	£3 0s 8d
Wylson *alias* Wetton, Thomas	1561	ditto	V Abbots Bromley, Staffs.			69	1519: Lich. gild member Inst. 13.12.1526: V Abbots Bromley 1533: Abbots Bromley	£29 17s 4d
Yate, John	1549	ditto	P Fletchamstead, Warks.	S 19.9.1528	Halesowen, Worcs.	43		£8 11s 4d

8 *Lancashire and Cheshire Wills and Inventories: Third Portion*, 48–51.
9 Bowker, *Henrician Reformation*, 115.

Bibliography

Place of publication is London unless otherwise stated

Manuscript Sources

Lichfield Joint Record Office
  B/A/1/14, Register of Geoffrey Blythe, Bishop of Coventry and Lichfield, 1503–31.
  B/A/1/14ii, Ordination Register, Diocese of Coventry and Lichfield, 1503–31.
  B/A/17/1(1), Clerical Subsidy for the Archdeaconry of Stafford, 1531.
  B/C/2/1–3, Lichfield Consistory Court Books, 1524–31.
  D.30/1–4, Lichfield Dean and Chapter Act Books.
  D.30/18, Clerical Subsidy for the Archdeaconry of Stafford, 1533.
  D.77/1, Register of the Gild of St Mary and St John the Baptist, Lichfield.
  P/C/11, Wills and Inventories
London, British Library
  Harleian Ms 594, fos. 116r–154v, Clerical Subsidy List for the Diocese of Coventry and Lichfield, 1533.

Primary Sources in Print

Act Book of the Ecclesiastical Court of Whalley, ed. A.M. Cooke, Chetham Society, Remains Historical and Literary Connected with the Palatine Counties of Lancaster and Chester, new series, vol. 44 (1901).

Bishop Blythe's Visitations c.1515–1525, ed. P. Heath, Staffordshire Record Society, Collections for a History of Staffordshire, 4th series, vol. 7 (1973).

Calendar of Papal Letters Relating to Great Britain and Ireland, vol. XVIII (Pius II & Julius II: Vatican Registers, 1503–13, Lateran registers, 1503–1508), ed. M.J. Haren (Dublin, 1989).

Calendars of Wills and Administrations in the Consistory Court of the Bishop of Lichfield and Coventry 1516 to 1652, ed. W.P.W. Phillimore, Index Library, vol. 7 (1892).

The Churchwardens' Accounts of Prescot, Lancashire, 1523–1607, ed. F.A. Bailey, Transactions of the Lancashire and Cheshire Record Society, vol. 104 (1953).

Churchwardens' Accounts of All Saints, Walsall, 1462–1521, ed. G.P. Mander, William Salt Society, Collections for a History of Staffordshire, 3rd series (1930).

A History of the Chantries Within the County Palatine of Lancaster, ed. F.R. Raines, Chetham Society, Remains Historical and Literary Connected with the Palatine Counties of Lancaster and Chester, vols LIX, LX (1862).

Lancashire and Cheshire Wills and Inventories from the Ecclesiastical Court, Chester: The Second Portion, ed. G.J. Piccope, Chetham Society, Remains Historical and Literary Connected with the Palatine Counties of Lancaster and Chester, 51 (1860).

Lancashire and Cheshire Wills and Inventories from the Eccesiastical Court, Chester: The Third Portion, ed. G.J. Piccope, Chetham Society, Remains Historical and Literary Connected with the Palatine Counties of Lancaster and Chester, 54 (1861).

Letters and Papers Foreign and Domestic, Henry VIII, 1509–47, ed. J.S. Brewer, J. Gairdner, R.H. Brodie, 21 vols (1862–1910).

The Lisle Letters, An Abridgement, ed. M. St Clare Byrne (Harmondsworth, 1985).

Melton, William, *Sermo Exhortatorius Cancelarii Eboracensis hii qui ad Sacros Ordines Petunt Promoveri* (c.1510).

A List of Families in the Archdeaconry of Stafford 1532–3, ed. A.J. Kettle, Staffordshire Record Society, Collections for a History of Staffordshire, 4th series, vol. 8 (1976).

A List of the Clergy in Eleven Deaneries of the Diocese of Chester 1541–42 together with a List of the Tenths and Subsidy Payable in Ten Deaneries circa 1538, ed. W.F. Irvine, Record Society for the Publication of Original Documents Relating to Lancashire and Cheshire, xxxiii (1896).

Probate Inventories of Lichfield and District 1568–1680, ed. D.G. Vaisey, Staffordshire Record Society, Collections for a History of Staffordshire, 4th ser., 5 (1969).

The Register of John Morton, Archbishop of Canterbury 1486–1500, vol. II, ed. C. Harper-Bill, Canterbury and York Society, vol. LXXVIII (1991).

The Regulations and Establishment of the Household of Henry Algernon Percy, the Fifth Earl of Northumberland, at his Castles of Wressle and Leckonfield in Yorkshire begun Anno Domini MDXII, ed. T. Percy (1905 edn).

A Selection from the Prescot Court Leet and Other Records 1447–1600, ed. F.A. Bailey, Record Society for the Publication of Original Documents relating to Lancashire and Cheshire, vol. 89 (1937).

Solihull Parish Book, 1525–1720, transcribed by G.L. Bishop, duplicated typescript, University of Birmingham Dept. of Extramural Studies (1977).

Staffordshire Incumbents and Parochial Records (1530–1680), ed. W.N. Landor, The William Salt Society, Collections for a History of Staffordshire (1915).

Star Chamber Proceedings, Henry VIII and Edward VI, William Salt Society, Collections for a History of Staffordshire (1912), 3–207.

Supplement to Bishop Blythe's Visitations, ed. P. Heath, Staffordshire Record Society, Collections for a History of Staffordshire, 4th series, vol. 13 (1988).

Valor Ecclesiasticus Temp. Henrici VIII Auctoritate Regia Institutus, ed. J. Caley and J. Hunter (Record Commission), 6 vols (1810–34).

Secondary Sources

Aveling, J.C.H. 'The English Clergy, Catholic and Protestant, in the 16th and 17th Centuries', in Haase, W., ed., *Rome and the Anglicans: Historical and Doctrinal Aspects of Anglican-Roman Catholic Relations* (Berlin, 1982), 56–142.

Bainbridge, V.R. *Gilds in the Medieval Countryside: Social and Religious Change in Cambridgeshire c.1350–1558* (Woodbridge, 1996).
Barron, C.M. and Harper-Bill, C. eds, *The Church in Pre-Reformation Society; Essays in Honour of F.R.H. du Boulay* (Woodbridge, 1985).
Bennet, H.S. 'Medieval Ordination Lists in the English Episcopal Registers', in Conway Davies, J., ed., *Studies Presented to Sir Hilary Jenkinson* (1957), 10–34.
Bennett, M.J. 'The Lancashire and Cheshire Clergy, 1379', *Transactions of the Historic Society of Lancashire and Cheshire*, 124 (1972), 1–30.
Bernard, G.W. 'The Pardon of the Clergy Reconsidered', *JEH*, 37 (1986), 258–87.
Bill, P.A. *The Warwickshire Parish Clergy in the Later Middle Ages*, Dugdale Society Occasional Papers, no. 17 (Oxford, 1967).
Bossy, J. 'The Mass as a Social Institution', *Past and Present*, 100 (August, 1983), 29–61.
Bowker, M. 'Non-Residence in Lincoln Diocese in the Early Sixteenth Century', *JEH*, 15 (1964), 40–50.
—— *An Episcopal Court Book for the Diocese of Lincoln, 1514–1520*, Lincoln Record Society Publications, vol. 16 (1967).
—— *The Secular Clergy in the Diocese of Lincoln, 1495–1520* (Cambridge, 1968).
—— 'The Henrician Reformation and the Parish Clergy', *Bulletin of the Institute of Historical Research*, 50 (1977), 30–47.
—— *The Henrician Reformation: The Diocese of Lincoln under John Longland, 1521–47* (Cambridge, 1981).
Bradshaw, B. and Duffy, E., eds, *Humanism, Reform and the Reformation: The Career of Bishop John Fisher* (Cambridge, 1989).
Bridgeman, G.T.O. *The History of the Church & Manor of Wigan in the County of Lancaster, Part I*, Chetham Society, New Ser., vol. 15 (1888).
Brigden, S. 'Tithe Controversy in Reformation London', *JEH*, 32 (1981), 285–301.
—— 'Religion and Social Obligation in Early Sixteenth-Century London', *Past and Present*, 103 (May, 1984), 67–112.
—— *London and the Reformation* (Oxford, 1989).
Brooke, C.N.L. 'Rural Ecclesiastical Institutions in England: The Search for their Origins', *Settimane di studio del centro Italiano di studi sull'Alto Medioevo*, 28 (1982), 'Cristianizzazione ed Organizzazione Ecclesiastica delle Campagne nell'alto Medioevo: Expansione e Resistenze', 685–711.
Burgess, C. ' "For the Increase of Divine Service": Chantries in the Parish in Late-Medieval Bristol', *JEH*, 36 (1985), 46–65.
—— 'A Service for the Dead: The Form and Function of the Anniversary in Late Medieval Bristol', *Transactions of the Bristol and Gloucester Archaeological Society*, 105 (1987), 183–211.
—— ' "By Quick and by Dead": Wills and Pious Provision in Late Medieval Bristol', *English Historical Review*, 102 (1987), 837–58.
—— 'The Benefactions of Mortality: The Lay Response in the Late Medieval Urban Parish', in D.M. Smith, ed., *Studies in Clergy and Ministry in Medieval England*, Borthwick Studies in History, 1 (1991), 65–86.
—— 'Strategies for Eternity: Perpetual Chantry Foundation in Late Medieval

Bristol', in Harper-Bill, C., ed., *Religious Belief and Ecclesiastical Careers in Late Medieval England* (Woodbridge, 1991), 1–32.
Burson, M.C. ' "... For the Sake of My Soul": The Activities of a Medieval Executor', *Archives*, 13 (1977–8), 131–6.
Carpenter, C. *Locality and Polity – A Study of Warwickshire Landed Society, 1401–1499* (Cambridge, 1992).
Chambers, D.S. *Cardinal Bainbridge in the Court of Rome, 1509 to 1514* (Oxford, 1965).
Clough, C.H., ed., *Profession, Vocation and Culture in Late Medieval England; Essays Dedicated to the Memory of A.R. Myers* (Liverpool, 1982).
Cobb, P.G. 'The Architectural Setting of the Liturgy', in Jones, C., Wainwright, G., Yarnold, E., eds, *The Study of Liturgy* (1978), 473–87.
Cooper, T.N. 'The Papacy and the Diocese of Coventry and Lichfield, 1360–85', *Archivum Historiae Pontificiae*, 25 (1987), 73–103.
———— 'The Secular Clergy of the Diocese of Coventry and Lichfield in the Early Sixteenth Century', unpublished Ph.D. Thesis, University of Birmingham (1992).
———— 'Oligarchy and Conflict: Lichfield Cathedral Clergy in the Early Sixteenth Century', *Midland History*, 19 (1994), 40–57.
———— 'Children, the Liturgy and the Reformation: The Evidence of the Lichfield Choristers', *SCH*, 31 (Oxford, 1994), 261–74.
Crehan, J.H. 'Medieval Ordinations', in Jones, C., Wainwright, G., Yarnold, E., eds, *The Study of Liturgy* (1978), 320–31.
Crichton, J.D. 'The Office in the West: The Later Middle Ages', in Jones, C., Wainwright, G., Yarnold, E., eds, *The Study of Liturgy* (1978), 378–82.
Cross, C. *Church and People, 1450–1660: The Triumph of the Laity in the English Church* (1976).
———— 'The Incomes of Provincial Urban Clergy, 1520–1645', in O'Day, R., Heal, F., eds, *Princes and Paupers in the English Church 1500–1800* (Leicester, 1981), 65–89.
———— 'Ordinations in the Diocese of York 1500–1630', in Cross, C., ed., *Patronage and Recruitment in the Tudor and Early Stuart Church*, Borthwick Studies in History, 2 (York, 1996), 1–19.
Davis, V. 'Rivals for Ministry? Ordinations of Secular and Regular Clergy in Southern England, c.1300–1500', *SCH*, 26 (Oxford, 1989), 99–109.
———— 'Medieval English Clergy Database', *History and Computing*, 2 (1990), 75–87.
Dickens, A.G. *The English Reformation* (1964).
———— 'The Shape of Anti-Clericalism and the English Reformation', in Kouri, E.I. and Scott, T., eds, *Politics and Society in Reformation Europe: Essays for Sir Geoffrey Elton on his Sixty-Fifth Birthday* (1987).
———— 'The Early Expansion of Protestantism in England 1520–1558', *Archiv für Reformationsgeschichte*, 79 (1988), 187–221.
Dickens, A.G. and Carr, D., eds, *The Reformation in England to the Accession of Elizabeth I* (1967).
Dobson, R.B. *Durham Priory, 1400–1450* (Cambridge, 1973).

Dohar, W.J. 'Medieval Ordination Lists: The Origins of a Record', *Archives*, 20, no. 87 (1992), 17–35.

Donaldson, R. 'Sponsors, Patrons and Presentations to Benefices – Particularly those in the Gift of the Priors of Durham – During the Late Middle Ages', *Archaeologia Aeliana*, 4th series, 38 (1960), 169–77.

Duffy, E. *The Stripping of the Altars: Traditional Religion in England 1400–1580* (Yale, 1992).

Dunning, R.W. 'Patronage and Promotion in the Late-Medieval Church', in Griffiths, R.A., ed., *Patronage, the Crown, and the Provinces in Later Medieval England* (Gloucester, 1981), 167–80.

Dyer, C. *Standards of Living in the Later Middle Ages: Social Change in England c.1200–1520* (Cambridge, 1989).

Emden, A.B. *A Biographical Register of the University of Oxford to 1500*, 3 vols (Oxford, 1957–9).

———— *A Biographical Register of the University of Oxford, A.D. 1501 to 1540* (Oxford, 1974).

———— *A Biographical Register of the University of Cambridge to 1500* (Cambridge, 1963).

Fines, J. 'An Incident of the Reformation in Shropshire', *Transactions of the Shropshire Archaeological Society*, 57 (1961–4), 166–8.

———— 'Heresy Trials in the Diocese of Coventry and Lichfield, 1511–12', *JEH*, 14 (1963), 160–74.

Foss, D.B. 'John Mirk's "Instructions for Parish Priests"', *SCH*, 26 (Oxford, 1989), 131–40.

Frankforter, A.D. 'The Reformation and the Register: Episcopal Administration of Parishes in Late Medieval England', *Catholic Historical Review*, 63 (1977), 204–24.

Fuggles, J.F. 'The Parish Clergy in the Archdeaconry of Leicester 1520–1540', *Transactions of the Leicestershire Archaeological and Historical Society*, 46 (1970–71), 25–44.

Grisbrooke, W.J. 'Vestments', in Jones, C., Wainwright, G., Yarnold, E., eds, *The Study of Liturgy* (1978), 488–92.

Guy, J.A. 'Sir Thomas More and the Heretics', *History Today*, 30 (1980), 11–15.

———— 'Henry VIII and the *Praemunire* Manoeuvres of 1530–31', *English Historical Review*, 97 (1982), 481–503.

———— 'Law, Lawyers and the English Reformation', *History Today*, 35 (1985), 16–22.

———— *Tudor England* (Oxford, 1988).

Gwyn, P. *The King's Cardinal: The Rise and Fall of Thomas Wolsey* (1990).

Haigh, C. *Reformation and Resistance in Tudor Lancashire* (Cambridge, 1975).

———— 'Anticlericalism and the English Reformation', *History*, 68 (1983), 391–407.

———— ed. *The English Reformation Revised* (Cambridge, 1987).

———— *English Reformations: Religion, Politics, and Society under the Tudors* (Oxford, 1993).

Haines, R.M. 'The Associates and *Familia* of William Gray and His Use of Patronage While Bishop of Ely, 1454–78', *JEH*, 25, no. 3 (1974), 225–47.

—— 'A York Priest's Notebook', in Haines, R.M., *Ecclesia Anglicana – Studies in the English Church of the Later Middle Ages* (Toronto, 1989), 156–79.

Hair, P.E.H. 'Mobility of Parochial Clergy in Hereford Diocese c.1400', *Transactions of the Woolhope Naturalists' Field Club*, 43 (1979–81), 164–80.

—— 'Chaplains and Chapels of N.W. Herefordshire c.1400', *Transactions of the Woolhope Naturalists' Field Club*, 46 (1988–89), 31–64, 246–88.

Harper-Bill, C. 'Dean Colet's Convocation Sermon and the Pre-Reformation Church in England', *History*, 73, no. 237 (February, 1988), 191–210.

—— *The Pre-Reformation Church in England 1400–1530* (Harlow, 1989).

—— 'Who Wanted the English Reformation?', *Medieval History*, 2, no. 1 (1992), 66–77.

Hartridge, R.A.R. *A History of Vicarages in the Middle Ages* (Cambridge, 1930).

Harwood, T. *The History and Antiquities of the Church and City of Lichfield* (1806).

Heal, F. and O'Day, R. eds, *Church and Society in England, Henry VIII to James I* (1977).

Heal, F.M. *Of Prelates and Princes: A Study of the Economic and Social Position of the Tudor Episcopate* (Cambridge, 1980).

Heath, P. *Medieval Clerical Accounts*, St Anthony's Hall Publications, no. 26 (York, 1964).

—— *The English Parish Clergy on the Eve of the Reformation* (1969).

—— 'The Medieval Archdeaconry and Tudor Bishopric of Chester', *JEH*, 20 (1969), 243–52.

—— 'Staffordshire Towns and the Reformation', *North Staffordshire Journal of Field Studies*, 19 (1979), 1–21.

—— 'Between Reform and Reformation: The English Church in the Fourteenth and Fifteenth Centuries', *JEH*, 41, no. 4 (October 1990), 647–78.

Helmholz, R.H. 'Canonical Defamation in Medieval England', *American Journal of Legal History*, 15 (1971), 255–68.

—— 'Crime, Compurgation and the Courts of the Medieval Church', *Law and History Review*, I (1983), 1–26.

Hope, D.M. 'Liturgical Books', in Jones, C., Wainwright, G., Yarnold, E., eds, *The Study of Liturgy* (1978), 65–9.

Hosker, P. 'The Stanleys of Lathom and Ecclesiastical Patronage in the North-West of England During the Fifteenth Century', *Northern History*, 18 (1982), 212–19.

Houlbrooke, R.A. *Church Courts and the People During the English Reformation 1520–1570* (Oxford, 1979).

Howorth, H.H., ed., *The Vicars of Rochdale, Part I, By the Late Rev. Canon Raines* Chetham Society, New Ser., vol. 1 (1883).

Hughes, J. *Pastors and Visionaries: Religion and Secular Life in Late Medieval Yorkshire* (Woodbridge, 1988).

—— 'The Administration of Confession in the Diocese of York in the Fourteenth Century', in D.M. Smith, ed. *Studies in Clergy and Ministry in Medieval England*, Borthwick Studies in History, 1 (1991), 87–163.

Jack, R.I. 'The Ecclesiastical Patronage Exercised by a Baronial Family in the Late Middle Ages', *Journal of Religious History*, 3 (1964–5), 275–95.

Johnson, A.M. 'The Reformation Clergy of Coventry and Lichfield, 1536–1559', unpublished Ph.D. dissertation, Emory University (1976).
—— 'The Reformation Clergy of Derbyshire 1536–1559', *Derbyshire Archaeological Journal*, 100 (1980), 49–63.
Jones, D. *The Church in Chester, 1300–1540*, Chetham Society, Remains Historical and Literary Connected with the Palatine Counties of Lancaster and Chester, 3rd series, vol. VII (1957).
Jones, M.K. and Underwood, M.G. *The King's Mother – Lady Margaret Beaufort, Countess of Richmond and Derby* (Cambridge, 1992).
Keen, M. *English Society in the Later Middle Ages, 1348–1500* (1990).
Kettle, A.J. 'City and Close: Lichfield in the Century Before the Reformation', in Barron, C.M. and Harper-Bill, C., eds, *The Church in Pre-Reformation Society* (Woodbridge, 1985), 158–69.
Kitching, C. 'Church and Chapelry in Sixteenth-Century England', *SCH*, 16 (Oxford, 1979), 279–90.
Knowles, D. and Hadcock, R.N. *Medieval Religious Houses; England and Wales* (1953).
Kreider, A. *English Chantries; The Road to Dissolution*, Harvard Historical Studies, 91 (Cambridge, MA and London, 1979).
Kümin, B. 'Parish Finance and the Early Tudor Clergy', in Pettegree, A., ed. *The Reformation of the Parishes – The Ministry and the Reformation in Town and Country* (Manchester, 1993), 43–62.
—— *The Shaping of a Community: The Rise and Reformation of the English Parish c.1400–1560* (Aldershot, 1996).
Lehmberg, S.E. *The Reformation Parliament 1529–1536* (Cambridge, 1970).
—— *The Reformation of Cathedrals: Cathedrals in English society, 1485–1603* (Princeton, NJ, 1988).
Le Neve, J. and Jones, B. *Fasti Ecclesiae Anglicanae 1300–1541*, vol. X, *Coventry and Lichfield Diocese* (1964).
Lepine, D. *A Brotherhood of Canons Serving God: English Secular Cathedrals in the Later Middle Ages* (Woodbridge, 1995).
Luxton, I. 'The Lichfield Court Book: A Postscript', *Bulletin of the Institute of Historical Research*, 44 (1971), 120–5.
Lytle, G.F. 'Patronage Patterns and Oxford Colleges c.1300–c.1530', in Stone, L. ed. *The University in Society*, 2 vols (Oxford, 1975), i, 111–49.
—— 'Religion and the Lay Patron in Reformation England', in Lytle, G.F. and Orgel, S., eds, *Patronage in the Renaissance* (Princeton, NJ, 1981), 65–114.
Mackie, P. 'Chaplains in the Diocese of York, 1480–1530: The Testamentary Evidence', *Yorkshire Archaeological Journal*, 58 (1986), 123–33.
Marshall, P. *The Catholic Priesthood and the English Reformation* (Oxford, 1994).
—— *The Face of the Pastoral Ministry in the East Riding, 1525–1595*, University of York Borthwick Paper No. 88 (York, 1995).
—— 'The Dispersal of Monastic Patronage in East Yorkshire, 1520–90', in Kümin, B., ed. *Reformations Old and New: Essays on the Socio-Economic Impact of Religious Change c.1470–1630* (Aldershot, 1996), 124–46.

Mason, E. 'The Rôle of the English Parishioner 1100–1500', JEH, 27 (1976), 17–29.
McHardy, A.K. 'Careers and Disappointments in the Late-Medieval Church: Some English Evidence', SCH, 26 (Oxford, 1989), 111–30.
—— 'Clerical Taxation in Fifteenth-Century England: The Clergy as Agents of the Crown', in R.B. Dobson, ed., *The Church, Politics and Patronage in the Fifteenth Century* (Gloucester, 1984), 168–92.
Mertes, K. *The English Noble Household 1250–1600* (Oxford, 1988).
Moran, J.A.H. 'Clerical Recruitment in the Diocese of York 1340–1530: Data and Commentary', JEH, 34 (1983), 19–54.
—— *The Growth of English Schooling 1340–1548: Learning, Literacy, and Laicization in Pre-Reformation York Diocese* (Princeton, NJ, 1985).
Morris, C. 'The Commissary of the Bishop in the Diocese of Lincoln', JEH, 10 (1959), 50–65.
Morris, R. *Churches in the Landscape* (1989).
Nicholas, A.E. 'The Etiquette of Pre-Reformation Confession in East Anglia', *Sixteenth Century Journal*, 17 (1986), 145–63.
O'Day, R. 'The Law of Patronage in Early-Modern England', JEH, 26 (1975), 247–60.
—— 'Cumulative Debt: The Bishops of Coventry and Lichfield and their Economic Problems', *Midland History*, 3 (1975), 77–93.
—— 'Ecclesiastical Patronage: Who Controlled the Church?', in Heal, F. and O'Day, R., eds, *Church and Society in England: Henry VIII to James I* (1977), 137–155.
—— *The English Clergy: The Emergence and Consolidation of a Profession, 1558–1642* (Leicester, 1979).
—— *The Debate on the English Reformation* (1986).
O'Day, R. and Heal, F., eds, *Continuity and Change: Personnel and Administration of the Church of England 1500–1642* (Leicester, 1976).
Ordnance Survey, *Monastic Britain* (2nd edn, 1954).
Orme, N. *English Schools in the Middle Ages* (1973).
—— 'Education and Learning at a Medieval English Cathedral: Exeter, 1380–1548', JEH, 32 (1981), 265–83.
—— 'Schoolmasters, 1307–1509', in Clough, C.H., ed., *Profession, Vocation and Culture in Late Medieval England – Essays Dedicated to the Memory of A.R. Myers* (Liverpool, 1982), 218–41.
—— *Education and Society in Medieval and Renaissance England* (London and Ronceverte, WV, 1989).
—— 'Sufferings of the Clergy: Illness and Old Age in Exeter Diocese 1300–1540', in Pelling, M. and Smith, R.M., eds, *Life, Death and the Elderly: Historical Perspectives* (1991), 62–73.
Owen, D.M. *Church and Society in Medieval Lincolnshire*, History of Lincolnshire, 5 (Lincoln, 1971).
—— 'The Records of the Bishop's Official at Ely: Specialization in the English Episcopal Chancery of the Later Middle Ages', in Bullough, D.A. and Storey,

R.L., eds, *The Study of Medieval Records: Essays in Honour of Kathleen Major* (Oxford, 1971), 189–205.

—— 'An Episcopal Audience Court', in Baker, J.H., ed., *Legal Records and the Historian*, Royal Historical Society, Studies in History (1978), 140–9.

—— *Medieval Records in Print: Bishops' Registers*, Historical Association, Helps for Students of History, 89 (1982).

Parish, H.L. ' "By This Mark You Shall Know Him": Clerical Celibacy and Antichrist in English Reformation Polemic', *SCH*, 33 (1997), 253–66.

Platt, C. *The Parish Churches of Medieval England* (1981).

Pound, J. 'Clerical Poverty in England: Some East Anglian Evidence', *JEH*, 37 (1986), 389–96.

Rex, R. *The Theology of John Fisher* (Cambridge, 1991).

Rigby, S.H. *English Society in the Later Middle Ages: Class, Status and Gender* (1995).

Robinson, D. 'Ordinations of Secular Clergy in the Diocese of Coventry and Lichfield, 1322–1358', *Archives*, 17 (1985–6), 3–21.

Rodes, R.E., jr. *Ecclesiastical Administration in Medieval England: the Anglo-Saxons to the Reformation* (1977).

Rose, R.K. 'Priests and Patrons in the Fourteenth-Century Diocese of Carlisle', *SCH*, 16 (1979), 207–18.

Rosser, A.G. 'The Guild of St Mary and St John the Baptist, Lichfield: Ordinances of the Late Fourteenth Century', *Staffordshire Record Society, Collections for a History of Staffordshire*, 4th series, vol. 13 (1988), 19–26.

Russell, J.C. 'The Clerical Population of Medieval England', *Traditio*, 2 (1944), 177–212.

Scarisbrick, J.J. 'Clerical Taxation in England, 1485 to 1547', *JEH*, 11 (1960), 41–54.

—— *Henry VIII* (Harmondsworth, 1968).

—— *The Reformation and the English People* (Oxford, 1984).

Sheils, W.J. *The English Reformation 1530–1570*, Seminar Studies in History (Harlow, 1989).

Skeeters, M.C. *Community and Clergy: Bristol and the Reformation c.1530–c.1570* (Oxford, 1993).

Smith, D.M. *Guide to Bishops' Registers of England and Wales: A Survey from the Middle Ages to the Abolition of Episcopacy in 1646*, Royal Historical Society, Guides and Handbooks, II (1981).

—— 'Suffragan Bishops in the Medieval Diocese of Lincoln', *Lincolnshire History and Archaeology*, 17 (1982), 17–27.

Starkey, D., ed., *Rivals in Power: Lives and Letters of the Great Tudor Dynasties* (1990)

—— ed., *Henry VIII: A European Court in England* (1991).

Stevens Benham, L.M. 'The Durham Clergy, 1494–1540: A Study of Continuity and Mediocrity Among the Unbeneficed', in Marcombe, D., ed., *The Last Principality: Politics, Religion and Society in the Bishopric of Durham 1494–1660*, Studies in Regional and Local History, no. 1 (Nottingham, 1987).

Storey, R.L. *Diocesan Administration in Fifteenth Century England*, Borthwick Papers, 16 (2nd edn, York, 1972).

―――― 'Ordinations of Secular Priests in Early Tudor London', *Nottingham Mediaeval Studies*, 23 (1989), 122–33.

Swanson, R.N. 'Universities, Graduates and Benefices in Later Medieval England', *Past and Present*, 106 (February, 1985), 28–61.

―――― 'Titles to Orders in Medieval Episcopal Registers', in Mayr-Harting, H. and Moore, R.I., eds, *Studies in Medieval History Presented to R.H.C. Davies* (1985), 233–45.

―――― 'Learning and Livings: University Study and Clerical Careers in Late Medieval England', *History of the Universities*, 6 (1986), 81–103.

―――― 'Episcopal Income from Spiritualities in Late Medieval England: The Evidence for the Diocese of Coventry and Lichfield', *Midland History*, 14 (1988), 1–20.

―――― 'Lichfield Chapter Acts, 1433–61', *Staffordshire Record Society, Collections for a History of Staffordshire*, 4th series, vol. 14 (1988), 27–46.

―――― *Church and Society in Late Medieval England* (Oxford, 1989).

―――― 'Problems of the Priesthood in Pre-Reformation England', *English Historical Review*, 417 (October, 1990), 845–69.

―――― 'Chaucer's Parson and Other Priests', *Studies in the Age of Chaucer*, 13 (1991), 41–80.

―――― 'Standards of Livings: Parochial Revenues in Pre-Reformation England', in Harper-Bill, C., ed., *Religious Belief and Ecclesiastical Careers in Late Medieval England* (Woodbridge, 1991), 151–91.

―――― 'Clergy in Manorial Society in Late Medieval Staffordshire', *Staffordshire Studies*, 5 (1993), 13–33.

―――― 'Medieval Liturgy as Theatre: The Props', *SCH*, 28 (Oxford, 1992), 239–53.

―――― *Catholic England: Faith, Religion and Observance Before the Reformation* (Manchester, 1993).

―――― ' "Speculum Ecclesiae"? Sources for the Administrative History of the Late Medieval English Church', *Ricerche di Storia Sociale e Religiosa*, 48 (1995), 13–32.

Tanner, N.P. *The Church in Late Medieval Norwich*, Pontifical Institute of Mediaeval Studies, Studies and Texts, 66 (Toronto, 1984).

Thompson, A.H. *The English Clergy and their Organization in the Later Middle Ages* (Oxford, 1947).

Thomson, J.A.F. 'Tithe Disputes in Later Medieval London', *English Historical Review*, 78 (1963), 1–17.

―――― *The Later Lollards 1414–1520* (Oxford, 1965).

―――― 'The Bishop in his Diocese', in Bradshaw, B. and Duffy, E., eds, *Humanism, Reform and the Reformation: The Career of Bishop John Fisher* (Cambridge, 1989), 67–80.

―――― *The Early Tudor Church and Society 1485–1529* (Harlow, 1993).

Townley, S. 'Unbeneficed Clergy in the Thirteenth Century: Two English Dioceses', in D.M. Smith, ed., *Studies in Clergy and Ministry in Medieval England*, Borthwick Studies in History, 1 (1991), 38–64.

Tupling, G.H. 'The Pre-Reformation Parishes and Chapelries of Lancashire', *Transactions of the Lancashire & Cheshire Antiquarian Society*, 67 (1958), 1–16.

Venn, J. and J.A. *Alumni Cantabrigienses*, 4 vols (Cambridge, 1922–27).
Victoria History of the County of Stafford, vol. 3, ed. M.W. Greenslade (Oxford, 1970).
Victoria History of the County of Stafford, vol. 14, ed. M.W. Greenslade (Oxford, 1990).
Whiting, R. *The Blind Devotion of the People: Popular Religion and the English Reformation* (Cambridge, 1989).
Williams, N. *The Cardinal and the Secretary* (1975).
Woodcock, B.L. *Medieval Ecclesiastical Courts in the Diocese of Canterbury* (Oxford, 1952).
Wood-Legh, K. *Perpetual Chantries in Britain* (Cambridge, 1965).
Wright, S.J., ed., *Parish, Church and People: Local Studies in Lay Religion, 1350–1750* (1988).
Wunderli, R.M. *London Church Courts and Society on the Eve of the Reformation*, Speculum Anniversary Monographs, 7 (Cambridge, MA, 1981).
Wybrew, H. 'The Setting of the Liturgy: Ceremonial', in Jones, C., Wainwright, G. and Yarnold, E., eds, *The Study of Liturgy* (1978), 432–9.
Youings, J. *Sixteenth-Century England* (Harmondsworth, 1984).
Zell, M.L. 'The Personnel of the Clergy in Kent in the Reformation Period', *English Historical Review*, 89 (1974), 513–33.
——— 'The Use of Religious Preambles as a Measure of Religious Belief in the Sixteenth Century', *Bulletin of the Institute of Historical Research*, 50 (1977), 246–9.
——— 'Economic Problems of the Parochial Clergy in the Sixteenth Century', in O'Day, R. and Heal, F., eds, *Princes and Paupers in the English Church 1500–1800* (Leicester, 1981), 19–43.

Index

NB: Places are identified according to their pre-1974 county designations.

Abbots Bromley (Staffs.)
   chapel of St Nicholas in church   148
   chaplains of *see* Beche, John; Wainwright, Stephen
   vicars of *see* Wylson, Thomas
Abell, John, curate of Kingstone
   agricultural concerns of   125
   bequest to godchildren   159
   bequest to poor   163
   biography   190
   commendation of soul   147
   length of tenure of post   108
   ownership of livestock   119
Absenteeism *see* Non-residence
Acolytes   17, 18
Acton (Chesh.)
   vicar of *see* Caulyn, Robert
Acton Trussell (Staffs.)
   curate of *see* Gryme, Robert
Adams, Oliver, Abbot of Combe   86
Adbaston (Staffs.), chaplain of   54
Adderton:
   John, sponsor of Robert Adderton   98 (n.20)
   Robert, stipendiary priest of Leigh   98 (n.20)
Advowsons   43
Affinity   157
Agriculture, involvement of clergy in   81 (n.230), 82, 84 & n.238, 85, 91, 92, 118, 119, 125, 157, 163, 166, 184-7
   beehives   85, 119, 166
   see also Marketing
Alb   145
Alderley Edge (Chesh.)
   rector of *see* Mainwaring, M. Robert
Aldridge (Staffs.)
   rectors of *see* Walker, Edmund; Weldon, M. Philip
Alen:
   Robert, vicar of Seighford   59
   Thomas, rector of Kingswinford
     biography   190
     commendation of soul   147
     ownership of chalice   134

     valuation of benefice   80
Alexander VI, Pope   64
Allestree (Warks.)
   curate of *see* Fowler, Gilbert
   vicar of *see* Darley, M. William
   vicarage of   61
Almonry schools   10
Alrewas (Staffs.), vicar of *see* Collier, M. William
Alspath (Warks.), vicar of   116 (n.108)
Alstonefield (Staffs.), tithe disputes in parish   167, 169
Altar:
   portable   134
   removal of   148
Altham (Lancs.), curate of   96
Alvecote Priory (Warks.)   23, 28
Anticlericalism   35-6
Antiphoner   9, 134
Antiphons   134
Apparitors   171 (n.151), 172, 174, 176, 178, 181
Appleby, Thomas, vicar of Atcham   171 (n.151)
Appropriation, monastic *see* Monasteries
Aquinus, Thomas   130
Arbury Priory (Warks.)   26
Arley (Warks.), rectory of   46
Asche, Richard, chantry priest of Beighton
   bequest of corinal   134
   bequest to godchildren   160
   bequests of   99, 150-1
   biography   190
   stipend   151
   value of probate inventory   151
Ashbourne (Derbs.)
   vicar of *see* Tykhill, William
Ashley (Staffs.)
   rector of *see* Bowyer, Andrew
Ashley:
   Thomas, ordinand   17 (n.48)
   William, chaplain   172
   William, vicar of Moreton Corbet   151

INDEX

Ashton-under-Lyne (Chesh.)
   rector of *see* Molyneux, M. Edward
Assistant clergy *see* Stipendiary clergy
Astbury (Chesh.), clerical provision of 96 (n.13)
Astley, William, chaplain of Wigan 109, 119–20 (n.122)
Astley (Warks.), collegiate church 44
Aston (Warks.)
   clerical provision of 97
   tithe dispute in parish of 167, 169
   vicar of 54
Astronomy, clerical interest in 170
Atcham (Salop)
   chaplain of *see* Ashley, William
   curate of *see* Cotton, Richard
   vicar of *see* Appleby, Thomas
Atkinson, Stephen, chaplain of Bramshall 104
Audlem (Chesh.)
   chaplain of *see* Hoxleye, Thomas
   rector of *see* Strethay, M. Edmund
Audley (Staffs.)
   chaplain of *see* Smyth, Hugh
Aughton (Chesh.)
   rectors of *see* Bradshaw, William; Morecroft, Brian
Augustinian Order
   appropriation of churches by 38
   as providers of titles to orders 23–6
Austen (Nr. Doncaster, Yorks.)
   parish priest of *see* Rogers, William
   vicar of 153
Avery, Thomas, clerk of Holy Trinity, Coventry 71
Avon Dassett (Warks.)
   curate of *see* Warner, William
   rector of *see* Dalison, Thomas
   rectory of 72, 73

Bablake collegiate church 133, 190
Babyngton, William, curate of Stanton 151 (n.77)
Bachelor, Edmund, rector of Sheinton
   agricultural concerns of 84–85, 92
   bequest to church 92
   bequest to patron 41 (n.19)
   bequest to relatives 157
   bequests to colleagues 152
   bequests to godchildren 159
   burial request 92
   career 92, 112, 190
   charitable bequests of 163–4
   commendation of soul 147
   funeral arrangements 92, 147
   house 87–8
   ownership of books 139
   ownership of imagery 145
   value of benefice 80
   value of probate inventory 83, 84–5, 92
Bacon, William, rector of Standon 58
Baddesley Clinton (Warks.)
   rector of *see* Pyffert, M. John
Bagge (*alias* Bage), William, chaplain of Chesterfield 150 (n.71), 187
Bagshaw, Gervase, vicar of Colwich and Sedgley 60
Bailey, William, clerk of Holy Trinity, Coventry 71
Bainbridge, Christopher, Cardinal Archbishop of York 73
Bakewell (Derbs.)
   presentations to vicarage 49 & n.64
   vicars of *see* Wilcocks, M. John
Bakewell, Thomas, curate of Checkley 105 (n.58)
Balam, Thomas, chaplain of Hillmorton 116
Ball, M. Roger, vicar of Harborne 54
Banados (Thrace), suffragan bishops of 28 & n.85
   and *see* Wele, Thomas
Banaster, Thomas, criminous clerk 176 (n.171)
Bangor, bishop of 153
Bangor-is-y-coed (Flint)
   curate of *see* Wyllington, Maurice
   rectors of *see* Knight, William; Straitbarrel, James
Baptism 141, 160
Barefote:
   Robert, merchant of London 47
   Robert, vicar of Mancetter 47 (n.55)
      accumulation of cash by 87
      biography 190
      houses 88
      ownership of books 139–40
      ownership of alabaster head of St John the Baptist 145
      priest of gild of St Mary 83
      property ownership and leasing by 87
      value of probate inventory 83
Barker, Thomas, prior of Newburgh and rector of Eckington 38
Barlborough (Derbs.)
   rector of *see* Tatton, Ralph

INDEX 207

'Rood Guild' in parish of 163
Barlow, Robert, curate of Burton upon Trent and Walsall 108
Barnes, John, vicar of Leighton 152 & n.87
Barrow upon Trent (Derbs.)
   parishioners of 48
   rector of *see* Layton, Ambrose
   tithe litigation in parish 168
   vicar of *see* Franks, William
   vicarage house and garden 88
Barton-under-Needwood (Staffs.)
   birthplace of John Taylor, royal diplomat 51–2
   church of 52
   curate of *see* Grene, William
Baschurch (Salop)
   chaplain of *see* Wycherley, Richard
Basingwerk Abbey (Flint) 23
Bassingbourne (Cambs.), Trinity Gild in 99
Baswich Priory (*alias* St Thomas, Stafford)
   titles to orders from 22, 25, 104, 105, 112
Battman (*alias* Bateman), John, chaplain of St Michael's, Coventry 151 (n.75)
Beauchief Abbey (Derbs.) 22, 25
Beaufort, Lady Margaret 44, 46, 48
Bebington (Chesh.)
   rector of *see* Chauntrell, Nicholas
Beche, John, rector of Maer etc. 110
Bee, John, chantry priest of Uttoxeter
   bequest to serving boy 123, 171
   bequests to women 170–1
   biography 190
   charitable bequests of 163
   commendation of soul 147
   ownership of beehives 119
   property ownership by 118
   provision of funeral doles by 126
Beighton (Derbs.)
   chantry priest of *see* Asche, Richard
Bellet, John, stipendiary priest of Cheadle 104–5
Bells 53, 146, 148
Bellyster, Simon, curate of Shilton 150 (n.70)
Benedictine Order, as providers of titles to orders 23–6
Benefice(s)
   availability of 37–9
   definition of 39
   deprivation from 37–8
   episcopal foundation of 39
   exchange of 60
   houses appurtenant to 81, 83, 87–8, 90
   leasing of 82, 85
   see also Leasing
   mobility between 60–2
   papal provisions to 40
   pensions payable from, *see* Pensions
   tenure of 56–60
   unions of 72–4, 92
Benefit of Clergy 35, 175–6 (n.171)
Berdemore, John, chaplain of Grindon, chantry priest and schoolmaster of Kingsley 109
Beresford, M. James, canon of Lichfield etc. 61
Berrington (Salop)
   curate of *see* Luter, Roger
Bexwyke, Richard, curate of Middleton
   bequest to alewives 183
   bequest for mass, *dirige* and prayers for his soul 101, 146
   bequest for a priest to say masses at his church 101–2
   bequest to scholars 163
   biography 190
   outstanding pension 125
Bible 140, 142, 143, 152, 153, 185
Bickenhill (Staffs.), parishioners of 136
Biddulph (Staffs.), parishioner of 86
Birkenhead Priory (Chesh.), titles to orders from 22
Birkenshaw, M. Maurice, tutor to Thomas Winter and rector of St Mary on the Hill, Chester 54
Birmingham (Warks.) 3, 97
   rector of *see* Sutton (*alias* Dudley), Richard
Bishop's Itchington (Warks.) 97
Bishop's Tachbrook (Warks.)
   vicar of *see* Hopton, John
Blackburn (Lancs.)
   chaplain of *see* Deane, Richard
Blessed Virgin Mary
   antiphons to 134
   commendation of soul to 144, 147, 148, 185, 188
   hours of 9
Blithfield (Staffs.)
   rector of *see* Kynnersley, M. Francis
Blockley, Richard, vicar of Wolvey
   bequests to godchildren 160
   biography 190

208   INDEX

devotion to St John the Baptist   144
provision for funeral doles for priests   102
lease of land by   86
testamentary provision for support of a priest   102
Blore (Staffs.)
   rector of *see* Ward, John
Blount, William, Lord Mountjoy   47
Blymhill (Staffs.)
   chaplain of *see* Collins, John
   parsonage house at   81
   rectory   81
Blythe:
   Geoffrey, bishop of Coventry and Lichfield   3, 4, 16, 28, 29, 30, 40 (n.18), 47, 52
     consistory court of   69, 70, 122, 123, 125, 130, 134, 155, 165, 171, 179, 182–3
     dispute with dean and chapter of Lichfield Cathedral   49
     Official Principal of   64, 180
     presentation to benefices by   49–50
     vicars-general of *see* Cantrell, Ralph; Sneyd, Ralph
     visitation of Repton Priory   153 (n.89)
   John, archdeacon of Coventry and Stafford   47, 64–5
   Robert, vicar of Dunchurch
     agricultural concerns   84
     biography   190
     employment of curate by   91
     executors   149–50
     value of probate inventory   91
   M. Robert, vicar of Shirley   49 (n.63)
   Thomas, warden of the hospital of St Nicholas, Nantwich   55
Bobbington (Staffs.), parish of   170
Boleyn:
   Anne   47 (n.53)
   William, rector of Winwick   45
Bologna, university of   50
Bolsover (Derbs.)
   vicar of *see* Cartleage, Robert
Bolton (Lancs.)   96 (n.13)
   chaplain of *see* Ramsbothom, Henry
Bond, John   53
Bonde, William, priest   64
Bonsall (Derbs.)
   rector of *see* Lililow, M. Thomas

Books, ownership by clergy   138–40
Books of Hours   9
Borows, Richard, vicar choral of Lichfield Cathedral   104 & n.48
Boston (Lincs.)   13
   gild of St Mary in   99
Bosworth, William, priest   27
Bothe:
   Robert, rector of Thornton   55
   Sir William   55
Bowker, Thomas, chaplain of Eccles   116
Bowring, M. Ralph, vicar of Plemstall   70 (n.167)
Bowyer, Andrew, curate of Keele, later vicar of Wolstanton and rector of Ashley   111–12
Boydell, Ralph, vicar of Rostherne   54
Boylestone (Derbs.)
   chaplain of *see* Latham, Edmund
   rectory   46
Bradburne, Isobel, Lady of Boylestone   46
Bradley (Staffs.)
   vicar of *see* Dyngley, Roger
Bradocke, M. George, priest   88 (n.252)
Bradshaw:
   Peter, rector of Eccleston etc.   44
   Thomas, rector of Hamstall Ridware etc.   113
   Thurstan, chaplain of Cheddleton   105
   William, curate of Penwortham, rector of Aughton   74, 75, 77
Brailsford (Derbs.)   102
Bralyford, John, chaplain   154
Brampton (Derbs.)
   curate of chapel of *see* Somersall, Thomas
Bramshall (Staffs.)
   chaplain of *see* Atkinson, Stephen
Breadsall (Derbs.), rectory   81, 87
Breadsall Park Priory (Derbs.)   23
Bredwall, Thomas, chaplain, later vicar of Stoke and Newcastle   112
Brereton, M. John, rector of Christleton etc., Royal Chaplain   44, 66, 67, 69
Brett, Richard, chaplain   77, 154, 180
Bretunner, Joachim, Archdeacon of Shrewsbury   16
Breviary   103, 134
Brewood (Staffs.)
   vicar of *see* Flemyng, Henry   93

White Ladies Priory
   employment of chaplains by   101
   titles to orders from   22, 104, 190
Brewster, M. William, vicar of Etwall
   accumulation of cash by   87
   bequest to chaplain   150
   bequest to church   146
   bequests to colleagues   152, 153
   bequest to godchildren   159
   bequest to sister   157–8
   bequest to successor at former vicarage   90, 153
   biography   190
   burial arrangements   146–7
   charitable bequests   162, 163
   commendation of soul   146
   ownership of books   140
   provision for funeral doles for clergy and poor   102
Bridges, William, chaplain of Macclesfield and master of Macclesfield Grammar School
   as schoolmaster   10
   bequest to church   145
   bequest to servant   123
   bequests to godchildren   160
   bequest to scholars   163
   biography   190
   charitable bequest of   161
   debts owed to   164
   debts written off by   124
   discharge clause in will   183
   funeral arrangements   146
   memorial to   131
   ownership of property   118
   provision for clergy to say funeral offices   102–3
Bristol, parishes of All Saints and St Nicholas   10
Broke, Griffin, rector of Darlaston   58, 59
Brook, James, fellow of collegiate church of Bunbury   93
Broughton Astley (Leics)
   rector of see Reed, M. John
Bruce, Robert, rector of Kingsley   58, 59
Bryddocke, Richard, priest of Manchester
   bequest of corinal   134
   biography   190
   commendation of soul   147
   provision of funeral dole for clergy   102, 147
Bucke, Charles, priest of Coventry   153, 190
Buckingham, archdeaconry of   63

Buildwas Abbey (Salop), titles to orders from   22, 104, 112, 190, 192
Bulcombe, M. John, rector of Church Eaton   60
Bunbury (Chesh.), collegiate church of
   fellow of see Brook, James
Burdet, Amer, vicar of Middlewich   42
Burgh, John de, *Pupilla Oculi* of   15
Burnaston (Derbs.), parishioners of   162
Burnley (Lancs.), chapel of   96
Burscough Priory (Lancs.)
   canons of as vicars of Ormskirk   38
   titles to orders from   22, 38 (n.10)
Burton, Robert, priest of York
   commonplace book of   133
   including:
      astronomical calculations   170
      exercises in grammar and etymology   139 (n.44)
      exposition of doctrine of transubstantiation   135 (n.25)
      form of the Mass of the Five Wounds   146 (n.62)
      preparations for celebration of Mass   135 (n.21)
      ready reckoner   164
      riddles   170
      summaries of belief   137 (n.37)
Burton Lazars hospital (Leics)   163
Burton upon Trent (Staffs.)
   chaplain of see Hyll, John
   curate of see Barlow, Robert
   Abbey, titles to orders from   23, 24, 185
Bury (Lancs.)
   rectors of see Smyth, Richard
Bushbury (Staffs.)
   parishioners of   162–3
   vicar of see Slany, Henry
   vicarage   81
Butler:
   Thomas, sub-prior of Shrewsbury   43 (n.28)
   Sir Thomas   97 (n.20)
   William, vicar of Wrockwardine
      accommodation arrangements   90
      appointment of servant as executor of will   89
      biography   190
      indebtedness of   91–2
      possible connection with Shrewsbury Abbey   43 (n.28)

210 INDEX

    presentation to benefice   26 & n.74
    valuation of benefice   81
    value of probate inventory   91
    wages outstanding to servants 89–90
  M. William, vicar of Pattingham   59 & n.117
Butts, Dr William, royal physician   47 & n.53
Byrche, Sampson, vicar of Stretton   112
Byrde, John, vicar of St Mary's, Lichfield   93, 112
Byshoppe, Henry, vicar of Moreton Corbet, 144, 190

Calton (Staffs.)
  curate of see Hode, Thomas
Calton, Robert   48
Calwich Priory (Staffs.)   23
Cambridge:
  university   13, 21, 32, 44, 50, 63
    colleges:
      Clare   44–5
      Jesus   21
      King's   16, 21, 190
      Michaelhouse   48, 59 (n.117)
      St John's   21
      Trinity   45
  see also titles to orders
Campion, William, rector of Breadsall
  biography   190
  hire of assistant   90
  value of benefice   81, 90
  value of glebe and house   87
  value of probate inventory   90
Candlemass   148 (n.63)
Canterbury:
  archbishop of   122
  convocations   8, 51, 52 (n.74), 55, 138
  diocese of   62, 63, 95 (n.3), 166
Cantrell, Ralph, canon of Lichfield, dean of St John's, Chester, vicar-general of Bishop Blythe   16
Canwell Priory (Staffs.)   23, 192
Carlisle, diocese of   95
Cartleage, Robert, vicar of Bolsover, later chantry priest of Dronfield   76, 77
Cartwright, John, chaplain of Wolstanton   186
Catechism   8, 9, 137 & n.37
Caulyn, Robert, rector of St Oswald's, Chester etc.   44

Caverswall (Staffs.)
  curate and vicar of see Wildblood, John
Celibacy   17, 130, 170, 171
Chad farthings   80 & n.226
Chadwick, John, criminous clerk   176 (n.171)
Chalice   30, 134
Chalner, John, curate of Cheswardine   172
Chancel
  furnishings of   143
  prohibition of laity from   135–6
Chancery   55
Chantry certificates and returns   9, 10, 96 (n.13), 98, 106, 108
Chantry priests (chantrists)   8, 11, 36, 96 (n.13), 98
Chantries   34, 37, 53, 97
Chapels   95, 107
  domestic   100
Chaplain(s)
  employment of   90, 95
  in service of houses of female religious   101
  in service of monastic oratories   101
  'riding'   100
  use of term   56
  see also Household chaplains; Stipendiary clergy
Charity, of clergy   92, 125–6, 161–4
Chauntrell, Nicholas, rector of Bebington   76
Chaverham, John, vicar of Cuckney   152
Cheadle (Staffs.)
  rector of see Norres, M. Richard
  rectory of   48, 58, 59
  stipendiary priest of see Bellet, John
Chebsey (Staffs.)   49 (n.64), 83
  vicar of see Hall, M. John
Checkley (Staffs.)
  curate of see Bakewell, Thomas
  rector of see Draycott, M. Anthony
  rectory   80
Cheddleton (Staffs.)
  chaplains of see Bradshaw, Thurstan; Forde, Richard; Goodwyn, John
Chelaston (Staffs.)
  curate of see Peyrson, Roger
Chelwaw, Matthew, ordinand   17 (n.53)
Chepping (Yorks.)   73
Chester
  abbey (St Werburgh's)
    presentations to benefices by   42

INDEX 211

titles to orders from 22, 24, 25, 26, 190
usurpation of presentation rights of 54
archdeaconry of 4
   clerical stipends in 115, 117
   employment of stipendiary clergy in 91, 95, 96 & n.13
   significance of lay patronage within 42, 43
   schools in 11
   value of livings in 78
Benedictine nunnery in 101
city 3
collegiate church of St John
   dean of see Cantrell, Ralph; canon of see Strete, Richard
Holy Trinity
   rectors of see Caulyn, Robert; Pommell, Thomas; Smyth, Richard
St Mary on the Hill
   rectors of see Birkenshaw, M. Maurice; Davenport, M. John; Straitbarrel, James
   usurpation of presentation rights to 54
St Oswald
   vicar of see Caulyn, Robert
Chesterfield (Derbs.)
   bequests to church 163
   chaplains of see Bagge, William; Tryge, Henry
   curate see Whitworth, Richard
   'St Katherine's Quere' in church of 188
   vicars of see Flint, Oliver; Lililow, M. Thomas
Cheswardine (Salop)
   curate of see Chalner, John
Chetwynd (Salop)
   rector of see Grene, Ralph
Child's Ercall (Salop) 168
Childwall (Lancs.)
   stipendiary priest of see Ireland, Christopher
Chilvers Coton (Warks.)
   vicar of see Keldermere, John
Chorlton, Henry, chaplain of Wellington 137
Christleton (Chesh.)
   vicar of see Brereton, M. John
Church, prohibition on layman entering 168

Church (Lancs.), chapel of 96
Church Eaton (Staffs.)
   rector of see Bulcombe, M. John
Church Gresley Priory (Derbs.)
   canon of 38
   titles to orders from 23
Church Lawton (Chesh.), clerical provision of 96 (n.13)
Churchwardens' accounts 99, 166
Cistercian Order, as providers of titles to orders 23–6
Clay, Humphrey, vicar of Loppington 177
Clergy
   accommodation costs of 90, 122, 123
   age profile of 57 & n.102, 58, 82, 125, 190–3
   concubines of 171, 173 & n.167, 174, 175, 178, 181
   family relationships 156–8
   funeral and burial arrangements 131–3
   marriage of 173
   migration of 33–4 & n.105
   performance of secular work by 99, 100–1, 117–22
   see also Agriculture
   practice of medicine by 170
   property ownership by 87, 118
   relations between 148–55
   see also Poverty, clerical; Stipendiary clergy; Unbeneficed clergy
Clerical subsidies 37
Clerical violence 86, 154, 180–1, 182
Clifton Campville (Staffs.), rectory 79
Clint (Yorks.) 24 (n.70)
Clinton, Sir Thomas, patron of Arley 46
Clitheroe (Lancs.),
   chaplains of 96 & n.12
Closet, clerk of 100
Cloth see Textile production
Clothall (Herts), rectory 73
Clough, Roger, chaplain 54
Clowne (Derbs.)
   rector of see Hewat, Robert
Clyff, William, Warden of the collegiate church of Manchester 16
Cockersand Abbey (Lancs.) 23
Cockson, Hugh, chaplain of Wigan 98, 109
Coddington (Chesh.)
   rector of see Porte, M. Thomas

Codgrave, Robert, vicar of Elmton 59 (n.115)
Coke, John, ordinand 17 (n. 48)
Cokke, Thurstan, ordinand 17 (n.48)
Coleshill (Warks.) 48
Colet, John, Dean of St Paul's 15, 34, 36, 52 (n.74), 129–30
College of Physicians 51 (n.73)
Collegiate churches 11, 110–11
Collet, Richard, vicar of Holy Trinity, Coventry 53, 69, 74, 76
Colley, Henry, chaplain of Prescot
   actions contrary to manorial by-laws 165
   dispute with fellow-chaplain 165
   length of tenure of post 109
   ownership of property 118
   sued for outstanding debt 125
Collier, M. William, vicar of Alrewas and St Peter's, Derby 60
Collins, John, rector of Weston-under-Lizard etc. 102, 112
Colmore, John, Succentor of Lichfield Cathedral, vicar of Penn 64, 167–8
Colne (Lancs.)
   chaplains of 96
Colton (Staffs.)
   rectors of see Tatton, George; Tatton, Thomas
Colwich (Staffs.)
   vicar of see Bagshaw, Gervase
Colyer, George, Warden of the collegiate church of Manchester etc. 16
Combe Abbey (Warks.)
   abbot of see Adams, Oliver
   titles to orders from 23, 24
Comberford, Richard, vicar of Hartington 14 (n.29)
Combermere Abbey (Chesh.) 22
Communion 135, 136
   Easter 136, 145
   see also Eucharist
Compurgation 137, 172, 175 & n.171, 181
Confession 136–7
   alleged charge for hearing 137, 181
   alleged revelation of 136–7
   failure of curate to hear 136
   imposition of penance following 136
   irregularity in hearing of 174
Confirmation 160
Confraternities, religious
   employment of priests by 99

   of the Holy Trinity, Wisbech 99
   of St Mary, Boston 99
   proliferation of 34
   testamentary bequests to 145
Consanguinity 157
Constantine, George 142
Copnall, John, chaplain of Wolstanton 186
Cornwall, archdeacon of 55
Corporal case 134
Corveser, William, vicar of Stanton upon Hine Heath
   bequest to godchildren 160
   bequests to servants 89
   biography 191
   commendation of soul 147
   household 89
   executor 151
Coryer, Robert, ordinand 17 (n.53)
Cottingham (Northants)
   rector of see Draycott, M. Anthony
Cotton, Richard, curate of Atcham 141–2
Cound (Salop)
   chaplain of see Bachelor, Edmund
   rebuilding of church 164
   rector of see Shaw, Ralph
Coundon (Salop)
   chaplain of see Turner, Thomas
Coventry (Warks.):
   archdeacon of see Blythe, John
   archdeaconry of 4, 114
   cathedral priory 24, 26, 47
     appropriation of church by 82
     chantry of William Copston in 53
     presentations to benefices by 42
     transfer of patronage by 46
   chaplains of see Fisher, Thomas; Wells, John
   Charterhouse, 'Brother John' of 153
   city of 3
   craft gilds 132
   heretics of 4, 130, 135, 141
   Holy Trinity 69
     chantry priests of see Molyneux, William
     chaplain of see Marler, Henry
     clerical provision 70, 71, 97
     clerks of see Avery, Thomas; Bailey, William; Dalbye, John; Lambard, William; Morres, Thomas; Robothum, Robert
     stipendiary clergy 71

vicars of *see* Collet, Richard;
    Darrington, M. Nicholas; Orton,
    Thomas
  priest of *see* Bucke, Charles
St Michael 46, 132
  chaplain of *see* Battman, John
  clerical provision 97
  remuneration of assistant clergy
    116
  vicars of *see* Vesey, John
Coventry and Lichfield, diocese of
  subsidy return 94, 95
  value of livings 78
Credit, parish clergy as providers of 87,
  164 & n.115, 165, 186–7
Creed 8, 9
Crich (Derbs.)
  chantry priest of *see* Swynte, Robert
  chaplain of *see* Marett, John
  vicar of *see* Richardson, William
  vicarage house 88
Criminous clerks 175–6 (n.171)
Crosse, John, vicar of Offchurch 172
Croxden Abbey (Staffs.), titles to orders
  from 21, 22, 104, 109, 190, 192
Cruets 134
Cubley (Staffs.)
  rector of *see* Hodgkinson, John
Cuckney (Notts.)
  vicar of *see* Chaverham, John
Curacy, perpetual 95
Curate(s)
  definition 95
  employment of 90, 95
  taxation of 36
  see also Stipendiary clergy
Curdworth (Warks.)
  vicar of *see* Flemyng, Thomas
Cusmere, William, ordinand 21

Dalbury with Lees (Derbs.)
  rector of *see* Ottaway, Robert
Dalbye, John, clerk of Holy Trinity,
  Coventry 71
Dale Abbey (Derbs.), titles to orders from
  22
Dalison, Thomas, rector of Avon Dassett
  etc. 72, 73–4
Darlaston (Staffs.)
  rector of *see* Broke, Griffin
  valuation of rectory 79
Darley Abbey (Derbs.)
  grant of nomination to benefice by
    49 (n.63)

presentations to benefices by 43
titles to orders from 22
Darley, M. William
  canon of Lichfield Cathedral 76
  vicar of Allestree 61–2, 76
  rector of Ladbroke 61–2, 76
Darrington, M. Nicholas, canon of
  Lichfield etc. 66, 69, 74, 75
Darwin, M. George, vicar of Dilhorne
  86 & n.244
Dashwen, Thomas, curate of Enville
  170
Davenport:
  Hugh, proxy for M. John Davenport
    53
  M. John, rector of St Mary on the Hill,
    Chester 53
Daventry Priory (Northants), title to
  orders from 91 (n.262)
Dawley (Salop)
  curate of *see* Podmore, Richard
Deane, Richard, chaplain of Blackburn
  171 (n.151)
Debts:
  owed by clergy 91–2, 123, 124–5
  owed to clergy 85, 87, 120, 124,
    186–7
  see also Credit
Defamation 130, 154
Delf, William, curate of
  Newcastle-under-Lyme 108
Denston (Staffs.)
  chaplain of *see* Fletcher, Edward
Deprivation of benefice 37–8
De Profundis 8, 9, 148, 160
Derby (Derbs.):
  Abbey, titles to orders from 23
  archdeaconry of 4, 115
  archdeacons of *see* Strete, Richard;
    Taylor, John
  collegiate church of All Saints
    canons of *see* Lililow, M. Thomas;
      Newton, Robert
  St Peter's
    ordination ceremony held in 28
    vicar of *see* Collier, M. William
  St Werburgh's, vicar of 59 (n.117)
  and see Hodgkinson, John
Dethick:
  family, patrons of church of
    Hartshorne 38
  John, rector of Hartshorne 38
Diason (*alias* Dyson), William, rector of
  Harley and Sheinton 61, 152 & n.86

Dieulacres Abbey (Staffs.), titles to orders from   17 (n. 48), 22, 25, 104, 105, 110, 143 (n.55), 186, 192
Dilapidations   153
Dilhorne (Staffs.)
  dispute between parishioner and vicar   86
  vicars of see Darwin, M. George; Tomkinson, Thomas
Dirige (placebo and dirige, otherwise dirge)   101, 103, 146
Dispensation(s)
  forged   134
  papal   14 (n.29), 29, 64, 67
    by legatine authority   29, 67, 134
    for defect of age   64
    for defect of birth   73
    for holding benefices in plurality   44, 45, 64, 66, 67
    for multiple orders   29
    for non-residence   135
    grant of royal pardon for acquisition of   66
Doddleston (Chesh.)
  rector of see Porte, M. Thomas
Dodycott, William, rector of Kinnersley   191
Dodycotte, Richard, chaplain of Wroxeter
  biography   191
  charitable bequest of   126, 161
  debts owed to   124
  funeral arrangements   125, 146
  ownership of sheep flock   118
  provision for funeral doles for clergy   102
Donnington (Salop)
  vicar of see Hill, Richard
Dore:
  Edward, priest   156
  Robert, chantry priest of Walsall   156, 191
Doveridge (Derbs.)
  curates of see Holme, Richard; Wayne, Richard
  vicar of see Fitzherbert, John
  vicarage   81, 88
Drakford, Thomas, curate of Leigh   108
Draycott (in the Moors) (Staffs.)
  curate of see Wildgoose, Thomas
  rector of see Draycott, M. Anthony
Draycott, M. Anthony, rector of Checkley etc.   66, 69–70, 179
Dronfield (Derbs.)
  chantry priest of see Cartleage, Robert
Dudley (Staffs.)
  lords of the manor of see Sutton family
  priory, titles to orders from   23, 190
Dunchurch (Warks.)
  chaplain of see Swanne, John
  remuneration of curate   116
  vicar of see Blythe, Robert
Durham Cathedral Priory   42
Dyngley, Roger, vicar of Bradley etc.   50–1

East Riding (of Yorks.), archdeaconry of
  clerical stipends in   113, 115
  incidence of pluralism in   62, 63
  number of stipendiary clergy   94, 95 (n.9)
Easter:
  communion   145
  confession   136
  dues   81, 82, 154
Eastham (Chesh.)
  chaplain of see Moile, William
Eccles (Lancs.)
  chaplains of see Bowker, Thomas; Sydall, Thomas
  remuneration of assistant clergy   116
Eccleshall (Staffs.)
  chaplain of see Jackson, Edmund
  episcopal manor of   28
  prebend of   51
Eccleston (Lancs.)
  rector of see Bradshaw, Peter
Eckington (Derbs.)
  rector of see Barker, Thomas
Education   7–13
  by stipendiary clergy   120, 163
  elementary   8–11, 98
  secondary   11
  standard, of clergy   106
  university   12–13, 138
Egerton, M. Richard, canon residentiary of Lichfield Cathedral etc.   66, 67, 69–70, 169
Eggington (Derbs.)
  rector of moiety see Smith, Richard
  rectory of   48
Elevation (of host)   136 (n.26)
Ellenhall (Staffs.)
  curate of see John Beche
Elmton (Derbs.)
  vicar of see Codgrave, Robert

Ely:
    bishop of 21
        and see Stanley, James
    diocese of
        incidence of pluralism in 62, 63
        ordinations in 32
Enfield (Staffs.)
    rector of see Egerton, M. Richard
Enville (Staffs.)
    curate of see Dashwen, Thomas
Epistles 140
Etwall (Derbs.)
    bequest to church 146
    vicar of see Brewster, M. William
Eucharist 136
    alleged denial of to parishioner 136
    canon law restriction on celebration 134
    judicial suspension from 166, 167
Evangelists, book on 185
Evesham Abbey (Worcs) 42
Examination see Ordination
Excommunication:
    illegal by incumbent 180
    judicial:
        of clergy 123-4, 180, 182
        of laity 166, 167, 176
Exeter (Devon):
    bishop of see Vesey, John
    diocese of 55
        value of pensions in 74 (n.191)
Eyre, Edmund, vicar of Tideswell 64, 135

Fald, John, chaplain 134
Farewell Priory (Staffs.), titles to orders from 23, 105, 108
Farnworth (Lancs.)
    chapel of 91, 121
    curate of see Johnson, Thomas
    master of grammar school at see Hatton, Thomas
    see also Prescot
Fazakerley, Robert, curate of Walton 122
Fernhead, John, curate and later rector of Lymm 150
Ferrara, university of 51
Field of the Cloth of Gold 51
Filiation 172
First Fruits 55
Fish, Simon, author of *Supplicacyon for the Beggers* 34
Fisher:
    John, Bishop of Rochester 129
    Thomas, chaplain of Coventry

        bequest to the Bishop of Bangor 153
        biography 191
        burial arrangements 132
        good debts of 124
        ownership of bells to adorn statues 145
        relationship with godson 160
    William, chaplain 123
Fitzherbert:
    John, vicar of Doveridge
        agricultural concerns of 84
        bequest of surplice 133, 150
        bequest to chaplain 150
        bequest to curate 150
        bequests to godchildren 160
        biography 191
        charitable bequests of 162, 163
        brother in his house 158
        household of 89
        ownership of books 140
        value of house and glebe 81
        value of probate inventory 84
    Thomas, precentor of Lichfield Cathedral 21 (n.66), 97, 108
Five Wounds (of Christ), devotion to 146 and n.62
Flemyng:
    Henry, vicar of Brewood 93
    Thomas, chaplain of Walsall 105, 166
    Thomas, vicar of Curdworth 172
Fletchamstead (Warks.)
    priest of see Yate, John
Fletcher:
    Edward, vicar of Rugeley etc. 111
    Roger, curate of Patshull 105 (n.58), 108
Flint, Oliver, vicar of Chesterfield 187
Forde, Richard, chaplain of Cheddleton 105
Formulare Instrumentorum 140
Fowler, Gilbert, chaplain, later curate of Allestree 174
Fox, Thomas, vicar of Penn etc. 110
Francis, Ralph, vicar of Willington 26 & n.75
Francklyn, Robert, recipient of multiple orders 29
Franks, William, vicar of Barrow upon Trent
    biography 191
    economic concerns of 85

poverty of   168
tithe litigation by   168
Frankton (Warks.), rectory of   46
  rector of *see* Strethay, M. Edmund
Frinde, William, chaplain of Wybunbury   175
Frodsham (Chesh.)
  rural deanery   96
  vicars of *see* Egerton, M. Richard; Wolley, John

Funeral doles   102, 103, 161, 163

Galeston? (Lancs.)   47
Gamlingay (Cambs.), gild priest of   99
Garendon Abbey (Leics), titles to orders from   23
Garnett, Edward, chaplain of Prescot
  action taken for recovery of debt   120
  alleged illegal felling of tree   165
  dispute with fellow chaplain   165
  length of tenure of post   109
  property ownership   118
Geoffrey the Grammarian   139
Gerrard, Thomas, sponsor of Hugh Cockson, chaplain of Wigan   99
Gifford, Sir John   47
Gilds:
  civic   40 (n.18)
    employment of clergy by   99
  St Mary and St John the Baptist, Lichfield *see* Lichfield
  religious *see* Confraternities
Glasgow, diocese of   21
Glebe   52, 81, 83, 84, 86, 87, 184
Glossop (Derbs.)
  vicar of *see* Talbot, John
  vicarage   72
Glover, M. John, priest   88 (n.252)
Gnossall (Staffs.), collegiate church   191
Godchildren   159–61
Golden Legend   140
Goldshaw Booth (Lancs.), chapel of the royal forest of Bowland in   96 (n.12)
Goodwyn, John, vicar of Ilam etc.   110, 143
Gospel, reading of   100
Grace Dieu Priory (Leics.)   124 (n.153)
Grange, Henry, chaplain of Wigan
  length of tenure of post   109
  listed as pauper   127
Grappenhall (Chesh.), rectory of   46
Gratwich (Staffs.)
  chaplain of *see* Fletcher, Edward

clerical provision of   70
rector of *see* Ward, John
Great Barr (Staffs.)
  curate of *see* Schelfeld, William
Great Budworth (Chesh.)
  chapels in parish of *see* Lower Peover, Witton
  number of clergy   96
Great Houghton (Northants)
  rector of *see* Throgmorton, M. William
Great Packington (Warks.)
  vicar of *see* Wright, John
Great Schism   40
Green:
  William, scholar of Wanlet (Lincs.)   13
  Sir William   21
Gregory, George, chaplain of Rossendale
  bequest to colleague   151
  bequest towards repair of chapel   126
  biography   191
  debts of   124
  hire of colleague to pray for his soul   102, 126
  ownership of kersey by   119
  poverty of   126
  remuneration of   117, 124
  share in beehives owned by   119
Grene:
  Ralph, rector of Chetwynd   93
  Richard, vicar of Longdon   58
  Roger, perpetual curate of Rodington   26 & n.75
  William, curate of Barton-under-Needwood   152
Gresley, John, rector of Norton in Hales and Ruthin   64–5
Grindon (Staffs.)
  chaplain of *see* Berdemore, John
  rector of *see* Egerton, M. Richard
  value of rectory   80
Grygge, John, rector of Wolstanton   72–3
Gryme, Robert, curate of Acton Trussell   105

Hadfield, William, ordinand   17 (n.48)
Hail Mary   8, 9
Halesowen Abbey (Worcs), titles to orders from   22, 104, 193
Hall, M. John, vicar of Chebsey
  agricultural concerns   85
  biography   191
  commendation of soul   147

INDEX 217

income 59
length of tenure of benefice 58 &
  n.112
value of probate inventory 59, 83
Halsall (Lancs.)
  curate of see Kirkby, Thomas
  members of Halsall family as rectors of
  43
Hampton in Arden (Warks.), vicarage of
  48
Hamstall Ridware (Staffs.)
  rectors of see Bradshaw, Thomas;
    Merton, William
Hanbury (Staffs.)
  rector of see Throgmorton, M. William
Handsworth (Staffs.)
  rector of see Throgmorton, M. William
Harborne (Staffs.)
  vicarage of 49 (n.64), 54
  vicars of see Ball, M. Roger; Hospis, M.
    Reginald; Waterward, Thomas;
    Wyrral, George
Hardwick, William, vicar of Rostherne
  54
Harley (Salop)
  rector of see Diason, William
Harrington, Richard, vicar of Sutton
  Maddock
  admission to vicarage 93
  charged with non-residence 64, 77,
    180
  charged with violence against
    parishioners 180
  disputes with parishioners 77
  involvement in violent dispute with
    chaplain 77, 154, 180
  pension on retirement 77, 180
Harrison, Nicholas, rector of Pleasley
  173
Hartington (Derbs.)
  vicar of see Comberford, Richard
Hartshorne (Derbs.)
  patrons of church see Dethick family
  rector of see Dethick, John
Haslingden (Lancs.)
  curate of see Holden, John
Hatford (Berks)
  rector of see Brereton, M. John
Hatton:
  Richard, curate of Shifnal
    bequest of a 'workday jacket' 126
    bequest to serving boy 123
    bequests to family 187
    biography 187, 191

charitable bequest of 162, 187
clerical connections 152–3
choice of executors 150, 155, 187
commendation of soul 147–8
debt owed to 187
funeral arrangements 147–8, 187
length of tenure of post 109
ownership of quiver and arrows
  187
Thomas, master of Farnworth
  Grammar School, 12, 106
Haughmond Abbey (Salop), titles to
  orders from 23, 24
Hawarden (Chesh.)
  rector of see Pole, Ranulph
Hawardyn, Humphrey, vicar of Tarvin
  49 (n.63), 53
Haydock, Gilbert, vicar of Rochdale 173
Hayward, Richard, chaplain 122
Henbury (Chesh.), perpetual curacy of
  50
Heneage, George, rector of Sutton
  Coldfield and Dean of Lincoln 50
Henry VII 4
Henry VIII 4
  chaplains to see Brereton, M. John;
    Draycott, M. Anthony; Taylor,
    John
  chaplain and secretary to see Knight,
    William
  diplomats to see Taylor, John; Vesey,
    John
  divorce proceedings of 51
  physicians to see Butts, Dr William;
    Linacre, Thomas
  solicitor to see Porte, John
  tutor to see Hone, William
Hereford, diocese of 8 (n.7)
  number of unbeneficed clergy 95
Heresy 141–2
  and see Cotton, Richard; Coventry,
    heretics of
Hertford Priory (Herts) 47
Hewat, Robert, rector of Clowne 76
Hey, Matthew, chaplain of Wigan 109
Heynson, Robert, chaplain of Middlewich
  123
Heyton, Henry, chaplain 172
Higgins, Richard, rector of Kemberton
  187
High Ercall (Salop)
  bequest of breviaries to church 134
  chaplain of see Pyxley, Thomas

Hill:
    Richard, vicar of Donnington 26 & n.75
    William, priest of Lichfield 105
Hillmorton (Warks.)
    chaplain of see Balam, Thomas
Hinstock (Salop)
    rector of see Holwaye, John
Hobard, John, priest of the Trinity Gild, Bassingbourne 99
Hobbroyle, Robert, ordinand 17 (n.53)
Hode, Thomas, curate of Calton 105 (n.58)
Hodgkinson, John, rector of Cubley etc. 61
Holden:
    John, curate of Haslingden 152 (n.80)
    Thomas, priest 151 (n.80)
Holderness, deanery of, incidence of pluralism in 62
Holinshed, Raphael, historian 10
Holland, Nicholas, ordinand 21
Holme, Richard, curate of Doveridge 150 (n.72)
Holwaye, John, rector of Hinstock
    bequest of book of debts by 164
    bequest to servant 89
    bequests to his family 157
    biography 184–5, 191
    clerical connections 152–3
    commendation of soul 148
    livestock owned by 85
    ownership of books 139
    ownership of weapons 185
Holy Name (of Jesus), devotion to 144
Holy See 40
Hone, William, tutor to Henry VIII, Dean of Tamworth 50
Hood, William, priest 102
Hope (Derbs.)
    presentation to vicarage of 49 (n.64)
    vicar of see Lililow, M. Thomas
Hopkins, Thomas, vicar of Long Itchington 26 & n.75
Hopton, John, vicar of Bishop's Tachbrook 49 (n.63)
Hopton (Staffs.)
    chaplains of see Fox, Thomas; Walker, Edmund
Hordley, William, vicar of Holy Cross in Shrewbury Abbey 55
Hoskayne, William, ordinand 17 (n.53)
Hospis, M. Reginald, vicar of Harborne 54
Hospitality 89 & n.254
Households, aristocratic and gentry
    education in 11
    employment of clergy by 100, 101
Household chaplains 100–1
Households, clerical 86, 88–90, 170–2, 186
Housekeepers see Servants
Howell, Michael, chaplain of Shifnal 150 (n.68), 155, 187
Howll, Thomas, chaplain of Whitmore 108
Hoxleye, Thomas, chaplain of Audlem 117 (n.116)
Huddleston, Miles, ordinand 29
Hughson, Thomas, chaplain of Warrington 117 (n.116)
Hull (Kingston upon Hull) (Yorks.), chantry priest of 98
Hulton (Hilton) Abbey (Staffs.), titles to orders from 22, 25, 104, 108, 109, 111
Hulton, Roger, recipient of multiple orders 29
Hunne's Case 35–6
Hunt, M. Thomas, rector of Mucklestone 60
Hyll, John, chaplain of Burton upon Trent 108
Hymnal 134

Ightfield (Salop)
    rector of see Mainwaring, M. Robert
Ilam (Staffs.)
    church 143
    lord of the manor see Porte, John
    rector of see Littonne, John
    vicar of see Goodwyn, John
Images:
    adornment of 145
    'Our Lady' 146
    St John the Baptist 144, 145
    the Trinity 148
    veneration of 141
Induction, ceremonies of 52–3
Ingestre (Staffs.)
    curate of see Underhill, John
    perpetual curate of see Egerton, M. Richard
Institution to benefices 52–5
    by proxy 53–4
    charge for 55
    documents of 64
Interdict 182

Inventories, probate 82, 83–4 & n.237, 86
Ireland:
    Christopher, stipendiary priest of Childwall 98 (n.20)
    Roger, curate of Radcliffe 101
    Thomas, sponsor of Christopher Ireland 98 (n.20)

Jackson:
    Edmund, chaplain of Eccleshall, vicar of Offley 111
    Robert, vicar of Penn 40 (n. 18)
James of Voragine, semon collection by 140, 185
Jennings, Roger, rector of Weston-under-Lizard 58
Jenyns, William ap, ordinand of the diocese of York 21
Johnson, Thomas, curate of Farnworth 148 (n.63)

Keble, M. Edward, rector of Warrington 98 (n.20)
Keele (Staffs.), chapel of
    curate of see Bowyer, Andrew
Keldermere, John, vicar of Chilvers Coton 59 (n.115), 168
Kemberton (Salop), rector of see Higgins, Richard
Kenilworth (Warks.)
    Abbey 23, 24, 48, 56
    vicars of see Pulteney, John; Wright, John
Kent, Richard, chaplain of Newcastle-under-Lyme
    bequest to godchildren 159
    biography 191
    rosary beads owned by 145
Kingsley (Staffs.)
    chantry priest and schoolmaster of see Berdemore, John
    rectors of see Bruce, Robert
    rectory of 59
Kingstone (Staffs.)
    curate of see Abell, John
Kingswinford (Staffs.), rectory 80
    rector of see Alen, Thomas
Kinnersley (Salop)
    rector of see Dodycott, William
Kirkby, Thomas, curate of Halsall 122
Kirk Ireton (Derbs.)
    rector of see Smyth, Richard
    rectory 80, 82, 86

Knight:
    Henry, chaplain of Wilmslow 151
    William, chaplain and secretary to Henry VIII 51
Knowle (Warks.), curate of 116
Kynnersley, M. Francis, rector of Blithfield and Leigh 59 (n.116)

Ladbroke (Warks.)
    rector of see Darley, M. William
    rectory 61
Lambard, William, clerk of Holy Trinity, Coventry 71
Langley Priory (Leics.), titles to orders from 23
Langton, Thomas, patron of Wigan 51
Lark:
    Mistress, mistress of Cardinal Wolsey 45 (n.41)
    Thomas, chaplain and secretary to Cardinal Wolsey and rector of Winwick 45 & n.41
Latham:
    Edmund, chaplain of Boylestone 151
    John, master of Malpas Grammar School 12, 71, 106
    Lawrence, chaplain of Prescot 118
Launde Priory (Leics.)
    appropriation of rectory of Rostherne by 54, 96 (n.13)
    titles to orders from 17 (n.48), 23
Lawton see Church Lawton
Layton, Ambrose, rector of Barrow upon Trent 168
Lea (Derbs.), chantry at
    see Roston, M. Richard
Leasing, statutory limitation of clerical involvement in 86
Leckonfield (Yorks.) 100
Lee:
    Edward, Archbishop of York 113, 138
    John, priest of York 9
    Roger, chaplain of Wroxeter
        bequest to church 146
        biography 191
        charitable bequest of 161
        funeral arrangements 146
        inclusion of sacred monogram in will 144
Lees (Derbs.) see Dalbury with Lees
Legh:
    Alexander, curate of Ryton-on-Dunsmore

accommodation in parsonage 123
bequest to his vicar 150
bequest towards rood loft 145
biography 191
burial arrangements 132
choice of executor 150
contribution towards choir stalls 124–5
debts owed by 124, 126
hire of colleague to pray for his soul 126
ownership of livestock 119
remuneration of 117, 124
rent and tax arrears of 123, 124
testamentary hire of priest 102, 120
M. Peter, ordinand 21
Leicester:
Abbey 48
archdeaconry of, incidence of pluralism in 62, 63, 68
Leigh (Lancs.)
stipendiary priest of *see* Adderton, Robert
Leigh (Staffs.)
curate of *see* Drakford, Thomas
rector of *see* Kynnersley, M. Francis
Leigh, Roger, rector of Lymm
bequest to chaplain 150
bequest to curate 150
bequests to godchildren 160–1
biography 192
charitable bequest of 162, 163
commendation of soul 147
request for burial 147
Leighton (Salop)
vicar of *see* Barnes, John
Lenton Priory (Notts.) 42
Leson, William, rector of Newton Regis
dispute with parishioner 135–6
tithe action by 167
Letters dimissory 21, 32
Leyland (Lancs.)
vicar of *see* Molyneux, M. Edward
Lichfield (Staffs.):
bishop's palace 181
Cathedral:
chancellor of 50
see also Whitehead, Ralph
chantry priests of *see* Fletcher, Edward; Tatton, Richard; Tatton, Thomas
chantries in:
St Radegund 49

St Thomas 111
chapel of Stowe annexed to 156
choir school at 10, 11
choristors' house 137, 177
dean and chapter of:
act books of 41
appropriation of churches by 49, 135
charge of absenteeism by 64
dispute with bishop 49
presentation to benefices by 49, 54, 75, 111
incidence of pluralism among canons of 65
library at 10
non-residentiary canons of *see* Bretunner, Joachim; Collet, Richard; Darley, M. William; Darrington, M. Nicholas; Strethay, Edmund; Taylor, John; Vesey, John
ordination ceremonies in 28, 29, 30
penitential procession around 142
precentor of *see* Fitzherbert, Thomas
prebends and prebendal churches:
annexed to archdeaconries of Coventry and Stafford 65
Colwich 60
Eccleshall 51, 111
Offley 111
Ryton 117
Tarvin (Tervin) 49 (n.63), 53
Ufton 42
rebuilding work 172
residentiary canons of 10
see also Beresford, M. James; Cantrell, Ralph; Egerton, M. Richard; Sneyd, Ralph
succentor of *see* Colmore, John
vicars choral of 40 (n.18)
see also Borows, Richard
citizens of 83 (n.237)
Franciscan friary 28
Gild of St Mary and St John the Baptist
clerical membership of 40–1 (n.18), 52 (n.74), 112, 156, 170, 192, 193
hire of priests by 99
hospital of St John
warden of *see* Egerton, M. Richard

INDEX   221

priests of see Hill, William; Whitehead, Thomas
St Mary's chapel (later vicarage)   99
 vicar of see Byrde, John
Lililow, M. Thomas, canon of All Saint's Derby etc.   61, 67, 75
Lilleshall Abbey (Salop), titles to orders from   22, 155 (n.95), 184, 187, 191
Linacre, Thomas, rector of Wigan and royal physician   47 (n.53), 51 & n.73
Lincoln (Lincs.):
 bishop of   21
  and see Longland, John
 cathedral of, prebends in   50
 dean of see Heneage, George
 diocese of:
  archdeacon of Buckingham in see Taylor, John
  examination of ordinands in   15
  incidence of pluralism in   62, 63, 68
  clerical stipends in   113, 115
  number of ordinations in   30
  number of pensions arrangements in   74
  number of stipendiary clergy   94–5
  remuneration of stipendiary clergy in   71
  subsidy returns of   79
  titles to orders in   25–6
  visitation returns   63
Lisle, Lady   100
Lister, Ralph, curate of Norbury   116
'Little Clerks'   8
Little Packington (Warks.)
 rector of see Wilkins, John
Littonne, John, rector of Ilam   76
Liverpool (Lancs.) see Walton and Liverpool
Lollards   141
 see also Coventry, heretics of
London:
 alleged anticlericalism in   35–6
 All Hallows the Great, rector of   51
 dean of St Paul's Cathedral see Colet, John
 diocese of:
  church courts   182
  migration of clergy to   33 & n. 104
  ordinations in   31, 33
  unfounded criminal charges against clergy in   178 (n.179)
  incidence of pluralism in   62, 63

 merchant of see Barefote, Robert
 size of clerical population   34
 Stratford-at-Bow Priory, title to orders from   17 (n.48)
Longdon (Staffs.)
 episcopal manor of   28
 vicars of see Grene, Richard; Rawson, Robert
Longford (Derbs.)
 rector of   38
  see also Redfern, Edward
 vicars of see Redfern, John; Strethay, Edmund
Longford, Ralph   46, 49 (n.63)
Long Itchington (Warks.)
 vicar of see Hopkins, Thomas
Longland, John, bishop of Lincoln   28 & n.87
 chaplain to see Heneage, George
Longton, Robert, ordinand   17 (n.53)
Loppington (Salop)
 churchwardens of   177
 vicar of see Clay, Humphrey
Lower Peover (Chesh.) chapel of   96
Ludolph of Saxony see Vita Christi
Lullington (Derbs.)
 chaplain of see Malabur, Henry
 vicar of   38
Luter, Roger, curate of Berrington   174
Luther, Martin   141
Lutheranism see Cotton, Richard
Lydda (Palestine), suffragan bishop of see Smith, Roger
Lymm (Chesh.)
 chaplain of see Sefton, John
 curate of see Fernhead, John
 rectors of moiety of see Fernhead, John; Leigh, Roger; Werburton, Richard
Lyndwood, William see Provinciale

Macclesfield (Chesh.):
 chapel in parish of see Pot Shrigley
 chaplain of see Bridges, William
 deanery   96
 grammar school   163
 perpetual curacy   96
 schoolmaster of see Bridges, William
Machyn, Ralph, curate of Stone   105
Mackworth (Derbs.), vicar of   154
Maer (Staffs.)
 rector of see Beche, John
Mainwaring, M. Robert, rector of Alderley Edge etc.   68 & n.160

Malabur, Henry, chaplain of Lullington and of the Royal Free Chapel, Stafford 124, 125
Malpas (Chesh.)
  clerical provision of 70
  master of grammar school at 70
    and see Latham, John
  rector of moiety of *see* Brereton, M. John
Mancetter (Warks.)
  gild priest of *see* Barefote, Robert
  'guild house' 88
  vicars of *see* Barefote, Robert; Ward, Henry; Whittington, William; Wylett, William
  vicarage house 88
Manchester (Lancs.)
  collegiate church:
    chaplains of *see* Trafford, M. Henry
    examination of ordinands at 15
    fellow of *see* Turton, Henry
    ordination ceremony held at 28
    wardens of *see* Clyff, William; Colyer, George
  grammar school 12
  priest of *see* Bryddocke, Richard
Manuals for parish clergy 15, 128, 133, 136, 140 (n.47)
  see also Burgh, John de; Mirk, John
Marchington (Staffs.)
  chaplain of *see* More, William
  St Katherine's altar 145
Marett (alias Maryat), John, chaplain of Crich 150 (n.67)
Marketing, statutory restriction on clerical involvement in 84, 118
  see also Agriculture, Textile production
Marler, Henry, chaplain of Holy Trinity, Coventry
  biography 192
  burial arrangements 132
  commendation of soul 144
  remuneration 116, 124
Marshall, John, criminous clerk 176 (n.171)
Mary *see* Blessed Virgin Mary
Mass:
  book 99, 134
  celebration in church under interdict 182
  celebration in unlicensed chapel 135
  daily 134
  funerary 35, 146
  increasing focus of devotion on 34
  intercessory, for the dead 34, 36, 97 & n.20, 101–2, 103, 134, 145, 152
  irregularity in celebrating 174, 181
  of the Five Wounds 146 & n.62
  of 'Our Lady' 100
  of St Gregory 103, 146
  suggested parody of by heretics 135
  suspension of priests from celebrating 136, 154, 172, 174, 180, 181
  teaching of boys to assist priest in 10
  trental of 101, 102, 103, 146, 152
  see also Obits
Matlock (Derbs.)
  rectors of *see* Beresford, M. James; Lililow, M. Thomas
Matrimony, irregular performance of 137
Mavesyn Ridware (Staffs.)
  rector of *see* Merton, William
Maxstoke Priory (Warks.), titles to orders from 26 & n.75
Mayo, John, suffragan bishop of 28
Melbourne (Derbs.)
  vicar of *see* Reed, M. John
  vicarage house and garden 88
Melton, William, chancellor of York 14–15, 34, 36
Memo, Dionisio, organist of St Mark's, Venice, and perpetual curate of Henbury 50
Mere, Thomas, curate of Norton in the Moors 108
Merevale Abbey (Warks.), titles to orders from 22, 25
Merton, William, rector of Hamstall Ridware and Mavesyn Ridware 58, 60–1
Mickleover (Derbs.)
  chaplain of *see* Webster, Randall
Middleton (Lancs.)
  curate of *see* Bexwyke, Richard
  employment of priest to say masses at 101
  parish clerk 146
Middlewich (Chesh.)
  chaplain of *see* Heynson, Robert
  vicar of *see* Burdet, Amer
  'wich house' in 123
Mirk, John, manual for parish priests of 133
Mobberley (Chesh.)
  rector of *see* Sherman, M. Henry

INDEX 223

Moile, William, chaplain of Eastham and Warrington 117 (n.116)
Molder, William, rector of Rolleston 76
Molyneux:
  family, lords of Sefton 43–4
  M. Anthony, priest of 'Copston's Chantry', Coventry Cathedral Priory 53
  M. Edward
    accusation of misappropriation by 122
    indebtedness of 69
    litigation by 12 (n.24), 68–9
    pensions payable by 68, 75
    pluralism of 67, 68
    rector of Ashton-under-Lyne 68
    rector of Sefton 43, 68
    rector of Walton and Liverpool 68, 70
    vicar of Leyland 42 & n.27, 68
  James, lord of Sefton 43
  Thomas, rector of a moiety of Wallasey 42
  William, chantry priest of Holy Trinity, Coventry 71
Monasteries:
  almonry schools in 10
  appropriation of churches by 38, 39, 47, 81, 92, 96 (n.13)
  educational provision by 10, 11
  grants of nomination rights by 48, 49 (n.63)
  grants of nomination rights to 48
  grants of presentation rights by 47
  presentation to benefices by 41–3
  titles to orders from 17 & n.48, 19–27, 33, 104–5
Moneyash (Derbs.), chantry of the BVM in parish church of 49 (n.64)
Monks Kirby (Warks.)
  patron of 53
  vicars of see Newton, Robert; Stockwith, William
Montgomery, Sir John 47
Month's mind 103, 120
More:
  Sir Thomas 15, 27, 34, 36, 100, 173 (n.163)
  William, chaplain of Marchington
    accumulation of cash by 119
    bequests to church 145
    biography 192
    charitable bequest of 162
    debts owed by 124
    hire of colleague to pray for soul 126
    ownership of livestock by 119
    ownership of share in sheep flock 118
    remuneration of 125
Morecroft, Brian, rector of Aughton 74, 75
Moreden, John, chaplain 175
Morehall, John, vicar of Sutton Maddock 154
  biography 186, 192
  debts owed to 164
  dispute with chaplain 180
  pension payable by 186
Moreton, John, rector of Stockton 153, 184, 187
Moreton Corbet (Salop)
  vicars of see Ashley, William; Byshoppe, Henry
Morley (Derbs.)
  rector of see Tatton, Bartholomew
Morres:
  Robert, priest of York 9
  Thomas, clerk of Holy Trinity, Coventry 71
Morrey (alias Morray), Thomas, chaplain of Swynnerton 150 & n.73
Mortuaries 122, 166, 167, 168, 178
Mounteagle, Lord see Stanley, Edward
Mountjoy, Lord see Blount, William
Much Wenlock Priory (Worcs) 23
Mucklestone (Staffs.)
  curate and vicar of see Wildblood, John
  rector of see Hunt, M. Thomas
Music see Song
Muster Rolls 114
Myddle (Salop)
  rector of see Tong, Thomas
  tithe litigation in parish 168
Mylner, John, chaplain 154
Mynshull, Richard, rector of Warrington 38–9

Nantwich (Chesh.)
  clerical provision of 96 (n.13)
  warden of hospital of see Blythe, Thomas
Newburgh Priory (Yorks.)
  prior of see Barker, Thomas
Newcastle (Staffs.), deanery of 110, 111

224 INDEX

Newcastle-under-Lyme (Staffs.)
   curate of 71; see also Delf, William
   chaplain of see Kent, Richard
   householders of 165 (n.116)
   see also Stoke and Newcastle
Newstead Priory (Notts.), titles to orders from 22, 187, 193
Newton Regis (Warks.)
   dispute between parishioner and rector 135–6
   rector of see Leson, William
   the dispute in parish 167
Newton, Robert, vicar of Monks Kirby and canon of Derby 77
Non-residence 62–72 & n.176, 73, 91, 135, 136, 169, 177, 180
   see also 'Reformation Parliament'
Norbury (Derbs.)
   curate of see Lister, Ralph
Norfolk, clerical standards of living in 114
Norres, M. Richard, rector of Cheadle 48, 58, 59, 172
Northumberland, Earl of see Percy, Henry
North Wingfield (Derbs.)
   chantry priest of see Wylson, John
   chaplain of see Whitehead, Thomas
Norton (Derbs.) 4
Norton Priory (Chesh.)
   examination of ordinands at 15
   ordination ceremony held at 28
   titles to orders from 12, 22, 25, 104, 190
Norton in Hales (Salop)
   rector of see Gresley, John
Norton in the Moors (Staffs.)
   curate of see Mere, Thomas
Norwich (Norf.) 13
   diocese of 55
      incidence of clerical immorality in 177–8
      tithe and mortuaries litigation in 166
Nowell, M. John, rector of Swynnerton
   accused of removing bible from church 142–3
   alleged undervaluation of benefice 78–9
   biography 192
   bequest of whisky still 170
   bequest to chaplain 150
   bequest to poor children 163
   bequest to servant 89
   testamentary bequests 143

Nuneaton (Warks.) 46
   priory of, employment of chaplains by 101
   vicar of see Whittington, M. Robert
Obits
   establishment of 102
   performance of by clergy 120
   proliferation of 34
   see also Month's mind
Oculus Sacerdotis (of William of Pagula) 140 (n.47)
Offchurch (Warks.)
   vicar of see Crosse, John
Offley (Staffs.)
   vicar of see Jackson, Edmund
Oratories, private 100
Order of the Garter 51
Orders (Holy) see Ordination; Titles to Orders
Ordination(s):
   ceremonies 14, 15, 27 (n.80), 28–30
   examination for 14, 15–18
   impediments to receiving 13–14, 64
   letters of testimony to support 14
   numbers of 30–6, 37
Ormskirk (Lancs.)
   appropriation of church by Burscough priory 38
   number of clergy in parish 96 & n.13
   vicars of 38
Orton, Thomas, vicar of Holy Trinity, Coventry, and Ufton 42
Ortus Vocabulorum 139
Ottaway, Robert, rector of Dalbury 152
Oxford:
   university 21, 32, 50, 53, 63, 65, 106
      colleges:
         All Souls 21
         Balliol 21
         Magdalene 21
   council of 13
   see also Titles to orders

Pagham (Sussex)
   vicar of see Bradshaw, Peter
Pagula, William of 15
Palin, Richard, stipendiary priest of Trentham 106
Papal dispensations, see Dispensations, papal
Papal provision
   by Wolsey's legatine authority 54
   to benefices 40, 54

INDEX 225

to bishopric of Exeter *see* Vesey, John
Paplowe (*alias* Poppye), John, ordinand 21
Parish priests *see* Stipendiary clergy
Parishes, origins of 39
Parker, Ralph, chaplain of Shenstone and curate of Yoxall 108–9
Parr, John, criminous clerk 176 (n.171)
Parson, Robert, gild priest of Gamlingay 99
Pastoral care, by stipendiary clergy 72, 128
Paten 30, 134
Pater Noster 8, 9
Patronage 39–52, 93, 150
   exercised by the crown 39, 46, 50–2
   purchase of rights of 53–4
   transfers of 45–8, 55–6
Patshull (Staffs.)
   curate of *see* Fletcher, Roger
Pattingham (Staffs.)
   vicar of *see* Butler, M. William
Peak, deanery of the 49
Penance:
   judicial, imposed on clergy 137, 175, 177, 182
   judicial, imposed on laity 167
   unwarranted imposition following confession 136
Pendle (Lancs.)
   chapel 96 (n.12)
   chaplain of the royal forest of 96 (n.12)
   curate of *see* Seller, William
Penkridge (Staffs.)
   royal free chapel of
      chapel of Denston annexed to 111
      chapel of Stretton annexed to 112
Penn (Staffs.)
   vicars of *see* Colmore, John; Fox, Thomas; Jackson, Robert
Pensions 52, 60 (n.119), 68, 69, 74–7, 80, 92, 125, 180, 186
Penwortham (Lancs.)
   curate of *see* Bradshaw, William
Percy, Henry, Fifth Earl of Northumberland, employment of household chaplains by 100
Peyrson (*alias* Pereson), Roger, curate of Chelaston 151 (n.77)
Pickering, William, ordinand 17 (n.48)
Pilgrimage 141
Pinxton (Derbs.)
   rector of *see* Shurley, Richard

Planknay, M. George, recipient of multiple orders 29
Pleasley (Derbs.)
   rector of *see* Harrison, Nicholas
Plemstall (Chesh.)
   clerical provision of 70 (n.167)
   vicar of *see* Bowring, M. Ralph
Plumton, George, ordinand 17 (n.48)
Pluralism 38, 44, 45, 50–1, 59 & n.117, 62–72, 92, 112, 181
   see also 'Reformation Parliament'
Podmore, Richard, curate of Dawley
   agricultural concerns of 125
   bequest for a priest to sing mass 102
   biography 192
   commendation of soul 144
   remuneration of 125
   ownership of sheep flock 118
Pole, Ranulph, lord of Poole and rector of Hawarden 46 & n.50
Polesworth (Warks.)
   clerical provision of 97
   Abbey:
      abbess of 60 (n.119)
      employment of chaplains by 101
      titles to orders from 23, 26
Poll Tax returns, clerical 95
Pommell, Thomas, rector of Holy Trinity, Chester 44–5
Pontisbury, Leonard, vicar of Shawbury 192
Poole (Chesh.), manor of 46
Porte:
   John, solicitor to Henry VIII 47
   John, lord of Ilam 143
   Sir John 87
   M. Thomas, rector of Coddington and Doddleston 60
Porteus see Breviary
Postillae super Bibliam (of Nicholas of Lyra) 140 (n.47)
Pot Shrigley (Chesh.), chapel of 96
Potter, Richard, chaplain and churchwarden of Prescot 121
Poverty, clerical:
   alleged by incumbent 86
   among pluralists 68
   evidenced by level of stipends 114, 116, 117, 125, 168
   evidenced by modest funeral arrangements 125–6
   evidenced by probate inventories 83, 90, 125, 126, 168
   evidenced by subsidy return 127, 180

226   INDEX

testamentary bequest to a 'poor priest' 101–2
Prayers:
　in elementary syllabus   10
　for the dead   101, 102, 126, 145, 158, 163
　　see also *De profundis*; *Dirige*; *Hail Mary*; Obits; *Pater Noster*
Preaching   137–8, 142
Premonstratensian Order, as providers of titles to orders   23, 25
Prescot (Lancs.)
　chapels in parish of *see* Farnworth, Rainford
　chaplains of *see* Colley, Henry; Garnett, Edward; Latham, Lawrence; Potter, Richard; Sherdeley, John; Traves, James; Webster, John
　churchwardens' accounts of   165
　curate of *see* Sherdeley, Henry
　decorations made for rood screen of church   121
　employment of assistant clergy within parish   91
　involvement of clergy in legal work   120
　lease of vicarage   82
Prestbury (Chesh.)
　number of stipendiary clergy   96
　perpetual curacy of Henbury in parish of   50
Pricksong   141 (n.47)
Primers   9, 99
Processions   134
　penitential   137, 142, 167, 172, 174, 175, 177, 182
Procurations   80
Provinciale (of William Lyndwood)   139
Psalms
　exposition of by St Augustine   140
　in elementary syllabus   10
Psalter   10, 102, 152
Pulford (Chesh.)
　rector of *see* Werburton, Richard
Pulteney, John, vicar of Kenilworth   56
Pupilla Oculi (of John de Burgh)   140 (n.47)
Purgation *see* Compurgation
Purgatory   34
Putney (Surrey)
　warden of collegiate church of St Lawrence in *see* Roston, M. Richard
Pyffert, M. John, rector of Baddesley Clinton   53, 56

Pynnyngton, George, ordinand   17 (n.48)
Pyxley, Thomas, chaplain of High Ercall
　accumulation of cash by   119
　bequest of breviaries   134
　biography   192
　burial arrangements   132–3
　ownership of sheep flock   118

Quatt (Salop)
　rector of *see* Tomkins, Thomas

Radcliffe (Lancs.), curate of *see* Ireland, Roger
Rainford (Lancs.), chapel of   91
Ramsbothom, Henry, chaplain of Bolton   102
Ranton Priory (Staffs.), titles to orders from   22, 104, 109
Rawson, Robert, chantry priest of Lichfield Cathedral and vicar of Longdon   49
Real presence, doctrine of   135
Redfern:
　Edward, rector of Longford   39, 46, 49 (n.63)
　John, vicar of Longford   39
　　bequest to colleague   151
　　bequest to a woman   171
　　biography   192
　　charitable bequest of   162
Reed, M. John, vicar of Melbourne
　absenteeism   91
　biography   192
　employment of assistant clergy by   91
　indebtedness of   91
　ownership of books   139
　ownership of rosary beads   145
　rector of Broughton Astley   91
　value of probate inventory   83, 91
'Reformation Parliament'   55, 62, 63
　legislation limiting clerical involvement in leasing and marketing by   84, 86
　legislation limiting pluralism and non-residence by   65–6, 68, 72
Repton (Derbs.)
　gild priest of *see* Stolys, John
　priory:
　　bequest to   163
　　monks of   153 (n.89)
　　ordination ceremonies held at   28
　　prior of *see* Young, John
　　request for burial in   132

INDEX 227

titles to orders from 17 (n.48), 22, 26 & n.75, 192
Richardson, William, vicar of Crich 88
  bequests to family 157
  bequests to servants 89
  biography 192
  executors 149–50
  witness of will 150
  employment of assistant clergy by 91
Roberts, James, chaplain of Rossendale 137
Robothum, Robert, clerk of Holy Trinity, Coventry 71
Rocester Abbey (Staffs.), titles to orders from 22, 192
Rochdale (Lancs.)
  vicar of see Haydock, Gilbert
Rochester, diocese of
  incidence of pluralism in 62, 63
  number of stipendiary clergy 95 (n.3)
Rodington (Salop)
  perpetual curate of see Grene, Roger
Rogers, William, parish priest of Austen 153
Rolleston (Staffs.)
  rector of see Molder, William
  rectory 79, 80
  school at 10
Rolleston, Richard, rector of Stoney Stanton and Weston 61
Rome 13
  embassies to see Knight, William
  English hospital in 51
  papal *curia* in 64
Rood screen 121
Roode, Andrew, rector of Wistaston 70 (n.167)
Rosary beads 145 & n.61
Rossendale (Lancs.)
  chapel of the royal forest of Blackburnshire in 96 (n.12), 137
  'chapel reeves' of 124
  chaplains of see Gregory, George; Roberts, James
  curate of see Smith, Stephen
Rostherne (Chesh.)
  appropriation of church by Launde Priory 54, 96 (n.13)
  clerical provision of 96 (n.13)
  vicarage of 54
  vicars of see Boydell, Ralph; Hardwick, William
Roston, M. Richard, chantry priest of Lea 61, 73

Rowlowe, Richard, rector of Ryton
  bequest to household and servants 88
  biography 192
  charitable bequest of 162
  hire of plough-team to parishioners 85
  house 88
  household 89
  request for burial 147
Rugby (Warks.)
  curate of see Wainwright, Stephen
  manor 48
  rectory 48
Rugeley (Staffs.)
  ordination ceremony held in parish church 28
  vicarage 49 & n.64
  vicars of see Fletcher, Edward; Tatton, Thomas
Rural deans 28
Rushton (Staffs.)
  curate of see Sutton, Robert
Ruthin (Denbigh)
  rector of see Gresley, John
Rylay, Richard, rector of Swarkestone
  agricultural concerns of 81 & n.230
  bequest of paten 134
  bequest to layman 153
  bequests to godchildren 159
  bequests to servants 88
  biography 192
  burial arrangements 132
  colleagues as witnesses of will 151
  ownership of rosary beads by 145
  value of benefice 81
Ryton (Salop)
  rector of see Rowlowe, Richard
Ryton-on-Dunsmore (Warks.)
  choir stalls of church 124
  curate of see Legh, Alexander
  rood loft of church 145
Ryve, Richard, vicar of South Wingfield
  bequest to godchildren 159
  bequest to patron 43
  bequests to parish confraternity and church 145
  biography 192
  charitable bequest of 163
  colleagues as overseers of will 155
  establishment of obit 102, 120
  hire of priest to say mass at Brailsford 102
  memorial to 131
  pluralism of 70 (n.167)

Sacraments:
    importance to laity of performance of 135, 137
    in relation to priesthood 133–7
    see also Confession, Eucharist, Matrimony, Ordination
St Chad 41, 50
St Cleer (Cornwall), vicarage of 73
St George, play of 99
St John the Baptist 144, 145
Saints, commendation of soul to 144–5, 147, 148, 185, 187, 188
Saints' days 141
Sallust (C. Sallustius Crispus), works of 140
Salop, archdeaconry of see Shrewsbury
Salt (Staffs.), chapel of
    chaplains see Fox, Thomas; Walker, Edmund
Sandwell Priory (Staffs.), titles to orders from 23, 105
Sandwich (Kent), imprisonment of recalcitrant priest by parishioners of 98 (n.21)
Schelfeld, William, curate of Great Barr 105 (n.58)
Schoolmasters 70, 99
    see also Berdemore, John; Bridges, William; Hatton, Thomas; Latham, John; Lee, John; Staple, John; Whitworth, Richard
Schools 10, 35
    chantry 9
    informal 9, 35
    in the diocese of York 9, 11
    in Lancashire 11
    grammar 11
    see also Macclesfield, Malpas, Rolleston, Wanlet, York Minster
Seaman, Edward, chaplain of Solihull 122–3
Sedgley (Staffs.)
    vicar of see Bagshawe, Gervase
Sefton (Lancs.)
    allegation of misappropriation from rectory 122
    clerical provision of 96 (n.13)
    rectors of see Molyneux, M. Edward
Sefton, John, chaplain of Lymm 117
Seighford (Staffs.)
    vicar of see Alen, Robert
Seller, William, curate of Pendle 136
Sermon collections 140
Sermones Discipuli 140

Servants, of clergy 88–9, 123, 157, 160, 170–1, 186
    see also Households, clerical
Service books 163
    see also Antiphoner, Breviary, Hymnal
Seven Corporate Acts of Mercy 9
Seven Deadly Sins 9
Sextus Decretalum 139
Sexual immorality, alleged against clergy 38, 171–8, 180–2
Sharp, John, ordinand of Glasgow diocese 21
Shaw, Ralph, rector of Cound 152
Shawbury (Salop)
    vicar of see Pontisbury, Leonard
Sheinton (Salop)
    church 92
    poor of 92
    rectors of see Bachelor, Edmund; Diason, William
    rectory 80
Shenstone (Staffs.)
    chaplain of see Parker, Ralph
Sherdeley:
    Henry, curate of Prescot 121, 156
    John, chaplain of Prescot 118, 156
Sheriffhales (Salop)
    curate of see Collins, John
    vicar of see Walker, John
Sherington, Anthony, recipient of multiple orders 29
Sherman, M. Henry, rector of Mobberley 53
Shifnal (Salop)
    chaplain of see Howell, Michael
    curate of see Hatton, Richard
    'great bell' in church of 148
Shilton (Warks.)
    curate of see Bellyster, Simon
    vicar of see Smyth, John
Shirebroke, Thomas, vicar of Tibshelf
    dispute with vicar of Mackworth 154
    disputes with parishioners 179–80
    false procurement of evidence by 167
    poverty of 180
    tithe and mortuaries litigation by 167, 169
Shirley (Derbs.)
    vicar of see Blythe, M. Robert
Shrewsbury (Salop):
    Abbey
        alleged misappropriation of income from Wrockwardine vicarage by 43 (n.28)

INDEX   229

sub-prior of see Butler, Thomas
ordination ceremony held at   28
presentation to benefices by   41,
    43 (n.28)
sub-prior of see Butler, Thomas
titles to orders from   23, 24, 26 &
    n.75, 190
vicarage of Holy Cross in   55–6
    chaplain of   152 (n.87)
vicar of see Hordley, William
archdeacon of see Bretunner, Joachim
archdeaconry of (alias Salop)   4, 78
    clerical stipends in   115
    number of dependent chapels in
        97
collegiate church of
    deans of see Strete, Richard
    ordination ceremony held at   28
Shurley, Richard, rector of Pinxton   49
    (n.63)
Shustoke (Warks.), vicar of
    tithe litigation by   168, 169
Simony   47, 48
Slany:
    Henry, vicar of Bushbury
        agricultural concerns   85
        bequest of corn by   82
        bequests to relatives   156, 158
        biography   192
        charitable bequest of   162–3
        commendation of soul   144, 145
        length of tenure of benefice   58
        rent of field by   82
        valuation of benefice   81
        value of probate inventory   83
    Richard, priest   158
Smith:
    Richard, rector of moiety of
        Eggington   48
    Roger, suffragan bishop of Lydda   28
        & n.87
    Stephen, curate of Rossendale   122
Smyth:
    Hugh, chaplain of Audley   93, 108
    John, vicar of Shilton
        accommodation arrangements of   90
        bequest of vestments   133–4
        biography   192
        burial arrangements   132
        income of   82
        ownership of books   139
        ownership of vestments   90
        poverty of   90
        witness of will   150
    Richard, priest   185
    Richard, rector of Holy Trinity,
        Chester, and Bury   44, 61
    Richard, rector of Kirk Ireton
        accumulation of cash by   87
        biography   192
        lease of benefice by   82, 85, 87
        ownership of chalice   134
        ownership of mass book   134
        valuation of benefice   80
    Thomas, vicar of Uttoxeter   172
Sneyd, Ralph, canon residentiary of
    Lichfield Cathedral etc.   67, 69–70
Solihull (Warks.)
    chaplain of see Seaman, Edward
Somersal (Herbert) (Derbs.), rectory of
    47
Somersall, Thomas, curate of Brampton
    chapel   109
Song, teaching of   11, 98, 141 (n.47)
South Walsham (Norf), rectory of   72
South Wingfield (Derbs.)
    church, Lady chapel in   145
    clerical provision of   70 (n.167)
    Holy Trinity Gild   145
    vicar of see Ryve, Richard
Southall, Thomas, clerk   154
Sparke, Thomas, canon lawyer   16 &
    n.45
Spofforth (Yorks.), memorial inscription
    in church, 8
Stafford (Staffs.):
    archdeacon of   37, 80 and see Blythe,
        John
    archdeaconry of   4
        clerical stipends in   114
        number of dependent chapels in
            97
        subsidy returns of   79–80, 114
        tenure of benefices within   56–62
        value of benefices in   78, 80
    hospital of St John
        warden of see Egerton, M. Richard
    priory of St Thomas see Baswich
    royal free chapel
        canon of see Colyer, George
        chapels annexed to see Hopton, Salt
        chaplain of see Malabur, Henry
Stafford family, patronage policy of   44
Standish (Lancs.)
    rector of see Bradshaw, Peter
Standish, Sir Alexander   87
Standon (Staffs.)
    rector of   143

and *see* Bacon, William
Stanley of Lathom, family, ecclesiastical patronage of   43, 44
Stanley:
    Edward, Lord Mounteagle (d.1524)   103, 120
    James, bishop of Ely and rector of Winwick   44, 45, 46
    Sir John   46
    Thomas, Earl of Derby (d.1521)
        grant of right of presentation by   47
        presentations to benefices by   44–5
    see also Stanley of Lathom
Stanton (Staffs.)
    curate of *see* Babyngton, William
Stanton upon Hine Heath (Salop)
    vicar of *see* Corveser, William
Staple, John, chaplain of Walsall   11, 98
Stapleton (Salop)
    rector of *see* Webb, Richard
Star Chamber   69, 142, 179
Starismore, William
    chaplain of Walsall   105 (n.57)
    chantry priest of Walsall   112
    vicar of Wednesbury   112
Statues *see* Images
Statute of Labourers   8 (n.4)
Sterky, William, ordinand   17 (n.53)
Stipendiary clergy
    accommodation of   122–3
    age profile of   71
    employment of   50 (n.70), 70, 90–1, 97–103, 107, 135
    mobility   106–13
    numbers   94–7
    performance of secular work by   99–101, 117–22
    property ownership by   118
    provenance   103–5
    quality of   70–2, 127–8
    remuneration of   71, 74, 90–1, 101, 102, 113–17, 124
    sources of stipendiary income   117, 127
    standard of living   125–7
    status   105–6
    taxation of   36
    use of term 'parish priest' to designate   95
    see also Unbeneficed clergy
Stockton (Salop)
    rector of *see* Moreton, John

Stockton (Warks.), rectory of   47
Stockwith, William, vicar of Monks Kirby   53
Stoke and Newcastle (Staffs.), parish of
    chaplain of *see* Bredwall, Thomas
    rector of *see* Egerton, M. Richard
    rectory of   80
    vicar of *see* Bredwall, Thomas
    see also Newcastle; Newcastle-under-Lyme
Stoke Dry (Leics), rectory of   72, 73
Stoke-on-Trent (Staffs.) *see* Stoke and Newcastle
Stolys, John, gild priest of Repton   101
Stone (Staffs.)
    curate of *see* Machyn, Ralph
    Priory, titles to orders from   23, 105, 192
Stoneleigh Abbey (Warks.), presentation to benefices by   26
Stoney Stanton (Derbs.)
    rector of *see* Rolleston, Richard
Stowe (Staffs.), chapel annexed to Lichfield Cathedral
    chaplain of *see* Walker, Edmund
    curate of *see* Tatton, Thomas
Straitbarrel, James, rector of Bangor-is-y-coed etc.   73
Strete, Richard, archdeacon of Derby, dean of collegiate church of Shrewsbury   16, 47
Strethay, M. Edmund, canon of Lichfield etc.   38, 46, 66–7, 68
Stretton (W. Staffs.)
    vicar of *see* Byrche, Sampson
Subdiaconate   17
Subsidies, clerical, *see* Taxation
Summa Angelica   139
Supplicacyon for the Beggers see Fish, Simon
Sutton (*alias* Dudley):
    family, lords of Dudley   43–4
    Richard:
        pension payable to   68, 75, 76
        rector of Birmingham   76
        rector of Walton and Liverpool   43–4
    Robert, curate of Rushton   109
Sutton Coldfield (Warks.)
    bequest to church   134
    John Vesey of   52
    rectors of *see* Heneage, George; Taylor, John; Wendon, M. Ralph
Sutton Maddock (Salop)
    disputes in parish   180–1

vicars of see Harrington, Richard; Morehall, John
Swanne, John, chaplain of Dunchurch 150 (n.67)
Swarkestone (Staffs.), rectory of 81, 87
rector of see Rylay, Richard
Swynerton, William, rector of Blymhill
agricultural concerns 84
appointment of servant as executor of will 89
biography 192
charitable bequests of 163
commendation of soul 144
employment of colleague to say intercessory masses 102
parsonage house of 81
valuation of benefice 81
Swynnerton (Staffs.)
chaplain of see Morrey, Thomas
parishioner of 142
rector of see Nowell, M. John
Swynte (alias Swynestoh alias Swynstoo), Robert, chantry priest of Crich 150 (n.70)
Sydall, Thomas, chaplain of Eccles 116
Synodals 80

Talbot, John, vicar of Glossop 72, 73
Talboys, Gilbert, lord of the manor of Rugby 48
Taliare, Oliver, ordinand 17 (n.53)
Tamworth (Staffs.), royal free chapel of
canon of see Dyngley, Roger
dean of see Hone, William
Tarvin (Chesh.)
vicar of see Hawardyn, Humphrey
Tattenhall (Chesh.)
rector of see Sneyd, Ralph
Tatton:
Bartholomew, rector of Morley 156
George, rector of Colton 156
Ralph, rector of Barlborough
bequest for intercessory masses 101
bequest of stole 134
biography 192
burial arrangements 132
charitable bequests of 163
connections with the Prior of Repton 153 & n.89
family relationships 156
membership of Lichfield Civic Gild 156

Richard, chantry priest of Lichfield Cathedral 101, 156
Thomas, vicar of Rugeley etc. 101, 111, 156
Taxation, of clergy 36, 92, 103, 123-4
Taylor:
John, rector of Sutton Coldfield, royal diplomat 51-2 & n.74
Nicholas, chantry priest of Warrington 98 (n.20)
Richard, master of Warrington Grammar School 12 & n.24, 98 (n.20)
Robert, priest 93
Ten Commandments 9
Textile production etc., involvement of clergy in:
cloth 85, 119
flax 81 (n.230), 84, 85, 157, 185
hemp 81 (n.230), 84, 85, 157
linen 84, 186
sheep 84, 85, 118, 119, 186
spinning and weaving 84, 85, 119, 187-8
wool 84, 85, 87, 118-19, 187-8
yarn 118, 121, 158, 185
see also Agriculture
Thornton (-le-Moors) (Chesh.)
rector of see Bothe, Robert
Thorpe (Derbs.)
rector of see Lililow, M. Thomas
Thorpe Constantine (Staffs.)
curate of see Walker, Hugh
Throgmorton, M. William, rector of Handsworth etc. 66
Thurgarton Priory (Notts.), titles to orders from 23
Tibshelf (Derbs.)
dispute over Easter dues 154
tithe litigation in parish 167, 169, 179-80
vicars of see Shirebroke, Thomas; Vyes, Thomas
Tideswell (Derbs.)
complaint of parishoners concerning lack of sacramental provision 135
vicar of see Eyre, Edmund
Tithe(s) 52, 168
hay 87
coal 167
corn 82
lambs and wool 81, 84, 119, 168
litigation 75, 165-9, 179-80

milling   168
small (or petty)   81, 82, 83, 167, 168
Titles to Orders   17 & n.48, 19–27
   as evidence of provenance of clergy
      17, 21, 43, 104
   to benefice   20, 35, 65
   to choral vicar's stall   104
   monastic   17 & n.48, 19–27, 104–5
   patrimonial   19, 35
   from university colleges   21
Tomkins, Thomas, rector of Quatt   64
Tomkinson, Thomas, vicar of Dilhorne
   dispute arising from lease of vicarage
      and glebe   86
Tong (Salop), collegiate church   192
Tong, Thomas, rector of Myddle   152
Tonsure   130
Trafford, M. Henry, rector of Wilmslow
   etc.   16
Transubstantiation, doctrine of   135
   (n.25)
Traves, James, chaplain of Prescot   121
Trentham (Staffs.)
   Priory, titles to orders from   23, 175
      (n.170)
   stipendiary priest of *see* Palin, Richard
Tryge, Henry, chaplain of Chesterfield
   bequest of books to colleague   151
   bequest to godson   160
   bequest to serving boy   123
   bequests to church   163
   biography   192
   burial arrangements   126, 132
   involvement in wool trade   118–19
   legal work undertaken by   121
   ownership of books   140
   poverty of   125, 126
   remuneration   116, 117, 124
Tunstall, Thomas, curate of Wolstanton
   bequest to servant   123, 158
   bequests to godchildren   159, 187
   bequests to relatives   186
   bequests to his children   158, 186
   biography   186–7, 192
   colleagues as witnesses of will   186
   commendation of soul   148
   funeral arangements   148
   hire of plough-team by   119
   involvement in wool trade of   118
   length of tenure of post   108
   loans to parishioners   165, 186–7
   ownership of linen shop   118, 186
   relationship to housekeeper   173
   rent of property by   118
   remuneration   116, 117, 124, 165
   value of probate inventory   165
Turin, University of   16
Turner, Thomas, chaplain of Coundon
   102, 152
Turton, Henry, fellow of the collegiate
   church of Manchester   103
Tutbury (Staffs.):
   Priory:
      appropriation of Doveridge church
         by   81
      titles to orders from   23
   vicarage   79
Tutbury and Tamworth, deanery of
   79–80
Twyste, M. Thomas, proxy for M. Roger
   Ball, vicar of Harborne   54
Tykhill, William, vicar of Ashbourne
   153 (n.89)
Tyndale, William   142, 173 (n.163)

Ufton (Warks.)
   vicar of *see* Orton, Thomas
Unbeneficed clergy   94–128
   modest funeral arrangements of
      125–6
   numbers   94–7
   standard of living   125–7
   taxation of   103
   use of term 'chaplain' to designate
      56
   use of term 'clerical proletariat' for
      127–8
Underhill, John, curate of Ingestre
   105–6 (n.58), 112
Upholland Priory (Lancs.)
   examination of ordinands at   15
   titles to orders from   22, 25, 190
Utley, Hugh, ordinand   17 (n.53)
Utraquism   135
Uttoxeter (Staffs.)
   chantry priest of *see* Bee, John
   curate of   175 (n.170)
   parish clerk of   172
   vicar of *see* Smyth, Thomas

Vale Royal Abbey (Chesh.)
   presentation to benefice by   41
   titles to orders from   17 (n.48), 22, 25,
      26, 190
Valle Crucis Abbey (Denbigh)   191
Valor Ecclesiasticus   3, 75, 77, 78–81
Venice
   ambassador of   34

INDEX 233

organist of St Mark's *see* Memo, Dionisio
Vernon:
  M. George, rector of Whitchurch 182
  Sir Henry, patron of the Vernon chantry, Walsall 11
Vesey (Veysey), John, vicar of St Michael's, Coventry, later bishop of Exeter 52, 53
Vestments 90, 133
  alb 145
  amice 134
  chasuble 30
  cope 90, 133
  corinal 134
  rochet 134
  stole 134
  surplice 133, 150
Vicar of Bray 188 & n.3
Virgin Mary *see* Blessed Virgin Mary
Visitation, parochial 172
Vita Christi (of Ludolph of Saxony) 140, 185
Vocation 7, 17
Vyes, Thomas, vicar of Tibshelf 76

Wainwright, Stephen, chaplain of Abbot's Bromley, curate of Rugby 107
Walker:
  Edmund, rector of Aldridge etc. 110
  Hugh, curate of Thorpe Constantine 106 (n.58)
  John, vicar of Wombourne etc. 37, 67
Wallasey (Chesh.)
  rector of *see* Molyneux, Thomas
Walsall (Staffs.):
  books belonging to church 140 & n.47
  chantry in church of *see* Vernon, Sir Henry
  chantry priests of *see* Dore, Robert; Starismore, William
  chaplains of *see* Flemyng, Thomas; Staple, John; Starismore, William
  churchwardens 140
  citizens of 11
  complaint by parishioners 136
  curate of *see* Barlow, Robert
  school at 11, 98
  St Clement's altar in church of 166
Walton and Liverpool (Lancs.), parish of
  clerical provision of 70, 96 & n.13
  curate *see* Fazakerley, Robert
  rectors of *see* Molyneux, M. Edward; Sutton, Richard
  remuneration of assistant clergy of 71
Wanlet (Lincs.), school at 13
Ward, Henry, vicar of Mancetter 170
Ward, John, rector of Blore and Gratwich 67, 69
Wardship 47, 49
Warley, Thomas, member of the Lisle household 100
Warner, William, curate of Avon Dassett 74
Warrington (Lancs.)
  Austin friary, ordination ceremony held at 28
  chantry of Sir Thos. Butler in parish church of 12
  priest of *see* Taylor, Nicholas
  chapel of Eastham in parish of *see* Moile, William
  chaplains of *see* Hughson, Thomas; Moile, William; Wright, Robert
  deanery 96
  grammar school 12
    schoolmaster of 97 (n.20) and *see* Taylor, Richard
  provision of stipendiary priest by Sir Thos. Butler in 97 (n.20)
  rectors of *see* Keble, M. Edward; Mynshul, Richard; Wingfields, Thomas Mary
Waterward, Thomas, vicar of Harborne 54
Warton, Geoffrey, ordinand 17 (n.53)
Wayne, Richard, curate of Doveridge 150 (n.72)
Weaponry, owned by clergy 89, 160 & n.106, 185, 187
Webb, Richard, rector of Stapleton
  accumulation of cash by 87
  bequest to a chaplain 152
  bequest of portable altar 134, 152
  bequest of a psalter 102
  biography 192
  employment of colleague to say masses for his soul 102, 152
  lease of benefice 85
  lease of land by 85–6
  loan to parishioner 165
  purchase of roof tiles 90
  rent owed to 85
  value of probate inventory 85

Webster:
    John, chaplain of Prescot 118
    Randall, chaplain of Mickleover 152
Wednesbury (Staffs.)
    vicar of see Starismore, William
Welbeck Abbey (Notts.) 152
Weldon, M. Philip, rector of Aldridge 58
Wele, Thomas, suffragan bishop of Banados 28
Wellington (Salop)
    chaplain of see Chorlton, Henry
Wells, John, chaplain of Coventry
    bequest of books to colleague 151
    bequest of breviaries 134
    bequest of surplice 133
    biography 192
    funeral and burial arrangements 102, 131-2
Wendon, M. Ralph, rector of Sutton Coldfield
    bequest of liturgical equipment 134
    bequests to relatives 158
    bequest of service books 134
    biography 192
    commendation of soul 148
    ownership of books 139
    request for burial 158
Werburton, Richard, rector of Pulford and Lymm 68 & n.160
Westminster, prebend of St Stephen's chapel in palace of 51
Weston (-on-Trent) (Derbs.)
    rector of see Rolleston, Richard
Weston-under-Lizard (Staffs.)
    curate of see Collins, John
    rectors of see Collins, John; Jennings, Roger
Weyme, John, ordinand 17 (n.53)
Whalley (Lancs.):
    Abbey
        accusation of interference in mortuary rights by 122
        citation of chaplains by 135
        jurisdiction of 96 (n.12)
        titles to orders from 22, 24, 25
    parish
        chapels in see Altham; Burnley; Church; Clitheroe; Colne
        chaplains of the royal forests in see Clitheroe Castle; Goldshaw Booth; Pendle; Rossendale
        see also Wolfenden Booth

Whitbroke, William, recipient of multiple orders 29
Whitchurch (Salop)
    rector of see Vernon, M. George
Whitehead, Ralph, chancellor of Lichfield Cathedral 65, 108, 176
Whitehead, Thomas, chaplain 105, 108
Whitewell (Lancs.)
    chapel of the royal forest of Trawden at 96 (n.12)
Whitmore (Staffs.)
    chaplain of see Howll, Thomas
Whittington:
    M. Robert, vicar of Nuneaton 176-7
    William, vicar of Mancetter
        admission of non-residence by 64
        charges against 181-2
        deprived of benefice 38, 76, 181
        misconduct whilst hearing confessions 136-7
Whitworth, Richard, curate of Chesterfield
    bequest of books by 138, 187
    bequest of school fees by 9, 120
    bequest from colleague 151 (n.75)
    biography 187-8, 193
    choice of witness of will 150, 187
    commendation of soul 148, 188
    length of tenure of post 109, 187-8
    ownership of livestock 119
    ownership of shears, looms and spinning wheel 119, 187-8
    request for burial 188
Wigan (Lancs.)
    chaplains of see Astley, William; Cockson, Hugh; Grange, Henry
    rectors of see Linacre, Thomas; Wyott, M. Richard
    rectory of 78
        dispute concerning tithes of 119-20 (n.122)
Wilcocks, M. John, vicar of Bakewell 49-50
Wildblood, John, vicar of Caverswall etc. 110
Wildgoose, Thomas, curate of Draycott 179
Wilkins, John, rector of Little Packington 137
Willington (Derbs.)
    vicar of see Francis, Ralph
Willock, Nicholas, vicar of Biddulph 86

INDEX 235

Wilmslow (Chesh.)
  chaplain of see Knight, Henry
  rector of see Trafford, M. Henry
Wilson, John, priest 93
Wiltshire, archdeaconry of 55
Winchester, diocese of
  incidence of clerical immorality in 177
  ordinations in 31
Windsor (Berks), Royal Free Chapel of St George
  canon of see Butler, M. William
Wingfields, Thomas Mary, rector of Warrington 53–4
Winter, Thomas, rector of Winwick, son of Cardinal Wolsey 45 & n.41, 54
  tutor to see Birkenshaw, M. Maurice
Winwick (Lancs.)
  rectors of see Boleyn, William; Lark, Thomas; Stanley, James; Winter, Thomas
  rectory 45, 78
Wirksworth (Derbs.)
  vicars of see Beresford, M. James; Draycott, M. Anthony
Wisbech (Cambs.), Trinity Gild of 99
Wishaw (Warks.), rector of 116 (n.108)
Wistaston (Chesh.)
  clerical provision of 70 (n.167)
  rector of see Roode, Andrew
Witton (Lancs.), chapel of 96
Wodnut, Ranulph, chaplain of Wybunbury 53
Wolfenden Booth in parish of Whalley (Lancs.) 151
Wollaton hospital (Notts.) 193
Wolley, John, vicar of Frodsham 26 & n.74, 41
Wolsey, Thomas, Cardinal Archbishop of York
  appeal from Lancashire chaplain to 122
  appeal to court of audience of 168
  downfall of 51
  forged dispensation from 134
  intervention in a case in Lichfield consistory court 176
  legatine authority of 14 (n.29), 29
  mistress of see Lark, Mistress
  presentation to benefices by 54
  secretary and chaplain to see Lark, Thomas
  usurpation of presentation rights of Chester Abbey 54

Wolstanton (Staffs.)
  chaplains of see Cartwright, John; Copnall, John; Goodwyn, John
  curate of see Tunstall, Thomas
  householders of 165 (n.116)
  'Our Lady's aisle' in church 165
  'Our Lady's chancel' in church 148
  rectors of see Grygge, John
  vicar of see Bowyer, Andrew
Wolverhampton (Staffs.), royal free chapel of
  chaplain of see Bradshaw, Thomas
Wolvey (Warks.)
  church 144
  vicar of see Blockley, Richard
Wombourne (Staffs.)
  chaplain of see Bradshaw, Thomas
  vicar of see Walker, John
Wombridge Priory (Salop), titles to orders from 23, 186, 191
Woodchurch (Chesh.)
  rector of see Sneyd, Ralph
Worcester, diocese of 8 (n.7)
Worfield (Salop)
  presentation to vicarage of 49 (n.64)
  vicar of see Walker, John
Wressle (Yorks.) 100
Wright:
  John, vicar of Great Packington and Kenilworth 60
  Robert, chaplain of Warrington 117 (n.116)
Wrockwardine (Salop)
  vicar of see Butler, William
  vicarage 43 (n.28), 81
Wroxeter (Salop)
  chaplains of see Dodycotte, Richard; Lee, Roger
  parish funeral custom 146
  statue of 'Our Lady' in church of 146
Wybunbury (Chesh.)
  chaplains of see Frinde, William; Wodnut, Ranulph
  vicar of see Darrington, M. Nicholas
Wycherley, Richard, chaplain of Baschurch 152
Wylett, Thomas, rector of Hamstall Ridware, vicar of Mancetter 76, 181
Wyllington, Maurice, curate of Bangor-is-y-coed 106
Wylson, John, chantry priest of North Wingfield 193
Wylson (alias Wetton), Thomas, vicar of Abbots Bromley

bequest of bible and book on the evangelists 185
bequest to children attending funeral 8
bequests to colleagues 185
bequests to church 185
bequests to godchildren 159–60
bequests to servants 89
biography 185–6, 193
charitable bequest of 162
commendation of soul 148
debts owed to 186
length of tenure of benefice 58, 185–6
ownership of sermon collection 140
provision for funeral dole for clergy 102
request for burial 148, 185
Wyott, M. Richard, rector of Wigan 87
Wyrral, George, vicar of Harborne 54
Wyttour, John, ordinand 17 (n.53)

Yate:
John, priest of Fletchamstead
bequest to a woman 171
biography 193
burial arrangements 132, 147

property ownership 118
William, ordinand 18
York (Yorks.):
archbishops of *see* Bainbridge, Christopher; Lee, Edward; Wolsey, Thomas
clergy of 9
diocese of:
education in 10
emigration of clergy from 33
incidence of clerical immorality in 177
ordinand of 21
ordinations in 8, 30–1
private oratories and domestic chapels in 100
Gild of St John 9
Minster
chancellor of *see* Melton, William
grammar school 10
Ouse Bridge Civic School 9
St Mary's Abbey 10
Young, John, Prior of Repton 153 & n.89
Yoxall (Staffs.)
curate of *see* Parker, Ralph
tithe litigation by rector 169

Other Volumes in
Studies in the History of Medieval Religion

I
Dedications of Monastic Houses in England and Wales 1066–1216
Alison Binns

II
The Early Charters of the Augustinian Canons of
Waltham Abbey, Essex, 1062–1230
Edited by Rosalind Ransford

III
Religious Belief and Ecclesiastical Careers in Late Medieval England
Edited by Christopher Harper-Bill

IV
The Rule of the Templars: the French text of the Rule of
the Order of the Knights Templar
Translated and introduced by J. M. Upton-Ward

V
The Collegiate Church of Wimborne Minster
Patricia H. Coulstock

VI
William Waynflete: Bishop and Educationalist
Virginia Davis

VII
Medieval Ecclesiastical Studies in honour of Dorothy M. Owen
Edited by M. J. Franklin and Christopher Harper-Bill

VIII
A Brotherhood of Canons Serving God: English Secular
Cathedrals in the Later Middle Ages
David Lepine

IX
Westminster Abbey and its People c.1050–c.1216
Emma Mason

X
Gilds in the Medieval Countryside: Social and
Religious Change in Cambridgeshire c.1350–1558
Virginia R. Bainbridge

XI
Monastic Revival and Regional Identity in Early Normandy
Cassandra Potts

XII
The Convent and the Community in Late Medieval England: Female Monasteries in the Diocese of Norwich 1350–1540
Marilyn Oliva

XIII
Pilgrimage to Rome in the Middle Ages: Continuity and Change
Debra J. Birch

XIV
St Cuthbert and the Normans: the Church of Durham 1071–1153
William M. Aird